National Literacy Campaigns

Historical and Comparative Perspectives

National Literacy Campaigns
Historical and Comparative Perspectives

Edited by

ROBERT F. ARNOVE

Indiana University
Bloomington, Indiana

and

HARVEY J. GRAFF

The University of Texas at Dallas
Richardson, Texas

Plenum Press • New York and London

Library of Congress Cataloging in Publication Data

National literacy campaigns.

Bibliography: p.
Includes index.
1. Literacy—History. 2. Literacy—Cross-cultural studies. 3. Comparative education. I. Arnove, Robert F. II. Graff, Harvey J.
LC149.N33   1987   374'.012   87-10873
ISBN 0-306-42458-4

© 1987 Plenum Press, New York
A Division of Plenum Publishing Corporation
233 Spring Street, New York, N.Y. 10013

Printed in the United States of America

Contributors

Robert F. Arnove   School of Education, Indiana University, Bloomington, Indiana

H. S. Bhola   School of Education, Indiana University, Bloomington, Indiana

Ben Eklof   Department of History, Indiana University, Bloomington, Indiana

Richard L. Gawthrop   Department of History, University of South Carolina, Columbia, South Carolina

Arthur Gillette   UNESCO, Paris, France

Harvey J. Graff   School of Arts and Humanities, University of Texas at Dallas, Richardson, Texas

Charles W. Hayford   Department of History, Northwestern University, Evanston, Illinois

Rab Houston   Department of Modern History, University of St. Andrews, St. Andrews, Fife, Scotland

Egil Johansson   Demografiska Databasen, Umeå University, Umeå, Sweden

Marvin Leiner   Department of Elementary and Early Childhood Education, Queens College, Flushing, New York, New York

Leslie Limage   UNESCO, Paris, France

Edward Stevens   College of Education, Ohio University, Athens, Ohio

Jeff Unsicker   World College West, Pedaluma, California

v

Preface

We came to the task of editing this book from different disciplines and backgrounds but with a mutuality of interest in exploring the concept of literacy campaigns in historical and comparative perspective. One of us is a professor of comparative education who has participated in and written about literacy campaigns in Third World countries, notably Nicaragua; the other is a comparative social historian who has written on literacy campaigns in Western history. Both of us believed that literacy could only be understood in particular historical contexts. As Harvey Graff has noted, "to consider any of the ways in which literacy intersects with social, political, economic, cultural, or psychological life . . . requires excursions into other records."[1]

Thus, we have set out in this edited collection to explore some five hundred years of literacy campaigns in vastly different societies: Reformation Germany, early modern Sweden and Scotland, the nineteenth-century United States, nineteenth- and early twentieth-century Russia and the Soviet Union, pre-Revolutionary and Revolutionary China, and a variety of Third World countries in the post-World War II period (Tanzania, Cuba, Nicaragua, and India). In addition, we have included studies of the UNESCO-sponsored Experimental World Literacy Program and recent adult literacy efforts in three industrialized Western countries (the United Kingdom, France, and the United States).

The framework of a campaign facilitates analysis of literacy goals and outcomes in specific contexts. It enables us to better understand the relations between individual and societal transformations. This focus also enables us to distinguish the quantitative and qualitative dimensions of literacy activities, such as the difference between the spread of literacy and patterns of its use. Further, focusing on literacy campaigns allows us to escape the blinders of concentrating only on the recent period in literacy's history. Literacy campaigns have a surprisingly long history, contrary to current perceptions. In the West, they date from at least the Protestant Reformation of the sixteenth century.

Key common elements unite literacy campaigns across time and space. These elements comprehend mission, organization, pedagogy, and content; they are discussed in greater detail in the introductory overview chapter. The chapter, while attempting to identify the common components of an ideal model of a

[1] Harvey Graff, *The Literacy Myth; Literacy and Social Structure in the Nineteenth-Century City* (New York: Academic Press, 1979).

literacy campaign, also points out that there are a number of "paths" to changing levels of literacy—that no one path is necessarily destined to succeed in the achievement of mass literacy.

The theoretical overview is followed by a series of discrete case studies that represent major historical examples and significant recent campaigns. The different studies involve historical, social scientific, and comparative educational analyses and use diverse research methods: for example, archival, observational, and ethnographic approaches. Despite the different approaches and analyses, all the authors are concerned with contributing to an understanding of the multiple meanings of literacy for individuals and the more comprehensive communities of which they are a part. The chapters chronicle and illuminate the uses of literacy by individuals in different contexts as they attempt to forge a livelihood, make sense of the world, and pursue prosaic as well as aesthetic and spiritual goals. They also document the organized attempts of political and religious authorities to inculcate, if not impose, their views and goals.

While the various contributing authors have dedicated more than a decade to literacy studies or have recently completed a dissertation on the subject, the common enterprise of this book stimulated them to expand their previous research to include a comparative dimension; and in two of the historical studies, the researchers extended their analysis of literacy movements in nineteenth- and early twentieth-century Russia and China into the postrevolutionary periods. If some of our goals were unmet, the collection, at least, represents a first systematic attempt to examine, critically and comparatively, the concepts and facts of large-scale literacy campaigns in more than a dozen societies over nearly five-hundred years.

Other provisos: Although we have attempted to select what are widely considered to be significant historical and contemporary examples of literacy campaigns, we also are cognizant that a number of major country studies had to be omitted. We make no claim to encyclopedic exhaustiveness or definitiveness of treatment. It is our hope that the book will lead to further research on the social, cultural, political, and economic correlates of literacy, as well as, more generally, on the role of education in social control and social change.

ROBERT F. ARNOVE
HARVEY J. GRAFF

Contents

CHAPTER 1

Introduction

ROBERT F. ARNOVE AND HARVEY J. GRAFF

> *History has shown that, up to the present time, revolutionary regimes have been the only ones capable of organizing successful mass literacy campaigns. From the Soviet Union to China, from Vietnam to Cuba, all revolutionary governments have given high priority to the war on illiteracy.*[1]

> *The magnitude of the problem in many countries calls for massive efforts. Only specific campaigns with clearly defined targets can create the sense of urgency, mobilize popular support and marshal all possible resources to sustain mass actions, continuity, and follow-up.*[2]

The idea of a campaign to promote massive and rapid increases in rates of literacy is not unique to the twentieth century. We contend, and this work illustrates, that major and largely successful campaigns to raise levels of literacy have taken place over the past four hundred years from the time of the Protestant Reformations, and that they share common elements. Our belief is that

All textual references below to essays by Richard Gawthrop, Rab Houston, Egil Johansson, Edward Stevens, Ben Eklof, Charles Hayford, Jeff Unsicker, Marvin Leiner, Arthur Gillette, H. S. Bhola, Robert F. Arnove, and Leslie Limage refer to their contributions to this volume, unless otherwise noted. These essays examine most of the important examples of national literacy campaigns over the past four hundred years; any major omissions are due to our inability to secure a contribution. We do think that we deal with the essential cases, however. In all that follows, the term "literacy," when used without qualification, refers to basic or elementary levels of alphabetic reading and/or writing. We also wish to note that, although we discuss "wars on ignorance" and use other such terminology derived from various historical campaigns, we firmly believe that individual adults who cannot read or write have a rich reservoir of knowledge and skills. Similarly, largely illiterate societies with oral traditions have a richness of culture, involving alternative ways of perceiving, interpreting, and communicating views of the world, that should not be downplayed or denigrated.

[1] Lê Thành Khôi, "Literacy Training and Revolution: The Vietnamese Experience," in *A Turning Point for Literacy*, ed. Leon Bataille (Oxford: Pergamon), 1976, pp. 125–26.

[2] Udaipur Conference, "Campaigning for Literacy: Proceedings," International Council for Adult Education, Unesco, Uadipur, India, January 1982.

ROBERT F. ARNOVE • School of Education, Indiana University, Bloomington, Indiana 47405. HARVEY J. GRAFF • School of Arts and Humanities, University of Texas at Dallas, Richardson, Texas 75083-0688.

contemporary literacy campaigns can be better understood in a historical and comparative perspective.

Historically, large-scale efforts to provide literacy have not been tied to the level of wealth, industrialization, urbanization, or democratization of a society, nor to a particular type of political regime. Instead, they have been more closely related to efforts of centralizing authorities to establish a moral or political consensus, and over the past two hundred years, to nation-state building.[3]

What may be said of literacy campaigns is that, both historically and comparatively, they have formed part of larger transformations in societies. These transformations have attempted to integrate individuals into more comprehensive political and/or religious communities. They have involved the mobilization of large numbers of learners and teachers by centralizing authorities, who have used elements of both compulsion and social pressure to propagate a particular doctrine.

Campaigns, since the Protestant Reformations of the sixteenth century in Western Europe, have used a variety of media and specially developed materials, commonly involving a special cosmology of symbols, martyrs, and heroes. They often have been initiated and sustained by charismatic leaders and usually depend on a special "strike force" of teachers to disseminate a particular faith or world view.

A belief in the efficacy of literacy and the printed word itself has been an article of faith. Then as now, reformers and idealists, shakers and movers of societies and historical periods, have viewed literacy as a means to other ends— whether a more moral society or a more stable political order. No less today than four hundred years ago, individuals have sought and used literacy to attain their own goals.

In the twentieth century, particularly during the period from 1960 on, pronouncements about literacy deem it a process of critical consciousness-raising and human liberation. Just as frequently, such declarations refer to literacy, not as an end itself, but as a means to other goals—to the ends of national development and to a social order that elites, both national and international, define.[4]

This work examines continuities as well as changes in literacy campaigns over the past four hundred years. It also points to persisting issues related to literacy campaigns, their goals, organization, processes, and outcomes. The overarching goal of this work is a historically, comparatively, and dialectically based reconceptualization of the idea of a literacy campaign. By implication, we also call for a reconceptualization of literacy in theory and practice.

---

[3]Harvey J. Graff, *The Legacies of Literacy: Continuities and Contradictions in Western Society and Culture* (Bloomington: Indiana University Press, 1986); see also Randall Collins, "Some Comparative Principles of Educational Stratification," *Harvard Educational Review* 47 (February 1977), pp. 1–27, John Boli, Francisco O. Ramirez, and John W. Meyer, "Explaining the Origins and Expansion of Mass Education," *Comparative Education Review* 29 (May 1985), pp. 145–70, Yehudi Cohen, "Schools and Civilization States," in *The Social Sciences and the Comparative Study of Educational Systems*, ed. J. Fischer (Scranton, PA: International Textbook, 1970).

[4]G. Carron and Anil Bordia, *Issues in Planning and Implementing National Literacy Programmes* (Paris: Unesco and IIEP, 1985), esp. p. 18.

THE IDEA OF A CAMPAIGN

In a Unesco-commissioned review of twentieth century national literacy campaigns, H.S. Bhola defines the literacy campaign as "a mass approach that seeks to make all adult men and women in a nation literate within a particular time frame. Literacy is seen as a means to a comprehensive set of ends—economic, social-structural, *and political*." According to Bhola, "a campaign suggests urgency and combativeness; it is in the nature of an expectation; it is something of a crusade." Sometimes, this becomes the moral equivalent of war. By contrast, a "'literacy program', which even though planned, systematic and designed-by-objectives, may lack both urgency and passionate fervor."[5]

Although a limited time frame is considered to be a defining characteristic of a mass campaign, those national cases frequently pointed to as exemplars of twentieth-century literacy mobilizations commonly took two or more decades. Bhola's examples include the USSR (1919–1939), Vietnam (1945–1977), the People's Republic of China (1950s–1980s), Burma 1960s–1980s), Brazil (1967–1980), and Tanzania (1971–1981). Only the Cuban literacy campaign spanned a period of one year or less. The Nicaraguan Literacy Crusade of 1980, not studied by Bhola, lasted but a brief five months. Despite the variable time spans, they all had "an intensity of purpose expressed in a series of mobilizations and were highly combative in trying to achieve their goals."[6]

What distinguishes twentieth century literacy campaigns from earlier educational movements (such as those of Germany, Sweden, and Scotland, which spanned over two hundred years) is the telescoped period of time in which the mobilizations occurred, stemming from the fact that political power can be more effectively centralized than in earlier periods. The transformation of communications, including electronic technologies and economies of scale in the publishing industry, further facilitates printing and dissemination of literacy texts, and transmission of messages and symbols relating to a campaign. The combination of technology and concentration of political power also may portend greater opportunities for the monitoring of, and social control over, the uses of literacy.

There also are international dimensions to the types of literacy activities characterizing the second half of the twentieth century, and increasing opportunities for countries to learn from one another. Despite these differences, the similarities between literacy campaigns over the past four hundred years are strongly evident. Insufficiently recognized among these similarities is the increasing tendency of countries to borrow from other campaigns, a process of mimesis. This is what Graff terms the "legacies of literacy."

In the following pages, we review similarities between contemporary campaigns and the literacy drives and movements of the sixteenth through nineteenth centuries. The characteristics on which we focus are the contexts, goals,

---

[5] H. S. Bhola, *Campaigning for Literacy: A Critical Analysis of Some Selected Literacy Campaigns of the 20th Century, with a Memorandum to Decision Makers* (Paris: Unesco/ICAE Study, 1982), p. 211.
[6] Ibid.

mechanisms, organization, materials and methods, teachers, and consequences of campaigns. Another important common feature is the relationship between literacy efforts and the institutionalization of schooling. The chapters contained in this book place literacy efforts in historical context while also searching for common patterns over time and across different social, economic, and political configurations. Theorists and planners of literacy campaigns may learn much of value from these patterns, from the past successes and failures documented in the national case studies.

CONTEXT AND TRIGGERING EVENTS

Historically, the initiation of a literacy campaign has been associated with major transformations in social structures and belief systems. Typically, such campaigns have been preceded and accompanied by more gradual changes, such as the spread of religious doctrine, the growth of market economies, the rise of bureaucratic and legal organizations, and the emergence of national political communities. But usually there is a profound, if not cataclysmic, triggering event: a religious reformation or a political revolution, the gaining of political independence and nationhood.

The German, Swedish, and Scottish campaigns from the middle of the sixteenth century were intimately connected to the Protestant Reformations and the subsequent Catholic Counter-Reformation. In the German case, the Treaty of Augsburg of 1555 established that the religious preference of the ruling elite of each city or territory determined whether the population of that political entity would adhere to the Catholic or the Lutheran Church. Shortly thereafter, the Catholic Church, reinvigorated by the Council of Trent and the founding of the Order of Jesuits, responded to the threat of religious heterodoxy. According to Gawthrop, the Protestant rulers, in conjunction with religious authorities, systematically set out to establish schools "to indoctrinate the general population and thereby ensure religious conformity."

For Scotland, the Reformation of the 1560s is described by Houston as a political event with religious overtones. Anti-French and anti-Catholic nobility, concerned with the establishment and protection of their faith, advocated a national effort to educate the population in the principles of Protestantism.

Literacy efforts in Sweden, according to Johansson, must also be understood in the context of the Protestant Reformation. The Swedish experience should be taken as part of a process of nation building following a series of great wars. Military defeat contributed to renewed emphasis on mass literacy in Prussia in 1807, France in 1871,[7] and Russia in 1905.

Literacy efforts in the nineteenth century, for example in the United States, represent a convergence of various social forces and widely held beliefs: the competition of various religious denominations to capture souls, and a belief in republican government, with its need for an educated citizenry. But a key catalyst

---

[7] Boli, Ramirez, and Meyer, p. 165

was the extension of the franchise to the working class during the first three decades of the century, a trend which coincides with the beginning of the common school movement.

In Russia, the abolition of serfdom in 1861 unleashed enormous energies, both at the local and state levels, that were channeled into literacy activities. At the same time, national elites, of both progressive and conservative tendencies, began to make linkages between literacy and the process of modernization and the strengthening of the Russian State.[8]

The campaigns of the twentieth century are usually associated with revolutionary upheavals and attempts by state authorities to create a new political culture and accelerate the process of economic development. The most striking cases of massive mobilization that pivot on the provision of literacy and adult education are the USSR, following the October 1917 revolution; the People's Republic of China, following the 1949 "liberation"; Cuba, following its 1959 revolution; and Nicaragua, after the "triumph" of 1979. Other notable cases involving large-scale literacy as part of the struggle for independence from colonial domination include Vietnam from 1945 on, and the actual attainment of independence followed by the restructuring of a society in accordance with a new model of development—Tanzania after 1967.[9]

The wealth and resources of a country have not been the critical factor in shaping the scope and intensity of a war on ignorance. Rather, the political will of national leaders to effect dramatic changes in personal beliefs, individual and group behaviors, and major institutions emerges as the key factor. Cases in which a strong political will has been lacking include India, with approximately one-half of the world's more than 800 million illiterate adults, and the advanced industrialized countries of the U.S., the U.K., and France, which, according to Limage, have profound illiteracy problems.[10]

GOALS

The transformations that provide the context for most mass literacy campaigns usually embrace the formation of a new type of person in a qualitatively different society. In the contemporary period, there is frequent reference, for example, to the creation of the "New Socialist Man [Woman],"[11] in a society

[8]Ben Eklof, *Russian Peasant Schools: A Social and Cultural History, 1861–1914* (Berkeley: University of California Press, 1986); see also Chapter 6 below.

[9]See Bhola, *Campaigning*, Lê Thành Khôi, "Literacy Training", and Chapter 10 below.

[10]See Chapters 11 and 13 below. See also Graff, *Legacies*, Brian Street, *Literacy in Theory and Practice* (Cambridge: Cambridge University Press, 1984), Jonathan Kozol, *Illiteracy in America* (Garden City: Doubleday, 1985), and Kenneth Levine, "Functional Literacy: Fond Illusions and False Economies," *Harvard Educational Review* 52 (1982), p. 252.

[11]Whatever the reasons, revolutionary societies following the socialist path to development almost invariably refer to the formation of the new "socialist man," equating the masculine gender with humanity. We feel uncomfortable with this formulation and therefore purposely refer to the new "socialist female" as well. The terminology used by new revolutionary regimes merits considerably

organized according to principles of cooperation, egalitarianism, altruism, sacrifice, and struggle (the USSR, the People's Republic of China, Vietnam, Cuba,
Ethiopia, Nicaragua). In the period of the great Protestant reforms, educational
goals were joined, according to Strauss, "to that grand design of a spiritual
renewal of state, society, and individual which endowed earlier Lutheranism
with its strongest source of appeal."[12] The Lutheran Reformation in Germany,
Strauss continues, was particularly important because

> It embarked on a conscious and, for its time, remarkably systematic endeavor to develop
> in the young new and better impulses, to implant inclinations in consonance with the
> reformers' religious and civic ideals, to fashion dispositions in which Christian ideas of
> right thought and action could take root, and to shape personalities capable of turning
> the young into new men—into the human elements of a Christian society that would
> live by evangelical principles.[13]

An important legacy of the German campaign is Luther's shift in attention
to shaping the young, as opposed to his earlier focus on all members of the
community. The dilemma faced by Luther, whether to concentrate literacy efforts
on the young or on adults, is a strategic issue in almost all subsequent mass
campaigns. In twentieth-century campaigns, despite initial large-scale efforts
aimed at entire populations, a narrowing eventually occurs with greater emphasis
placed on the formal education of the young. Literacy and basic education, over
time, become conflated (confused?) with state organized and regulated systems
of schooling.

Luther's emphasis on youth reflects the widespread and persisting belief
that youth is less corrupt and more easily molded. Gawthrop points to the
pessimistic views of German religious reformers concerning the malleability of
human beings. Whereas many of the earlier reformers did not believe it was
possible to effect any permanent, positive alteration in human nature—given
their belief in the imminence of the Day of Judgment—they embraced, according
to Gawthorp, "the molding power of education only in so as it assisted their
efforts to combat the spread of heretical doctrine." The early Protestant reformers attempted to make basic instruction available to the largest possible number
of youths, not only for the sake of their salvation, but for the common welfare.

In Scotland, political order and doctrinal conformity were the goals of
centralizing authorities. In Sweden, according to Johansson, all educational efforts
were concentrated on comprehending, understanding, and putting the word
into practice in everyday life.

In the nineteenth-century United States, the rapid spread of literacy served
similar purposes of religious propagation, maintenance of political order, and

---

more examination and discussion, and the sexist implications of key expressions should not be
glossed over.

[12] Gerald Strauss, *Luther's House of Learning: Indoctrination of the Young in the German Reformation*
(Baltimore: Johns Hopkins University Press, 1978), p. 8.

[13] Ibid., p. 2; see also Strauss, "Lutheranism and Literacy: A Reassessment," in *Religion and Society
in Early Modern Europe*, ed. Kaspar von Greyerz (London: Allen & Unwin, 1984), pp. 109–23, and
Richard Gawthrop and Gerald Strauss, "Protestantism and Literacy in Early Modern Germany,"
Past and Present 104 (1984), pp. 31–55.

the formation of a national character. According to Stevens, "the process of becoming literate was itself a process of socialization promulgated by those interested in using the school to resolve social, economic, and political tensions arising from a culturally pluralistic and emerging industrial society. The process of schooling and hence the process of becoming literate are seen in relation to nation-building, a fervent evangelical Protestantism, and technological innovation." What is of special significance in the U.S. case is that the reformers advocated a republican form of government, based on more active citizen participation in political governance.

In Russia, following the 1917 Revolution, Lenin noted that "the illiterate person stands outside politics. First it is necessary to teach the alphabet. Without it, there are only rumors, fairy tales, prejudice, but not politics."[14] The society of worker collectives ("soviets") that the socialist reformers envisioned depended on a literate citizenry that could understand the nature of their past exploitation, grasp the organizing principles of the new society, and participate in the necessary transformations.

In all the above cases, literacy is almost never itself an isolated or absolute goal. It is rather one part of a larger process *and* a vehicle for that process. Literacy is invested with a special significance, but seldom in and of itself. Learning to read, possibly to write, involves the acquisition or conferral of a new status—membership in a religious community, citizenship in a nation-state. Literacy often carries tremendous symbolic weight, quite apart from any power and new capabilities it may bring. The attainment of literacy per se operates as a badge, a sign of initiation into a select group and/or a larger community.

Historically, there has been constant tension between the use of literacy for achieving individual versus collective goals. Inseparable are the questions of (a) whether to select the individual or the group as the target of a campaign and (b) whether to aim at transforming individuals in order to change societies or at transforming collectivities in order to reform individuals. Changes at one level do not necessarily bring about a corresponding transformation at the other.

Throughout history, the provision of literacy skills to reform either individuals or their societies rarely has been linked to notions of people using these skills to achieve their own ends. To the contrary, reformers advocating the extension of education to the populace have attempted to restrict the ability to read to learning a particular text or doctrine. They commonly feared that unbridled literacy would lead people to new visions, to new ways of perceiving and naming the world that were not acceptable.[15]

Houston notes that in the sixteenth- to eighteenth-century literacy campaigns, "The individual [had] no right to learning for its own sake. The overall aim was societal advancement." John Knox, the great Protestant divine, stressed that "all should be educated in the doctrines of Calvinism . . . the preservation

---

[14] Peter Kenez, "Liquidating Illiteracy in Revolutionary Russia," *Russian History* 9 (1982), p. 175, quoted in Chapter 6 below.

[15] Harvey J. Graff, *The Literacy Myth: Literacy and Social Structure in the Nineteenth-Century City* (New York: Academic Press, 1979).

and extension of Protestantism was central to the literacy campaign."[16] Similarly, Resnick and Resnick note that the goal of Protestant religious instruction in the United States was not enlightenment in the general sense, but rather "a particular way of viewing the world."[17]

In the contemporary period, especially in those mobilizations that occur in socialist societies, the acquisition of literacy is linked integrally to "political education" in a particular ideological doctrine, Marxism–Leninism or (Mao-Zedong Thought) or nationalist variations such as Sandinismo. In the People's Republic of China, Mao Zedong stressed "political literacy," even though, as Hayford points out, peasants and workers remained unable to read books, magazines, and newspapers. Lenin noted, "As long as there is such a thing in the country as illiteracy it is hard to talk about political education". Even prior to the 1917 revolution, political elites in Russia, who were promoting literacy efforts as part of modernization, evinced, according to Eklof, a fear of "wild" popular literacy. Eklof's analysis of literacy campaigns after the revolution shows that it was precisely at the time of massive extension of education in the early 1930s that Stalin also drastically tightened up censorship and surveillance to control the uses of literacy.

The post–World War II era is particularly interesting because of a change in the rhetoric, and sometimes the ideology, of literacy campaigns and the goals that are announced in international conferences such as that of Tehran in 1965. The Tehran Conference declared that literacy, rather than being an end in itself, "should be regarded as a way of preparing man for a social, civic and economic role . . . reading and writing should lead not only to elementary general knowledge but to training for work, increased productivity, a greater participation in civil life and a better understanding of the surrounding world, and should . . . open the way to basic human culture."[18]

A year before the Unesco-sponsored Tehran Conference, the 1964 session of Unesco's General Conference called for a "five-year experimental world literacy program designed to pave the way for the eventual execution of a world campaign in the field of literacy."[19] The Experimental World Literacy Campaign (EWLP, 1967–73) was distinguished both by its selectivity (reaching one million adults in eleven countries) and by its stress on "functionality." As Gillette notes, the central criterion in the program was narrowly oriented functionality—with major emphasis being given to industrial, agricultural, and craft training for men, and homemaking and family planning for women.

The only country to expand immediately its EWLP pilot project into a major campaign was Tanzania. The goals of the Tanzanian campaign are

[16]See Rab Houston, *Scottish Literacy and the Scottish Identity* (Cambridge: Cambridge University Press, 1986). See also Kenneth Lockridge, *Literacy in Colonial New England* (New York: Norton, 1974).

[17]Daniel P. Resnick and Lauren B. Resnick, "The Nature of Literacy: An Historical Explanation," *Harvard Educational Review* 47 (1977): 370–85.

[18]United Nations, Educational, Scientific and Cultural Organization, *World Conference of Ministers of Education on the Eradication of Illiteracy, Final Report* (Tehran, Iran, 1965).

[19]13th Session of Unesco's General Conference, quoted in *The Experimental World Literacy Program: A Critical Assessment* (Paris: Unesco Press and UNDP, 1976), p. 9.

noteworthy, for they reflect a different conceptualization of the methods and outcomes of literacy. They also reflect the pedagogical ideas of leading adult educators like Paulo Freire, who focus on literacy as a process of individual consciousness-raising and social change. Tanzanian declarations on the goals of literacy and adult education, for example, state that "one of the most . . . significant functions of adult education is to arouse consciousness and critical awareness among the people about the need for and possibility of change." The goal of adult education programs, according to Kassam and Hall, was to "help people in determining the nature of the change they want and how to bring it about."[20]

Paulo Freire's conception of the adult literacy process as "cultural action for freedom" is relatively open-ended. It is also clear that those countries that have embraced Freire's language and some of his pedagogical methods in their national campaigns, for example Tanzania and Nicaragua, have a more specific notion of the desired end-state of literacy promotion and acquisition. Literacy and adult education efforts are always informed and oriented by particular political world views of societal elites and dominant groups. In Tanzania and Nicaragua, as in other mass campaigns such as those of Vietnam and Ethiopia, literacy promotion is predicated upon socialist and populist notions. In Brazil, Freire's native country, a literacy campaign has been underway for years, frequently employing the rhetoric of "conscientizacion" but also very much tied to gaining acceptance for a technocratic, statist, and capitalistic approach to development.

The most eloquent international statement on the goals of literacy campaigns appears in the 1975 Declaration of Persepolis (Iran):

> literacy . . . [is] not just the process of learning the skills of reading, writing, and arithmetic, but a contribution to the liberation of man and to his full development. Thus conceived, literacy creates the conditions for the acquisition of a critical consciousness of the contradictions of society in which man lives and of its aims; it also stimulates initiative and his participation in the creation of projects capable of acting upon the world, of transforming it, and of defining the aims of an authentic human development[21]

Such goals are articulated by a number of national literacy campaigns (Cuba, Tanzania, Nicaragua, Guinea Bissau). Nagging questions remain. The translation of these goals into outcomes very much depends on the mechanisms, methods, materials, and teachers that are employed in large-scale literacy efforts. Given the transformations and mobilizations that generally precipitate and accompany such campaigns, or "crusades," it is unlikely that literacy will be used only for ends exclusively determined by the individual or individuals collectively organized at the base. It is to these mechanisms and mobilizational strategies that we now turn.

[20] Yussaf Kassam and Bud Hall, "Tanzania's National Literacy Campaign: A Journey of Imagination, Energy, and Commitment," unpublished paper, International Council for Adult Education, Toronto, 1985, p. 7.
[21] United Nations Food and Agricultural Organization (FAO), "The Declaration of Persepolis," *Ideas and Action* 10 (1975), p. 43; also see Bataille, *Turning Point.*

PATTERNS OF MOBILIZATION

The initial literacy campaigns in Western Europe—Germany, Scotland, and Sweden—from the mid-sixteenth century on, and the nineteenth-century United States education movements reveal several distinctive patterns of mobilization. These patterns may be viewed in relation to (a) the degree of centralization of political and religious authority exercised over a campaign, and (b) the extent to which a literacy campaign's activities are institutionalized in schooling.

One legacy—that of state-directed activities—was established by the German literacy drives. Initially, literacy activities promoted by the followers of Luther were decentralized, domestically based, and informal. But by the 1550s, according to Gawthrop, there was an unmistakable trend toward coordination and direction of primary education by centralizing political and ecclesiastical authorities, and movement toward a uniform system of education. There was a corresponding shift to formal institutions and "carefully trained cadres of pastors and teachers operating under the aegis of benevolent, but strong willed, governments." Among the reasons offered for this shift are the disillusionment of Luther and his followers with the results of "uninformed enthusiasm." Gawthrop notes that "peasants justifying their rebellion of 1525 by misrepresenting (in Luther's eyes) his religious message turned the Great Reformer against any fostering of unsupervised book learning."[22]

Similarly, Scotland's literacy efforts were state-directed and even more comprehensive in scope. According to Houston, the literacy campaign "initiated in Scotland at the time of the Reformation and carried through by legislation in the seventeenth century (1616) was the first truly *national* literacy campaign." It was universal in coverage, religiously oriented, and school-based. Educational activities directed at literacy involved joint action of the Scottish State and the Protestant Kirk. What distinguishes the Scottish case from that of the German— as well as that of seventeenth-century New England—campaigns was that the latter were essentially more localized efforts.[23]

Another distinctive pattern was that of the Swedish campaign. Launched in 1686, it was national in scope but was carried out almost entirely *without* the use of schools. Sweden offers an example of a domestically based but politically and religiously sponsored and enforced campaign. The primary focus was on informal activities supervised by local religious authorities. Its unique features included a literacy based in reading ability but seldom in writing, and also a special stress on the mother's educational role in the home. In early modern Sweden, as a result, the exceptional pattern of women's rates of literacy paralleling men's was achieved. This represents a historical and indeed a contemporary anomaly.[24]

[22]See also Gerald Strauss, Luther's House of Learning.
[23]See also Houston, *Scottish Literacy;* Lockridge, *Literacy.*
[24]Egil Johansson, "The History of Literacy in Sweden," in *Literacy and Social Development in the West,* ed. Harvey J. Graff (Cambridge: Cambridge University Press, 1981), pp. 151–83.

	Centralization	
	Hi	Lo
Yes	Scotland	USA
School-based	Germany	
No	Sweden	Germany initially

Figure 1. Patterns of mobilization.

The nineteenth-century United States represents another pattern. Unlike the German, Swedish, and Scottish cases, according to Stevens, there was no centrally orchestrated policy that brought the power and resources of the nation-state to bear on the problem of literacy. Instead, the competition of religious denominations, the proliferation of religious and secular presses, the exhortation of leading secular and clerical authorities, and local civic initiative came together to promote literacy activities. Most activity was organized and directed by the individual states rather than the federal government.

These patterns may be represented graphically as in Figure 1. The lower right hand cell of centralized, non-school-based literacy campaigns essentially remains a highly preliminary stage from which campaigns pass as they develop. Historically and comparatively, state and religious authorities strive to move literacy promotion away from unregulated, unschooled situations.

In the twentieth century, the most striking examples of mobilization involve national, centrally organized efforts that are waged in terms of a "war on ignorance." But these efforts have also depended heavily on local initiative and popular organizations to recruit teachers and students and to implement instructional activities. The People's Republic of China, with the most massive mobilization of people (over 48 million), was, according to Bhola, "centrally instituted and nationally orchestrated, but carried out in a decentralized manner, leaving much to local choice and initiative."[25]

From the sixteenth century onward, political and religious authorities have used exhortation and appeals to moral and patriotic sentiments, as well as compulsion and social pressure, to induce people to acquire literacy. State legislation requiring local municipalities and religious institutions to offer instruction, hire teachers, and ultimately require illiterate individuals to attend schools or demonstrate knowledge of certain texts characterizes the early German, Swedish, and Scottish cases.

In the twentieth century, the Soviet Union stands out as the first case of a country adopting a war-seige mentality to combat illiteracy. The December 29, 1919 Decree on Illiteracy, for example, required all illiterates eight to fifty years

[25] See Bhola, *Campaigning,* pp. 89–90; see also Chapter 7 below and Robert F. Arnove, "Education in China and India," *Comparative Education Review* 28 (August 1984), pp. 378–401.

of age to study, empowering local Narkompros (People's Commissariats of Enlightenment) to draft literate citizens to teach, and making it a criminal offense to refuse to teach or study.[26] In June 1920, the All-Russian Extraordinary Commission for the Eradication of Illiteracy was created and given the power to issue regulations with the force of law. During the 1917–1921 period, as detailed by Eklof, an institutional framework was created to set up Likpunkty ("liquidation points") from which to attack illiteracy. The likpunkty were to provide 6–10 week literacy courses.[27] The "New Committee" that was established to conduct literacy efforts was called the *gramCheka* (*gram* being the abbreviation for literacy, and *Cheka* the initials for the secret police). And, as Eklof notes, looming large in adult literacy efforts was the Red Army.

Interestingly enough, the Russian army, at the end of the nineteenth century, also played an important role in state efforts to promote literacy. New recruits who could produce a primary school certificate or demonstrate reading ability had their terms of enlistment reduced. The French and U.S. armies, in the nineteenth century, also conducted significant literacy instruction among recruits.

However, social control and compulsion, as well as positive inducements to acquire literacy, are not unique characteristics of twentieth-century campaigns. In the case of Sweden, a church law of 1686 required children, farm hands, and maid servants "to learn to read and see with their own eyes what God bids and commands in His Word."[28] Every household person and villager was gathered once a year to take part in examinations supervised by the local clergy in reading and knowledge of the Bible. The adult who failed the examination could be excluded from communion, and denied permission to marry.

In Scotland, as in Sweden, the Church had the right to refuse admission to communion to the grossly ignorant. Other social pressures included efforts to shame illiterates.

In the German states of Saxony (1772) and Bavaria (1802), pastors were forbidden to confirm anyone who had not spent enough time in school to have learned reading and a certain amount of religious knowledge. Throughout the German states, according to Gawthrop, a series of regulations restricted numerous categories of jobs from the state administration to those who could read, write, and do sums. Prussia imposed such limitations on those who wished to enter a craft guild.[29]

---

[26] Kenez, "Liquidating Illiteracy," pp. 180–81, quoted in Chapter 6 below.

[27] There was similar imagery and sloganeering in the Cuban and Nicaragua campaigns, with terroritories being declared free of "illiteracy" when more than eighty percent in a hamlet, village, or city had achieved literacy. Illiteracy was viewed as a scourge to be eliminated by a conquering army of literacy brigades.

[28] Johansson, *The History of Literacy in Sweden* (Umeå: School of Education, Umeå University, Sweden, 1977), p. 11.

[29] See Max Weber's essay on "The Rationalization of Education and Training" for a later view of the reasons for educational requirements in the German civil service, in *From Max Weber*, ed. H. H. Gerth and C. Wright Mills (Oxford: Oxford University Press, 1946).

Compulsion is frequently counterproductive. The history of education in Western Europe and North America, as in other parts of the world, offers striking evidence of local initiatives of communities and grassroots movements to acquire literacy skills and establish schools. These efforts run parallel to and, in some instances, counter to the authority of state and religious authorities.[30]

In Scotland, for example, "adventure" or private fee-paying schools, although putatively illegal, comprised a parallel education system to the state-sponsored parish schools. These schools, as Houston indicates, were extremely important in extending education as the Scottish population increased.

In pre-1917 Russia, most peasants learned to read and write outside the formal school network. As Eklof documents, peasants set up informal village schools founded either by payments from individual households or by the entire commune. Formal school expansion in the 1861–1914 period was, according to Eklof, eventually a process of formal recognition and registration of extant peasant schools.[31]

By contrast, more recent campaigns tend to originate with centralized authorities, thus raising the question of the intent and will of national leaders. In his review of twentieth-century campaigns, H. S. Bhola stresses the importance of national political will in mass literacy campaigns:

> The political will of the power elite actualized by the institutional power of the state can work wonders—resocialize each and every member of the society, transform the fabric of a society and invent a new future. Cultural revolutions can be brought about; literacy campaigns can be launched and ensured of success.[32]

In the Soviet Union, five years after the passing of comprehensive legislation, the establishment of liquidation points, and the creation of gramCheka, Minister of Education Lunacharskii complained that "the society for the liquidation of illiteracy passes wonderful resolutions but the concrete results of its work are despicable."[33] Krupaskaya, Lenin's wife and a renowned educator, complained ten years after the 1919 literacy decree that not a single article had been implemented. More aptly, Bhola notes:

> There are no substitutes for the twin process of organization and mobilization. On the one hand, the government must undertake both the administrative and technical organization of its decision making in the implementation system. On the other hand, people

---

[30]On compulsion, see M. J. Maynes, *Schooling for the People: Comparative Local Studies of Schooling History in France and Germany, 1750–1850* (New York: Holmes and Meier, 1985), David Tyack, "Ways of Seeing: An Essay on the History of Compulsory Schooling," *Harvard Educational Review* 46 (1976), pp, 355–389, W. M. Landes and Lewis C. Soloman, "Compulsory Schooling Legislation," *Journal of Economic History* 32 (1972), pp. 36–61; Carl Kaestle and Maris Vinovskis, *Education and Social Change in Nineteenth-Century Massachusetts* (New York: Cambridge University Press, 1980), and the two books by Michael B. Katz, *The Irony of Early School Reform* (Cambridge, MA: Harvard University Press, 1968) and *Class, Bureaucracy and Schools*, 2nd ed. (New York: Praeger, 1975).

[31]On formal vs. informal and nonformal learning of literacy, see Sylvia Scribner and Michael Cole, *The Psychology of Literacy* (Cambridge, MA: Harvard University Press, 1981).

[32]Bhola, *Campaigning*, p. 57.

[33]Roger Pethybridge, *The Social Prelude to Stalinism* (London: 1974), p. 152, cited in Chapter 6 this volume.

must be mobilized; learners must be motivated to learn; those who can teach and contribute in other ways, must be enabled to do so.[34]

But how? A review of past campaigns suggests that the creative use of symbols, a variety of media, the sponsorship of charismatic figures, and the availability of relevant and interesting materials all contribute to the diffusion of literacy. Moreover, opportunities for grass roots organizations (mass organizations in socialist societies) to participate is critical to the success of a mass campaign.

MOTIVATING LEARNERS

As literacy campaigns—historically and comparatively—have been associated with major social movements and transformations, they have benefited from the unleashing of energies and the opening of opportunities that occur in periods of social transition. Concomitantly, they have suffered from the dislocations, disorganization, and upheavals that characterize such periods.

The Soviet Union reveals both the revolutionary zeal with which populations may be mobilized for educational purposes and the debilitating conditions of civil war, external aggression, and widespread famine that also typified post-1917 Russia. Post-1949 China, similarly, was wracked by the legacy of war, but also by mobilizations such as the Great Leap Forward (1958) and the Great Proletarian Cultural Revolution (1966–1976). Among other goals, these mobilizations sought to extend education to larger numbers. Yet they contradictorily resulted in more than 100,000,000 people being added to the ranks of illiterates due to schools being closed and literacy skills being frowned upon and therefore not used.[35] The cases of Vietnam, Ethiopia, and Nicaragua also underscore the twin phenomena of enormous energies being channeled into literacy efforts and to the necessity of diverting resources into national defense and reconstruction— with extreme difficulty in meeting both sets of demands at the same time.

In all of the major twentieth-century campaigns, as in past campaigns of the previous three centuries, charismatic figures have been associated with literacy campaigns. Notable among the early Protestant reformers are Martin Luther, John Calvin, and Johns Knox; among Americans of the early republican and common school era, Thomas Jefferson, Noah Webster, and Horace Mann; in the twentieth century, Vladimir Illich Lenin, Mahatma Gandhi, Mao Zedung, Ho Chi Minh, Fidel Castro, and Julius Nyerere.[36]

The stature of these figures and the symbols that they represent to their followers are tied to notions of salvation, redemption, recreation. Notions attached to the saving of individual souls in the Reformation and Post-Reformation periods

---

[34] Bhola, *Campaigning*, p. 57.

[35] Arnove, "Education in China and India," p. 382.

[36] R. W. Scribner, "Incombustible Luther: The Image of the Reformer in Early Modern German," *Past and Present* 110 (1986), pp. 38–68.

of Western Europe, and the common school "crusade" of nineteenth century U.S., become linked in the twentieth century (especially in the post-World War II period) to the goals of redemption of a society that had suffered under colonialism, to the birth of a nation, and to the creation of a new and more just (moral?) society.

In the twentieth-century campaigns, to mention some of the more salient cases, literacy workers have been variously designated as *kultarmeitsy* (cultural soldiers) in the Soviet Union and as *brigadistas* (brigade workers) in the Cuban and Nicaraguan campaigns. Posters and billboards portray literacy workers as fighting a war with pencils, blackboards, and notebooks as their weapons against the "dark forces" of ignorance. (Pencils had very real meaning as weapons of war in Nicaragua: counter-revolutionaries who attacked literacy workers as agents of the transformations occurring in the country actually drove pencils through the cheeks of some of the "brigadistas" whom they had killed.)

Arnove describes the symbolization of the 1980 Nicaraguan National Literacy Crusade (CNA) in this way:

> The imagery and vocabulary of struggle and a national war loomed large in the symbolism of the CNA. Just as six guerrilla armies victoriously converged on Managua on 19 July (1979), in the wake of Somoza's flight from the country, so, on 24 March 1980, six "armies" left Managua to wage war on illiteracy. The six national fronts of the people's Literacy Army consisted of some 55,000 brigadistas (literacy workers), mostly high-school students, who would live in the rural areas of the country. . . . The six fronts were divided into "brigades" at the municipal level, and the brigades in turn were divided into "columns" at the hamlet level. The columns had four "squadrons" of thirty brigadistas each.[37]

Emotionally charged words and generative themes characterize the literacy primers in societies that are undergoing radical change. Appropriately, the first words of the Nicaraguan primer are *la Revolución* (the Revolution), which also contain all the vowels of the Spanish alphabet. Other key words include *liberación*, *genocidio*, and *masas populares*. Similarly, significant words are found in the Cuban literacy primer. The Soviet literacy text began with this dramatic exclamation: "*My ne raby, ne raby my.*" ("We are not slaves, slaves we are not.") The campaigns of early modern Germany, Sweden, and New England all had parallel features. Scribner shows this especially well in the German Reformers' use of pictorial imagery.[38]

In the twentieth-century campaigns, slogans abound and frequently are very similar. (Whether this indicates mutual borrowing or similar phenomena is difficult to determine.) In Cuba, various slogans centered on the notion that "if you were literate you could teach; if you were illiterate you could study."[39]

---

[37] See Chapter 12 this volume.

[38] R. W. Scribner, *For the Sake of Simple Folk: Popular Propaganda for the German Reformation* (Cambridge: Cambridge University Press, 1981); see also "History of Literacy" in Jòhannson, *The History of Literacy in Sweden.*

[39] Richard Fagen, *The Transformation of Political Culture in Cuba* (Stanford: Stanford University Press, 1969), p. 56; see also Jonathan Kozol, *Children of the Revolution* (New York: Delacorte, 1978 and Chapter 8 below.

In Ethiopia, the saying was: "Let the educated teach the uneducated, and the uneducated learn."[40] In Nicaragua, billboards and posters proclaimed:

> *En cada casa un aula*
> *En cada mesa un pupitre*
> *En cada Nica un Maestro!*

> Every home a classroom.
> Every table a school desk
> Every Nicaraguan a teacher!

Billboards, posters, flyers, specialized newspapers and publications—and, historically, pamphlets, handbills, and boards—have been an integral part of literacy campaigns. For example, pamphleteering littered early-to-mid-sixteenth-century Germany; in the second half of the seventeenth century, as Gawthrop documents, governments and private reformers disseminated leaflets to parents extolling the benefits of education. In Germany, as later in the United States, religious messages as well as technical information were disseminated widely in the form of simply written works and tracts for adults. Print media included specialized periodicals, calendars, almanacs, and also cheap novels and newspapers. This glut of print enjoyed great popularity but did not necessarily represent the interests of societal elites and their designs for literacy in the masses.

Print assumed a symbolic power and significance aside from individuals' ability to read it. For example, possession of a Bible, and its location in a prominent place in the home, was a goal of many. In the late eighteenth and early nineteenth centuries, in England and the U.S., Tom Paine's works held such power among literates and illiterates alike.

In many countries, traditional art forms—theatrical groups, dance troups, and musical ensembles—have been used to arouse popular interest in the literacy campaign. In China, wall murals, bulletin boards, and public blackboards have been used to raise interest in reading. Historically, wall plaques, printed cards, and pictorial icons played this part.

Tanzania, which has emphasized postliteracy maintenance and development activities more than most countries in recent years, has imaginatively used a variety of media and vehicles to promote reading and writing skills: the radio, mobile book libraries, and locally and inexpensively produced newspapers. Critical to the success of the Tanzanian program has been the development of textbooks that represent different areas of interest to learners and that are designed according to level of reading difficulty.[41]

Linguistically suitable reading materials and appropriate forms of adult education have not always characterized literacy campaigns.[42] Continuities that derive from the German campaign, however, include the attempt to impart a

---

[40] Bhola, *Campaigning.*

[41] Kassam and Hall, "Tanzania's Campaign." For historical situations, see Scribner, "Incombustible Luther," Peter Clark, *English Provincial Society from the Reformation to the Revolution* (Hassocks: Harvester, 1977), and E. P. Thompson, *The Making of the English Working Class* (New York: Pantheon, 1963).

[42] On the notion of "andragogy" see Chapter 9 below.

uniform and socially significant message (world view) to all students, the selection of teachers with special traits, and the use of a common language to do so.

MATERIALS AND METHODS

In Germany, following the Treaty of Augsburg (1555), government leaders supported the clergy of their territories in creating an expanded network of primary schools. School ordinances set forth a standard curriculum—consisting above all of catechism, drill, and psalm saying—followed, in descending order of importance, by reading, writing, and much less often arithmetic. Gawthrop notes that in his concern with religious conformity, Luther created a pedagogical instrument, the shorter catechism, to guide teaching efforts of parish sextons "to gather the children at least once a week to teach them the commandments, the Creed, the Lord's Prayers, and some hymns." Emphasis was also placed on selecting carefully trained cadres of pastors and teachers. But generally, the level of knowledge required of the teachers was little more than "that which their pupils would learn if their instruction were successful." In Württemberg, nominees for teachers were required to pass an examination testing their literacy, singing ability, and knowledge of the catechism. It was not until the mid-eighteenth century that emphasis was placed on teacher training and the comprehension of teachers. Pedagogy consisted of "constant reiterations of immutable formulas."[43]

In Sweden, materials consisted of special psalm books (combining catechism, biblical motifs, and texts of the ecclesiastical calendar). Special syllabary were developed, such as "The Golden ABCs" with 24 verses, each of which began with a letter of the alphabet. The most widely distributed book was the 1689 Catechism with Luther's "Explanations." The text included 303 questions and answers, scriptural passages, questions for young persons and bridal couples, and rules for home worship.

In Scotland, according to Houston, "Because of its religious and moral emphases, the form of education was dictated by the wish to transmit an approved body of knowledge and doctrine to the pupil rather than to stimulate critical understanding." Rote learning involved catechism, reading, writing, and, especially for girls, training in domestic vocational skills such as sewing, knitting, and weaving. In the United States, as Resnick and Resnick have observed, the earliest mass literacy effort, Protestant religious instruction, was intended to develop, not a generalized capacity to read, but mastery of a very limited set of prescribed texts.[44]

---

[43] Gerald Strauss, *Luther's House of Learning*, p. 22; see also Chapter 2, this volume, Gawthrop and Strauss, "Literacy and Protestantism," Strauss, "Lutheranism," and Maynes, *Schooling*.

[44] Resnick and Resnick, "Nature," Lockridge, *Literacy*; see also Lee Soltow and Edward Stevens, *The Rise of Literacy and the Common School* (Chicago: University of Chicago Press, 1982). For English comparisons, see David Cressy, *Literacy and the Social Order* (Cambridge: Cambridge University Press, 1980) and Richard Altick, *The English Common Reader* (Chicago: University of Chicago Press, 1957). In general, see Graff, *Legacies*.

From viewing these earlier campaigns, we learn that new and carefully crafted materials were developed to convey prescribed content. Attempts were made to simplify texts and also to use mnemonic and other heuristic devices. Concomitantly, most pedagogy was dominated by basic drill and repetition, with a goal of uncritical internalization of revealed truth or doctrine or unquestioning patriotism. Aligned with this pedagogy was an experience of "training to be trained," a socialization in discipline, orderliness, and obedience.

While state and religious authorities were concerned with the uniformity of messages, religious groups also vied to place their particular view before the public. The result of this competition, and the increasing availability of inexpensive print materials—novels, vocational manuals and guides, religious materials, as well as fairy tales and political tracts—contributed to the diversity of information available to the literate. Sometimes, state and church pursued contradictory ends. Propagation of one particular religion or sectarian doctrine over another could, and did, conflict with the promotion of common citizenship in a nation-state supposedly based on consensus values. Important examples of this conflict include Scotland and England and, to a lesser extent, the United States and Canada.

Other issues surfaced in these early campaigns that still trouble planners of literacy campaigns. One problem—the language of instruction—emerged in the Scottish campaign. In the Lowlands, the more urbanized, economically developed, and Protestant section of the country, English was spoken; in the rural, relatively undeveloped, and Catholic Highlands, Gaelic was the primary language. Since the Lowlands were politically dominant, English was the language of instruction. As Houston points out, "The drive for conformity in beliefs and language usage was harmful to literacy attainment in Scotland." If anything, the language problem was even more complex in Ireland.

The language issue poses serious problems in twentieth-century campaigns. Gillette, in his essay on the Experimental World Literacy Program, notes that the opposition within various participating countries to "the use of international funds to promote literacy as a means of spreading the national language to assimilate (subdue?) minority groups . . . raised sensitive cultural, and thus political questions in certain instances." Among the eleven participating countries, Tanzania used Kiswahili, the official language, as the medium of instruction; in fact, the literacy campaign contributed to the dissemination and standardization of the use of Kiswahili in the school system and throughout the country. In India, Kenya, and Ethiopia various languages have been used. In Indonesia, learning in the national language was supplemented by materials in local languages.[45] The language problem is highly reminiscent of bilingualism and trilingualism that plagued literacy campaigns in the West from the late medieval period through the twentieth century.

In Vietnam, efforts to extend literacy to various ethnic minorities may be viewed in terms of "cultural uplift" and the creation of a common culture

---

[45] See Chapter 9, this volume, see also Carron and Bordia, *Issues.*

benefiting all persons.[46] It may also be seen as cultural imperialism, attempts to undermine traditional cultures.

In some cases, the nature of the language itself—Chinese, for example—poses serious problems for the widespread dissemination of literacy. Hayford's essay notes the long history of attempts to simplify the Chinese language system of orthography, and how literacy, in the past, was confined to elite stratum and was very much related to limited mobility opportunities for the gentry and to political rulers.[47] Hayford examines pre-1949 literacy efforts to design new readers in a simplified language with themes that appealed to mass and middle-brow audiences. The James Yen Movement of the 1930s and 1940s developed, for example, the "People's Thousand Character Primer," based on frequency of words in selected texts, street signs, and standard contracts. Mao Zedong, who was involved in the movement, employed many of the same methods but introduced socialist content into the texts. In Ya'nan, by 1939, he had introduced a new writing system and a phonetic alphabet to teach literacy to populations under the control of the Chinese Communist Party.[48]

The language of instruction leads to the question of *whose* language and values form the medium and content of a literacy campaign. The power of dominant groups to shape language policy and educational content is similarly reflected in what skills are developed in what populations as part of the literacy process. Historically and comparatively, rural populations, the working class, ethnic and racial minorities, and women have been the last to receive literacy instruction and to gain access to advanced levels of schooling. As various Unesco publications reiterate, "The world map of illiteracy is the map of poverty."

Women have been the most disadvantaged group. From the time of the Protestant Reformation, when household heads were held responsible by the state for literacy instruction and for supervising reading, men typically have benefitted most from education campaigns. Moreover, when reading was extended to women, men received preference in the teaching of writing.[49] However, in early modern Sweden and the nineteenth-century United States, perceptions of women's special educational "mission" at home, as mothers, and as school teachers propelled their rates of literacy upward, sometimes rivaling those of men.

Do significant differences in materials and methods characterize contemporary literacy campaigns? Over the past two decades, there has been a shift to concepts of literacy as individually or collectively empowering and liberating. In

---

[46]See Carron and Bordia, *Issues*, chapter on Vietnam.

[47]See Chapter 7, this volume; see also Cohen, "Civilizational States," Evelyn Rawski, *Education and Popular Literacy in Ch'ing China* (Ann Arbor: University of Michigan Press, 1979), Kathleen Gough, "Implications of Literacy in Traditional China and Indiana," in *Literacy in Traditional Societies*, ed. Jack Goody (Cambridge: Cambridge University Press, 1968), pp. 69–84. Rawski and Gough, in particular, argue that the orthographic obstacle to literacy has been exaggerated.

[48]See also Rawski, *Education*.

[49]See Chapter 13 this volume; see also Francois Furet and Jacques Ozouf, *Lire et écrire: L'alphabètisation des français de Calvin à Ferry* (Paris: Editions de Minuit, 1977), esp. Vol 1 (translated into English as *Reading and Writing* (Cambridge: Cambridge University Press, 1983).

some cases, this has meant developing different literacy primers that appeal to different interests. In Tanzania, for example, twelve different literacy primers were prepared—all but two, according to Kassam and Hall, based on the economic and social activities of the people of that country.[50] Elsewhere, it has meant the use of emotionally charged themes that awaken people to examine their past exploitation and to their role as agents of change in a society now reorganized along radically different principles.

Campaigns of the last two decades, in addition to employing notions derived from Paulo Freire's "pedagogy of the oppressed," are also based on borrowings from other countries. Current literacy programs take from the declarations of international conferences such as those of Persepolis and Udaipur. According to Gillette, the Experimental World Literacy Program, for example, contributed to instructional methodology specifically for adults. Appropriately designated as "andragogy," adult literacy efforts increasingly stress (1) an inductive approach, which starts with adults' own ideas and insights; (2) experiential learning, which derives from and relates to the prospects of applying newly acquired knowledge and skills; and (3) a variety of techniques and a flexible approach in which it is realized that there is "no magical solution to the problem." Other approaches, of course, focus on children and youth.[51]

Interestingly enough, statements by Lenin and Ho Chi Minh cautioned against too impetuous and inflexible an approach to literacy instruction. Both were aware of the dangers of authoritarian, and—in the case of Lenin—excessively political, instruction that ignored learners' interests and needs in the initial stages of literacy. Revealingly, Lenin, along with Marx and Gramsci, held to rigorous, very sound, seemingly traditional, education for all. Only a broadly based education would end the cultural dominance of previous elites and their social system.

Although contemporary campaigns seem to differ from past campaigns in their more learner-oriented approaches and their emphasis on participatory teaching methods, similarities also are important. An examination of mass mobilizations, such as that of Nicaragua, reveal, on the one hand, attempts to engage the learners in dialogue and to design texts that respect the linguistic universe and social interests of illiterates. But, on the other hand, national uniform texts were used, instruction was frequently teacher-centered and directive, and the acquisition of basic literacy skills was often based on various repetitive and mechanical means of teaching and learning.[52] Moreover, in mass mobilizations, teachers are often chosen for their allegiance to a particular party or regime, rather than for their pedagogical preparation.

In the mass mobilization literacy campaigns, all elements—materials, media, symbols, methods, instructional personnel—work together in theory to socialize the population into a new faith, sometimes a conserving one, sometimes a revolutionary one. Outcomes, however, may be something else.

[50] See Kassam and Hall, "Tanzania's Campaign."
[51] See, e.g. Arthur Gillette, *Literacy and Youth.*
[52] See Chapter 12 below.

OUTCOMES

Outcomes may be studied at the individual, group, and collective levels. Consequences may be assessed as immediate or over a longer term. They may be studied in quantitative or qualitative terms. The quantitative side generally refers to numbers of individuals reached by a campaign and the numbers who achieve literacy and continue on to postliteracy adult educational activities. Frequently, these figures are impressive, involving millions of people who participated in a campaign and dramatic decreases in illiteracy levels.[53]

As a result of earlier campaigns, an estimated eighty-five percent of the German population could read by 1850. A base had been established for the subsequent industrialization of the country. Similar figures are noted for Scotland and for much of the developed West.[54] In the twentieth century, the Soviet campaign claimed to have raised literacy levels to approximately eighty-two percent by 1939. In the post–World War II period, the studies in this volume note a decline in illiteracy in Tanzania, from sixty-seven percent in 1970 to fifteen percent in 1983; in Cuba, from twenty-four percent to four percent as the result of the 1961 campaign; and in Nicaragua, from fifty percent to approximately fifteen percent, as the result of the 1980 campaign in Spanish and the follow-up campaign in indigenous languages. A striking pattern emerges: with the exception of Cuba, the results are essentially the same. Regardless of date, duration, or developmental level, approximately eighty-five percent adult literacy is achieved. Nevertheless, an irreducible minimum remains of at least ten to twenty percent. This is a point to ponder.

Such figures tell little about the levels of literacy achieved or the uses and implications of literacy acquisition. The more interesting analyses, from our point of view, are those of a more qualitative nature. Literacy itself is too often viewed in only a dichotomous way: either a person is literate or not. But literacy may also be viewed along a continuum: a set of skills that may become more complex over time in response to changing social contexts, shifting demands on individuals' communication skills, or individuals' own efforts at advancement. Only in Tanzania did the campaign actually define as many as four levels of literacy acquisition that involved increasingly more complex uses of reading and writing skills.

Historically, reading has not always related closely to either comprehension or writing. In seventeenth-century Sweden, emphasis was placed on reading Holy Scripture, not on being able to use the skills of writing. Limage similarly draws attention to the difference between reading and writing skills in France. For the Soviet Union, Eklof distinguishes between literacy and "true education," which means use of reading and writing skills to understand the nature of one's society and being able to contribute to improvements in it—perhaps even to

---

[53] Sometimes the quantitative outcomes are not impressive. The results of the EWLP indicate that little more than ten percent of the one million individuals who participated in the program in eleven countries completed a test of literacy attainment; see Chapter 9 below.

[54] See following discussions and Graff, *Legacies*.

Quantity

		Low	High
	Low		Mass campaigns: collective advancement and individual benefits; political socialization and moral development
Quality	High	Selective campaigns: individual (often upper or middle class) benefits; cognitive skills; "gatekeepers"	

Figure 2. Quantity and quality in national literacy campaigns.

alter its very premises and structures. If comprehension, understanding what one reads, is a critical feature of literacy, then, even in the more wealthy school districts of the United States many teenagers may be classified as illiterate; they do not understand their school texts or major stories in newspapers. Arnove and Arboleda remark that if illiteracy refers to the ability to understand the basic issues confronting individuals in contemporary society, then illiteracy is pervasive in many industrially advanced nations with extensive systems of schooling.[55]

The relations between quantity and quality within campaigns, more generally, are represented schematically in Figure 2. That mass literacy campaigns almost invariably—indeed, virtually by definition—aim at quantitative rather than qualitative goals is grasped immediately. The contrasting strategy of emphasis on the quality of literacy skills, as the figure also illustrates, takes the individual as the target.

The goal of many literacy campaigns has been changes in individuals' belief systems as part of transformations in social systems. The outcomes that merit study include changes in self-concepts, ideological orientations, political dispositions, feelings of efficacy, and commitments to engage in social action. There have been some attempts to measure these outcomes using questionnaires and interviews.[56] Assuming that countries are willing to examine critically the course

[55]See following discussions, John Bormuth, *"Illiteracy in the Suburbs,"* mimeograph. Department of Education, University of Chicago, October 1970. Robert F. Arnove and Jairo Arboleda, "Literacy: Power or Mystification," *Literacy Discussion* 4 (December 1973), pp. 389–414, Street, *Literacy*, and Kozol, *Illiteracy*.

[56]On evaluation as a component of the EWLP, see Chapter 9 below; see also Jan L. Flora, John McFadden, and Ruth Warner, "The Growth of Class Struggle: The Impact of the Nicaraguan Literacy Crusade on the Political Consciousness of Young Literacy Workers," *Latin American Perspectives*, 36 (Winter, 1983), pp. 49–53, and Kassam, *Illiterate No More: The Voices of New Literates from Tanzania* (Dar es Salaam: Tanzania Publishing House, 1979). For earlier works on literacy, education, and modernization, see Alex Inkeles and David Smith, *Becoming Modern: Individual*

and outcomes of their campaigns, there are a number of serious problems. Changes in individuals are extremely difficult to assess, particularly with regard to the role of literacy as a causal factor. The instruments tend to be limited in their reliability and validity. For example, positive sentiments aroused by the experience of participating in a campaign may be reversed as government policies and circumstances change.

Importantly, the very process of participating in a campaign and achieving literacy may confer a new status on individuals, removing a stigma of inferiority.[57] The opposite side of the coin is that those who do not participate in a campaign or who continue to be illiterate may be labeled as deviant and denied full membership rights in a religious or political community. Historically as well as more recently, those who oppose literacy efforts may be viewed as dissident, unassimilated, counterrevolutionary, or enemies of the state.

The community-level outcomes of expanded literacy are more difficult to measure. Nevertheless, we must ask how diffusion of literacy affects the practices that traditionally have held communities together, if such practices are to be supplanted or reinforced by the cultural policies of new political regimes, how the spread of literacy modifies orality and other traditional means of communication, and whether or not, as Bhola claims, literate communities "by definition, will have to have a higher fund of symbolic skills."[58]

Historically, collective transformations have been sought through literacy campaigns. Therefore, outcomes must also be examined at the societal level. This level has up to now been studied least.[59]

The case studies in this book suggest a number of (intended as well as unintended) structural and cultural outcomes. Among these outcomes are the institutionalization of school systems, standardization of national languages, incorporation of marginal populations into national societies, and legitimation and consolidation of political regimes. Another consequence is the resistance of individuals and groups to centralizing tendencies on the part of national authorities. Despite apparent high-level generalizations across time and space, what is most important resides in specific contexts. Each social context shapes and conditions relations that can only be viewed as dialectical—tying all factors and actors together in complex fashion.

Institutionalization of Schooling

The development of state controlled or sponsored school systems is one legacy of the Reformation German and Scottish campaigns. The dissemination of literacy in most of Western Europe and North America, from the late seventeenth century, is the sometimes torturously slow and gradual story of the

---

Change in Six Developing Countries (Cambridge, MA: Harvard University Press, 1974) and Daniel Lerner, *The Passing of Traditional Society* (Glencoe: Free Press, 1958).
[57] See Bhola, *Campaigning*, p. 25 and Chapter 12 below.
[58] Bhola, *Campaigning*, p. 22.
[59] Carron and Bordia, *Issues*, p. 35

establishment of schools—and systems of schooling. Lurie testifies to the culmination of this history:

> Literacy education for adults and the provision of schooling for children must be seen as two sides of the same coin, and that consequently, the planning of education and the subsequent facilities of educational systems . . . must be redirected as to serve the aims of these two objectives more effectively.[60]

At times, literacy activities (as in late nineteenth-century Russia) outran the establishment of schools by state authorities. But the long-term historical trend has been for formal institutionalized education to either replace or incorporate nonformal (out-of-school) activities that also provided literacy.

Campaigns of the last three decades, such as those of Cuba and Nicaragua, have consciously attempted to develop a postliteracy system of adult education outside the formal school system. They nonetheless have contributed to tens of thousands of youths and young adults entering higher levels of the formal system after completing the adult education cycles. In many respects, the "popular education" system in Nicaragua, with progressively more levels being added to it, comprises a parallel, increasingly institutionalized education system.[61]

Literacy provision and socialization of individuals over time have merged and been institutionalized in state systems of formal education. From the earliest campaigns, the goals of literacy provision have been the propagation of a particular faith or world view, the reading of prescribed texts, under the supervision of teachers of a certain moral persuasion and of an upright character. Historically, the religious orientation of school systems has given way to a more secular faith in the nation-state and/or the propagation of an ideology such as capitalism or socialism.

Standardization of Languages

The widespread dissemination of mass literacy depends not only on common texts (hence inducements to all facets of publishing) but on the use of a common language. The histories of England, France, and Italy illustrate the importance of creating linguistic commonality as part of nation-state formation.[62] School systems in many countries today are viewed by national authorities as contributing to the forging of consensus values as well as teaching a national language. Gillette points out, for example, that one of the effects of the EWLP in Mali was standardization of the national language. In Tanzania, the literacy campaign that followed the EWLP helped develop a new written literature in Kiswahili. In pre- and post-1949 China, according to Hayford, literacy movements often attempted to simplify, and even romanize, traditional Chinese orthography.

[60]S. Lurie, "Preface," in Carron and Bordia, *Issues.*
[61]Arnove, *Education and Revolution in Nicaragua* (New York: Praeger, 1986), esp. Chapter 3.
[62]Historically, social class formation has been part and parcel of the same process; see Graff, *Legacies.*

Incorporation and Integration

One of the intended outcomes of recent campaigns, such as those of Cuba and Nicaragua, is also the integration of countryside and city. Not only recently, but also historically, literacy campaigns have been an important device for attempting to overcome geographical and social divisions within a society.

In twentieth-century campaigns, sending tens of thousands of urban high school and university students to live and teach in the countryside is a manifestation of a new political regime's intent to extend basic social services to marginal populations and to incorporate them into national efforts. These mobilizations also seek to teach urban, largely middle-class youths about the realities of rural life, and make them more appreciative of their rural brothers and sisters and more committed to rural development.[63]

Attempts to integrate society by means of literacy campaigns are not unique to the twentieth century. Describing the German literacy drives of the eighteenth and nineteenth centuries, Gawthrop remarks that "by the early nineteenth century the vast majority of peasants were receiving the same basic education as that given to all but the elite elements of Germany's middle classes." There was a narrowing of cultural disparity between town and countryside as people of different social strata had access to the same books—Bible, catechism, and hymnal.

The publication of scores of editions of the same religious texts—in the millions—in Germany, Sweden, and the United States, as well as popular books such as the McGuffey readers in the United States and Chairman Mao's Little Red Book in China, contributed to the population's reading common texts. But the inducements to diversification as well as economies of scale in publishing also contributed to specialized publications. This specialization resulted in the proliferation of tracts aimed at a multitude of audiences, with their differing belief systems and points of view. The proliferation and specialization of print materials has at times contributed to consensus building but at other times to the deepening of divisions within a society.

Legitimation and Consolidation of Regimes

The incorporation of people into a new moral or political order is always a desired outcome of mass campaigns. Regime legitimation at the national level is certainly an intended goal of nineteenth- and twentieth-century campaigns. Legitimation at the international level is a more recent and less studied phenomenon. According to Unsicker, campaigns apparently may contribute to a nation's standing in the international community and may facilitate greater readiness on the part of international technical assistance and donor agencies to provide aid.[64]

---

[63] See Fernando Cardenal and Valerie Miller, "Nicaragua 1980: The Battle of the ABCs," *Harvard Educational Review* 51 (1981): 1–26.

[64] Conversely, a regime may lose legitimacy if it fails to mount a successful literacy campaign. This issue also merits study.

The success of large-scale mobilizations is often the function of mass organizations, such as youth, worker, neighborhood, defense, and women's associations. In turn, one structural outcome of literacy campaigns in mobilizational
regimes, such as Nicaragua, Cuba, Ethiopia, the Soviet Union, and the People's
Republic of China, has been the strengthening of these mass organizations.

A national campaign, by mobilizing large numbers of people and strengthening mass organizations, creates opportunities for large-scale citizenship participation in decision making. But such mobilizations and organizations may also
serve as instruments for exercising cultural and political hegemony by dominant
groups or the state apparatus. The history of efforts at social control, of dominant
groups trying to control the uses of literacy and expanded communication skills,
offers countless examples of people, individually and collectively, resisting efforts
at either imposition or control.

Resistance

As literacy provision commonly forms part of efforts to impose centralizing
authority and attempts to change people's beliefs, it is not unusual to discover
instances of individuals and groups resisting perceived threats to their identity.
The German literacy drives elicited such responses from peasants from as early
as the sixteenth century. Russia offers abundant instances before and after the
1917 revolution of peasant populations setting up their own schools and employing reading materials that did not accord with the designs of state authorities.
Eklof chronicles peasant attacks on State appointed teachers in the late 1920s
and early 1930s. He also describes how, despite intense efforts at censorship,
readers pursue their own interests, frequently of an escapist nature: "Library
subscribers took out books on politics in far smaller number than their availability. Books checked out were concentrated in the areas of travel, biography
and history (primarily on World War II, military memoirs, spy documentaries,
regimental histories)."

Similar accounts of reading habits from Tanzania and the People's Republic
of China indicate that peasants and workers may be less interested in reading
about how to construct a latrine or organize a cooperative than they are in
romance and adventure stories. Gillette sums up the difficulty of controlling
outcomes of literacy campaigns: "Happily, literacy like education more generally
cannot be reduced to behavioral conditioning. It endows people with skills that
they can (although do not always) use to receive and emit messages of an almost
infinite range, a range that in any event escapes the control of those who imparted
literacy. . . . Literacy is potential empowerment."

Persisting Problems

In addition to the resistance of people to control, and the unpredictable
outcomes of literacy campaigns, there are other seemingly intractable problems.
Class, ethnic, racial, geographical, and gender differences in literacy acquisition
have been ubiquitous over the past four hundred years. The recent Cuban and

Nicaraguan campaigns, however, reveal a new potential for breaking this pattern. One particularly important change is the extent to which women are participants in and beneficiaries of literacy campaigns. In Cuba and Nicaragua, a majority of the literacy workers were women. As Arnove notes, one of the changes accelerated and magnified by the latter literacy crusade has been the liberation of women from their marginal positions in the society. The results from other campaigns, such as Tanzania, further indicate that women predominate at the lower levels of literacy attainment; at the highest levels, corresponding to functional literacy, males predominate.[65]

LESSONS

To ask of literacy that it overcome gender discrimination, integrate a society, eliminate inequalities, and contribute to political and social stability is certainly too much. Literacy may be empowering, especially when it can work in conjunction with other changes. Ultimately, the retention and uses of literacy depend on the context on the environment of opportunities available to people to use their literacy skills, transformations in social structures, and the ideology of leaders. Whether the materials and methods of literacy and postliteracy campaigns are truly designed to equip people to play more active roles in shaping the direction of their societies or, to the contrary, are intended to induct people into roles predetermined by others, is a telling indication of ideology and intent.

Literacy planners and political leaders are aware of a number of the factors that contribute to the success—as well as limitation—of current and past campaigns. The extent to which international and national authorities involved in literacy campaigns have fully grasped the implications of these lessons and are committed to applying them remains in question. One basic reason for doubting the resolve of political and educational leaders in many countries is that widespread possession of literacy by a populace may lead to unpredictable, contradictory, and conflictive consequences.[66]

There is a dialectic, an interaction, between individuals and the environment as they gain literacy, and between them and centralizing authorities. The dialectic is an ongoing process with the nature of that interaction being shaped by the expansion—and sometimes the transformation—of literacy itself. In the last thirty years, there has been a change in the ideology of literacy toward an emphasis on empowerment. Contributing to this shift have been the seminal work of Paulo Freire, the example of the Cuban literacy campaign, Unesco-sponsored conferences and declarations, and the emergence of a more critical and political scholarly literature. Whether this shift to empowerment and grassroots determination of literacy development will effectively counter long and

---

[65] Kassam and Hall, "Tanzania's Campaign."

[66] Henry M. Levin on "The Identity Crisis of Educational Planning," *Harvard Educational Review* 51 (1981): 85–93.

strong traditions of top-down centralized direction of literacy efforts remains to be seen.

The tension between the base and the top, between the masses and elites, between those who are the supposed beneficiaries of literacy and those who envision and organize for the populace, has been heightened by the telescoped period of time, the scale of mobilization, modern technologies and communication, and the refined instruments of state power. Also contributing to the tension is the new awareness of base and top alike of the political nature of literacy—not surprising given the rhetoric and ideology of recent campaigns concerning education for critical consciousness and liberation. This tension, as the essays in this volume illustrate, has a long history. We can perhaps understand the nature of the tension; it is very difficult to predict or prescribe the manifold outcomes of a campaign and the uses of literacy.

CHAPTER 2

Literacy Drives in Preindustrial Germany

RICHARD L. GAWTHROP

LITERACY CAMPAIGNS IN THE ERA OF THE REFORMATION

Among the chief assets Germany possessed by the time it had begun to industrialize was an uncommonly literate labor force. By 1850 Prussia's literacy rate—not unrepresentative of that of the rest of the German states—had reached eighty-five percent. This Prussian rate, which assumes a standard of literacy consisting of both reading and writing skills, compares with a mid-century rate of sixty-one percent for France (reading only) and fifty-two percent for England (reading and writing).[1] Although historians have assumed that high literacy rates played an important role in the rapidity of German industrialization in the nineteenth century,[2] they have failed to give a satisfactory explanation for this early achievement of mass literacy.[3] One reason for this failure is their unwillingness to view the literacy drives of the sixteenth and eighteenth centuries as having exerted a sufficiently powerful impact on society to account for the unusually high literacy rates of nineteenth-century Germany.

This attitude stems in part from the methodological limitations of traditional scholarship in this field. To appreciate why these deficiencies are so critical, it is necessary to consider the nature of the two sets of literacy drives in early modern Germany. These drives or "campaigns"—I use the two terms synonymously—are classic examples of state-led efforts to impose literacy on an

---

[1] Kenneth Barkin, "Social Control and the Volksschule in Vormärz Prussia," *Central European History* 16 (March 1983), p. 50. For a quantitative analysis of school enrollment in nineteenth-century Prussia, see Peter Lundgreen, "Educational Expansion and Economic Growth in Nineteenth-Century Germany: A Quantitative Study," in *Schooling and Society: Studies in the History of Education*, ed. Lawrence Stone (Baltimore: The Johns Hopkins University Press, 1976), pp. 20–66.
[2] David S. Landes, *The Unbound Prometheus: Technological Change and Industrial Development in Western Europe from 1750 to the Present* (New York: Cambridge University Press, 1969), pp. 340–48.
[3] For a critical assessment of the recent literature on late eighteenth- and early nineteenth-century Prussian primary education, see Barkin, pp. 32–37.

RICHARD L. GAWTHROP • Department of History, University of South Carolina, Columbia, South Carolina 29208.

often reluctant population in a preindustrial society. The leading role of the
state compels the historian assessing educational efforts of this sort to analyze
both the institutions fostered by the bureaucratic elite and the popular culture's
reaction to pedagogical pressure from above. The interdisciplinary approach
required for such a study is all too rare in German historiography, with its long-
standing separation of political and administrative history, on the one hand, and
social history, on the other. In 1968 Gerhard Oestreich proposed that the split
be overcome by concentrating on "the spiritual, moral, and psychological changes
which social discipline [during the preindustrial era] produced in the individual,
whether he was engaged in politics, army life, or trade."[4] Although Oestreich's
all-embracing concept of "social discipline" has received much critical attention,
it has not been able to break down the compartmentalization that continues to
inhibit the development of synthesizing perspectives among the practitioners of
German history.

     Another aspect of the inability to appreciate the significance of the German
literacy drives manifests itself in overly harsh evaluations of the content and
method of primary education in early modern Germany. At the root of this
difficulty is the culture-bound attitude of highly literate people toward the subject
of literacy. As Walter Ong has shown, individuals with this bias think in terms
of a dichotomy between literacy and "preliteracy."[5] Ong's own work demonstrates
that, on the contrary, literacy and oral tradition have coexisted throughout nearly
all of history in a variety of cultural configurations. Modern culture, defined as
being based almost exclusively on "highly interiorized" literacy, is in this sense
unique. Previous cultures, even literate high cultures, always possessed at least
a certain "residual orality," while predominantly oral, popular cultures have been
able to assimilate selectively some external uses of literacy.[6] When modern critics
of eighteenth-century schools condemn their religious content and emphasis on
memorization, they fail to realize that the failure of most of the school children
to acquire highly interiorized literacy need not imply that the schools had a
negligible, or even negative, impact on the development of mass literacy.

     In this essay I attempt to overcome these methodological barriers in order
to demonstrate that the literacy drives of early modern Germany contributed
decisively to the high rates of literacy achieved by the early nineteenth century.
The first step in this process, the series of literacy drives launched in the middle
of the sixteenth century, constituted perhaps the first state-led literacy campaigns
in European history. Economic and political factors played an important role in
the decision of city-states and territorial authorities in Germany to organize such
efforts at this early date. Inflationary prosperity in early sixteenth-century Europe
led to an expansion of the monetarized sector of the economy, especially in

[4]Gerhard Oestreich, "Strukturprobleme des europäischen Absolutismus," *Vierteljahrschrift für Sozial-
und Wirtschaftsgeschichte* 50 (1968), p. 338. An English translation of this article is included in Gerhard
Oestreich, *Neostoicism and the Modern State*, trans. David McLintock (New York: Cambridge University
Press, 1982), p. 265.
[5]Walter J. Ong, *Orality and Literacy: The Technologizing of the Word* (New York: Methuen, 1982),
pp. 10–15, 174–75.
[6]Ibid., pp. 115–16, 178–79.

Germany, where cities such as Augsburg and Nuremberg combined access to mineral resources with textile manufacturing, metal working, and banking strength to assume a leading place in the European economy as a whole.[7] Besides creating a greater demand for reading skills in German cities, economic growth also promoted literacy more indirectly. The extension of the market into previously self-sufficient economic units profoundly disrupted German society. The political authorities, hampered by archaic legal systems, were initially unable to arbitrate the conflicts that arose between the various social groups, of which the Peasant War of 1525 was only the most important example. The urgent need for order enabled the governments of territorial states and free cities to increase dramatically their legislative and judicial powers—a development whose success was powerfully aided by the adoption of Roman law by central authorities throughout Germany.[8] Thus, economic expansion led to a correspondingly rapid growth in the judicial and administrative bureaucracies of the sixteenth-century German states, whose need to exert control over their territories constituted a necessary condition for the initiation of the mid-century literacy drives.

The crucial impetus for seeking to impart a knowledge of reading to all segments of society came, however, from the Protestant Reformation, though not in the way usually suggested by historians of that movement. The spontaneous religious excitement generated by Luther died out within thirty years and did not in itself produce a permanent change in popular reading patterns. It is possible, to be sure, that the thousands of pamphlets supporting or condemning the Reformation, as well as Luther's initial insistence that Christians should read the Bible for themselves, played a part in increasing literacy in German towns during the 1520s and 1530s.[9] But the spectacle of peasants justifying their rebellion of 1525 by misrepresenting (in Luther's eyes) his religious message turned the Great Reformer against any fostering of unsupervised book learning, particularly on the village level.[10] The widespread ignorance of religious doctrine revealed by the visitation of Saxon parishes by Protestant church officials in the late 1520s further reinforced Luther's desire to restrain uninformed lay enthusiasm and led him to seek a safe means for instilling in the populace the essentials of the new faith.

In 1529 Luther created a pedagogical instrument, the Small Catechism, to guide the teaching efforts of parish sextons, whom the Lutheran church authorities were then compelling "to gather the children at least once a week to teach

---

[7] Peter Kriedte, *Peasants, Landlords and Merchant Capitalists: Europe and the World Economy, 1500–1800* (New York: Cambridge University Press, 1983), pp. 32, 35–39.

[8] Gerald Strauss, *Law, Resistance, and the State in Sixteenth-Century Germany* (Princeton: Princeton University Press, 1986).

[9] Rolf Engelsing, *Analphabetentum und Lektüre: Zur Sozialgeschichte des Lesens in Deutschland* (Stuttgart: Metzler, 1973), p. 35. For a sophisticated assessment of the impact of the Lutheran agitation on the popular mind, see R. W. Scribner, *For the Sake of Simple Folk: Popular Propaganda for the German Reformation* (New York: Cambridge University Press, 1981).

[10] Richard Gawthrop and Gerald Strauss, "Protestantism and Literacy in Early Modern Germany," *Past & Present* no. 104 (August 1984), pp. 33–35, 42.

them the Ten Commandments, the Creed, the Lord's Prayer, and some German hymns."[11] In these early Lutheran catechism classes, the usual method for teaching the catechism consisted of recitation and memorization. Although this oral form of learning retained its central place in German religious education far into the nineteenth century, the Lutheran reformers realized that the catechization of children would be more effective if the young people were also taught to read. By 1541 this more intensive curriculum had worked its way into church legislation. In that year regulations drawn up for Lutheran sextons in Brunswick obliged these church employees to teach their pupils reading as well as the catechism. In the following two decades, instruction in the catechism became a common feature of Lutheran church life in German villages, though in most cases this practice stopped well short of a program of full-time schooling designed to teach reading to every child of the village and its environs.[12]

What turned these fledgling church institutions into instruments for a full-scale literacy campaign was the tendency, unmistakable by the 1550s, toward the coordination and direction of primary education by centralizing political and ecclesiastical authorities. The desire of the governing elites to promote literacy by means of a uniform system of instruction stemmed from the nature of the relationship between church and state in post-Reformation Germany. The legal framework for accommodating the religious division of Germany between the Catholic and Lutheran faiths was established by the Treaty of Augsburg (1555). That document laid down the fundamental principle that the religious preference of the ruler or ruling elite of each city or princedom determined whether the population of that political unit would belong to the Catholic or the Lutheran Church. The treaty thereby created a unity of belief within each German territory and accelerated the process, already well advanced in both Catholic and Protestant principalities, by which the secular authority was acquiring the power to supervise the internal workings of the territorial church.[13]

The reason that this situation produced literacy drives throughout late sixteenth-century Germany was that the Augsburg settlement did not solve the problem of political and religious instability. From the early 1560s on, the Catholic church, reorganized at the Council of Trent and reinvigorated by the newly founded Jesuit order, sought to regain territories lost to Protestantism earlier in the century. On the Protestant side, an acrimonious split developed between a Lutheranism strongly committed to the *status quo* and the militantly anti-Catholic Reformed (Calvinist) church. As a result, both Catholic and Protestant states acutely feared religious heterodoxy within their borders because of the possibility of subversion from a neighboring state adhering to one of the other religious factions. The strong political need for uniform belief induced governments to use their ascendancy within their ecclesiastical administrations to establish schools

[11] Ernst Christian Helmreich, *Religious Education in German Schools: A Historical Approach* (Cambridge: Harvard University Press, 1959), p. 15. See also Gawthrop and Strauss, pp. 35–36.

[12] Helmreich, p. 15. See also Eugen Schmid, *Geschichte des Volksschulwesens in Altwürttemberg* (Stuttgart: Kohlhammer, 1927), pp. 14–16.

[13] For the best analysis of the relationship between church and state in consequence of the Reformation, see Strauss, *Law, Resistance, and the State*, Chapter 7.

designed to indoctrinate the general population and thereby ensure religious conformity.[14] With the enthusiastic support of the clergy within their territories, the leaders of German city-states and principalities therefore embarked on ambitious efforts to create or greatly expand networks of primary schools and place them under clerical supervision and control.

The institutional structures governing these school systems conformed to a common pattern. School ordinances promulgated by city or state authorities set forth a standard curriculum, consisting above all of catechism drill and psalm singing, followed, in descending order of importance by reading, writing, and, quite rarely, arithmetic.[15] The ordinances required that school be held up to five hours a day, five days a week. Parishes that did not already have a sexton were required to hire one and place him in charge of the school. The merging of the positions of sexton and schoolmaster, clearly spelled out in the widely copied Württemberg school ordinance of 1559, became the norm for small towns and villages throughout Germany.[16] The advantages of this arrangement were that it saved the community the extra expense of supporting another ecclesiastical employee and that it therefore kept tuition fees at a relatively low level. Although as a rule local communities financed the schools, the higher authorities did grant some financial help to poorer villages that really wanted a school.[17] The communities usually nominated a candidate for vacant schoolmaster positions, but the church consistory officially made the appointment. In Württemberg at least, nominees were required to pass an examination testing their literacy, singing ability, and knowledge of the catechism.[18] The modest size of most of the individual German polities permitted the central authorities to exercise close control over the teachers. In addition to the local supervision of the teacher by the pastor, it was common practice for the central clerical bureaucracy to send an official once or twice a year to inspect each school. The highest body within the church administration annually reviewed the inspectors' reports and took action whenever needed.[19]

The literacy drives of the mid-to-late sixteenth century not only established the structural framework for primary schooling in early modern Germany but were also responsible for a growth in the uniformity and size of the German school systems. In fourteenth- and fifteenth-century German cities, prosperous artisans and merchants sponsored vernacular, secular, private schools, in which utilitarian skills, such as reading and arithmetic, were taught.[20] As the sixteenth century progressed, some of these schools were suppressed by the established

---

[14]Gerald Strauss, *Luther's House of Learning: Indoctrination of the Young in the German Reformation*, (Baltimore: Johns Hopkins University Press, 1978), p. 21.

[15]The sixteenth-century Lutheran school ordinances have been collected and published in Reinhold Vormbaum, ed., *Evangelische Schulordnungen*, 1 (Gütersloh: Bertelsmann, 1858).

[16]For a detailed analysis of the Württemberg ordinance, see Schmid, pp. 17–29; for the text, see Vormbaum, 1, pp. 68–165.

[17]Strauss, *Luther's House of Learning*, p. 25.

[18]Schmid, pp. 46–49.

[19]For the inspection system in Württemberg, see ibid., pp. 79–80.

[20]Peter Lundgreen, *Sozialgeschichte der deutschen Schule im Überblick, Teil 1: 1770–1918* (Göttingen: Vandenhoeck und Ruprecht, 1980), p. 17. See also Schmid, p. 4.

churches; some survived despite official persecution, and many others added the catechism to their curriculum and gradually became indistinguishable from the publicly sponsored primary schools.[21] Another sign of increasing uniformity was the gradual disappearance, in most places, of the early Reformation pattern of the pastor or sexton's conducting weekly catechism for fairly small numbers of pupils. Their place was taken mainly by "constant," that is, full-time, schools.[22]

The growth in numbers of such schools constituted the most significant achievement of the sixteenth-century literacy drives. In electoral Saxony most of the larger villages had schools by the 1570s, but the authorities in the school ordinance of 1580 expressed their intention of providing instruction in catechism and reading for residents of the poorer and more isolated villages as well. By 1617 their determination resulted in the existence of a "far larger number" of schools than had been the case in the 1570s.[23] In Württemberg, another Lutheran territory, precise figures tell a similar tale. In 1559 there were 150 localities with vernacular schools, most of which were constant schools; in 1581 there were 240, and in 1600 some 400 communities possessed "German" schools.[24] Catholic principalities, such as Bavaria, followed the general trend. Though comparable statistics on rural schools are lacking, in Munich in the 1560s, "every parish had an elementary school."[25]

Although the creation of these centrally directed school networks was a tremendous achievement, particularly for the sixteenth century, the ability of these schools to teach literacy was seriously impaired by a series of obstacles, most of which ultimately derived from the poverty of the individual communities. In the first place, many families could not take advantage of the educational opportunities offered by the school systems. Particularly in the poorest, least populated areas, where villages were too small to have their own churches, the nearest constant school was often too far away to be of any use. These districts were served only by temporary schools, usually offshoots of a neighboring constant school; and the financing of such schools was usually so tenuous that they could not be relied on to provide even periodic schooling to the more remote hamlets.[26] Moreover, in areas where constant schools did exist, the need of farming families for their children's labor prevented school from being held between sowing and harvest and often obliged parents to remove their children from school during the winter months. Many poorer families chose not to enroll their children in school at all in order to save themselves the modest, but not inconsequential, tuition fee.

Unless there was strong peer pressure in the community in favor of schooling, the authorities could not force children to attend school. In most areas of

[21] Strauss, *Luther's House of Learning*, pp. 201–02; Schmid, p. 7. See also Christopher R. Friedrichs, "Whose House of Learning? Some Thoughts on German Schools in Post-Reformation Germany," *History of Education Quarterly* 22 (1982), pp. 371–78.

[22] Schmid, pp. 38–41.

[23] Strauss, *Luther's House of Learning*, pp. 21, 198.

[24] Schmid, pp. 29, 36.

[25] Strauss, *Luther's House of Learning*, p. 197.

[26] Ibid., p. 27; Schmid, pp. 44–45.

Germany, parents had no legal obligation to educate their children, and efforts in some places to impose fines on recalcitrants met with failure.[27] One of the many reasons for that outcome was the reluctance of teachers to report parents to the authorities for fear of communal disapprobation, since the schoolmaster's livelihood depended not only on his tiny salary and the tuition payments, but also on use of village land and forms of payment in kind, for which the good will of the community was essential.[28]

This is not to say that popular support for the sixteenth-century school system was totally lacking, that the authorities simply imposed this institution on an unwilling population. On the contrary, when the consistory in Württemberg attempted to close some schools for reasons of economy, the affected communities stubbornly resisted the loss of their school. Although the precise reasons for such grass roots support for schooling are a matter for speculation, clearly elite groups in villages and small towns saw some value in having a local school.[29]

Nevertheless, for the overwhelming majority of people in this preindustrial society, the costs of sending their children to school outweighed the benefits youngsters received from their education. Peasants and artisans did not need skill in reading to learn the techniques required for making a living, which were transmitted orally. Nor were most peasants and poorer townspeople inclined to pay for schooling simply for the religious and moral training it would provide their children. As Gerald Strauss has shown, popular attitudes toward the churches in the second half of the sixteenth century ranged from apathy to antipathy. Until at least the Thirty Years' War (1618–1648), the traditional folk culture of the peasantry on the whole resisted successfully the influence of the urban-based piety of both the Protestant and Catholic reformations.[30] In addition to this culturally based indifference or opposition to the religious message of the schoolmaster, the latter may also have had to contend with a general sense of alienation among the common people resulting from the rising taxes, declining real wages, and rapidly increasing population characteristic of late sixteenth-century Germany.[31]

---

[27] Strauss, *Luther's House of Learning*, p. 23; Schmid, pp. 133–34.

[28] For the best account of the system used to finance primary schooling in Germany from the late sixteenth to the early nineteenth century, see Mary Jo Maynes, "The Virtues of Archaism: The Political Economy of Schooling in Europe, 1750–1850," *Comparative Studies in Society and History* 21 (1979), pp. 613–25.

[29] Strauss, *Luther's House of Learning*, p. 21. The village elite may have wanted simply to have such schooling available for their children or to maintain a school out of a sense of local pride. In the Württemberg material presented by Schmid, foundings of village schools are often attributed to existence of large numbers of school-age children. This suggests that possibly the village elites were acting out of a desire to use the school as a means of controlling excess numbers of young people that may have been threatening village cohesion in the late sixteenth century. Schmid, pp. 33–35.

[30] Strauss, *Luther's House of Learning*, pp. 302–08. See also David Sabean, *Power in the Blood: Popular Culture and Village Discourse in Early Modern Germany* (New York: Cambridge University Press, 1984).

[31] Kriedte, pp. 50–54.

A final limitation on the effectiveness of these literacy campaigns was the generally poor quality of instruction in the schools. Some of the factors responsible for this state of affairs were beyond the control of the schoolmaster. The impoverished communities could commonly afford to spare only the most primitive, one-room building to serve as a school house. Besides the problems posed by deficient heating and lighting, the lack of spatial division obliged teachers either to instruct all their pupils at once or to work with one child at a time while the others noisily waited. The combination of voluntary attendance and remuneration through tuition fees forced most schoolmasters to adopt a lax approach toward maintaining order.[32] Such external constraints on classroom productivity were compounded by the low level of performance on the part of teachers themselves. In the sixteenth and seventeenth centuries, most schoolmasters were artisans who assumed their teaching positions without any form of apprenticeship, let alone teacher training. The certifying examinations did not even touch on pedagogical method and required of candidates no more knowledge "than that which their pupils would learn if their instruction were successful."[33]

In addition to possessing frequently modest capabilities, teachers were unable to devote their full attention to their classroom duties. If they were also sextons of the parish church, they usually had to serve as assistant pastor, custodian of the church, bell ringer, organist, and choir director.[34] Furthermore, many continued to pursue their handicraft work on the side or else devote considerable time to farming the small plot of land given to them. This latter activity provided another reason why school was not in session during the warmer months, so that in many cases what little learning took place during the preceding winter was lost over the summer. By the time most pupils left school for good, usually after only one to three winter terms, they had acquired little more than a memorized repertoire of prayers and portions of the catechism, as well as enough reading ability to leaf through the pages of a calendar or almanac that relied primarily on illustrations to provide entertainment and information.[35]

Problems stemming from low levels of attendance, popular resistance to schooling, and inadequate teaching remained endemic in German primary education throughout the early modern period. What seems surprising is that authorities in the sixteenth century did not even attempt to overcome these systemic difficulties, contenting themselves rather with making sure that individual teachers were not grossly negligent and that each school had adequate financial support. To be sure, these day-to-day concerns were vitally important and consumed large portions of the time and energy of the central bureaucracies. But the reluctance of official bodies to pursue the goal of mass literacy too persistently also resulted from the negative and defensive character of the goals that had originally induced them to organize the sixteenth-century literacy drives. In both Catholic and Protestant areas at that time, the clerical elites sought to

---

[32] Schmid, pp. 149–50.
[33] Ibid., 322–23, 347.
[34] Helmreich, p. 16.
[35] Schmid, p. 150.

maintain their monopoly on doctrinal truth and perpetuate the laity's dependence on them for religious understanding. That even the Lutheran laity was not encouraged to read the Bible on its own is suggested by the scarcity of Biblical commentary written in German and by the low volume and high cost of printed Bibles.[36] It was no accident that the Lutheran primary schools were oriented toward pupils' memorizing the catechism and not toward their learning to read the Bible.[37]

Still more fundamentally, the framers of late sixteenth-century school legislation did not desire or think it possible to effect any permanent, positive alteration in human nature. They embraced the molding power of education only in so far as it assisted their efforts to combat the spread of heretical doctrines. As long as this aim was being achieved, little else mattered. A complete explanation for this characteristic attitude of that age cannot be attempted here, but among the Lutheran clerics it took the form of a widespread belief in the imminence of the Day of Judgment. The effect of this doctrine was to prevent the development of a philosophy of education based on the malleability of human beings. Thus, the pessimistic eschatology of the Lutheran establishment served to rationalize the limitations of their pedagogical achievements and justify their lack of initiative in seeking substantive improvements in their educational institutions.[38]

The inadequacies of the primary school systems, combined with the inertia shown by the authorities once the new school networks were in place, prevented the sixteenth-century literacy campaigns from substantially broadening the social composition of the German reading public. This supposition is difficult to test quantitatively, as historians have no figures on school attendance at their disposal, and only fragmentary, inconclusive data on literacy.[39] At first glance, figures on numbers of book titles in print, the most informative indicator available, suggest an expansion in literacy. The number of new titles grew steadily throughout the second half of the sixteenth century, and the total number of available editions reached extremely impressive levels by the 1610s. But the fact that in 1600 over seventy percent of the editions in print were in Latin indicates strong demand for learned works by the rapidly growing legal and clerical elites and a strictly limited appetite for reading material on the part of the overwhelming majority of the population.[40] Even in the largest cities, where perhaps one-third to one-half of the male citizenry possessed some skill in reading, surviving book inventories of prosperous merchants demonstrate that their reading interests, like those of other urban dwellers, did not extend beyond the psalter or New Testament, a devotional work or two, and an occasional journal or newspaper.[41]

[36] Miriam U. Chrisman, *Lay Culture, Learned Culture: Books and Social Change in Strasbourg, 1480–1599* (New Haven: Yale University Press, 1982), pp. 153–55.

[37] Gawthrop and Strauss, pp. 36–37.

[38] Strauss, *Luther's House of Learning*, pp. 31, 33, 46–47, 300–01.

[39] Ibid., p. 200.

[40] Rolf Engelsing, *Analphabetentum und Lektüre: Zur Sozialialgeschichte des Lesens in Deutschland* (Stuttgart: Metzler, 1973), pp. 31, 42–43.

[1] Rolf Engelsing, *Der Bürger als Leser: Lesergeschichte in Deutschland, 1500–1800* (Stuttgart: Metzler, 1974), p. 340.

In the countryside, where the bulk of the population lived, the percentage of those unable to read was, of course, far higher, and the proficiency level of those who could was even lower. By the time that the Thirty Years' War ended the expansion of primary school networks, it was clear that the first series of German literacy drives had not succeeded in producing a mass reading public. Only after the major constitutional and cultural changes produced by the wars and depressions of the seventeenth century could the German elites initiate literacy drives capable of surpassing the limited achievements of their sixteenth-century forebearers.

LITERACY DRIVES IN EIGHTEENTH-CENTURY GERMANY

For a century after 1618, the German lands endured a long series of wars. Even after the enormous destruction and catastrophic demographic losses of the Thirty Years' War, the weakened, still politically fragmented country was forced to confront continued external aggression from the west, north, and southeast—often simultaneously. In terms of schooling and literacy, what is remarkable about this period is not the decline in printed books, nor the embarrassing number of illiterate city mayors, but the survival of the primary school networks created in the sixteenth century.[42] To be sure, governments distracted by war could not invest any time or capital in improving the qualitative performance of the school network, which was being adversely affected by invading armies and by uncertain or deteriorating economic conditions.[43] Nevertheless, when peace finally arrived in the 1710s and persisted, with only two fairly brief interruptions, until the 1790s, the institutional foundation for new, more aggressive literacy drives was still in place.

That the literacy drives of the eighteenth century differed in kind from those of the Reformation era was the consequence, first of all, of changes in the constitutional structure of the German states. The continual pressures of war and economic depression, while ruining the prosperity and precipitating the decline of the German city-states, led to the emergence of the larger territorial principalities as the leading forces in German politics. These states were able to gain this position because in the military emergency of the seventeenth century they alone were able to institute permanent, standing armies. The cost of maintaining such forces, however, was so prohibitive that it led to bitter confrontations between the princes and those representative bodies, or estates, which had traditionally represented the interests of local ruling groups. Although during the

---

[42] In Württemberg, for example, which lost half of its population in the 1630s and 1640s and suffered repeated invasions by French armies in the 1680s and 1690s, more communities had schools in 1700 than in 1600. Schmid, pp. 111, 193.

[43] The atmosphere of crisis in the seventeenth century led to a temporary lack of interest in primary education among state administrators. According to Veit Ludwig von Seckendorff, a bureaucrat and early cameralist, such an interest was regarded as "indecent" among the bureaucratic elite. Seckendorff, *Deutscher Fürstenstaat*, Neudruck der Ausgabe Jena 1737 (Aalen: Scientia, 1972), p. 335.

sixteenth century the estates had generally voted to accede to the princes' demands
for additional revenue and had even collected the taxes themselves, their refusal
to vote the funds for the new armies incited the princes in most of the larger
territories to refrain from calling the estates, to levy taxes without their consent,
and to establish new bureaucratic officers, or commissars, to act as tax collectors
and local administrators. This destruction of the estates as a territory-wide political force led the princes to assert—and justify—their absolute power of command over all their subjects. Whereas, in the sixteenth century, the estates claimed
to represent the good of society at large, in the two succeeding centuries absolutist
princes largely succeeded in undermining this claim of the estates and in identifying their own interest with that of the body politic as a whole.[44]

To reinforce their ideological position, absolutist princes adopted the pos-
ture of being outside or above the social hierarchy, portraying themselves as
impartial arbiters capable of balancing the interests of the various groups in
society. In practice, this supremacy of the prince meant the subordination to his
political interest, to *raison d'état*, of every other institution, including, most significantly, the church.[45] Two results of this process were the destruction of the
traditional church–state symbiosis, which had still existed in the sixteenth century
despite the growing power of the state, and, concomitantly, a drastic change in
the prince's sense of his own mission. The typical absolutist prince reigning after
the Thirty Years' War no longer perceived himself, even in theory, as the guard-
ian of his subjects' salvation.[46] Instead, what mattered most was now the "common
good," usually equated with an increase in the power of the state. Since, in the
late seventeenth century, German territorial states were all suffering to a greater
or lesser extent from the effects of near-constant war and of economic backwardness vis-à-vis Western Europe, the princes' ability to increase their power
depended ultimately on an expansion of the tax base of their territorial economies. Hence, the absolutist rulers and their bureaucracies strove not just to
regulate the economic life of their realms (such regulation in itself was common
in the sixteenth century) but to do so in order to encourage manufacturing,
increase population, and improve the infrastructure of the economy.[47]

For this program of "modernization" to succeed, absolutist governments
realized that they needed to do more than merely impose an external discipline
on their subjects. The detailed, comprehensive development plans pursued by
the central authorities required people from every level of society to learn new
skills and go along willingly with what the state had in mind for them. Consequently, the professional theorists who advised state administrations on policy
matters, the cameralists, were inclined to assume that human beings were essentially malleable, that through education they could become obedient, energetic,

[44]Oestreich, *Neostoicism and the Early Modern State*, pp. 195, 234–37; for the relationship between
princes and estates in the sixteenth century, see Strauss, *Law, Resistance, and the State*, Chapter 8.

[45]John G. Gagliardo, *From Pariah to Patriot: The Changing Image of the German Peasant, 1770–1840*
(Lexington: The University Press of Kentucky, 1969), pp. 85–86.

[46]Hermann Conrad, "Staat und Kirche im aufgeklärten Absolutismus," *Der Staat* 12 (1973), p. 62.

[47]Marc Raeff, *The Well-Ordered Police State: Social and Institutional Change through Law in the Germanies
and Russia, 1600–1800* (New Haven: Yale University Press, 1983), pp. 171–72.

and productive people, capable of contributing their share to the common good.[48] In accordance with the cameralists' emphasis on the transforming power of education, the absolutist states sought to add a pedagogical dimension to every institution under their direct control, whether it be the army, the court, the civil service, or the newly established workhouses. Above all, the cameralists hoped that the primary schools could be the instruments for imparting knowledge applicable to daily life and for inculcating a religious morality that would encourage hard work and a willingness "to accommodate one's dealings with the laws of society."[49]

Unfortunately for the cameralists' vision of primary-school education, the disruption of the close relationship between church and state characteristic of the sixteenth century had led to a partial separation of the two institutions. Moreover, as part of the price for achieving their political monopoly, the princes had been obliged to recognize the privileged autonomy of many traditional organizations such as the church. Therefore, since the various churches had maintained their control over the primary school networks, the state administrations normally could exert only indirect influence over educational policy in the late seventeenth and eighteenth centuries. As the Lutheran and Catholic orthodoxies did not generally share the desire of the secular governments to remake society, the states—in order to mount literacy campaigns based on cameralist criteria—had to identify, encourage, and collaborate with movements within the churches that shared their basic objectives.

Two such movements in particular played key roles in shaping the specific goals of the eighteenth-century literacy drives and in fashioning the means for achieving them. The first of these, Lutheran Pietism, arose in the last quarter of the seventeenth century, intending to reform church and society by inducing spiritual conversions on the part of individuals, who would thereafter strive continuously to raise their own level of piety and seek to convince others to adopt their "active" Christianity.[50] Although the Pietists originally conceived of their reform as an internal matter within the church, by the 1690s the resistance of Lutheran orthodoxy to their innovations had compelled the Pietists to seek protection from secular governments. A few regimes, notably those of the Prussian kings Frederick I and Frederick William I (d. 1740), did come to the support of the Pietists, enabling them to survive as a movement, but compelling them to reevaluate their formerly negative attitude toward collaborating with the state.[51]

Once established in Prussia, the Pietists began to advocate a more intensive form of primary schooling as the most effective means of bringing about a more "Christian" society. Backed by the Prussian state, the Pietist leader August Hermann Francke began, in the mid-1690s, to establish in the city of Halle a network of schools, which quickly acquired an excellent reputation throughout Germany

[48] Ibid., pp. 177–78.
[49] Joseph von Sonnenfels, *Grundsätze der Policey, Handlung und Finanzwirtschaft*, 5th ed. (Munich: 1787), p. 54.
[50] Richard Gawthrop, "*For the Good of Thy Neighbor: Pietism and the Making of Eighteenth-Century Prussia*" (Indiana Univ. diss., 1984), pp. 90–95, 119–33.
[51] Ibid., pp. 145–73, 271–90.

and beyond. Two characteristics in particular distinguished Francke's schools from the typical German primary school at that time. One was an emphasis on selecting teachers who would serve as role models for the type of piety that the Pietists wished to inculcate. The other was a commitment to making the children understand the meaning of the religious material being presented to them. This latter goal, in turn, forced the Halle Pietists to place an unprecedented emphasis on instructional methods and on the training of teachers in those methods. In conjunction with this pedagogical experiment at Halle, Francke composed detailed instructions for his teachers, which dealt exhaustively with matters pertaining to curriculum, teaching methods, conduct of teachers, standards of pupil behavior, monitoring of pupils, and classroom discipline.[52]

As Francke also dominated the theological faculty at the University of Halle, and as his hundreds of students often supported themselves by working as teachers in his primary school system, theology graduates of the university who became pastors, professors, and clerical administrators throughout Germany tended to rely on Francke's regulations to guide their efforts to reform the educational systems in their own principalities. Consequently, from roughly 1725 to 1775 new school ordinances more or less based on the Halle model were decreed in practically every Lutheran territory in Germany, constituting in most cases the first substantive change in the basic school law since the sixteenth century.[53] Francke's influence also reached into Catholic areas as his pedagogical instructions were adapted in the 1740s by the Silesian educator Felbiger for use in Catholic primary schools. Felbiger's prescriptions were widely copied in the Habsburg empire and in southern and western Germany.[54]

Although Pietism served as the prime mover of educational reform in the late seventeenth and early eighteenth centuries, in the second half of the latter century it was gradually superseded in that role by the German Enlightenment. It is important to emphasize the "German" character of that movement by pointing out that nearly all its advocates and sympathizers were members of the establishment, that in other words the German Enlightenment drew its major support from the universities, the secular bureaucracies of the princely states, and the clergy, both Protestant and Catholic.[55] Far less antireligious than its French counterpart, the German Enlightenment worked, in the field of education, within the framework of the Pietist school ordinances, sharing both the Pietists' confidence that education could produce a moral citizenry and their

[52] Ibid., pp. 199–212; for the text of Francke's regulations, see August Hermann Francke, *Schriften über Erziehung und Unterricht*, ed. Karl Richter (Leipzig: Max Hesse, 1880), pp. 393–460.

[53] For the texts of these ordinances, see Reinhold Vormbaum, ed., *Evangelische Schulordnungen*, III (Gütersloh: Bertelsmann, 1864).

[54] Max J. Okenfuss, "Education and Empire: School Reform in Enlightened Russia," *Jahrbücher für die Geschichte Osteuropas* 27 (1979), pp. 44–46; Fritz Neukamm, *Wirtschaft und Schule in Württemberg von 1700 bis 1836* (Heidelberg: Quelle & Mayer, 1956), pp. 55–60.

[55] Joachim Whaley, "The Protestant Enlightenment in Germany," in *The Enlightenment in National Context*, ed. Roy Porter and Mikulas Teich (New York: Cambridge University Press, 1981), p. 111. The same relationship between the Enlightenment and society was true in the Catholic states as well. See T. C. W. Blanning, "The Enlightenment in Catholic Germany," in *The Enlightenment in National Context*, pp. 122, 125.

determination to make sure that schoolchildren actively understood the essentials of religion. Though the common adherence to these values by the two reform movements ensured considerable continuity in educational policy throughout the eighteenth century, the ultimate goals of the German Enlightenment differed fundamentally from those of the Pietists. For the Pietists, the state of a person's religious life mattered more than political ends; for partisans of the Enlightenment, religion served, in the final analysis, merely as a disciplinary force that would help people become hardworking and obedient. As a result, the Enlightenment pedagogues went beyond the Pietists in emphasizing the teaching of practical skills and responsible citizenship. These priorities reflected the commitment of the Enlightenment to educating subjects who would conform to the demands placed on them by "modernization," not in a spirit of mechanical obedience, but "from a rational understanding of rights and duties."[56]

In attempting to realize these ideals in practice, eighteenth-century officials demonstrated a systematic, persistent, and pragmatic approach in addressing the weaknesses of school systems inherited from the sixteenth century. One such problem, that of low attendance, lent itself particularly well to methods of this kind. As part of the difficulty was due to the unavailability of schooling to large portions of the population, eighteenth-century governments employed a number of strategies to make primary education accessible to all members of society. Beginning before 1700, the Pietists founded several dozen workhouses and orphanages in German cities. Servicing these institutions, and open to the general public as well, were so-called "poor schools," which provided rudimentary instruction to low-class children in urban areas.[57] As for the more remote, impoverished rural districts, some eighteenth-century regimes aggressively subsidized the founding of new schools in such places—the best known example of which was the building of over nine hundred schools in East Prussia by Frederick William I in the late 1730s.[58] Early eighteenth-century Prussia also pioneered in establishing schools for the children of soldiers and in making available schools of different faiths to accommodate the religiously diverse population of the larger cities. Later in the century, the emphasis throughout Germany switched to educating hitherto unschooled or inadequately schooled adults. Night schools or Sunday schools, taught by either the pastor or the schoolmaster, became extremely common in the 1780s and 1790s.[59]

In addition to providing more access to education, eighteenth-century governments also applied more pressure on parents to send their children to school. Especially in the second half of the century, governments and private reformers disseminated leaflets addressed to peasant parents extolling the benefits of education. Such exhortation was reinforced by a series of coercive measures. As

---

[56] Gagliardo, pp. 94–96. See also Whaley, pp. 112–13.

[57] Engelsing, *Analphabetentum und Lektüre*, pp. 48–49.

[58] Fritz Terveen, *Gesamtstaat und Retablissement: Der Wiederaufbau des nördlichen Ostpreussens unter Friedrich Wilhelm I, 1714–1740* (Göttingen: Musterschmidt, 1954), p. 115.

[59] Helmreich, p. 35. For the role that night schools played in a rural Swiss district, see Rudolf Braun, *Industrialisierung und Volksleben: Die Veränderungen der Lebensformen in einem ländlichen Industriegebiet vor 1800* (Erlenbach-Zürich and Stuttgart: Eugen Rentsch, 1960), pp. 139–46.

early as the 1640s, Saxe-Gotha and Württemberg declared it obligatory for children to attend school. They were joined by most other German states in the course of the eighteenth century (Prussia in 1717, Saxony in 1772, Bavaria in 1802).[60] Such "school-compulsion" laws gained in effectiveness as the authorities issued other, complementary legislation on school attendance. One of the major Pietist contributions was the introduction of confirmation in most Lutheran areas during the eighteenth century. This practice became particularly significant for the spread of literacy because, as was also the case in Sweden, pastors were forbidden to confirm anyone who had not spent enough time in school to have learned reading and a certain amount of religious knowledge.[61] Another important innovation was the holding of school during the summer. Although the most common arrangement was for school to meet only two or three times a week for a couple of hours at a time, even this limited summer schedule maintained continuity between winter terms and made it possible for pupils to make steadier progress.[62] A final incentive used by governments to promote school attendance was a series of regulations restricting numerous categories of jobs in the state administration to those who could read, write, and do sums. Prussia even went so far as to impose the same requirements on those who wished to enter a craft guild.[63]

As the purpose behind the school attendance laws of the eighteenth century was to improve the morality and productivity of the population, upgrading classroom performance also received a great deal of attention by school administrators.[64] Both Pietist and Enlightenment pedagogues recognized the central role played by the schoolmaster, and the authorities consistently sought to raise the teachers' level of competence. Although only a small number of teacher-training programs existed before 1800, eighteenth-century administrators did at least formalize the existing system of apprenticeship by regulating admission standards for apprentices and finding places for journeymen to practice their trade. In Württemberg, for example, after 1750 schoolmasters who had more than one hundred pupils or were engaged in too many outside activities were required to take on at least one journeyman.[65] In addition to undergoing this guildlike system of training, candidates had to pass more demanding examinations in order to become certified than had been the case in the sixteenth century. Thus, in Württemberg by the 1780s, prospective teachers had to demonstrate proficiency in catechization (i.e. in teaching method), competence in arithmetic, knowledge of the content of the various books of the Bible (as opposed

---

[60]Schmid, p. 109; Engelsing, *Analphabetentum und Lektüre*, p. 62.

[61]Gawthrop and Strauss, p. 52. For the Swedish system of clerical monitoring, see Egil Johansson, "The History of Literacy in Sweden," in *Literacy and Social Development in the West: A Reader*, ed. Harvey J. Graff (New York: Cambridge University Press, 1981), p. 159.

[62]In Württemberg villages, by 1750 the holding of a summer school was the rule rather than the exception. Schmid, p. 370.

[63]Engelsing, *Analphabetentum und Lekture*, p. 62.

[64]This relationship between the "morality of literacy" and sought-for improvements in classroom instruction is discussed in Harvey J. Graff, *The Literacy Myth: Literacy and Social Structure in the Nineteenth-Century City* (New York: Academic Press, 1979), pp. 22–48, 272–92.

[65]Schmid, pp. 327–28.

to mere ability to recite the catechism), and sufficient literacy to pass a dictation (instead of writing down a proverb or familiar religious verse).[66] Finally, in the last decades of the eighteenth century, the initial steps toward the profession-alization of teachers were taken. The Württemberg teachers formed a society in 1780 that began to hold yearly conferences in 1798. Under the influence of the Enlightenment, teachers in the same area also started a pedagogical journal in 1786 through which news of innovations such as wall blackboards, slates, inkwells, and report cards could be passed along to local schoolmasters.[67]

More frequent and prolonged pupil attendance, as well as more qualified teachers, made feasible what both reform movements desired most–an inten-sification in the program of study. In terms of curricula prescribed for primary vernacular schools, the sixteenth-century school ordinances barely went beyond listing the subjects to be taught, whereas their eighteenth-century counterparts gave teachers detailed instructions on how to teach each subject and lesson plans spelling out how to utilize each hour of every day of the week.[68] Even more importantly, the eighteenth-century ordinances placed a far greater emphasis on reading. To be sure, memorization was still very important, and, in preparing for confirmation, eighteenth-century German children typically learned to recite much more religious material than ever before.[69] But they were also taught to read this same material, along with books of Biblical verses, Bible story books, and the Bible itself. In the last quarter of the eighteenth century this religious reading was supplemented by collections of fairy tales and an early example of an all-purpose primer, Rochow's *Kinderfreund*.[70] In contrast, pupils in the six-teenth and seventeenth centuries in many cases did not have printed copies of even the catechism, having to learn it as best they could through mimicking recitations by teachers whose own grasp of the text was frequently far from perfect.[71]

This is not to claim that the reality of what, in the late eighteenth century, came to be called the *Volksschule* ("people's school") lived up to the expectations of the reformers. As the philosopher Herder noted in 1787, "the children under-stand nothing of what they sound out and read; they learn therefore without zest and love, rather with daily suffering."[72] In addition to this common criticism, cameralist and Enlightenment pedagogues faulted the school systems for the slowness with which they introduced practical subject matter into the reading

---

[66] Ibid., pp. 347–49.

[67] Ibid., pp. 233–35; Gerd Friederich, *Die Volksschule in Württemberg im 19. Jahrhundert* (Weinheim and Basel: Beltz, 1978), p. 19.

[68] For a comparison of the curriculum of the Württemberg school ordinance of 1559 with that of 1729, see Vormbaum, ed., I, pp. 160–61 and Vormbaum, ed., III, pp. 320–32.

[69] This emphasis on memorization is consistent with a culture that, despite an increasing prevalence of printing, still possessed a strong "residue of orality." In Ong's words, "the residual orality of a given chirographic culture can be calculated to a degree from the mnemonic load it leaves on the mind, that is, from the amount of memorization the culture's educational procedures require." Ong, p. 41.

[70] Braun, p.136; Engelsing, *Analphabetentum und Lektüre*, p. 59; Gagliardo, p. 108.

[71] Schmid, p. 124.

[72] Quoted in Engelsing, *Analphabetentum und Lektüre*, p. 65.

curriculum.[73] These same critics also pointed to the modest remuneration received by teachers—not to mention the pitiful sums given to their assistants—as undermining popular respect for learning and resulting in the failure of the teaching vocation to attract the most qualified people.[74] Finally, reformers complained bitterly about the attitudes of parents: the reluctance with which they sent their children to school, their frequent refusal to pay for larger, more comfortable schoolhouses, and their vehemence in protesting any shift in the program of study from religious instruction to secular subjects.[75]

Taking their cue from such contemporary observers, whose values corresponded closely to their own, modern historians have tended to focus on these deficiencies, while underestimating what the eighteenth-century literacy campaigns did achieve. The most obvious accomplishment was a dramatic improvement in school attendance. Complaints of overcrowded school buildings and high pupil-to-teacher ratios reflected levels of attendance that toward the end of the eighteenth century probably averaged about forty percent of all children eligible to attend school, a figure that included everyone from ages five to thirteen or fourteen. In the duchy of Baden, where the government aggressively promoted the primary education of both its Catholic and Protestant subjects, enrollment figures around 1800 were "between seventy and ninety percent of school-aged children." Even in East Prussia, one of the poorest areas in Germany, forty percent of the peasants could sign their names in 1800. In the first decades of the nineteenth century, moreover, attendance continued to improve rapidly. In Prussia, a kingdom with considerable diversity of religions and socioeconomic structures, some sixty percent of eligible children attended school in 1816. By the 1830s this percentage was close to 100 percent, a level that, according to Mary Jo Maynes's calculations, had been reached in Baden as well.[76]

These enrollment figures indicate that, by the early nineteenth century, the vast majority of peasants were receiving the same basic education as that given to all but the elite elements of Germany's middle classes. This narrowing of the cultural disparity between town and countryside was reflected in the similarity in books possessed by peasant and artisanal households. In both categories of household, book holdings nearly always consisted of a Bible, a catechism, a hymnal, and other devotional or instructional materials.[77] Figures pertaining to numbers of book editions reveal the universality of these particular books; the most common religious school book, a collection of Bible stories, went through over one hundred editions between 1714 and 1828, while a Bible foundation sponsored by Halle Pietism alone sold over two million low-cost complete

[73] J. G. Justi, *Grundfeste zu der Macht und Glückseligkeit der Staaten, Neudruck der Ausgabe Königsberg 1761* (Aalen: Scientia, 1965), II, pp. 116–17. See also Engelsing, *Analphabetentum und Lektüre*, p. 69.
[74] Seckendorff, p. 335; Sonnenfels, p. 56.
[75] Gagliardo, pp. 102–03; Engelsing, *Analphabetentum*, p. 66.
[76] Lundgreen, *Sozialgeschichte der deutschen Schule*, p. 37; Maynes, p. 613; Engelsing, *Analphabetentum*, p. 62; Peter Lundgreen, "Industrialization and the Educational Formation of Manpower in Germany," *Journal of Social History* 9 (1975–76), p. 67.
[77] Helmut Möller, *Die kleinbürgerliche Familie im achtzehnten Jahrhundert* (Berlin: de Gruyter, 1969), p. 248; Engelsing, *Der Bürger als Leser*, p. 340; Braun, pp. 136–37.

Bibles in the course of the eighteenth century.[78] In both social groupings, more-over, the same mores regulated the use of these materials within the family. The head of the peasant or artisanal family typically read to his assembled family passages from a religious text that in many cases he had partially or completely memorized. The prevalence of this custom in the eighteenth century shows that, while the primary schools indeed did not always graduate pupils with much more reading ability than that required to stage these ceremonial performances, at the very least, an important step in the transition from oral tradition to highly interiorized literacy had been taken. It was of no small significance that the capacity to manipulate a printed text had become linked with the authority of the father in the German family.[79]

The rapid spread of a literacy used for ritualistic purposes was not, how-ever, the only result of expanding enrollments in the German *Volksschulen*. Thou-sands, perhaps millions, of late eighteenth-century Germans, though continuing to be rooted in an essentially oral culture, also began to apply their reading skills to texts designed to meet the personal needs of this newly literate mass audience. The years after 1770, for example, saw a spectacular rise in the purchases of cheap novels, usually adventure stories. Demand was so strong that the available editions of such works at the Easter book fair in Leipzig increased from forty-six in 1770 to three hundred in 1800, the latter figure representing roughly twelve percent of the total number of editions sold at the fair that year.[80] After the 1760s, moreover, the circulation figures of certain newspapers became so large that their readership must have extended far beyond highly educated elite groups. In 1803, printings of the *Hamburgische Correspondent* numbered some fifty thousand copies, and it can be assumed that ten people read each copy of this one newspaper.[81]

The ready availability of other types of informative material was due to the efforts of social reformers, who consciously sought to overcome the short-comings of the school systems by producing useful, inexpensive, and simply written printed works for adults. As German governments in the last quarter of the eighteenth century strove to induce farmers to introduce new crops and farming techniques, these socially concerned publicists worked particularly hard to communicate the advantages of the new methods to the peasantry. Thus, in the 1780s, peasant newspapers began to appear in large numbers; by 1790, at least 104 different periodicals relating to the technical side of farming had been founded.[82] Though the circulation of these newspapers is unknown and probably not that extraordinary, the agrarian reformers did reach a large audience with R. Z. Becker's peasant calendar, which, unlike earlier examples of this genre, contained a tremendous quantity of practical information. First published in

[78]Gawthrop and Strauss, pp. 49–51.

[79]Möller, p. 259; Engelsing, *Analphabetentum und Lektüre*, p. 54.

[80]Rudolf Jentzsch, *Der deutsch-lateinische Büchermarkt nach den Leipziger Ostermesskatalogen von 1740, 1770 und 1800 in seiner Gliederung und Wandlung* (Leipzig: Voigtländer, 1912), Tafel III.

[81]Engelsing, *Analphabetentum und Lektüre*, p. 60.

[82]Gagliardo, pp. 104–05.

1788, Becker's almanac had sold 150,000 copies by 1798 and one million by 1811.[83]

Aggregate figures on numbers of editions published in late eighteenth-century Germany likewise reflected the enormous number of new readers produced by the second set of preindustrial literacy drives. The demand for books and periodicals generated by this new reading public resulted in at least a quadrupling of available editions between 1750 and 1800. Assuming a rough equality in number of editions available in the 1610s and the 1740s, the significance of the expansion in publications after 1750 is heightened still further when one considers that all but a tiny fraction of mid-to-late eighteenth-century books were written in German, that the number of copies per edition had in many cases doubled or tripled, especially with respect to devotional literature and popular novels, and that the number of readers per copy had also risen because of the existence of reading societies and lending libraries.[84] To be sure, this growth in the consumption of printed materials occurred in part because of the considerable social change that marked this period. But the population increase, the expansion of the market economy, and the development of cottage textile industries characteristic of the late eighteenth century could not have done more than help motivate individual Germans to develop further on their own the reading skills most of them had already acquired in the *Volksschulen*.

In summary, the German states by 1800 had experienced unusual success in promoting literacy within a traditional social framework by means of literacy campaigns sponsored by ideologically minded elites. To be sure, with respect to even the eighteenth-century literacy drives, the mobilization of the population was not nearly so intensive or fast-paced as the twentieth-century examples discussed later in this volume. Eighteenth-century Germany, though it was experiencing significant socioeconomic change, was still a predominantly agrarian, preindustrial society. In order to achieve aims such as mass literacy, which sprang from the desire of state officials to "modernize" their societies, governments had to rely on traditional organizations: the churches, for teaching personnel and supervisory staff, and the communal institutions of villages and small towns, for the financial support of the schools. Despite these limitations, however, German bureaucracies, displaying a persistent, problem-solving mentality, succeeded over the course of the eighteenth century in introducing reforms that greatly improved the performance of the primary schools. These innovations were the key factor in explaining why probably a majority of the population in early nineteenth-century Germany possessed and periodically used a functional literacy, despite the still-limited vocational need for this skill. German industrialization, which got under way in the 1840s and 1850s, benefited immensely from a labor force educated to be not only literate but also diligent, punctual, and obedient.[85]

The legacy of a state-controlled school system that developed under the auspices of religious zeal and secular ideology was not, however, without its

[83] Engelsing, *Analphabetentum und Lektüre*, p. 59.
[84] Jentzsch, pp. 15, 67, 146; Engelsing, *Analphabetentum und Lektüre*, pp. 55–57.
[85] Lundgreen, "Industrialization," pp. 78–79.

unsettling side. Already by the end of the eighteenth century, the schools had become a crucial battleground for the struggle between advocates of the Enlightenment and their conservative opponents.[86] This politicization of the schools—and the very ability of the *Volksschulen* to reach and mold the coming generation—encouraged every ideological movement in the following two centuries to attempt to manipulate the school system for its own ends. Sometimes these efforts succeeded all too well, but that is another story.

ACKNOWLEDGMENTS

I would like to thank Gerald Strauss for reading and commenting on an earlier draft of this chapter.

---

[86] Engelsing, *Analphabetentum*, pp. 67, 75.

CHAPTER 3

The Literacy Campaign in Scotland, 1560–1803

RAB HOUSTON

The literacy program that was initiated in Scotland at the time of the Reformation and carried through by legislation in the seventeenth century was the first truly national literacy campaign. Some principalities and city states of Protestant Europe had tried to encourage literacy from the beginning of the sixteenth century. However, these initiatives were small in scale and enjoyed little success compared with the Scottish aim to organize education at a national level. Government intervention helped to realize the aim of a controlled and systematized educational network at a much earlier date than in any other European nation state. This chapter assesses the aims, methods and achievements of the Scottish literacy campaign between the Reformation and the time of the French Revolution. Working side by side, church and state sought to create a national, universal, and religiously oriented educational system centered on a school in every parish.[1] Legislation between 1616 and 1696 set up the parochial school system, administered by the church in rural areas and by the secular authorities in the towns. It was designed to be available to all children, however poor their circumstances, and was to be paid for by a levy on the more prosperous inhabitants of particular parishes.

The activities of church and state in the field of education have afforded a model for more recent systems of instruction, of which the common schools of nineteenth-century North America offer an example.[2] In Britain, beliefs about what was achieved by the Scots during the seventeenth and eighteenth centuries

---

[1] The best overviews of education and society in Scotland are provided by the following publications: James Scotland, *The History of Scottish Education* vol. 1 (London: University of London Press, 1969), Rosemary O'Day, *Education and Society, 1500–1800* (London: Longman, 1982), pp. 217–37, and T. Christopher Smout, *A History of the Scottish People, 1560–1830* (London: Fontana, 1972), pp. 420–50. The nature and achievements of the Scottish literacy campaign compared with others before the nineteenth century are discussed extensively in Rab Houston, *Scottish Literacy and the Scottish Identity*.

[2] E. G. West, *Education and the Industrial Revolution* (London: Batsford, 1975), p. 59.

RAB HOUSTON • Department of Modern History, University of St. Andrews, St. Andrews, Fife, Scotland KY16 9AL.

have provided a confirmation and celebration of certain values concerning education and its importance to society. They have also been central to educational policy in the twentieth century. The apparently generous and successful provision of education in early modern Scotland has been used to justify both continuity and change in education in Britain and in other countries since the eighteenth century.[3] The perceived results of the drive for literacy, and the values it supposedly embodied, have formed an important focus of identity for the Scots as a people. The image of Scottish literacy and education was, as we shall see, an exaggeration and distortion of reality, but as a myth about what could be done in the field of learning it has proved of greater importance than an understanding of what actually occurred between 1560 and 1803 in that country. The Scottish system and its attainments have been used by historians and sociologists as a reference standard alongside New England, Prussia, and Sweden, which also had literacy campaigns, and which achieved high levels of literacy among their populations during the eighteenth century.

Action by the Scottish state and the Protestant Kirk to implement a national education program based on the parochial schools was seen as the key to Scotland's successes in literacy. Adam Smith, the father of classical economics, opined that "the establishment of . . . parish schools has taught almost the whole common people to read, and a very great proportion of them to write and account."[4] This is, however, only an assumption which arises from a deep faith in institutions as a way of perfecting humanity and from the preoccupations of historians and legislators over the last century with the creation of planned and controlled educational systems. In the last three decades of the nineteenth century, most countries of northwestern Europe instituted compulsory education under centralized organization. This created the framework for educational debates and legislation in the twentieth century and has produced the expectation that the straightest, perhaps the only, pathway to literacy is via a formally organized school system.

Scotland is a particularly useful example of a literacy campaign, for two reasons. First, the initiatives of the church and state were carried out in a country that was economically backward and socially primitive. Until the end of the eighteenth century, Scottish agriculture was largely traditional, industrial production was low, and the strongly patriarchal society was highly polarized between a small number of large landowners and the mass of the peasantry. The population totalled approximately one million in 1700, settlement was dispersed, and there were few large towns or "burghs". Until 1603, Scotland had its own

[3] John Gray, Andrew McPherson, and David Raffe, *Reconstructions of Secondary Education. Theory, Myth and Practice since the War* (London: Routledge, 1983), especially pp. 36–44. Donald J. Withrington, " 'Scotland a half-educated nation' in 1834? Reliable Critique or Persuasive Polemic," in *Scottish Culture and Scottish Education, 1800–1980*, ed. Walter M. Humes and Hamish M. Paterson (Edinburgh: John Donald, 1983), pp. 55–74.

[4] Adam Smith. *An Inquiry into the Nature and Causes of the Wealth of Nations*, II, (Oxford: Clarendon Press, 1976), p. 785. See also G. Strauss, *Luther's House of Learning*, Kenneth A. Lockridge, *Literacy in Colonial New England* (New York: Norton, 1974), and Egil Johansson, "The History of Literacy in Sweden."

monarchy and until 1707 its own parliament. The country was politically unified and relatively untroubled by divergent religious opinions of the kind which racked continental Europe. There was, nevertheless, a fundamental cultural divide between Highland and Lowland Scotland, of which the most obvious manifestation was the different languages spoken by Highlanders (Gaelic) and Lowlanders (Scots English). As late as the 1750s, one third of Scotland's population lived in the Highlands. Over the seventeenth and eighteenth centuries, the partial legal independence, continuing violence, and strong Catholicism of the area became an increasingly embarrassing anomaly in the Scottish state and thus came under attack from secular and ecclesiastical authorities alike.

Second, despite its backwardness, Scotland joined England as the first country in the world to experience an industrial revolution. Some authorities argue that Scotland's parochial school system created a very literate population that was highly receptive to economic and social change. In view of Scotland's poorly developed society and economy, its achievement in education and literacy is all the more remarkable, and, because of that country's early industrialization, all the more interesting for historians and for policy makers in the twentieth century.

The aspirations of the secular and religious Reformers who created the campaign were embodied in the Calvinist manifesto, *The Book of Discipline*, in legislation, and in the records of both central and local bodies of the Protestant church.[5] They are neatly summarised in the following extract from the register of the Privy Council of Scotland in 1616, announcing the first legislative step toward a national system.

> For as much as the King's Majesty having a special care and regard that the true religion be advanced and established in all parts of this kingdom, and that all His Majesty's subjects, especially the youth, be exercised . . . in civilitie, godliness, knowledge and learning . . . and whereas there is no means more powerful to further this his Majesty's princely regard and purpose than the establishing of schools in particular parishes of this kingdom where the youth may be taught at the least to write and read and be catechised and instructed in the grounds of religion; therefore the King's Majesty has thought it necessary and expedient that in every parish a school shall be established and a fit person appointed to teach the same upon the expense of the parishioners.[6]

The Scottish Reformation of 1560 was essentially a political event with religious overtones. It was brought about by a group of nobles disaffected with the pro-French policies of the Catholic monarch. The nobles' military and political success allowed the religious changes desired by their Protestant allies to be implemented. Mass support for the new creed was limited.[7] The overriding concern of the Calvinists was therefore the establishment and protection of their faith. The religious Reformers had to win both political backing for their point of view and also to conquer the hearts and minds of a populace largely indifferent

[5] John Knox, *The History of the Reformation in Scotland with which are included Knox's Confession and the Book of Discipline*, ed. Cuthbert Lennox (London: Andrew Melrose, 1905).

[6] *The Register of the Privy Council of Scotland*, vol. 10 *1613–16*, ed. David Masson (Edinburgh: Neill, 1891), pp. 671–2.

[7] Ian B. Cowan, *Regional Aspects of the Scottish Reformation*, Historical Association Pamphlet, General Series, 92 (London: Historical Association, 1978).

to, or ignorant of, their message. The great Protestant leader John Knox stressed that all should be educated in the doctrines of Calvinism. Indeed, the preservation and extension of Protestantism was central to the literacy campaign.

Religion, however, was not the only goal. Teachers licensed to teach in the parish schools had to be "sound in the knowledge of God," but they had also to be properly qualified and "honest in lyf."[8] Teachers had to be Protestants, sympathetic to the existing secular regime, and supporters of the established form of church government, whether episcopalian or presbyterian. The moral and political aspects of education and literacy were important to church and state alike. The aim of the campaign was to establish total political and religious conformity among Scotland's population. What started as a means of creating a new order became a way of preserving an established one. In his political testament, Knox stressed that the nation's youth were to be restrained from idle temptations, and, by their good behavior and learning, were to provide an example for the older generation.[9] At one level the Scottish campaign was designed to be national and integrative, but the goal was to serve the needs of the Calvinist church and of the existing political regime rather than to democratize the political culture.

Nor did the Reformers ignore the notion of the commonwealth. They were careful to point out the advantages to society as a whole of having an educational system which covered all social groups and could generate the most able people to staff the institutions of church and state. It was hoped that everyone would gain access to education in the interests of society at large. Importantly, the individual had no right to learning for its own sake, and the campaign's primary aim was societal advancement rather than the promotion of personal adequacy through education. Poor but gifted children could receive financial aid from local administrative bodies to ensure that they were educated, but this was not the product of any committment to social equality. Church and state worked to ensure that widespread education would generate an ample supply of secular and ecclesiastical officials. Basic education was to enhance religious knowledge and social order; more advanced types of schooling were to help create a service elite. In short, the Protestant reformers of the later sixteenth century argued vigorously for the provision of schools "for the preservation of religion" and for the general good of society through the cultivation of talented individuals. Literacy was not essential for political participation, which was in any case restricted to a tiny minority of society.

The literacy campaign was designed to create a unified national religious, moral, and political community. Church and state were related symbiotically, the former requiring the legislative and judicial backing of the secular authorities, who, on their part, were happy to have the church overseeing a drive toward the establishment of a godly, obedient and useful population. The church provided the initial impetus for the campaign, but state action was essential to overcome the problems of cost, motivation and organization.

---

[8]*The Records of the Synod of Lothian and Tweeddale, 1589–96, 1640–9*, ed. James Kirk, Stair Society, vol. 30 (Edinburgh: William Hodge, 1977), p. 68.
[9]Lennox, pp. 383–4.

In implementing their aims, the Protestants were fortunate in being able to build on a long-established tradition of education. There were schools in the larger towns of Lowland Scotland from the beginning of the sixteenth century, if not earlier, and the Catholic church was active in trying to promote literacy and education in the decades before the Protestant Reformation of 1560. Universities had been established at St. Andrews, Glasgow, and Aberdeen before the Reformation, with Edinburgh following soon after. Legislative precedents for the seventeenth-century statutes also existed in the form of the 1496 act of the Scottish parliament, which required the major landowners to educate their heirs.[10]

The educational aspirations of the Scottish Calvinists were common to much of Europe, Catholic and Protestant alike, and their methods had been tried in cities like Geneva and in the German principalities where *Schulordnungen* were widely promulgated from the early sixteenth century onwards.[11] In contrast, the distinctiveness of Scotland's educational system lay in the way it became centralized and controlled through state legislation at an early date. The campaign was a truly national one in conception, embodied in sovereign legislation and aimed at mass literacy through the medium of schools. In this form, it had no parallel before the nineteenth century. The New England school laws of the seventeenth century, like the German ordinances of the post-Reformation period, were essentially local, and the Swedish campaign that began in 1686 was to be carried through almost entirely *without* the use of formal schools.

The legislative framework for the campaign comprised four acts of the Scottish Parliament in the seventeenth century and one in the early nineteenth century. In 1616 an act of the Scottish parliament specified that a school should be established in every parish "where convenient means may be had" for supporting one, and that a suitably qualified teacher should be found to staff it. A further act of 1633 ratified this statute and gave to the bishops the task of overseeing its implementation. The act of 1646 was more explicit in requiring landowners to pay for the creation of a school and to provide a salary for the teacher. Church authorities were to oversee the foundation of schools. All these acts were designed to create schools and to provide the economic basis for a teacher in every one of the nine hundred or so Scottish parishes.

The economic dislocations of the 1690s produced the final and most important act of the seventeenth century, that of 1696, which settled the salary for existing teachers and compelled rural landowners (heritors) or burgh councils to fund them. The act made a legal provision for the capital cost of a school and teacher. Finally, an act of 1803 was passed to augment salaries fixed in 1696 but severely eroded by the inflation of the eighteenth century, and to tighten up official control of the schools in a period of social and ideological flux created by the French Revolution. In contrast to the Cuban or Nicaraguan literacy campaigns, which involved mass mobilization to promote literacy in a brief time span, the Scottish literacy drive involved a series of mobilizations. These had

[10]Scotland, pp. 38, 43–53; John Durkan, "Education in the Century of the Reformation," *Innes Review* 10 (1959), pp. 67–90.
[11]Strauss, *Luther's House of Learning*, pp. 1–27.

broadly the same aims but were carried through over a long period of years and in a variety of economic and political contexts. The sense of urgency which is clear in many twentieth-century literacy campaigns was muted in seventeenth and eighteenth-century Scotland.

As was the case with all early modern legislation, local initiatives and adaptations by church and burgh authorities were important in ensuring the success of the education acts.[12] The state passed legislation to enable and direct change, but financing of schools and teachers was left to the localities. Control of the running of the parochial schools was entrusted to the burgh authorities and to the Presbyteries and Kirk Sessions: the local agents of the Protestant Reformation in village communities. This sort of delegation from center to locality was a characteristic feature of administration in early modern Europe. Centralized control might exist but was hard to exert in practice because of the limited coercive powers of the government and the problems of communication. The significance of local initiatives and circumstances remained considerable and explains the chequered pattern of school placements into the eighteenth century. The system was nationally centralized, and legislation was undoubtedly important, but the situation in individual parishes remained vitally important to the campaign's success or failure. This, then, was the legislative and administrative framework. What of teaching methods and curricula?

Because of its religious and moral emphasis, the form of education was dictated by the wish to transmit an approved body of knowledge and doctrine to the pupil, rather than to stimulate critical understanding. Rote learning was central to the didactic process, which, for most children, involved catechism, reading, writing and (especially for girls) training in practical skills such as sewing, knitting, and weaving.[13] Elementary education for most children might give a foundation for later learning but did little to instill more than the simplest skills. At more advanced levels, Latin, mathematics, and other subjects were taught. Due to mass demand, a much greater emphasis on practical forms of education became apparent from the later seventeenth century. Bookkeeping and navigation, for example, gained ground against the more traditional classical education, especially in the growing commercial towns. Developments in course content at the postelementary level were a function of changing popular tastes and had little to do with the secular and ecclesiastical authorities, for whom political order and religious conformity continued to be the overriding concerns.

The educational drive did not stop in the schools. The core of the national literacy campaign was the parochial school system, but the church also instigated

---

[12]"Acts of the Parliament and of the Privy Council of Scotland relative to the establishing and maintaining of schools from the year 1496 to the year 1696," *Miscellany of the Maitland Club* 2,1 (1840), pp. 5–37; James Grant, *History of the Burgh and Parish Schools of Scotland, Burgh Schools* (Glasgow: Collins, 1876); *Extracts from the Records of Dunfermline in the 16th and 17th centuries*, ed. Andrew Shearer (Edinburgh: Constable, 1951).

[13]William Boyd, *Education in Ayrshire through 7 centuries* (London: University of London Press, 1961), pp. 25–30 gives a transcript of the school regulations for the parish school of Dundonald in Ayrshire in the early seventeenth century. These offer the fullest seventeenth century account of the curriculum, discipline, and organization of a parish school.

plans to promote learning at home. Recognizing the importance of socialization in the home for religious awareness, the Kirk was anxious that ministers of religion should catechize their flocks regularly and should ensure that masters of families (usually the husband and father) conducted religious instruction. All families were supposed to have a printed directory (reader) of family worship, which the household head was to use for instructing wife, children, and servants.

At first sight, this attempt to promote home learning is remarkably reminiscent of the late seventeenth-century Swedish literacy campaign. The Swedish church instigated a literacy program almost entirely without the aid of formal schools, but founded instead on a system of home learning of reading and the catechism. This was enforced by regular examinations of proficiency and sanctions against the ignorant.[14] We have no way of knowing how effective the home learning campaign actually was in Scotland, since there is no record of the standard of achievement reached by elements of the Scottish population. Basic religious knowledge was required to enjoy certain church rites. The Church might, for example, refuse admission to communion to the grossly ignorant, meaning that they would be denied the sacrament of marriage or baptism for their children.[15] To this spur were added attempts to shame illiterates. However, tests of religious knowledge were conducted orally, without any direct investigation of reading skills, meaning that we have no way of measuring attainments. As far as we can tell, the sort of facility demanded must have been very low. Simple rote learning of a few basic religious tenets—the Lord's Prayer, Creed, and the Ten Commandments—was all that was required. In contrast to the Swedish model, the Scottish reformers stressed public action as the core of the campaign. Home education was a second string to their bow, unlike the Swedish case, where it was central to the literacy program.

These were the aims of the literacy campaign and its methods. What the religious Reformers wanted was a system in which rural parishes had elementary schools for children up to the age of eight years, town grammar schools which would teach reading, writing, Latin, and arithmetic from age eight to twelve and, finally, colleges and universities in the principal towns. They strove for a school in every parish that all children could attend, in order to provide a basic education for as wide a spectrum of society as possible. Passage from elementary to grammar school to university was dependent on literacy attainments, on displayed facility in learning, and on financial resources. The provision of funds by burgh councils and Kirk Sessions for the children of the very poor was

[14] Johansson, "The History of Literacy in Sweden," pp. 161–74, 181–2. T. Christopher Smout, "Born Again at Cambuslang: New Evidence on Popular Religion and Literacy in Eighteenth Century Scotland," *Past &Present* 97 (November 1982) argues from a highly suspect source—110 cases specially selected by a clergyman from among the thousands who attended a religious revival meeting in 1740–1742—that Scotland was like Sweden: everyone could read by the middle of the eighteenth century, but writing was still firmly related to the social hierarchy and to economic needs. This case is by no means proven.

[15] Kirk, p. 230; Houston, ch. 5. For examples of the level of understanding required see *Register of the Minister, Elders and Deacons of the Christian Congregation of St. Andrews, 1559–1600*, ed. D. Hay Fleming (Edinburgh: Constable, vol. 1 1889, vol. 2 1890), vol. 1, pp. 196, 340–341, 439, and vol. 2, pp. 794, 809.

supposed to remove any financial obstacles that needy but gifted children would face in achieving elementary and higher education. Inevitably, the Reformers had to compromise, and their goals were not achieved overnight. How successful were they in providing schools and increasing the literacy of the Scottish population during the seventeenth and eighteenth centuries?

Until the second half of the seventeenth century there were only modest successes in establishing parish schools. The educational situation was probably much the same as in the pre-Reformation period. A survey of certain Lowland parishes in 1627 revealed that only twenty-nine out of forty-nine had a settled school. In the northeast Lowlands, thirty-five percent of Aberdeenshire parishes had schools in 1650, and twenty percent of those in part of Angus could boast one.[16] Some parish schools had been set up, but only in a minority of Lowland communities. This is not to say that no education was available in parishes without an official school. Even in the early seventeenth century, there were certainly schoolteachers in many Lowland areas who would in all likelihood have escaped official investigations into the provision of schools and salaries. Often poorly paid and peripatetic, these men provided an education in any building available to them—barn, alehouse or dwelling—in return for fees. We shall discuss their importance shortly. What we can conclude is that the formal provision of a schoolhouse and salaried teacher, a "settled school," was only achieved in a minority of parishes, even in the most favored areas of Scotland. Success was patchy because of financial restrictions, shortage of teachers, religious dissent after 1660, and the different attitudes of local landowners who had to pay for the schools: some stonewalled for decades.

By the end of the seventeenth century, the situation was much better. The goal of a school in every Lowland parish was close to being attained. More than ninety percent of parishes in the eastern counties of the Lothians, Fife and Angus (the most economically advanced parts of Scotland) had a school, and, in most of these, teaching of Latin was available, indicating that instruction had advanced beyond the three Rs.[17] In the rural Lowlands and in the small towns, the literacy campaign seems to have achieved a considerable measure of success by the end of the seventeenth century. Per capita educational resources were better in these environments than in the Highlands. A report of the General Assembly of the Church of Scotland in 1758 showed that a large proportion of Highland parishes were without schools. Until well into the nineteenth century, most formal education was provided by the Society in Scotland for Propagating Christian Knowledge (SSPCK), an Edinburgh-based charitable body that was independent but that shared the same goals as church and state in promoting education. Perhaps

---

[16]Scotland, p. 52; J. C. Jessop, *Education in Angus* (London: University of London Press, 1931), p. 58; Ian J. Simpson, *Education in Aberdeenshire before 1872* (London: University of London Press, 1947), p. 19.

[17]Donald J. Withrington, "Lists of Schoolmasters Teaching Latin, 1690," *Scottish History Society Miscellany* 10 (1965), pp. 121–42. J. M. Beale, "A History of the Burgh and Parochial Schools of Fife from the Reformation to 1872" (Ph.D. thesis, University of Edinburgh, 1953).

as many as 300,000 children in the Highlands got the only schooling they would ever receive from the SSPCK's foundations during the eighteenth century.[18]

Education in the Highlands was hindered by a shortage of money and of teachers, and by the often large size of the parishes and the difficulties of communication in that region. This meant that, even where a parish or SSPCK school did exist, not all eligible children would necessarily be able to gain access to it, due to the physical obstacle of distance. In addition, there were often too many children of school age to be accommodated in the parish school. This was also true of parts of the Lowlands. St. Ninians parish in Stirlingshire, for example, some ten miles by five in size, contained perhaps one thousand children of school age in the 1750s.[19] A further strain on the parochial school system was imposed by the population growth of the eighteenth century and the increasing concentration of Scotland's people in large towns. The notion of a single parish school in the growing industrial towns of the central Lowlands was increasingly inappropriate.[20] The literacy campaign retained a parochial focus which was increasingly out of step with social and demographic conditions.

Fortunately, private or "adventure" schools provided a valuable supplement to the state-instituted parish system. These were usually small, fee-paying schools that provided basic instruction in reading, writing, and sometimes arithmetic to younger children. Though often enjoying a tenuous existence, they were numerous, and their importance for Scottish education was enormous. An 1818 survey found that six percent of Scotland's school children were in private, endowed schools (the backbone of contemporary English education), thirty-one percent were in tax-supported parochial schools (the core of the Scottish national literacy campaign), while the remaining three-fifths were being educated in private, fee-paying schools.[21] These types of independent schools had been part of the educational scene since the sixteenth century. Private adventure schools preceded the national literacy campaign and continued to be important until the late nineteenth century. They were quite independent of the parochial system and depended on mass demand for basic education. Strictly speaking, private, fee-paying schools were illegal. Kirk Session and burgh authorities attempted to curb their activities in order to preserve official control over what was taught and by whom. They wished also to ensure that the parish schoolmaster received as large an income as possible from fees. Official attitudes toward private adventure schools reveal a concern for conformity and monopoly stronger than the desire to promote education for itself. Private schools nonetheless continued to be a central feature of Scottish education throughout the seventeenth century. Population growth in the following hundred years made them even more vital

---

[18]Scotland, pp. 60, 101. Charles W. J. Withers, *Gaelic in Scotland, 1698–1981: The Geographical History of a Language* (Edinburgh: John Donald, 1984), pp. 120–37.

[19]Smout, *History of the Scottish People,* p. 425.

[20]Ibid., pp. 441–3. E. G. West, "Resource Allocation and Growth in Early Nineteenth Century British Education," in *Applied Historical Studies,* ed. Michael Drake (London: Methuen, 1973), p. 61.

[21]Thomas W. Laqueur, "The Cultural Origins of Popular Literacy in England, 1500–1850," *Oxford Review of Education* 2 (1976), p. 256.

as the parochial network came under increasing strain. During the later seventeenth and eighteenth centuries, some local authorities were prepared to tolerate parish schools, but only those which taught girls or which provided only the most basic literacy.

It is essential to understand that the state's literacy campaign was not the only type of educational provision in seventeenth- and eighteenth-century Scotland. There was a national school system, but it was far from comprehensive. As in contemporary England, private schools that charged fees for learning were an important part of Scottish education. Additionally, work schools, poor-hospital schools and, from the late eighteenth century, Sunday Schools provided a measure of instruction in basic literacy. Indeed, the variety of types of school was considerable, and the public, parish schools formed only part of a complex educational mosaic. This makes it difficult to assess the precise importance of the national literacy campaign, since there were many educational establishments outside its province that existed to serve a widespread demand for education.

Schools, moreover, were not the only means of learning. A person might learn to read and write from other members of the family, from his or her peer group, as a servant or apprentice, or through autodidactic methods such as using a basic book of spelling and grammar. People may have employed the limited schooling they obtained as a foundation for deeper and more extensive self-teaching later in life. In the Highlands, old women gathered groups of children around them to teach reading, and, on the whole, informal learning was more important than in the Lowlands.[22] The state campaign supplied education, but there was also a clear demand for it in the Lowlands, shown both by the existence of adventure schools and in examples of learning by nonscholastic means. These three areas—parish schools, private schools, and informal teaching or autodidactic methods—overlapped in a complex way, sometimes complementary, sometimes supplementary.

In the Lowlands of Scotland, the aspiration of establishing a school in every parish had been achieved, in a large measure, by the end of the seventeenth century. By the middle of the eighteenth century most of the eligible population could, in theory, have had access to at least some elementary education.[23] What then did this mean in terms of literacy among ordinary men and women?

[22]Smout, "Born Again at Cambuslang," pp. 123–7; Houston, ch. 2, 4; John Sinclair, *Analysis of the Statistical Account of Scotland*, part 2 (London: John Murray, 1826), appendix, p. 19; F. G. Thompson, "Technical Education in the Highlands and Islands," *Transactions of the Gaelic Society of Inverness* 48 (1972–4), p. 248; Victor E. Durkacz, *The Decline of the Celtic Languages* (Edinburgh: John Donald, 1983). It was only in the Highlands and Islands that any systematic use was made of the literate people to teach their illiterate peers in the same way as the *brigadistas*, the principal agents of the Cuban national literacy campaign in the 1960s. See, for example, Andrew McKerral, *Kintyre in the Seventeenth Century* (Edinburgh: Oliver and Boyd, 1948), p. 155. The use of children or young adults who possessed reading and writing skills to teach illiterates was seen as a temporary expedient only.

[23]Smout, *History of the Scottish People*, p. 426. Figures on literacy are drawn from Houston, ch. 2, 3. Two types of document have been used. To derive figures for the mid-seventeenth century, national oaths of loyalty subscribed by all adult males have been analysed. For the period 1650–1780, signed or marked criminal court depositions offer the best source for statistical analysis of Scottish literacy.

Judged by the universal, standard, and direct measure of ability to sign a name in full on a document, we must conclude that the achievements were far from complete. In the period 1638–1644, seventy-five to eighty percent of adult males who lived in the rural Lowlands and who subscribed to the oaths of politico-religious loyalty circulating at that time were illiterate. The figure for town-dwellers was much better, close to fifty percent, but we have no information on women or the Highlands. By the third quarter of the eighteenth century, this figure had improved substantially to around thirty-five percent illiterate, with some fifty-five to sixty percent of men in the Highlands unable to sign their names on court depositions. Rates of improving literacy were much, much slower than in some twentieth-century campaigns such as Nicaragua, where, in the course of a nine-month period during 1979 and 1980, illiteracy was cut from fifty percent to fifteen percent.

Improvements did not take place in any steady fashion. The timing and extent of changing literacy levels varied among social groups: the main advances for the middling groups—craftsmen, tradesmen, and tenant farmers—occurred in the third quarter of the seventeenth century and again in the second quarter of the eighteenth. Among the lower classes—labourers, servants, and subtenants—the only improvement took place in the first period, and the subsequent century saw literacy rates stagnate. If the state educational system were responsible, it seems that it benefitted all classes in the seventeenth century but favored the middling groups in the eighteenth.

Environmental factors remained extremely important even in the mid-eighteenth century. The great cities of Edinburgh and Glasgow were the most literate milieu, followed by smaller burghs; most professional men, craftsmen, and tradesmen lived in these types of community. Rural dwellers were lowest in proportions literate. A person's socioeconomic standing continued to exert a powerful influence on his opportunities to learn and on his ability to write. Gentry and professionals were all literate in the 1750s and 1760s and had been since the early seventeenth century. Craftsmen and tradesmen were only twenty percent illiterate, farmers around one third, but nearly seventy percent of the working classes could not sign their names in full. The social hierarchy of literacy is clear.

Oaths of loyalty, the famous Covenants, covered all adult male householders. Witnesses before the courts were required to authenticate their testimonies with a personal subscription. Court depositions provide a good cross section of the population, and information about their age, occupation, social status, gender, and residence can be used to examine the importance of these variables for literacy. In both cases, the type of literacy being measured is simply the ability to subscribe to a document in person. Those who signed their names in full are held to be literate, those who made initials or a crude mark such as a cross are deemed illiterate. This criterion is the best available for analyzing literacy in Europe and North America before the nineteenth century, since it is found in documents all over those areas; it is a standard test which does not require interpretation of, say, questions about literate skills posed to individuals; and, finally, it is a direct measure of literacy which involves no problems of inference. In Britain, systematic studies of reading and writing ability among the population as a whole were not conducted until the nineteenth century, and even then their interpretation is far from straightforward. See West, *Education and the Industrial Revolution*, ch. 1–3 and Houston, ch. 5.

This is the best side of Scottish literacy. When we turn to women and to
the Highland region the achievements were more restricted. Women were much
less literate than men—seventy percent could not sign at a time when only thirty-
five percent of their husbands, fathers, and brothers were illiterate. Improvements in female literacy were slower than for men, but the influence of residence
and status was equally important in stratifying literacy attainments. Women who
lived in towns and cities were more literate than their rural sisters, and the wives,
widows, and daughters of landowners or professionals had far higher literacy
than those associated with craftsmen, tradesmen, or peasant farmers. Women
from the lowest classes were almost completely illiterate, even in the mid-eighteenth
century.

The reason for the inequality can be found in the strongly masculine
emphasis in Scottish society, which meant that girls received less education than
boys and that what they were taught was mainly reading and practical skills
thought to be appropriate to their station in life. In the Highlands they received
hardly any formal education at all. An eighteenth-century commentator observed
of the region: "the Parents consider Learning of any kind as of little Moment
to the Girls, on which Account, great Numbers of them never go to any School."[24]
Women's inferior status in Scottish society was both justified and reinforced by
their restricted education and low literacy. The religious Reformers wished that
both boys and girls would receive a basic education, but prevailing social attitudes
about women's role proved to be more powerful than their pious exhortations.
There was a formal committment to gender equality in elementary education,
but in reality female education was often restricted in scope and duration compared to that of males. In this area, the national literacy campaign's impact was
tempered by the cultural values of Scotland's people.

The other social and geographical sector in Scotland where the effects of
the literacy campaign were much attenuated was the Highland zone. In this
area, illiteracy among all social classes was some twenty to thirty percent higher
than in the Lowlands in the eighteenth century. Possessing a primitive economic
and social structure, few schools, and poor communications, the Highlands suffered from a number of disadvantages, and, as a consequence, literacy remained
very low until well into the nineteenth century. The literacy campaign that had
enjoyed success in the Lowlands by the end of the seventeenth century made
little headway even in the eighteenth century, but the reason for low literacy in
the Highlands is more complex than simply the lack of schools or economic and
geographical factors.

Most people in the Highlands spoke a different language from the Lowlanders: Gaelic. This had been the predominant language throughout Scotland
until the fifteenth century but was gradually replaced by Scots English. By the
beginning of the seventeenth century, Gaelic only existed in pockets of the
southwest of Scotland and in the Highlands. The association of Gaelic with
Catholicism and with disorder caused the law-abiding Lowlanders who ran the

[24]Charles W. J. Withers, "Education and Anglicization: the Policy of the SSPCK towards Gaelic in
Education, 1709–1825," *Scottish Studies* 26 (1982), p. 40.

SSPCK to insist on teaching in English, so that, in the words of the 1616 Education Act, "the Irish language which is one of the chief, principal causes of barbarity and incivility . . . may be abolished and removed." The campaign failed in the Highlands as a result of economic and geographical difficulties, and because the program of anglicization, protestantization, and pacification of which the drive for literacy was a part sought to destroy the culture of the Highlands. Rather than building on the popular tongue, church, state, and charitable bodies demanded that Highlanders learn English and thus, by definition, become "civilized." The Kirk did provide ministers who could speak Gaelic as religious instructors. But it also shared the presumptions of the government and SSPCK that Gaelic, Catholicism, and disorder were interlinked and must be eradicated. All three agencies insisted that learning should take place in English, with the result that Highlanders had to learn another language before they could tackle reading and writing. By divorcing language from literacy and insisting on education in a language which most people did not understand, the authorities condemned the campaign in the Highlands to be much less successful than that in the Lowlands in reducing illiteracy.[25] With little printed literature in Gaelic until the nineteenth century, Highlanders found it hard to make up defects in their education, and Highland culture remained predominantly oral.

The desire to assimilate the Highlands to the culture and polity of the Lowlands meant that an attack was mounted on existing Gaelic culture and language. Political, religious, and ideological goals worked against literacy, and it was only with a softening of official attitudes to education in Gaelic during the nineteenth century that any substantial progress was made. Gaelic was increasingly tolerated for religious purposes from the mid-eighteenth century, and from 1811 there was a Gaelic school society. During the seventeenth and eighteenth centuries, the demand by church, state and SSPCK for ideological supremacy militated against literacy. The campaign's drive for conformity to approved norms proved baneful for literacy in the Highlands.

Whatever its achievements, the national literacy campaign in Scotland was not able to remove distinctions between individuals based on class, gender, and geography. Lowland Scotland became one of the most literate zones in Europe, but the educational program was far from totally successful even by the third quarter of the eighteenth century. This was in marked contrast to the levelling effect of the Swedish national literacy campaign of the eighteenth century or those in late twentieth-century Nicaragua or Cuba, which succeeded in assimilating previously disadvantaged groups. Therefore, some of the extravagant claims made for Scotland's achievements in the early modern period are not justified. First, there was no linear progress in either ideas or attainments over the period 1560–1803. Some themes do run through the seventeenth century initiatives, notably the stress on basic, religiously oriented education, located in the parish schools and focused on the general good of society. The values expressed in the legislation were not, however, constant and regular, but were very much linked to political circumstances. For example, the act of 1646 that

---

[25] Durkacz; see also Charles Withers, *Gaelic in Scotland*, pp. 1–9, 100–15.

had specified that heritors should pay for parish schools was repealed in 1662, as part of the general reaction against the legislation of the "Scottish Revolution" period. Political concerns arising from the religious, dynastic, and constitutional dislocations of 1689–1690 explain, for instance, the act of the Scottish Parliament in 1690 to force grammar school teachers and university staff to swear allegiance to the crown and to presbyterian church government.[26] The attack on the Gaelic, Catholic Highlands was given added impetus by the Jacobite rebellions of 1715 and 1745, which threatened the politico-religious establishment. The 1803 act was strongly motivated by the perceived need to maintain the loyalty of school-masters in a period of disturbing political radicalism.

The effects of the legislation were cumulative but cannot be seen as part of anything except the simplest plan. And, as we have seen, the uneven progress of literacy is plain. Interestingly, however, political and religious upsets such as the Scottish Revolution of the 1640s or the Glorious Revolution of 1689 seem to have exerted only a temporary and slight negative impact on literacy trends. Again, this suggests either that the local system was extremely robust, or, more likely, that values remained unchanged and that *demand* was the critical factor. This demand was created by economic change, a desire for religious knowledge among individuals, contact with the administrative organs of church and state and landowner, cultural developments associated with the impact of printing, and deep pride among the Lowlanders about attaining basic literacy.

Second, education was not compulsory in Scotland until 1872. An early Calvinist hope was that "all must be compelled to bring up their children in learnynge and virtue," and indeed some burghs tried to enforce attendance for town children, backed up by the threat of fining recalcitrant parents or by promise of financial aid to overcome cost barriers.[27] Religious reformers hoped that no one would be able to use the excuse of poverty for failing to educate their children. Yet, compulsory education was an aspiration rather than an achievement before the late nineteenth century. We must conclude that many people wanted their children to become literate if they were sending them to parish, private, or charity schools. Church and state might provide some schools and some incentives, but without mass demand, it is hard to imagine that their initiatives would have gone very far.

Third, education was definitely not free until 1891. Virtually all parents had to pay fees to educate their children, and, even in cases where burgh or parish funds were used to finance the children of the very poor, there were incidental expenses to be met, and there was the important "opportunity cost" to be borne of child labour lost to its family. Children were useful workers from the age of seven or eight, and this explains the short duration of education for many of them coupled as it was with the clear seasonality in attendance: during harvest, the numbers at any given rural school would often be halved.[28] Not all eligible children would have been able to attend schools, and education was often

[26] Withrington, p. 121.
[27] Grant, pp. 309–11; Jessop, pp. 45–6.
[28] Smout, *History of the Scottish People*, p. 430; West, "Resource allocation," p. 61.

sporadic and short-lived for those who did. Poor children would be lucky to enjoy more than two years of elementary education, though the more fortunate might stay on until as late as twelve or even sixteen years of age, and the privileged few could attend the middle- and upper-class-dominated institutions of higher education.[29] Economic constraints continued to work against elementary learning. What is more, the stress on the general provision of basic education found in the parish schools was quickly transformed into a firmly elitist perception of literacy at the postelementary level.

Fourth, as we have seen, the achievements were not universal. Success was strictly limited in the Highlands for the lower classes and for women. True mass literacy was not achieved until the second half of the nineteenth century. It is clear that the Scottish national literacy campaign was not as successful as that of eighteenth-century New England where, for men at least, nearly all literacy differentials attributable to environmental factors had been eradicated by the second half of the eighteenth century. Nor have we any firm evidence that the mass reading ability achieved in Sweden by the same period was equalled in Scotland. The picture of signing ability that we have resembles much more closely that obtaining in contemporary northeast France, the Netherlands, and northern England.[30] All these regions lacked a systematic national literacy campaign. Dutch Protestants tried to insist on school provision, and, indeed, a large proportion of the eligible population attended schools in the Low Countries. This was not, however, an organized national campaign of the kind tried in Scotland. In France and England there was a religiously inspired drive for schooling, but nothing on the lines of the parish system in Scotland. In other words, similar results were obtained without systematic intervention and organization by the state.

The comparison with northern England is particularly intriguing. That region showed certain economic and cultural similarities with Lowland Scotland, but its educational history was quite different, being based on charitably endowed and fee-paying schools. Nevertheless, the northernmost English counties of Northumberland, Durham, Cumberland, and Westmorland had by the mid-eighteenth century achieved levels of signing ability that were on a par with Lowland Scotland. For women, the levels were slightly higher than in Scotland, and, for all social groups, they were superior to southern regions. We are left wondering whether the north of England and Lowland Scotland were areas where mass *demand* for education was strong, distinguishing this cultural zone from the Highlands and, to a lesser extent, from the southern parts of England. Schooling in the Highlands was poor, but this was not the only explanation for low literacy there. Eighteenth-century observers remarked on the apparent indifference of the Highlanders, and of the immigrant Irish of the western Lowlands, to learning as they defined it, but stressed the premium placed on basic literacy by what they saw as the worthy Protestant Lowlanders.[31] The achievement of the literacy campaign was to structure and control educational provision while

[29] Beale, p. 98; Smout, *History of the Scottish People,* p. 450.
[30] Houston, ch. 2, 4, 5 discusses school attendance and comparative literacy in European countries.
[31] Sinclair, pp. 19–22. Smout, "Born Again at Cambuslang," p. 126.

providing a foundation for literacy among a large proportion of the rural population. It created the potential for more elements of society to be assimilated to national culture and politics. Yet there remains the intriguing possibility that the national literacy campaign in Scotland achieved what it did because it built on a prevailing popular appreciation of literacy, rather than by imposing literacy on people. Demand rather than supply may be the crucial variable accounting for the Scottish success. In this respect, cultural values helped the literacy campaign, rather than hinder it as happened in the Highlands or in the case of women.

The paths to literacy which were available to the people of early modern Scotland were numerous and far from simple. Learning was transmitted and acquired in a variety of contexts, of which the national parish school system was only one. There were many different sorts of school, and the forms of learning were rather diverse. Efforts at promoting literacy and the methods employed overlapped in a complex way that makes it extremely risky to attribute the primary role to parish schools and thus to the national literacy campaign run by church and state. Traditionally, historians have assumed that if the aspirations and the legislation were successful, then it must have been due to the drive of church and state. But the coordinated parish system did not replace the range of other available schools, which in fact became more important under the impact of population increase and concentration during the eighteenth century. In conclusion, the successes which Scotland enjoyed in the seventeenth and eighteenth centuries were not simply the result of education provided and insisted upon by church and state. They must be seen as the product of overlapping efforts on the part of institutions and individuals. There was no one avenue to literacy, and the push of educational provision was vitally complemented by the pull of individual demand for learning. In fact, there is no compelling reason to attribute the primary role in changing literacy to the parish schools and thus to the religious and political campaign of the seventeenth and eighteenth centuries. At best, the campaign may have been important both in providing the opportunity for education to those otherwise unable to obtain it and in constituting an example that promoted the development of other types of school and thus encouraged Scotland's people to seek out literacy. Yet, it may have been the product of a broader desire for reading and writing, whose importance was more as a symbol of aspiration and an example of method for the nineteenth and twentieth century than as a concrete instance of successful achievement in the seventeenth and eighteenth.

CHAPTER 4

Literacy Campaigns in Sweden[1]

EGIL JOHANSSON

INTRODUCTION

The history of literacy in Sweden must be understood as two separate campaigns of popular education. The first one, the early church Campaign around 1700, was built upon informal instruction for everyone to read, sing, and pray the holy "Word" of God from books printed in Gothic type. The second one, the late school Campaign around and after 1850, was based upon formal schooling, so that everyone might read, write, and reckon the "world" from new books and texts printed or written in modern type. This is true for rural life and for the large majority of the population. But for towns and a small minority of the (male) people there always was a need for schools and reading, writing and elementary arithmetic in daily life, a continuing pattern of "functional" literacy.

To understand the church- and school-based literacy campaigns, and to recognize the intervening pattern of functional literacy for daily life, let us start with the background both in Sweden and in the whole of Scandinavia. I like to picture the region as an enormous tree on the map of cultural history,[2] the roots penetrating deeply into the livelihood and culture of the continent, the trunk marching through Denmark and southern Sweden, and the enormous crown stretching high up in the east, north and west, covering land and sea. This picture is of great help in trying to puzzle together the pieces of popular literacy and education in Scandinavia during the last three or four centuries, evoking not only the land itself, but its population growth, its economic, political, and cultural life, as well as the growth of popular literacy and education.

---

[1]This article compiles and completes some parts of four studies by the author: "Literacy Studies in Sweden: Some Examples," in Egil Johansson (ed.), *Literacy and Society in a Historical Perspective—A Conference Report*. Educational Reports, No. 2 (Umeå 1973); *The History of Literacy in Comparison With Some Other Countries*. Educational Reports, No. 12 (Umeå 1977), pp. 41–66; "Kunskapens träd i Norden" ("Popular literacy in Scandinavia. The picture of a growing tree"), in M. Jokipii and I. Nummela (ed.), *Ur nordisk kulturhistoria: Läskunnighet och folkundervisning före folkskolan (Cultural History in Scandinavia: Literacy and Popular Education before the Primary School System)*, XVIII, Nordic Historical Congress (Jyväskylä, Finland, 1981), pp. 263–267.
[2]Johansson, "Kunskapens," pp. 263–265.

EGIL JOHANSSON • Demografiska Databasen, Umeå Universitet, Umeå 901 87, Sweden.

The Growth in Population

The number of people living in Scandinavia around the year 1600 can be assumed to have been slightly more than two million. Of these, a third each lived in Denmark, Sweden, and the rest of the Scandinavian countries (e.g., Finland, Norway, Iceland, Greenland). By 1750 the number had increased by a million. In Denmark and Sweden, the population remained nearly steady, the increase being spread over the rest of Scandinavia. At the turn of the nineteenth century there were around five million Scandinavians. Almost half of them lived in Sweden and roughly a fifth each in Denmark, Norway, and Finland. The Danish population remained barely a million, and Norway and Finland, with their fast-growing populations, caught up with Denmark. During the next century, these three countries grew at the same rate, their populations almost tripling to approximately 2.5 million in each country by the end of the last century. During the same time, Sweden doubled its population to roughly five million. And since the eighteenth century, Iceland has doubled its population to approximately eighty thousand. Greenland's population was at that time around ten thousand. Thus, the population, its density and growth, could evoke the image of a growing tree on the map of Scandinavia, where first the trunk, then the branches, and finally the whole plant flourish. The real value of this picture emerges, however, in depicting the cultural and educational traditions of these countries.

Different Urban and Rural Educational Needs

Firstly, we can consider the conditions of Scandanavian lives and livelihoods. The proportion of city dwellers was significant: While a fifth of the population of Denmark lived in towns and cities, the urban population was barely a tenth in the rest of Scandinavia. Moreover, for a long time the merchants from Denmark and central Sweden dominated Scandinavia's towns and cities through privileges and mercantile rights. Copenhagen, with 100,000 inhabitants, and Stockholm, with its 76,000 in 1800, were at that time ten times bigger than either Oslo or Helsinki. Almost all of the other towns and cities remained rather small, but were set apart, even so, by a definite educational tradition. As on the continent, each town had its elementary schools, to some extent for the poorer children, as well as separate ones for the children of faculty at institutions for higher learning. Therefore, the development of life in the city can be pictured as an emerging tree of knowledge in the Scandinavian countries, with its roots and trunk in the south and with branches spread toward the east, north, and west. This is the case at least in regard to the educational requirements of both the authorities and the commercial and industrial life in the cities. Other aspects of industry and commerce strengthen this picture even more.

For the rural population—about ninety percent of all Scandinavians—there was another story. Naturally, this population remained strong where the towns and cities were weak, and vice versa. Even leaving aside considerations of fertility of the land and farming technique, it was typically the farmers in Denmark who lived under the most wretched conditions, especially during "Stavnsbaandet," in part a kind of villenage, in the eighteenth century. In Norway and Iceland, the farmers were given more breathing space under the same Danish rule. The farmers in Sweden and Finland lived perhaps more independently: they had self-government on the parish level and representation in the Swedish Parliament. But on the whole, the rural population believed that, for everyday use, they did not need much bookish education, literacy being saved for the church and Sunday life.

The Flowering of Popular Culture

Scandinavian indigenous culture branches off in a comparable manner. In Denmark and Scania, dependence on the continent was considerable, while further out over the Scandinavian map, the indigenous cultures lived on for a long time, the age-old customs, with their provincial characteristics, thus being preserved. The most noteworthy was Scandinavian popular poetry and, in particular, the oral and written popular literature of Iceland. A provocative question, similar to questions with our understanding of the runic tradition, is raised in the Icelandic history of popular literacy: namely, to what degree reading and writing of popular literature was once really widespread, only disappearing after the Reformation. We can also count spoken language among the indigenous popular culture. The many dialects were mainly left to live their own life. But in certain border areas, the confusion of tongues could be awkward, with German speakers turning into Danish ones, Danish speakers turning into Swedish ones, and Lapps turning into Norwegian speakers.

It was easier to control the written language, covering all dialects. Danish became the written language even in Norway, as was the case with Swedish in the Scanian counties. Danish and Swedish became the official languages in their respective political areas. But for popular literacy, the ordinary people—the Icelanders and the Greenlanders in the Danish kingdom, the Lapps and the Finns in the Swedish—saw their own mother tongues in print. In this respect, an interesting detail is that the popular literature was printed in Gothic script. At least in Sweden and Finland, this clearly revealed the range and form of both the religious and worldly popular literature. The learned literature, however, was printed in the Latin alphabet and for a long time, in Latin. This leads us to the problem of the role played by politics in the development of culture.

The Shifting Patterns of the Political Background

Politics, through war and peace, has drawn its dramatic lines over the Swedish and Scandinavian map. Danish land taken over by Sweden and Swedish land surrendered to Russia resulted in noteworthy linguistic, political, and cultural changes. Perhaps the Scanian countries, along with Karelia and the Norwegian Lappish province, were the ones to feel the political designs forced upon them the most. The power of the state and the missionary work of the church were the instruments in the distant west, north, and east in Greenland, Norway,

Sweden, and Finland. Such border areas witnessed the clash between earlier popular culture and the demands of a more modern age. Somewhere in the middle of this process still another pattern was at work, connected with the need for popular literacy within the church.

The Church Reading Tradition in Sweden and Finland[3]

It has been difficult in the past to make an accurate history of Swedish literacy known in other countries. In his *Statistik över Sverige (Swedish Statistics)*[4] (which is full of useful information), Carl af Forsell put the matter thus:

> Most foreign geographies and statistical works, e.g. those of Stein, Hassel, Crome, Malte Brun and others, maintain that the lower classes in Sweden can neither read nor write. As for the first statement, it is completely false, since there is not one in a thousand among the Swedish peasantry who cannot read. The reason for this is principally the directives of Charles XI that a person who is not well acquainted with his Bible should not be allowed to take Holy Communion and that a person who is not confirmed should not be allowed to get married. One might nowadays readily add that, in order to be confirmed, everyone should be able to prove that, besides reading from a book, he also possessed passable skills in writing and arithmetic. Even if in other respects the cottage of the farmer or the crofter gives evidence of the highest poverty it will, nevertheless, nearly always contain a hymn-book, a Bible, a collection of sermons, and sometimes several other devotional manuals. The English Lord Chancellor, Brougham, said in Parliament on May 1st 1816, that in the previous six years 9765 couples had been married in Manchester, among whom not a single person could either read or write. According to the *Revue Encyclopedique* of October 1832, seventy-four adolescents out of a hundred in the northern departments of France could read, whilst in the western ones it was twelve out of a hundred, and in the whole country only thirty-eight out of a hundred.

Af Forsell indignantly rejects foreign opinions about the low rate of literacy in Sweden, at the same time striking back by referring to low figures for England and France. The problem is still with us: It is difficult for foreign observers to understand the Swedish literacy scene, due to the special nature of the Swedish and Finnish reading tradition. First, the ability to read gained ground much earlier than the ability to write, whereas these two skills have followed each other closely in most other countries. Second, people were persuaded to learn to read by means of an actual campaign initiated for political and religious reasons; during the reign of Charles XI, for example, the Church Law of 1686 contained a ruling concerning a religious and Sunday-life reading for every man. Third, this reading campaign was forced through almost completely without the aid of a proper school system in the countryside. The responsibility for teaching children to read was ultimately placed on parents and godfathers. The social pressure was enormous. Everyone in the household and in the village gathered each year to take part in instructions and examinations in reading Gothic letters and

---

[3] Johansson, "History of Literacy," pp. 2–8.
[4] af Forsell, C., *Statistik över Sverige grundad pa offentliga handlingar (Statistics for Sweden Based on Official Documents)* (Stockholm 1833), p. 58.

biblical texts. The adult who did not succeed for a long time at these meetings would be excluded from both Holy communion and permission to marry.

These are the distinctive features that af Forsell points to as being traditionally Swedish. He hints, moreover, at the literate environment in these poor households, by referring to the large number of books. His statements are, of course, too optimistic in their generalizations about the ability to read as a whole. But the dilemma he describes is a real one: The distinctive Swedish reading tradition was, as happens, also observed by foreign travellers. The Scottish evangelist, John Patterson, writes about his trip to Sweden in 1807–1808:[5]

> From Malmoe I paid a visit to my friend, Dr. Hylander, in Lund, made the acquaintance of the bishop and some of the professors, and enlarged my knowledge of Sweden. As Dr. Hylander had a parish not far from Malmoe, I one day went with him to attend an examination of his parishioners. It was held in a peasant's house, in a large hall, where a goodly number were collected. The people, old and young, answered the questions put to them readily in general; those who were deficient in their knowledge were severely dealt with, and exhorted to be more diligent. On the whole the exercise was calculated to be useful. It was a pleasing circumstance that all could read. Indeed, this may be affirmed of the inhabitants of all the northern Protestant Kingdoms; you seldom meet one above ten or twelve who cannot read, and the most of them write their own language; yet at the time now referred to there was nothing like what we have in Scotland, a provision for the education of the people by means of parochial schools. The parents were the teachers of their children, till they reached the age of fourteen or thereabouts, when they attended the pastor or his assistant, to be prepared for confirmation and being admitted to the Lord's Supper. And as no person can be confirmed till he can read and repeat his catechism, or, until confirmed, can give his oath in a court of justice, or get married, a great disgrace is attached to not being able to read; indeed, one who cannot read is nobody in the eye of the law. This state of things has its advantages, as far as education is concerned; but, alas! it has its disadvantages, as it admits all to the enjoyment of religious privileges, and thereby tends to make a nation of religious formalists. After the examination was over, all the heads of families sat down to a sumptuous dinner provided for the occasion, and which gave me a little more insight into Swedish society among the peasantry. I was much pleased with the whole, and thanked my friend for the opportunity then offered me for seeing more of the people.

Patterson comments approvingly here on education for the masses in Sweden. The reading tradition was widespread. School instruction did not, however, exist in the same way as in Scotland, with parents being responsible for teaching their children. Another traveller, the German ecclesiastical historian Friedrich Wilhelm von Schubert, had the same impressions as Patterson during his tour of Sweden and Finland in 1811. He observed that the ability to read gained more ground after the first decade of the eighteenth century.[6]

The reading tradition in Sweden and Finland is also a problem for af Forsell's successors in the field of statistics today. The difficulty of comparing

[5] Paterson, J., *The Book of Every Land* (London 1858), pp. 51–52.
[6] Van Schubert has presented one of the most detailed descriptions of the custom of church examinations in Sweden and Finland. See *Resa genom Sverige*, Vol. I–II (Stockholm 1825), Vol. I, pp. 68–69 (Reise durch Schweden, 1–3) (Leipzig 1823). See also *Sveriges Kyrkoförfattning och Läroverk*, Vol. I–II (Lund 1822–1825), Vol. II, pp. 93–111 (*Schwedens Kirchenverfassung und Unterrichtswesen*) (Greifswald 1820, 1821).

Sweden and Finland with other countries has, in reality, increased. Since the Second World War, the accepted model has been to regard it as necessary that reading and writing follow each other closely, that formal school instruction be almost the only conceivable teaching method, and that economic models provide us with a decisive explanation of a functioning literate environment. A general ability to read in a poor, preindustrial, agrarian, developing country as was Sweden or Finland seems a sheer absurdity, and the notion that the ability to read gained ground there much earlier than the ability to write is completely foreign to this approach.

A typical expression of this outlook is given in the treatment of literacy in the Finnish censuses of 1880–1930. The figure for the adults who could neither read nor write was, according to these censuses, constantly lower than two percent. As late as the 1930s, these figures constituted no major problem for the statisticians in the League of Nations, who quoted the number of illiterate people in Finland in 1930 at 0.9%.[7] The Finnish authorities were, however, already subject at this time to inquiries about the meaning of these figures. As a result, the next census included, unfortunately, no information about cultural attainment, because of obscurities when making international comparisons. After the War, UNESCO's statisticians were harsher.[8] Those who were only able to read were classified as illiterate. The figure for the number of adult illiterates in Finland in 1930 thus became sixteen instead of one percent. For earlier periods, this figure became even higher. It was twenty-nine percent for 1920, forty-five percent for 1910, and sixty-one percent for 1900. The corresponding figure for 1880 was as high as eighty-seven percent. The contrast with Patterson's and von Schubert's observations of the Swedish and Finnish educational tradition is glaring.

But these contemporary UNESCO observers were also uncertain about the interpretation and use of the Finnish figures. An argument with the Finnish statisticians was described in a report published in 1957. Both sides were equally confused. The Finnish group tried to include those who were only able to read with those who were able to write, even if they had not been passed by the clerical examiners.[9] Such an adjustment to the contemporary definition of literacy need not necessarily be, however, the only way of escaping the dilemma of the Finnish figures. We might instead accept the reading traditions in Sweden and Finland as *historical realities* and then adjust our discussion of the concept of literacy accordingly. This article constitutes an effort at such an alternative.

Patterns of Analysis

To make a population literate requires some form of organized instruction and a number of literacy campaigns. This is true of all times and all countries. The ability to read and write became universal in the West only during the final

[7] *Aperçu de la Démographie des divers Pays du Monde 1929–1936* (Haag 1939), p. 28.
[8] *Progress of Literacy in Various Countries*. (UNESCO: Paris 1953), p. 88.
[9] *World Illiteracy at Mid-Century* (UNESCO: Paris 1957), pp. 177–188.

years of the last century, after the consolidation of compulsory schooling. The same result is sought in the developing countries today by means of large-scale mass-literacy campaigns.

Such *purposeful educational measures* always follow a typical pattern. The breakthrough of literacy is characterized by great differences—education gaps— between the age groups. The younger ones are, to large extent, subject to teaching. The total literacy growth is concurrent with the changeover of generations: the illiterate generations die off, the new generations are made literate by means of formal education, and the population will thus gradually become literate. This pattern is typical both of the past and of today, and is the result of strong teaching measures. It is also, of course, part of this pattern that in the end there are no noticeable differences between occupational groups, sexes, town and country, and so forth. All this is obvious. These observations are nevertheless extremely useful for testing and defining various stages of literacy in a population.

This first pattern, however, continually gives place to another, characterized by prevailing differences among a population in terms of *the demand and need* for functional literacy in daily life. These differences are defined principally by social and economic conditions. They appear primarily between various occupational groups, highly dependent on active literacy. A literate environment is obtained in these occupations *without* any particular teaching campaigns, with the teaching requirements supplied through private or limited social initiatives. Characteristic features appear here, too, with differences remaining to the very last between occupational groups, sexes, town and country, and so on. This is obvious for the male population of craftsmen and merchants in the towns all of the time, and also during the early church reading campaign. To trace and observe this pattern has proved profitable when analyzing the development of literacy. These two types of analysis for mass and functional literacy always work together in the process of educational programs, and they will be used below to analyze the two literacy campaigns in Sweden.

THE EARLY CHURCH CAMPAIGN: TO READ, PRAY, AND SING THE "WORD"

The early church campaign around 1700 focused not on schooling or writing, but on informal instruction at church and at home in reading, praying, and singing the "Word" of God—printed in books with Gothic type.

The Books

This old reading campaign required deep ideological immersion in the life of the church. The liturgy and instructions concerning devotions and continued education in church and at home were taken up principally in the psalter (hymnbook). Ever since the first editions in the 1530s, the psalter contained, besides psalms, the biblical texts of the ecclesiastical year, the Catechism with Luther's explanations, the "Hustavla," and prayers for home and church. The psalter of

1695 contained 413 psalms, some of them very long. The first twenty-one psalms were "catechetical psalms," corresponding to the five parts of the Small Catechism. Then followed psalms 22–112 with biblical motifs from the Book of Psalms and from the texts of the ecclesiastical year in psalms 113–215. The remaining half of the psalms were didactic psalms for everyday life, morning and evening psalms, and so forth. One of the most noteworthy psalms was number 260, "The Golden ABC." Each of the twenty-four verses began, in turn, with the letters of the alphabet. After the psalms followed the texts of the ecclesiastical year, the Small Catechism, the "Hustavla," the Athanasian Confession, David's seven Penitential Psalms, prayers for everyday use, and the regulations for baptism, marriage, and the divine service. The volume also included a long and penetrating discourse on how to interpret and follow the life and doctrine of the church.

This psalter appeared in at least 250 editions and in 1.5 million copies up to the introduction of the new psalter in 1819. The parishioners were recommended to sing from the book when sitting in the church. The rhythm was marked by this. Long pauses, between the verses, later a puzzle to music theorists, were supposed to allow time for reading the next verse.[10]

Widespread as well were the special editions of the ABC-book, following the medieval tradition for the education of children with the Lord's Prayer and the Creed as the first two parts (and after them the Ten Commandments, the Baptism, and the Holy Communion). This early type of ABC-book had the same function in the learning of the letters by small children as, for example, the Horn-books in England and the ABC-Tafeln in Germany.[11]

After the ABC-book came, for the children, the Small Catechism itself, with the famous explanations by Luther, along with special books with additional questions, answers, and words from the Bible. A number of editions of this kind were circulated during the seventeenth century, with an ever increasing content. Most widespread of these editions was the Catechism of 1689, edited by Archbishop J. Svebilius. It included the text of the Catechism, Luther's explanations, Svebilii expositions (including 303 questions and answers with biblical passages), daily prayers, the "Hustavla," the seven Penitential Psalms, additional questions for young people and others, and, finally, John Arndt's rules for Bible-reading at home.

Both the psalter and the Catechism stressed the importance of active and engaged reading and its application to life. The Catechism was regarded both as a book of devotion and as a compilation of biblical content. The Bible editions themselves were too expensive for these uses.

The books in a rural parish for example, in Dalecarlia, Rättvik, are listed for each household in the church examination register of the 1720s. In this parish of approximately six hundred families, around four hundred ABC-books, 650–750 Catechisms, more than 1100 psalters, twenty-nine Bibles and about

---

[10] B. Widen, "Literacy in the Ecclesiastical Context," in Johansson, *Literacy and Society.*

[11] I. Wilke, *ABC-Bücher in Schweden. Ihre Entwicklung bis Ende des 19. Jahrhunderts und ihre Beziehungen zu Deutschland* (Lund 1965), pp. 87–106. A. W. Tuer, *History of the Horn-book*, Vol. I–II (London 1896).

200 other religious books were registered. Of course, most of the young and adult people were also noted as "book-learned" or able to read.[12]

The Initiative from the Church and the Government

The Catechism and the psalter, together with the Almanac, became the most important books in the households during the seventeenth century. Along with the Church Law of 1686, they manifested the edicts that applied to everyone, stipulating a fully developed church education for the masses. There were also, apart from the Church Law, other ordinances applicable to the whole country. A royal degree of 1723 constrained parents and guardians to " . . . diligently see to it that their children applied themselves to book reading and the study of the lessons in the Catechism." Neglect could lead to payment of fines used for "the instruction of poor children in the parish." Such penalties give a good picture of the vertical outset of literacy on a central level. It was in the dioceses that theory became practice.

The Conventicle Edict of 1726 had a similar significance. It was best-known for its prohibition of the pietistical conventicles, with their devotional meetings outside the confines of the family household. Such spontaneous meetings were in themselves signs of increasing commitment to individual reading and devotion. But they were not to be included in the instruction in teaching and household order. In the place of such conventicles, the edict recommended and stressed regular family prayers in the home, but only for the family household.

Popular instruction was also often prescribed at the diocesan level, in diocesan decrees, and in resolutions passed by the clergymen's assemblies. Instruction was to be organized by the diocesan authorities. The local responsibility was placed on rural deans, vicars, and parish representatives. This vertical outset was completed by long and harsh examinations by the bishop and the rural dean during their visitations in the parishes. The recurrent instruction and examinations of the clergy enabled it to spread to the villages and homes.

The Horizontal Diffusion

The reading ability campaign in Sweden was carried through almost completely without the aid of proper schools. There were "school masters" in the parishes in, for instance, Skåne and Gotland. The parish clerks and other assistants were also, in some parts of the country, made responsible for the instruction of the children. But the main responsibility lay with the parents in the home. This, too, was one of Luther's original ideas. In the household order, the husband was responsible for education, in the same way as the clergyman was in the parish. The idea of the "general priesthood" made the household order into something of a teaching order as well.

[12]Rättvik Church Examination Register, 1723–59. *Church Archive*, litt A I:1, pp. 510–662.

A number of ABC-books with instructions for learning were published during the seventeenth century. Behind these instructions one finds the pedagogic ideas of Wolfgang Ratke and Amos Comenius. Ratke's *Didactica* was translated into Swedish in 1614. Comenius' first Swedish version of *Didactica Magna* appeared in 1642, and *Orbis Pictus* in 1683. Ratke and Comenius were both consulted about the educational problems in Sweden, the latter also visiting Sweden twice in the 1640s.

The reading instruction recommended in the ABC-books was the synthetic alphabetic method. The children were to learn the names of the letters first, and then gradually learn to combine them into syllables and words. The following instruction at a visitation in Norrbotten in 1720 provides a good illustration of this form of instruction.[13]

> The Rural Dean admonished the parish organist and others in the congregation involved in the instruction of young people to inculcate a firm knowledge of the lettered alphabet before proceeding with lessons in spelling. In like measure, they should not begin with basic reading before they have instructed the children in the correct and proper art of spelling. Furthermore, they should not impose any memorization exercise on the children before each is able to read directly from all books used in instruction. With respect to the first exercise in memorization, they should take heed that the children do not add or remove any letter of the written text, but rather that they faultlessly follow each letter verbatim. Similarly, a child should not be allowed to recite the second lesson before the first is securely fastened in his memory. From the very beginning, the children shall have become accustomed to reading clearly and diligently and to making firm observance of each sentence to its very end. Furthermore, they shall have become fully aware of the text they are reading and heed its utterance as if they heard it spoken by another [(!)]. In this manner, the children should gradually acquire a firm grasp of the textual meaning and content, and be able to articulate such in words other than those given in the text. In like measure, they shall answer with their own words to the questions posed them in the text.

The instruction is typical, corresponding well to leading thought of the time. Learning should pass from what was concrete for the eye, via memory, to a complete understanding and application.

It was possible to spread reading ability and catechetical knowledge horizontally because of strong social pressure. It was important to make progress within households and village communities, and those who were already able to read were supposed to instruct those who could not. Successes and failures became known at the recurring examinations. But it would be wrong to say that everything was a matter of compulsion in the Swedish reading campaign. Family prayers and village reading led many people to feel a need for religion. One sign of this was Pietism, which was just breaking through. Another were the "readers" in Norrland. Insight into both the difficulties and successes of the campaign is obtained from the Church examination registers, forming part of a noteworthy heritage from the time when Sweden was a major European power in the seventeenth century.

---

[13] A. Nordberg, *"Församlingsliv i Norrbotten under 1600- och 1700-talet"* ("Parochial Life in Northern Sweden during the 16th and 17th century"), *Kyrkohistorisk Årsbok*, No. 34 (Uppsala 1934), p. 270.

The Church Examination Registers

Popular instruction organized by the Church has been extremely well documented in Sweden and in Finland. Progress in reading and Catechism knowledge was noted in special examination registers. It is convenient to divide the oldest registers on the basis of dioceses and deaneries, since popular instruction was enforced vertically from the dioceses, via the rural deans and the vicars, and there out to the people.

The dioceses differ considerably from one another (Figures 1 and 2). The diocese of Västerås has the oldest examination registers, some dating as far back as the 1620s. There are at least some examination registers from this decade still extant for every deanery in this diocese. In the surrounding dioceses, Karlstad, Strängnäs, Uppsala, and Härnösand, and in the south, in Växjö and Visby, examination registers have been preserved for most of the deaneries since before 1720. The work in connection with the Church Law of 1686 is clearly reflected in the many registers from the 1680s. In the dioceses of Linköping, Kalmar, Skara, and Göteborg, there are examination registers dating from 1750 for the majority of the deaneries. The diocese of Lund is the exception, with a very early series of yearly so-called catechism registers from the 1680s and a considerably later collection of actual examination registers, with twenty-five percent of the deaneries having examples only from the nineteenth century. These sources consequently possess the oldest preserved examination register for every deanery, and indicate the pace of the enforcement of popular instruction, where diocese and deanery make up hierarchic units.

It is still uncertain to what extent the original examination registers have actually been preserved, and extensive studies are required to reduce this uncertainty. Nevertheless, the already existing surveys confirm the efforts of the clerical authorities for a more widespread popular education from the end of the

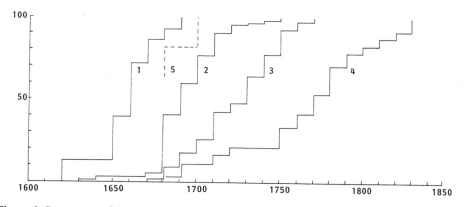

Figure 1. Percentage of deaneries in various dioceses within which at least one church examination register is known to have been begun, at various points in time. (For the diocese of Lund, a second line gives special catechism registers.) Urban areas excluded ($N = 170$). (1) The diocese of Västerås ($N = 15$). (2) The dioceses of Härnösand, Uppsala, Strängnäs, Karlstad, Växjö, and Visby ($N = 77$). (3) The dioceses of Linköping, Kalmar, Skara, and Göteborg ($N = 54$). (4) The diocese of Lund ($N = 24$). (5) The diocese of Lund, catechism registers ($N = 24$).

Figure 2. Sweden. Dioceses before 1900. *Biskopstown; some parishes in the study.

17th century. Examination registers from some rural parishes will be described as examples of this.

Example 1: The Church Reading Campaign in Möklinta in the 1690s[14]

The first example of the Church reading campaign is from the rural parish of Möklinta, in the diocese of Västerås. The oldest examination registers of parish catechistic meetings in Möklinta date from the periods 1656–1669 and 1686–1705. Both of these editions are reproduced below to show their authentic form and content. They will be explained and interpreted with reference to the various column entries. The illustrations provided here show one page from each edition covering one and the same family, that of the farmer Jöns Larsson

[14]Johansson, "Literacy Studies," p. 42–47.

in Gamleby. In the earlier register, such demographic data as years of birth are evidently of a secondary nature, inasmuch as the information is entered at some distance in the margins. On the other hand, the later register records the same material in a special column near the center of the page. The illustrations also show that a particular column for "Lit.," "literatus est" or "literas novit," eg., "reading from a book," has been introduced in the later register (Figure 3).

In the first registers from 1656 to 1669, the years of birth are entered in the margins. This information is followed by a column for family position (farmer, wife, son, daughter, son, son) and a column for the names of family members.

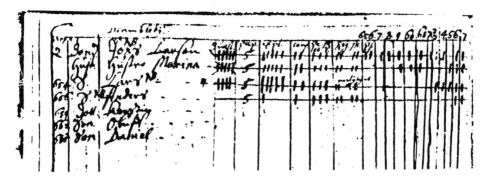

Figure 3A. Möklinta, Västerås diocese. Church examination registers (1656–1669) for the family of Jöns Larsson in the village of Gambleby. (Source: Möklinta Church Archive, Litt AI:1–2.)

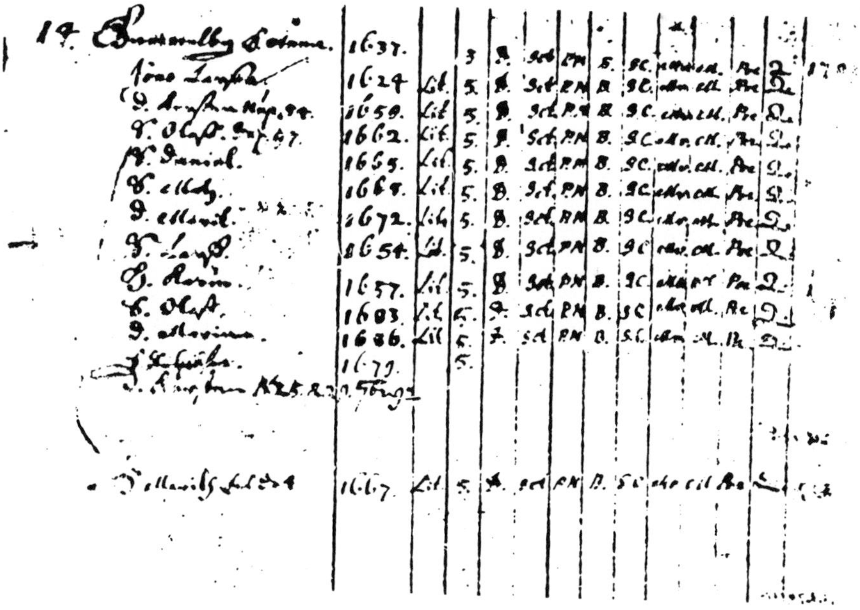

Figure 3B. Möklinta, Västerås diocese. Church examination registers (1686–1705) for the family of Jöns Larsson in the village of Gambleby. (Source: Möklinta Church Archive, Litt AI:1–2).

Subsequent columns register the extent of knowledge in the Catechism: *Questiones*, that is, questions about and answers to the extensive developments in the Catechism's five major headings, accounting for the highest degree of knowledge; *Praeceptiones*, the actual words in the text of the Small Catechism, or the least degree of knowledge; *Explicationes*, Luther's explanations of the words in the text; *Confessio*, the Confession of Sin; and *Preces Matutina et Vespertina*, morning and evening prayers, as well as *Regulea Mensae*, or prayers said at table. Finally there is a series of columns for each year—1656, 1657, and so forth—which apparently record attendance at catechistic meetings in the parish.

The later register, from 1686 to 1705, records the same family. The son Lars, born in 1654, has apparently established a family of his own with his wife Karin, born in 1657, and the births of two children in 1683 and 1686. The daughter Kerstin, born in 1659, and the son Olof, born in 1668, have also married, the latter with Marith, born 1667. The farmer Jöns Larsson has himself remarried with Anna, born in 1637, who died in 1701. Following the columns for names and years of birth appears the column which carries the most interest here, namely the notations "Lit," that is, "literate" or "able to read." This information is followed by the various degrees of catechetical knowledge, where "5" denotes the first articulate knowledge of the actual words in the text to the Catechism's five major headings. The five subsequent columns indicate knowledge of Luther's explanations of these headings: *Dekalogus, Symbolum Apostolicum, Pater Noster, Baptismus,* and *Sacra Coena* (Holy Communion). Three separate columns indicate prayers—*Matutin, Vesper,* and *Mensae* (i.e., morning, evening, and table prayers)—and the penitential psalms. *Psalmi Poenitentiae:* The last column records the greatest degree of knowledge, *Questiones,* or questions and answers to the Catechism's major headings.

In order to obtain a picture of literacy in Möklinta, I have compiled the notations "Lit"—"literate"—with information on sexes and years of birth provided by the registers of parish catechetical meetings from 1686 to 1705. I have included all persons born before or during 1694, totaling 1,410 persons. However, I have excluded those persons whose births are not recorded in the registers. Such is the case with 55 individuals. I have also excluded the younger children, born during or after 1695, in as much as the registers obviously do not record this age group to any detailed and thorough extent.

Table 1 gives the percentage of individuals listed with the notations "Lit" after their names, as arranged on the basis of year of birth. We see that a total of sixty-six percent of the Möklinta population was listed in the registers as "Lit," and that there is an obvious connection between literacy and age. The figures reflect a spread of almost three generations. Only one-fourth of the oldest residents, born in the early 1600s, are represented among the notations for "Lit." Almost half of those born during the mid 1600s are registered as "literate," whereas three-fourths of the youngest residents, born during the latter part of the century, are listed as "literate." This is a typical pattern for reading literacy and age groups, and it repeats itself, naturally enough, in studies covering the period in which literacy achieved its breakthrough in Sweden. Such a pattern

Table 1. The Notations "Lit" in Möklinta's Church Examination Register, 1686–1705, Arranged on the Basis of Year of Birth.[a]

Year of birth	Parishioners registered (N)	Notation "Lit" (%)
–1614	34	21
1615–1624	74	26
1624–1634	73	28
1635–1644	117	45
1645–1654	133	62
1655–1664	230	60
1665–1674	262	70
1675–1684	277	89
1685–1694	210	89
Total	1,410	66

[a]Percentage figures. (N = 1,440)

Table 2. Moklinta: The Notations "Lit" Distributed on the Basis of Sex and Year of Birth.[a]

	Men		Women	
Year of birth	Total (N)	Notation "Lit" (%)	D:o (N)	D:o (%)
–1614	19	26	(15)	13
1615–1624	37	38	(37)	14
1624–1634	32	38	(41)	20
1635–1644	56	48	(61)	43
1645–1654	50	66	(83)	59
1655–1664	101	62	(129)	58
1665–1674	127	71	(135)	69
1675–1684	138	86	(139)	92
1685–1694	110	85	(100)	73
Total	670	68	(740)	65

[a]Percentage figures. (N = 670)

also illustrates the way in which the literacy campaign has succeeded in penetrating the population both in terms of time sequence and age distribution.

The same general structure applies to a classification of the various age groups on the basis of sex, though with one significant difference for the oldest age groups (Table 2). On the whole, the men record a greater share of persons listed as "Lit" (sixty-eight percent), as compared with the women (sixty-five percent). This contrast is especially pronounced among the oldest age groups, but it grows less distinct in terms of the intermediate ones. The women record a greater share of the literacy figures among the youngest age groups. These figures may illustrate the way in which the men are most active in the introductory phase of the literacy campaign, while the initiative is subsequently taken over

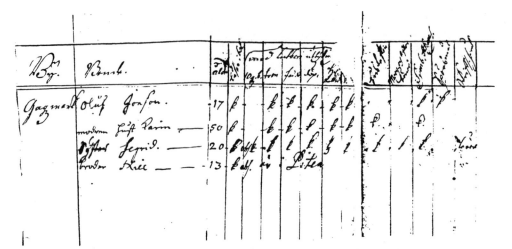

Figure 4. Skellefteå, Northern Sweden, church examination register, 1724. The first three columns indicate the village (Gagsmark), the family members, and their ages (Olof Jonsson, age 17, mother Karin, 50, sister Sigrid, 20, and brother Nils, 13). These columns are followed by a column for "reading from book" ("Läser i bok"), where "k" indicates "can." The subsequent columns contain a record of various skills in memorizing the catechism. (Source: Skellefteå, Church Archive, Litt AI:1–2.)

by the women in increasing numbers, until they finally assume the leading role in terms of book learning and home instruction under the auspices of the Church. The age distribution reflected by the process of book learning will be illustrated by a further example.

Example 2: The Church Reading Campaign in Skellefteå, 1724[15]

A further example from the period in which reading achieved its break-through is provided by the rural parish of Skellefteå in northern Sweden. The oldest extant examination register in Skellefteå parish dates from 1724. This is of the one-year type and thereby is concerned with a single instance of exami-nation. The register's form and content can be seen in the illustration (Figure 4).

During the 1700s, Skellefteå parish constituted the entire northern portion of Västerbotten's coastland. The following analysis covers the northern part of the old parish, equivalent to seven present parish districts of today: Skellefteå rural parish and Boliden, Norsjö, Jörn, Byske, Fällfors, and Kågedalen parishes. As was similarly done with Möklinta in the previous example, the present material on 1,489 individuals is grouped on the basis of year of birth (Table 3).

As a means of facilitating comparisons between the results in Skellefteå and those in Möklinta (see Table 1), the information on ages provided by the examination register has been converted into years of birth, calculated from the year 1724. The total number of persons with registered reading ability in Skel-lefteå (eighty-five percent) is higher than that in Möklinta (sixty-six percent).

[15] Ibid., pp. 47–49.

Table 3. Notations on Reading Recorded in the Skellefteå
Examination Register for 1724, Arranged on the Basis of
Year of Birth.[a]

Year of birth	Total (N)	Notations on reading (%)
−1644	35	43
1645–1654	64	52
1655–1664	152	64
1665–1674	189	74
1675–1684	169	84
1685–1694	189	89
1695–1704	288	95
1705–1714	403	98
Total	1489	85

[a]Percentage figures. Number = 1,489 (northern part of the parish).

However, one must take into account that the Skellefteå examination register
dates from a later period. A comparison between age groups reveals a striking
similarity: almost half of those born during the mid 1600s are able to read, and
this trend shows a marked increase among the younger age groups, with persons
born during and after the year 1675. This examination register provides a
further example of the way literacy achieves its breakthrough during the period
near the turn of the century, 1700.

Example 3: The Reading Campaign in Tuna in the 1690s[16]

The Church Law of 1686 led to the establishment of organized examination
registers in an increasing number of parishes, among these, Tuna in Medelpad.
Its oldest preserved examination register extends from 1688 to 1691 (Figure 5).

The parish was at this time divided into six examination districts (rotes).
The first pages are, unfortunately, missing in the register. The first district is,
therefore, not complete and is omitted from the following analysis. 397 persons
over the age of six are noted in the other five districts, the youngest children
not being noted until examined—an illustration of the examination function of
the register. The parishioners are arranged according to district, village, and
household. The social position is stated for every individual within the household: husband, wife, son, daughter, maidservant, farmhand, lodger, and so on.
Age, reading marks, and catechism knowledge are, together with names, noted
in special columns. The latter take up most of the space, with ten columns for
various types of knowledge: the words of the text, Luther's explanation of the
five articles, prayers, the "Hustavla," and specific questions. It is typical that these
last three or four columns are never filled in this first register, even if they are
always drawn up. They indicate the increasing knowledge of the Catechism

---

[16]Johansson, "History of Literacy," pp. 26–42.

Village	The fourth district: Farmer, Wife, Children, Servants	Age	Can read from a book	Simplic. partes Catech.	Dialogus cum explicatione	Symbolum cum explicatione	Orat. Dom. cum explicatione	Baptism cum explicatione	Sac. Caena cum explicatione	Confession of sin	Prayers	The "Hustavla"
Alstad	Jacob Eriksson	62	Can	Can	Can	Can	Can	Can	Can			
	(Wife) Ingeborg Eriksdotter	40	Cannot	Can	Accept	Badly		Can				
	(Son) Erik Jacobsson	14	Begun	Can	Can	Can	Can	Can	Can			
	(Daughter) Britta Jacobsdotter	16	Begun	Can	Can	Can	Can	Can	Can			
	(Son) Jacob Jacobsson	10	Begun	Can	Can	Can	Can	Can	Can			
	(Daughter) Karin Jacobsdotter	12	Begun	Can	Can	Can	Can	Can	Can			
	(Daughter) Anna Jacobsdotter	7	Begun		(died)							
	(Aunt?) Elin Eriksdotter	66	A little	Can								

Figure 5. The family of Jacob Eriksson in the parish of Tuna, in the fourth examination district and in the village of Alstad. Page 12 in the Church examination register for 1688–1691. The family includes parents, five children, and an elderly lodger, probably an aunt. The columns indicate age, reading ability, and, on one hand, knowledge of the words of the catechism (Simplic. partes) and, on the other, knowledge of the five articles, together with Luther's explanation (cum explicatione). Room is also left for confession, prayers, and the "Hustavla." At a later examination (in the Church examination register for 1696–1698), all children except Anna have been given higher grades in reading, in that "begun" has been altered to "can" read. (Source: Tuna, Medelpad, church examination register 1688–1691, p. 12.)

acquired because of an increase in reading ability, and bear witness, in their own way, to an intensified teaching campaign. Reading and catechism knowledge are noted with evaluations in plain language, that is, "intet"—*cannot* read, "begynt"— has *begun* to read, "lite"—can read *a little*, "någorlunda"—can read *acceptably*, and "kan"—*can* read. "Cannot read" and "can read" are presented separately in the following tables. "Has begun to read" is the most frequent of the other marks, used principally for children and young people. As regards Catechism knowledge, this report only indicates the number of Catechism items that had been learnt. A sketch of the material is presented in Table 4.

A total of about three quarters of the population was given reading marks ("begun," etc., or "can"). Reading and catechism knowledge are highly correlated. Most of those who got a high score in memorization also had high reading marks. The reverse is, on the other hand, not equally clear. The highest score in reading is not necessarily an indication of the highest degree of catechism knowledge. This illustrates the above-mentioned order of learning, reading being intended to precede memorization.

This observation is even more evident for those who have no marks. Nineteen persons have no reading marks, and for sixty-one persons there are no notes for catechism knowledge. Of these, 14 persons have no marks whatsoever. They have perhaps never been examined at all, since five of them are six-year-old children, whereas four of them are over sixty years of age. Only one of the two marks is missing for fifty-two persons. Forty-seven of these were examined in reading, but not in memorization. The reverse applies only to five persons. This is a further proof of the high priority given to reading instruction. The fact that several persons were given the mark "cannot read" does not contradict this: Reading from a book was given most emphasis at the examinations—a typical situation just before the breakthrough of reading in the parish.

This becomes clearer when the two marks are divided according to age. Twelve persons are omitted from Table 5 and the following tables, since there is no information concerning their age.

Here too, the oldest and the youngest differ greatly from each other. Among the oldest, both those who are able and those who are not able to read have marks in catechism knowledge (Table 6). If one examines the number of catechism items one will, however, discover a difference, in that, among the

Table 4. Reading Marks and Catechism Knowledge in Tuna, 1688–1691. ($N = 397$)

Columns about memorization (catechism item)	Reading marks				
	No note	"Cannot"	"Has begun," etc.	"Can"	N
6–8	1	12	27	74	114
5	1	21	35	52	109
1–4	3	30	37	43	113
No note	14	20	20	7	61
Total	19	83	119	176	397

Table 5. Reading Marks in Tuna, 1688–1691, Related to Age.[a]

Age	No note %	"Cannot" %	"Has begun," etc. %	"Can" %	Total %	N
> 60	9	43	7	41	100	42
61–60	0	47	13	41	100	32
41–50	5	35	20	40	100	40
31–40	0	21	37	42	100	43
26–30	3	20	31	46	100	39
21–25	2	13	22	63	100	59
16–20	3	16	26	55	100	38
11–15	2	2	46	50	100	50
< 11	12	5	62	21	100	42
Total %	5	21	30	44	100	385

[a]Percentage figures. ($N = 385$).

Table 6. Reading Marks and Catechism Knowledge in Tuna, 1688–1691, Related to Age.

Age	No note in catechism knowledge Not able to read	Able to read	Catechism knowledge Not able to read	Able to read	Total %	N
> 40	11	2	36	51	100	114
16–40	6	4	13	77	100	179
11–15	2	2	2	94	100	50
< 11	17	31	0	52	100	42
Total %	8	6	17	69	100	385

[a]Percentage figures. ($N = 385$).

oldest persons, those who are able to read also have a more extensive knowledge of the Catechism. For example, in the age group forty-one years and older, thirty-two persons got the highest catechism score, that is, a note for six items. Three quarters of these persons are also able to read. Those having marks in both reading and catechism in the age range 16–40 are as many as seventy-seven percent. In the second youngest age group, they are as many as ninety-four percent. Finally, the six- to eleven-year-old children once more illustrate the progressive educational campaign. Nobody obtained marks in memorization first, whereas thirty-one percent have, on the other hand, obtained such marks in reading.

All the events in a newly started reading campaign are depicted in the table. It is clear from the column for "cannot" that nearly half of the oldest and one fifth of the middle generation cannot read, whereas almost no one in the youngest group is illiterate. The advent of the learning process is indicated in the next column, "begun," with the first learning advance involving a passage from "begun" to "can" that always precedes catechism knowledge. Most of the youngest people are in the midst of the process of learning to read. On the other hand, the time for learning has passed for the oldest ones. They either lack ("cannot read") or possess reading ability ("can read"). Their results may, nevertheless, give us an idea of the preliminary stages in the reading campaign. As we know how little reading ability changes at a mature age, the oldest persons provide an indication of the number of people who were able to read, say, a quarter of a century earlier, in the 1660s: approximately forty percent, increasing in the 1690s to over seventy percent. The youngest children have not been included. Such a calculation also illustrates the drastic changes resulting from a purposeful reading campaign, becoming even more clear when reading and Catechism are put together in age groups.

A typical feature of one of the patterns of analysis has been illustrated with the material for Tuna. The reading campaign is documented principally in the form of education gaps between the generations. Another feature is that differences between the sexes become less obvious. The reading mark "can" was obtained by fifty-four percent of the men over fifty and by thirty-three percent of the women. The corresponding percentage figures for the youngest, twenty years and younger, are forty-four and forty-one percent respectively. A levelling-out is in operation. Women often have higher scores than men later on, in the eighteenth and nineteenth centuries.

The increasing number of women who were able to read brings us to the issue of home instruction, as it is depicted in literature and art, with either the mother or the father instructing the children in the home. To what extent did the children in Tuna have literate homes as early as in the 1690s? A sample from the third and fourth examination district provides an answer to this question. Out of 15 families with children who were sixteen years old and younger, there is only one family in which both the parents are illiterate. Both parents are able to read in ten families. It is hardly possible to discover any difference in the children's standard of reading, since this is more likely a function of age, as has already been indicated. It was possible to fulfill the demands placed on all the younger people to learn and use the printed word, if only the required pedagogic measures were taken.

Reading ability in Tuna has been analyzed primarily with the aid of the first model of analysis, starting from purposeful educational measures. The acquirement of reading is characterized by obvious differences in degree between the generations. Pedagogically, it is manifest as an intensified learning-to-read stage preceding catechism knowledge, principally in the case of children. The second model of analysis, based on differences in environment (e.g., between families) has already been suggested. A knowledge of the letters of the alphabet, however easily acquired, does not spread spontaneously within a given environment. The generational gaps and the differences between the sexes among the older people also suggest this. Instruction and learning had to be provided, not necessarily at great cost and in large quantities, but to a degree sufficient enough to make the basic skills of reading functional in an environment which was becoming more and more literate.

Systematic Studies of the Church Reading Campaign

The Church examination registers provide an enormous field for research. In spite of many sporadic efforts, however, this research has not adequately evaluated the distribution of reading ability. The evolving methodology has taken two directions. The first is an integrated system of information, keeping together the total amount of information in the Church archives of a certain parish over a long period of time. This method has been adopted and fulfilled in the interdisciplinary project. *Demografisk Databasen* (Demographic Database). The other method, adapted in these pages, aims at structuring and organizing the varied notes on reading and catechism knowledge in the examination registers. The distribution of reading marks is seen as a centrally directed campaign. On the basis of this, certain hypotheses are made, in their turn leading to a defined methodology for the adaptation of the sources. The contents of the examination register for Tuna were described in detail in the preceding example. It was, among other things, stressed that during a campaign period the time factor is the most important predictor of events. The differences can thus best be seen through a comparison between the generations, with the youngest becoming literate and many of the oldest remaining illiterate. Hence, as the older people die away, there are a growing number of literate persons in a population. Earlier differences in reading ability between the sexes, different social groups, town and country, various regions, and so forth also become less pronounced at the same time. The characteristic features of reading ability in the West will thus eventually disappear. This ability used to be very low, and was largely preserved by the immediate economic and cultural needs of the community.

Two different patterns of analysis thus become evident. In the first one, the time factor is decisive, the generation gaps being the most expressive factor. The social gaps provide the explanations in the second pattern. It is, nevertheless, vitally important to take both patterns into consideration in every analysis, as they always complement each other. They are, of course, equally valid for studies of present-day educational explosions.

These observations lead to the hypothesis that the reading marks in the examination registers, in their initial stage, are primarily correlated with the year of birth. This leads to a very simple methodology: the marks are distributed by birth cohorts, irrespective of when the examinations were carried out. This means that the same "generations" can be compared in different registers and between different parishes. The methodology will consequently also allow a certain amount of prediction of the past and the future, on the basis of the time for a certain examination.

The methodology can be illustrated with the results from some preliminary studies. Table 7 presents reading ability in Tuna, Möklinta, and Skellefteå c. 1700. The years of birth for Möklinta are given in the examination register. The indications of age for Tuna and Skellefteå have been converted into years of birth. According to the registers, the total number of people who could read

Table 7. Reading (Marks) in Tuna 1691, in Möklinta before 1705, and in Skellefteå in 1724, Related to Years of Birth[a].

Year of birth (approx.)	Reading ability (reading marks)		
	Tuna, 1691 %	Möklinta, 1705 %	Skellefeå, 1724 %
−1620	—	21	—
1620s	48	27	—
1630s	54	36	—
1640s	60	53	48
1650s	79	61	58
1660s	81	65	69
1670s	90	80	79
1680s	83	89	86
1690s	—	89	92
1700s	—	—	97
Total	74	66	85

[a]Percentage figures. (N = 385, 1,410, and 1,489, respectively.) Sources: The church examination registers, cited previously.

in the three parishes was between sixty-six and eighty-five percent. If distributed by decades of birth, the results show a great degree of similarity. Generation gaps can be discerned with marked leaps in the process. A graphic illustration (Figure 6) is even more explicit. The time axis indicates the measurements and the time of birth for the individuals. The curves represent a projection for every cohort back to its decade of birth. There is, again, a great degree of similarity among the three parishes, with the difference in time between the first and last measurement being still as great as thirty years. The advantage of this methodology, making it possible to compare various times and areas, is now apparent.

The methodology can be taken even further if there are results for several measurements in the same parish. Age, for example, is indicated for the young and adult people in the catechism registers for 1702, 1731, and 1740 for Skanör-Falsterbo. The total number of marks for reading increases during this time from fifty-eight to ninety-two percent. The difference in 1702, with sixty-seven percent for the men and forty-nine percent for the women, has been completely levelled out by 1740. The women have, by this time, even outdistanced the men to a certain degree, with ninety-three and ninety-one percent, respectively.

The result, however, becomes even more remarkable when reading ability to Skanör is projected back and forth in time on the basis of the different measurements. In one figure, the three results for 1702, 1731, and 1740 are related back in time to the respective periods of birth, and also between the measurement dates, to composite age groups common to all three (Figure 7). The total increase in reading ability is drawn as a line between the measurements. The slope of the line corresponds to the retrograde projection of reading ability distributed on birth cohorts. Such a projection apparently anticipates fairly well the total reading ability some thirty years later. It is thus apparent that the total reading ability of a population at a certain time is represented by the reading

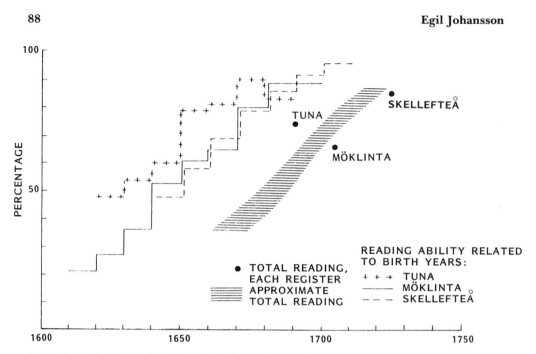

Figure 6. Reading ability in Tuna in 1691, in Möklinta in 1705, and in Skellefteå in 1724, according to the church examination registers. In total (74, 66, and 85 percent, respectively) and related to date of birth. Percentage figures.

ability of the middle generation—a rule of thumb just as useful for the ample reading-ability census material of later times. The extent of the education of older people must, of course, also be observed, since it can affect the validity of the rule.

Another confirmation of the usefulness of the method is finally given in a projection of reading ability for the birth cohorts in Tuna, Möklinta, and Skellefteå. The shaded field in Figure 6 indicates such a projection. It would, in other words, indicate the total growth of reading ability in the three parishes. Such projections of birth cohorts need not of course be used when there is a fairly long series of measurements for the same parish. This is, however, not often the case, because of gaps in the material. The methodology described above is, then, a useful complement, having been applied to a sample of parishes and examination registers for the whole country.

The Church Reading Campaign in Two Dioceses

The hypotheses and the methodology presented above have created opportunities for decisive research work on the hitherto confusing material of the church examination registers. The project has been awarded grants which have made it possible to plan and carry out a systematic study of a random sample of examination registers from parishes over the whole country. The parishes in every deanery have been arranged and numbered according to the deanery tables of 1805. One or two parishes for every deanery have then been selected with the aid of a table for random numbers. A division has been made into town

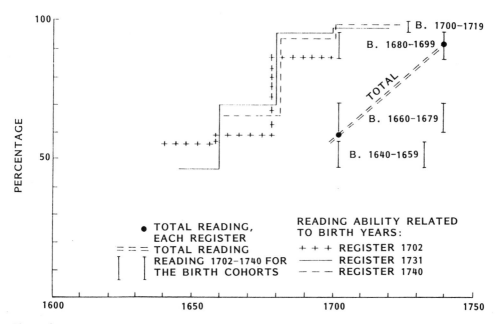

Figure 7. Reading ability in Skanör in 1702, in 1731, and in 1740, according to the catechism registers. In total (52, 81, and 92 percent, respectively) and related to date of birth. Percentage figures.

and country parishes. Only the country parishes have been studied so far; this is also where ninety percent of the population lived up to the middle of the nineteenth century.

Because of the differences between the dioceses, the sample was processed diocese by diocese and the sources examined minutely before the data was collected. Copies were made of typical combinations of marks. The data collection was made on forms, with the various types of marks as columns and the distribution of decades of birth as lines. This means that the results for every decade of birth compiled by dioceses, indicate the number of persons who had obtained some kind of grade or mark in reading. The total number of persons who were able to read at every examination was noted, as well as the distribution of birth cohorts. Consequently, double indications for reading ability were obtained. The easiest way of comparing them is to make a graphical survey. The result for the diocese of Västerås will be our first example.

The fifteen deaneries in the diocese of Västerås are each represented by a randomly chosen parish. The earliest register with both reading marks and information about age has been studied for every parish. There is, unfortunately, information about age in only six of the parishes before 1750, but after 1750 the number of measurements increases. In seven parishes the first useful registers have been checked against later ones. This means that a total of 23 examinations can be presented. The sources of error are, of course, numerous. There are, for example, some obscurities in a number of registers. That is why the doubling of some registers mentioned above has served as a check, great pains

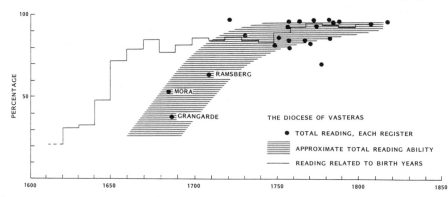

Figure 8. Reading ability in the diocese of Västerås, according to the church examination registers in a random sample of parishes. In total and related to time of birth. The population is about fifteen years of age and older. Sample: fifteen parishes, twenty-three church examination registers. Percentage figures (N = 4,371). The results for the sample of parishes in the diocese of Västerås correspond to the following registers, where both age groups and reading marks can be evaluated: Aspeboda (1775–1784), Björksta (1755–1774), Gagnef (1775–1784, 1785–1791), Grangärde (1653–1786, 1750–1761), Grytnäs (1723–1732, 1775–1784), Himmeta (1752–1762, 1763–1772), Hjulsjö (1766–1769, 1770–1779), Irsta (1731–1758, 1769–1775), Malung (1803–1814), Mora (1667–1685, 1775–1785), Odensvi (1748–1753), Ore (1740–1750), Ramnäs (1751–1758), Ramsberg (1699–1710) and V. Färnebo (1747–1759).

being taken to avoid the same persons appearing several times at any one measurement. Thus, if possible, only the last examination in every register has been studied.

Since some parishes in the diocese of Västerås were very densely populated, a sample of persons has been made within the registers. This, too, has been done at random. The result for the diocese of Västerås seems unambiguous. Both the notes for separate examinations and a projection of the birth cohorts by two or three decades illustrate a very distinct reading campaign circa 1670–1720. The conclusions are verified in many ways, for instance by the contemporary examination documents and by biographical data, as well as through literary sources.

There are also results for the diocese of Visby, although the examination registers studied for this diocese are much more recent—from 1750 onwards. The result is, nevertheless, comparable to the result for Västerås. All examination registers in the selection show a total reading ability of more than eighty percent. A retrograde projection of birth cohorts also indicates a high degree of similarity with the diocese of Västerås. The conclusion is that the actual reading campaign took place before 1750 in Gotland as well, which can also be tested on some registers from the beginning of the eighteenth century. These registers do not appear in the sample for the diocese of Visby.

These preliminary conclusions must now be tested and tried out for other dioceses. But at least they demonstrate the suitability of the program by means of a sample for the whole country. The results must, of course, also be combined with other contemporary source material and compared to other relevant research results, for example in literature and in anthropology. The quality of the reading must also be studied, since it was subject to detailed markings when the acquired reading ability was meant to be consolidated.

THE SCHOOL CAMPAIGN:
TO READ, WRITE, AND RECKON THE "WORLD"

The late school campaign around and after 1850 centered upon formal compulsory schooling to read, write, and reckon the "world" from new books and texts printed or written with modern type. There were some attempts to put writing into the early church reading campaign as well. Such attempts can be studied, for example, in the once Danish provinces of Scania, according to the more advanced tradition of infant schools in Germany, The Netherlands, and Denmark.

Writing in the Early Reading Campaign:
The Diocese of Lund (Scania) Around 1700[17]

The Church examination registers provide, on the whole, no information about writing ability. The exception is the diocese of Lund, where the efforts for national reconstruction coincided with the campaign for popular instruction. In the beginning, both reading and writing ability were sought. The aim was to place special teachers for children, students, and others in the villages, as was the custom on the continent. The children were to learn to read and write the Swedish language.

The town of Skanör-Falsterbo has already been mentioned in regard to reading skills from 1702 to 1740 (Figure 7). The results may be compared to six rural parishes for both reading and writing. The figure for reading rises to nearly eighty percent in 1740, at the same time as the gap between town and countryside becomes less pronounced (Figure 10). Writing in rural parishes continued at a low level, below ten percent. But in the town, there was something of a campaign—at first rising to more than twenty percent in 1731, with the increase coming to a stand-still after that, and the difference in writing between urban and rural parishes being more permanent on this lower level. But the total gap between reading in the church campaign and writing in the needs of daily life in the town increased to the typical Swedish pattern.

The significance of this interplay is best understood in terms of the double pattern of analysis described above. The reading campaign raises everyone to a wider level of ability. The differences between town and country, men and women, and so on, disappear. At first, writing was also concentrated on to a certain extent, at least among the boys in the towns. In fact, about seventy percent of the boys in Skanör, born in the 1680s and 1690s, became able to write, but only a few of the girls. After this, the campaign came to a standstill, at least as far as writing was concerned. For boys born in 1700 and later, the figure for those who mastered writing decreased, approaching that of an earlier practical need in town life. According to this pattern of analysis, it is also obvious from the registers that only a few women were able to write: they had no spontaneous need to learn the art.

[17] Ibid., pp. 55–57.

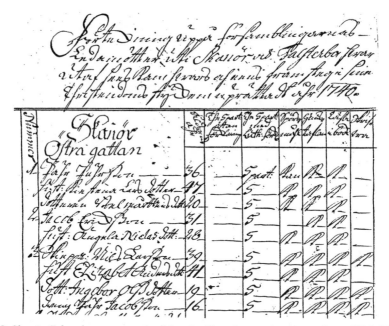

Figure 9. Skanör-Falsterbo, most south of Scania. Church examination register, 1740. The columns household number, names, age, catechism, Luther's explanations, further questions (spörsmål), "hustavlan," and, in the two last columns, reading from book (läser i bok) and writing (skriver). The marks "K" stand for "can" (Kan).

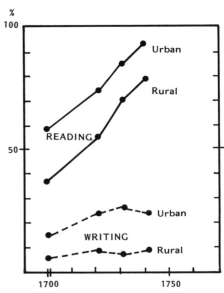

Figure 10. The deanery of Skytt, Scania. Reading and writing marks in the church examination registers for 1702, 1721, 1731, 1740 in two urban parishes (Skanör-Falsterbo) and six rural parishes (Hammarlöv, Vemmerlöv, Västra Alstad, Fru Alstad, Gyllie och Kyrkoköpinge). Young and adult people: Total about 1000–1150 individuals at each time. (Sources: church archives, katekisationslängder.)

The Differences between Reading and Writing up to the Nineteenth Century[18]

These early attempts to establish a writing campaign confirm the conclusion that there was a growing difference between reading and writing abilities, to last for more than a century. Our knowledge of this difference and what it was due to is, in reality, one of the most important contributions to the international debate on world literacy. Widespread literacy in a preindustrial country without formal schooling also presents alternatives for nonurban areas in the developing nations of today. Any support for the Swedish model is, therefore, important. Alexandersson has recently shown that the representatives of the peasantry in the Swedish Parliament in the 1760s could read but could not write. The questionnaire inquiries of 1813 also give ample information of the same kind. Since modern researchers often align themselves with the view that reading and writing are very much dependent on each other, nobody has been able to use the Swedish material. A debate on this issue needs to be set in motion. A contribution to this debate is offered in the following outline of the breakthrough of writing in Sweden in the century, since it at the same time verifies the existence of an earlier Swedish reading tradition.

Reading Ability for Convicts and Recruits and According to the Census of 1930[19]

Like many other countries, Sweden kept statistics about the literacy of convicts and recruits during the latter part of the nineteenth century. The idea of popular instruction as the best cure for criminal tendencies was propagated throughout Europe. In England, for example, the penalty could be more lenient if the criminal was able to read. A certain elementary education was also regarded as necessary for military service. Instruction in reading and writing was carried out very rigorously in France. Table 8 presents details concerning the number of convicts and recruits in Sweden who were *not* able to read, from 1860 onward. The table does not offer raw data, but only percentages. It is possible, to a certain extent, to anticipate the decrease in illiterate convicts. But both series point to literacy since the 1850s as clearly outdistancing the pace of the incipient schooling. In reality, the results of traditional home instruction are verified.

The censuses of many countries include information about literacy as early as the nineteenth century, but not until 1930 in Sweden. It is here, too, not a question of raw data, the statistics being offered per mille concerning deficient schooling. But these also provide results for the oldest persons. Table 9 presents the figures for the whole country in the census of 1930. One per mille of the population over fifteen years of age was illiterate in 1930, 5740 persons in all. Most of these are quoted as mentally deficient. They confirm, just like the convicts and recruits, a widespread reading ability. Even if eight percent of the oldest

---

[18] Ibid., pp. 52–54.
[19] Ibid., pp. 58–62.

Table 8. Number of Swedish Convicts and
Recruits Not Able to Read (1860–1925)

Year	Prisoners not able to read[a] (%)	Recruits[b] (%)
1860	5.1	—
1865	4.3	—
1870	2.9	—
1875	3.0	1.0
1880	2.3	0.7
1885	1.1	0.3
1890	1.5	0.1
1895	0.8	0.1
1900	0.5	0.1
1905	0.2	0.4
1910	0.2	0.2
1925	—	0.1

[a]Sources for the convicts: *Sveriges Officiella Statistik (BiSOS). B: Justitieministerns ämbetsberättelser 1859–1912. (The Official Statistics of Sweden. B: The Reports of the Minister of Justice.)*
[b]Military sources: *Kungliga Krigsvetenskapsakademins handlingar. (The Documents of the Royal Swedish Academy of Military Sciences)* 1874–86 (Stockholm: Beväringens kunskapsprov, 1887–1926) (the general knowledge tests for recruits).

Table 9. Deficient Schooling in Sweden According to the Census of 1930. (Census, 1930, Part VI, p. 47)[a]

Year of birth	No note (%)	Not able to read or write (%)	Able to read only (%)	Able to read and write without having gone to school (%)
–1859	0.7	0.3	3.9	3.4
1860–1869	0.1	0.1	0.5	0.9
1870–1879	0.1	0.1	0.1	0.3
1880–1914	0.0	0.1	0.1	0.1
Total	0.1	0.1	0.4	0.4

[a]*Sveriges Officiella Statistik. A: Folkräkningen 1930, Del V och VI* (the Census of 1930, Vols. V and VI).

persons had not attended school, they had nevertheless learned to read. It is, as we have seen, typical of earlier generations that they were only able to read. We will return to this table in our analysis of writing ability in Sweden.

The Breakthrough of Schooling, Modern Types and Writing (circa 1850–1900)

The best picture of the breakthrough of writing in Sweden is obtained when the official school statistics are combined with information about the writing ability of convicts and recruits, and with the information in the census of 1930. The latter information is projected back to the time that corresponds to the completion of schooling for every age group. Those who are over seventy years of age are assigned to the 1870s, those who are sixty to seventy years of age to the 1880s, etc. (Table 10).

The table summarizes the breakthrough of writing in Sweden. An earlier note from 1859 for convicts has not been included, since the basis for the division has not been made clear. The convicts seem to deviate completely in the table from the norm. This is, however, to some extent only an illusion, a fact which becomes quite clear when the contents of the table are transferred to a time diagram (Figure 11A).

The ability to read is general, according to all sources, which also confirm the progress of writing from the middle of the century. The information about the recruits and from the census coincides with that from the school statistics. In reality, schooling is the driving force. If the school children are allowed to represent the total number of persons able to write after a couple of decades, this curve also approaches that of the statistics for the convicts.

This sort of statistic is, however, so recent that the interpretation for the whole country may seem unreliable. It is, however, easily made more explicit if Norrbotten, for example, with its later stages of development, is considered (Figure 11B). Since Norrbotten was still in the main stage of literacy development at the end of the nineteenth century, its statistics also provide a clearer picture

Table 10. Sweden 1850–1910. Deficient writing ability and school instruction. Comparison between convicts, recruits, children with only home instruction, and birth cohorts in Census 1930. Percentage figures.

Year	Convicts[a] not able to write %	Recruits[b] not able to write %	Children[c] home instruction %	Census 1930 not able to write %	Birth cohorts[d] no school teaching %
1850	—	—	30	—	—
1856	—	—	30	—	—
1859	—	—	27	—	—
1865	60	—	23	—	—
1870	53	—	13	(4)	(8)
1875	41	11	9	—	—
1880	34	5	7	(1)	(2)
1885	22	2	6	—	—
1890	16	1	4	(1)	(1)
1895	11	1	4	—	—
1900	6	1	2	(1)	(1)
1905	4	1	1	—	—
1910	4	0	1	—	—

[a]Sources for the convicts: *Sveriges Officiella Statistik (BiSOS). B: Justitieministerns ämbetsberättelser 1859–1912. (The Official Statistics of Sweden. B: The Reports of the Minister of Justice.)*
[b]Military sources: *Kungliga Krigsvetenskapsakademins handlingar. (The Documents of the Royal Swedish Academy of Military Sciences) 1874–86.* Stockholm: Beväringens kunskapsprov, 1887–1926. (The General Knowledge Tests for the Recruits.)
[c]School statistics: Riksarkivet, Stockholm: *Ecklesiastikdepartementets statistiska avdelnings arkiv. Handlingar angående folkundervisningen (D): Sammandrag 1847–81.* (The National Swedish Record Office, Stockholm: *Documents on popular education (D): Summary 1847–81.) Sveriges Officiella Statistik. P: Folkskolorna 1868, 1882–1910. (The Official Statistics of Sweden. P: The Elementary Schools 1868, 1882–1910.)*
[d]*Sveriges Officiella Statistik. A: Folkräkningen 1930. Del V och VI (The Census of 1930, Vol. V and VI.)*

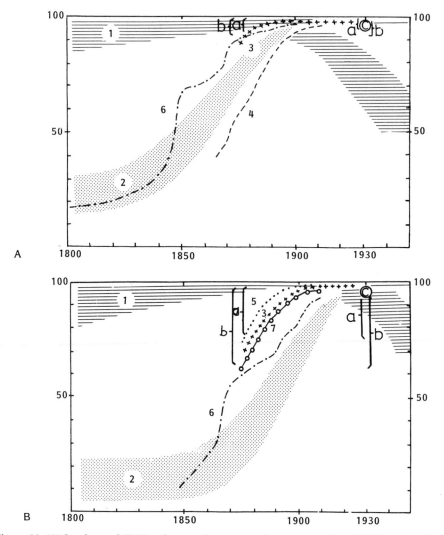

Figure 11. (A) Sweden and (B) Norrbotten, the most northern county. The shift from the old church reading tradition in Gothic style to the modern school campaign with reading and writing in modern style. 1, Church reading tradition (Gothic style). (Sources, see Table 10, notes a–d). 2, School campaign; reading and writing (modern texts). (Sources, see Table 10, notes a–d). 3, Writing ability, recruits 1874–1926 (Source, see Table 10, note b). 4, Writing ability, convicts 1865–1912 (Source, see Table 10, note a). 5, Writing ability, according to the census of 1930 with retrograde projection of the age groups back to the time when they were about 15 years of age (Source, see Table 10, note d). 6, School attendance 1800–1910 (1800–1850 estimations) (Source, see Table 10, note c) 7, School attendance according to the census of 1930 with retrograde projection of the age groups back to their schooltime (Source, see Table 10, note d). a = not able to write, the census of 1930, 70 years of age and older; b = no schooling, the census of 1930, 70 years of age and older; (c) total reading and writing ability, the census of 1930, 15 years of age and older.

of the process. The ability to read was general throughout Norrbotten, too, while the ability to write had increased from seventy to ninety-eight percent in thirty years. Schooling had also increased drastically during the same period. It is true that a lot of people had acquired the ability to write without the aid of proper schooling, but these three sources together still underline the unity of the Swedish writing campaign. They also provide an opportunity to make a rough outline of the spread of literacy in Sweden.[20]

The Shift from Informal Home Instruction to Formal School Teaching: The Swedish Model

The Swedish model based on home instruction was considered very important when the whole question of education was debated in the nineteenth century. Home instruction was to precede and supplement school instruction, which was the reason for the decree introducing compulsory school in 1842. It was not until 1858 that reading was included as a subject in special junior schools. This Swedish tradition was different from, for example, the German one, which stressed formal school teaching. Many people defended the merits of Swedish home instruction. Others maintained that the time had come for increased civic education through organized schooling.

One cannot get a firm grasp of the Swedish material, if one does not keep this debate in mind. A widespread reading ability before the introduction of organized schooling then seems quite reasonable, and it is also verified by the church examination registers, by the statistics for convicts and recruits, and by the census of 1930. The frame of research set up very early in the project has thus gained its full validity.

Toward the middle of the 19th century, a period of transition emerges between the two major, historical epochs in Swedish education. The traditional form of popular education, conducted under the auspices of the Swedish Church, was relieved of a good share of its responsibilities by the system of school education decreed in 1842. This process of transition is complicated and extended over a long period of time. The old system of education, characterized by parents instructing their children at home, remained in force for a long time. School instruction lacked a firm footing in many parts of the country. Continued operation between the two systems of education was often desired. The general scope of the problem can be visualized by means of a simplified illustration (Figure 12).

The following procedure is made use of here: firstly, the traditional form of popular education under the Church (A, C) is evaluated; secondly, it is combined with the new schooling (B, D, E). This procedure maps out the extent and significance of popular education (A) in its traditional form, and it specifies the reciprocity of home instruction (C) and school attendance (B). This reciprocity is difficult to interpret but was, nevertheless, approved of in the elementary school code. This procedure also confronts the actual function of the

[20]There are some historical sources on signatures in the marriage registers for convicts, etc. in Sweden as well. These sources require further studies.

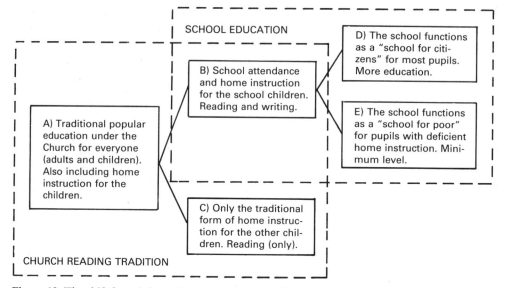

Figure 12. The shift from informal home instruction to formal school teaching in Sweden ca. 1850.

school as a superstructure of home instruction, "the school for citizens" (D), or as a complement to the insufficient home instruction, "the school for the poor" (E). It is not correct to present a biased description and emphasis of the varying growth and effectiveness of school attendance. The entire process must be studied with the aid of intensive comparisons between the various forms of education.

This approach has now been applied to many studies over the whole country. Reading ability is compared between school children and children who have only home instruction in the same villages, families, age groups, and so on within the project. The validity of the reading marks in the church register has been tested by the school data.

If the Swedish model of popular education is accepted, it also means that the Swedish material can be used for setting up new models for literacy campaigns in the developing countries. A very elementary reading ability for adults, acquired at home, will probably make school attendance much easier for the children.

CONCLUSION

This chapter tries to illustrate and discuss some results from a broad research project on the two literacy campaigns in Sweden. The old church reading campaign involved reading, singing, and praying the "Word" in the parish. The modern school reforms started as a campaign for reading, writing, and reckoning the "world" in modern daily life. In order to give a draft picture of these two cultural processes, some of the historical sources, problems, methods, and preliminary results have been discussed. The lessons for further historical studies of literacy campaigns in other countries and for practical discussions of problems in popular education are many and obvious.

CHAPTER 5

The Anatomy of Mass Literacy in Nineteenth-Century United States

EDWARD STEVENS, Jr.

When Samuel Goodrich, using the pseudonym "Peter Parley," looked back at his boyhood town of Ridgefield, Connecticut in 1790, he recalled a time when books were "scarce, [when they] were read respectfully, and [were read] as if they were grave matters, demanding thought and attention." "They were not," he continued, "toys and pastimes, taken up every day, and by everybody, in the short intervals of labor, and then, hastily dismissed, like waste paper." In the mid-nineteenth century, observed Goodrich, books and papers are "diffused even among country towns, so as to be in the hands of all, young and old."[1]

During the sixty years spanned by Goodrich's remarks, a large segment of the United States population had experienced a literacy campaign that permeated virtually every dimension of American culture. This essay presents a broad view of the conditions and actions supporting the campaign(s) for expanded literacy in the first seventy years of the nineteenth century. The nexus of literacy and schooling in nineteenth-century United States is emphasized. Both national and state level sources are used. In matters of educational reform per se, examples are used from both the midwest (Ohio) and New England (Massachusetts) to illustrate the strategies which led to common school expansion.

It is postulated that the process of becoming literate was itself a process of socialization promulgated by those interested in using the school to resolve social, economic, and political tensions arising from a culturally pluralistic and emerging industrial society. The actions of those who would control the process of schooling and hence the process of becoming literate are seen in relation to nation-building, a fervent evangelical Protestantism, and technological innovation. All of these provided a foundation upon which reformers could build. The strategies

---

[1] Samuel Goodrich, *Recollections of a Lifetime*, Vol. I (New York, 1857) cited in David D. Hall, "Introduction: The Uses of Literacy in New England, 1600–1850," in William L. Joyce, David D. Hall, Richard D. Brown, and John B. Hench, eds., *Printing and Society in Early America* (Worcester: American Antiquarian Society, 1983), p. 21.

EDWARD STEVENS, Jr. • College of Education, Ohio University, Athens, Ohio 45701-2979.

and precedents used by reformers and the *process* of convincing the American public that mass literacy was a worthwhile goal are emphasized. To a lesser extent, the structural constraints upon this ideal are discussed, as are the successes and failures of attempts to bring mass literacy to nineteenth-century America.

We are accustomed to thinking of the term "literacy campaign" as connoting a centrally orchestrated policy that brings the power and resources of state or church authority to bear on the problem of illiteracy. In this respect, the American experience differed markedly from the previous campaigns carried out by Swedish church authorities in the latter seventeenth century and attempts in eighteenth-century Scotland to bring about mass literacy. Likewise, it differed from mid-twentieth-century literacy campaigns in emerging African nations, Cuba, and Nicaragua.

If the term campaign is to be used, it must be understood that in nineteenth-century United States there was no single campaign, but rather several campaigns waged on different fronts. There were, of course, public funds committed to schooling, and the well-known common school reformers of the mid-nineteenth century sought to build a power base at the state level for disseminating their views and influencing state legislators. Nonetheless, power was diffuse when it came to implementation of school reform. Voluntarism and persuasion were still the modus operandi of reform in general, and state intervention was in its infancy.

The relative absence of centralized authority before mid-century in educational matters did not mean that efforts to eliminate illiteracy lacked focus. They did not. In fact, one of the basic features of the literacy campaigns after 1830 was their focus on the public school as the chosen instrument of reform. Thus, whereas power to influence educational matters was diffuse, the choice of the common school as the critical institution to bring about reform made it possible to both focus and generalize efforts to elevate and spread literacy in the United States. Schooling did not become a surrogate for literacy until the twentieth century, when years of schooling became an approximate measure of functional literacy. Yet, schooling and the achievement of literacy became closely associated by the fourth decade of the nineteenth century, when common school reforms succeeded in bringing schooling to most children aged ten and under. It is extremely difficult, then, to disentangle the effects of literacy from the effects of schooling, at least at the elementary level.[2]

The choice of the school as the major institution for reform also had a profound effect on the meaning of literacy, though the full effects of this choice would not be felt until the twentieth century. The choice of the school meant that the meaning of literacy would become increasingly standardized and associated with the process of schooling itself. The meaning, then, became an institutionalized one reflecting the motives and expectations of those who came to control the school. In this respect, it may be pointed out that the vertical and

---

[2]This problem of disassociating the effects of literacy from the effect of schooling is dealt with at length in Sylvia Scribner and Michael Cole, *The Psychology of Literacy* (Cambridge, Mass.: Harvard University Press, 1981).

individualistic structure of the school suited it well for the development of human capital and manpower sorting in the emerging industrial society of the nineteenth century. (The issue of social reproduction and its ideological and structural determinants, however, cannot be dealt with here.)[3] Suffice it to say that the process of becoming literate in the public school must be understood as part of the school's attempt to impose a particular form of socialization upon the young. As Robert Church has observed of nineteenth-century school reform: "[It] was primarily an effort to reach down into the lower portions of the population and to teach children there to share the values, ideals, and controls held by the rest of society."[4] At its best, school reform and the achievement of literacy carried with it a promise for upward mobility and a dream for success. At its worst, as Katz found in his study of early school reform in Massachusetts, "educational reform and innovation represented the imposition by social leaders of schooling upon a reluctant, uncomprehending, skeptical, and sometimes, as in Beverly [Massachusetts], hostile citizenry."[5]

At the opening of the nineteenth century, the United States was a literate nation by comparison to most of continental Europe. Between the years 1799 to 1809 the illiteracy rate (inability to sign one's name) among Army enlistees with an average age of 25.1 was forty-two percent as measured by signature (marker) counts; the illiteracy rate was twenty-five percent by 1850 and seven percent by 1895. (In the latter period, the average age of enlistees had dropped to 23.7.) Among merchant seamen in Philadelphia, the illiteracy rate was also forty-two percent in the years 1810 to 1820. These figures are probably biased upward for illiteracy, since enlistees and seamen included a disproportionate share of those in lower socioeconomic groups.

Other sources for estimating illiteracy rates also have been used. A sample of testators and witnesses to wills in Washington County, Ohio in 1800 yields lower illiteracy rates of thirty percent and ten percent, respectively. For grantors of deeds, the illiteracy rates was a low five percent. For Kent County, Delaware, a similar sample yields rates of fifteen percent for testators and witnesses and seventeen percent for grantors of deeds. Unlike army enlistee data, data from wills and deeds are likely to bias illiteracy rates downward, because those at the lower end of the wealth distribution were more likely to die intestate and more likely to be illiterate. Petitions yield a great variety of rates for late eighteenth-century America. One having 207 signatures and demanding an investigation into a land title held by Robert Livingston of New York showed forty-seven

[3] See Johan Galtung, "Literacy, Education and Schooling—For What?," in *Literacy and Social Development in the West, A Reader* (Cambridge, Eng.: Cambridge University Press, 1981), p. 271. The seminal work on social reproduction theory remains Samuel Bowles and Herbert Gintis, *Schooling in Capitalist America* (New York: Basic Books, 1976). For recent adaptations to curriculum theory see Michael Apple and L. Weiss, *Ideology and Practice in Schooling* (Philadelphia: Temple University Press, 1983), Jean Anyon, "Social Class and the Hidden Curriculum of Work," *Journal of Education* 162 (Winter 1980), 67–92, and Henry Giroux and David Purpel, eds., *The Hidden Curriculum and Moral Education: Deception or Discovery* (Berkeley, Ca.: McCutchan, 1983).
[4] Robert L. Church and Michael Sedlak, *Education in the United States, an Interpretive History* (New York: The Free Press, 1976), pp. 79–80.
[5] Michael B. Katz, *The Irony of Early School Reform* (Boston: Beacon Press, 1968), p. 112.

percent illiteracy. When the various sources of data (all of which are based on signature [marker] counts) and illiteracy rates are taken into consideration, a conservative estimate of twenty-five percent illiteracy in the United States in 1800 may be made.[6]

The general figures on illiteracy at the opening of the nineteenth century mask large regional variations. Illiteracy was far greater in southern states than in northern ones. To a lesser extent, a similar rise in illiteracy occurred on an East–West vector, though this was true more in the first half of the nineteenth century than by 1870. The great North–South discrepancies continued throughout the nineteenth century, even though an absolute decline in illiteracy occurred in both regions of the country.

Illiteracy was stratified by occupation, wealth, race, ethnicity, nativity, gender, age, and population density. This was true in the nineteenth century as it had been in the colonial period. Throughout the first seventy years of the nineteenth century, but especially until 1840, urbanity and literacy were strongly linked. As I have argued elsewhere, urbanity was a major factor in increased levels of literacy, and operated by making possible the building of schools, churches, and libraries. These, and the publishing activity which emanated from, but was not limited to, areas of high population density, made it possible, in turn, to spread the word that literacy and schooling were the intellectual foundations for economic success and the panaceas for America's social ills.[7]

By 1870, the gender gap had practically disappeared among the native born, nonfarm population. Among the foreign born, nonfarm population of women, however, illiteracy persisted at a rate considerably higher than among foreign born, nonfarm males. In 1870, the female–male literacy ratio was 1.26. Thus, for every four male illiterates there were five female illiterates.

Nativity was strongly associated with illiteracy. In 1860 and 1870 illiteracy was three times as great among foreign born women as among native born.[8] The impact of age and ethnicity on illiteracy, however, gradually declined, as more and more of the population received an elementary school education. These findings on the link between ethnicity and literacy in the United States may be contrasted with Graff's findings in *The Literacy Myth*, where the author emphasizes the importance of ethnic stratification in Canada as an important source of inequality. Ethnicity, along with race, age, and sex, says Graff, "represent[ed] the major structural features of illiteracy in urban Ontario in 1861."[9]

Wealth and occupation continued to be strongly associated with levels of literacy. Compared to 1800, when the illiteracy rate for those in the lower half of the wealth distribution was thirty to forty percent, the situation in 1870 had

---

[6]Lee Soltow and Edward Stevens, *The Rise of Literacy and the Common School in the United States: A Socioeconomic Analysis to 1870* (Chicago: University of Chicago Press, 1981), pp. 35, 39, 50, 52, 208n; Edward Stevens, "Literacy and the Worth of Liberty," *Historical Social Research* 34 (April 1985), pp. 65–81.
[7]Kenneth Lockridge, *Literacy in Colonial New England* (New York: W. Norton, 1974), passim; Soltow and Stevens, *Rise of Literacy*, pp. 55–56, 167–171, 175–176, 194–195.
[8]Soltow and Stevens, *Rise of Literacy*, p. 158.
[9]Graff, *The Literacy Myth*, p. 65.

eased somewhat. Even by 1870, however, the top fifty percent of wealthholders had only 7.8 percent of the illiterates. Though the illiteracy rate overall had declined dramatically by 1870, the distribution of illiterates among wealth classifications was uneven.[10] Illiteracy continued to be associated with lower wealth classifications, as illiterates were found in proportionately greater numbers at the lower end of the economic scale. The wealth/occupation/literacy linkage has been a finding common to many historical studies of literacy.[11]

PRECEDENTS AND STRATEGIES

The general level of illiteracy, its regional variations, and its relationship to demographic and socioeconomic variables helped to define the extent of the problem and the task of advocates of expanded common schooling and general public enlightenment in nineteenth-century United States. These variables also set the limits to its solution. Socioeconomic variables were not easily altered, demographic ones such as population density and fertility rate even less so in nineteenth-century United States.

From the standpoint of reform, then, the first step was to identify those points at which the illiteracy problem was susceptible to solution. The second step was to develop strategies that seemed likely to succeed. Of the first, it might be said that the solution was obvious. The future of literacy lay with the young, and the institution potentially the most powerful for intervening in the lives of *all* children was the public school. This point of attack was not exclusive of all others, such as family and church, but its public nature made it accessible to reformers. It was, in a sense, available—a tool which could be manipulated through the political process.

The second step, that of strategy, was not so obvious, and had many precedents upon which to rely. The evangelical Protestant tradition was easily adapted to the aims of increasing general public enlightenment through literacy. The presence of rhetorical studies in the classical liberal curriculum had also helped to train public officials who spoke for educational reform. In a society where oral persuasion counted for a good deal in public matters, the language-oriented curriculum of most nineteenth-century schools was a training ground for the art of persuasion. Print itself, and the already well-established use of books, newspapers, and documents for recording and disseminating information, provided another channel for reformist ideals. Reformers, then, had a practical base from which to work.

The effectiveness of reform methods, both oral and written, stemmed from the prior uses of, and expectations for, literacy laid down in the seventeenth

[10]Soltow and Stevens, *Rise of Literacy*, p. 201.

[11]See Graff, *The Literacy Myth*, Lockridge, *Literacy in Colonial New England*, David Cressy, *Education in Tudor and Stuart England* (New York and London: St. Martin, 1976), and William Gilmore, *Elementary Literacy on the Eve of the Industrial Revolution: Trends in Rural New England, 1760–1830* (Worcester, Mass.: American Antiquarian Society, 1982).

and eighteenth centuries. By the eighteenth century, for example, the ideal of progress through expanded knowledge was so well established (though not without its critics) that it had been reified to the point of being an article of faith in its own right. The spirit of scientific advance permeated Enlightenment thought. The faith that progress would ensue from expanded secular knowledge was generalized beyond science, however. For some, that faith was accompanied by the belief that progressive knowledge and the democratization of knowledge would go hand in hand. Speaking of the technological breakthrough of printing, Condorcet said in 1795 that "what formerly only a few individuals had been able to read, could now be read by a whole nation and could reach almost at the same moment everyone who understood the same language."[12] Fifty-eight years later, Josiah Holbrook, agricultural reformer and founder of the American Lyceum, expressed a similar faith in the power of the public press. Said Holbrook in his "Scientific Epoch": "The public press is destined soon to become one grand 'Scientific Journal.' The newspaper press and the book press have already made a visible and a reliable advancement towards such a character."[13]

The spirit of science and the morality of aspiration that accompanied efforts to raise the level of public enlightenment also were expressed well in the writings of late eighteenth- and early nineteenth-century agricultural reformers. In their efforts to promote a scientific and experimental approach to farming, agricultural reformers, like educational reformers, used the periodical press. Two early agricultural periodicals, the *Agricultural Museum* and *The Plough Boy*, urged farmers to apply the facts of chemistry to their practice. In the *Agricultural Museum*. A. Fothergill lamented the fact that the important science of agriculture "has been unformly committed to the sole management of the illiterate part of mankind" who "have obstinately pursued a routine of random practice, in imitation of their forefathers, without any settled principles."[14]

The number of agricultural periodicals grew rapidly, as did their circulation.[15] Periodicals like *The New England Farmer, The American Farmer, The Cultivator, The American Agriculturist*, and *The Southern Cultivator* frequently reminded farmers that they should read more and adopt an experimental attitude toward farming. Yet, the editors of these journals were continuously disappointed, if we are to judge by their laments. The frustration must have been great indeed over the next fifty years. In his work *Improving the Farm* (1867), Lucius Davis was not far removed from the exasperation of Fothergill fifty years earlier. Said

---

[12] Antoine-Nicolas de Condorcet, *Sketch for a Historical Picture of the Progress of the Human Mind*, trans. June Barraclough (New York: Noonday, 1955), pp. 99–100.

[13] Josiah Holbrook, "Scientific Epoch," *Journal of the United States Agricultural Society* 1 (July 1853), p. 84.

[14] A. Fothergill, "On the Application of Chemistry to Agricultural and Rural Economy," *Agricultural Museum* 2 (1811), p. 119.

[15] Estimates for the circulation of these periodicals are difficult to make. Jesse Buel optimistically estimated that in 1838, the thirty journals then in existence reached 100,000 (20%) of the farm families in the country. Demaree has estimated a total circulation of 350,000 in 1860. The great majority probably had less than 4,000 subscribers. The *American Agriculturist*, a leader in its field, printed 80,000 copies of its November, 1859 issue. (See Albert Lowther Demaree, *The American Agricultural Press*, 1819–1860 [New York: Columbia University Press, 1941], pp. 18, 56–57.)

Davis of the farmers who ignored books and periodicals on farming: "It will no longer do for a man to sneer at such publications . . . unless he is willing to be considered an ignoramus. . . . No farmer making the least claim to intelligence can afford to ignore the help of modern investigation and research."[16]

Foundations for nineteenth-century literacy campaigns were also laid in the theory and practice of constitutional government itself. Constitutionalism, as a political ideal, rested upon a theory of contract and consent. These, in turn, assumed that those subject to political and legal constraints acted as free, rational persons and willingly accepted the demands and constraints placed upon them. They had, then, the moral obligation to control their behaviors in accordance with the constraints. Both consent and its subsequent obligations rested upon the sharing of legitimate expectations (publicity). For free, rational consent to occur, it was assumed that an educated populace had to have access to information relevant to its consent. Thus the ideals of contract, consent, and moral obligation that were linked together in a theory of constitutional government had important implications for the educational attainment of the population in general.

When educational reformers and enthusiasts for public enlightenment spoke of the need for a literate and enlightened public, they stressed the link between education and a strong republican government. Both consent and stability were on the minds of those who promoted education. It was a "matter of the highest importance to republican government," said Academicus to Thomas Jefferson in 1797, "to disseminate knowledge and to keep the evenness of access to it open to all, and especially to the middle or even the lower class of people." And in 1798, the prizewinning essay of Samuel Harrison Smith, submitted to the American Philosophical Society, observed that a stable society and government were premised on the right of that society to "educate and acknowledge the duty of having educated, all children."[17]

Rush, Webster, and others warned the post-Revolutionary generation of Americans that the regionalism of colonial America must be put aside for the sake of national unity. McClellan has observed recently that the elite of late-eighteenth century American intellectuals "worried endlessly about the fragility of republics, about the absence of national traditions, and about a variety of divisions in the society."[18] Kaestle has noted also that "Americans of the 1830s and the 1840s inherited from the revolutionary generation an anxious sense of the fragility of republican government."[19] It was a fear noted earlier by Jefferson in his "Bill for the More General Diffusion of Knowledge":

[16] Lucius Davis, *Improving the Farm, or Methods of Culture that Shall Afford a Profit and at the Same Time Increase Fertility of the Soil* (New York: Rural Publishing Co., 1867), p. 12.

[17] Academicus to Thomas Jefferson, "Plan for the Education of Youth," c. Jan. 1797, Archives No. 10, American Philosophical Society Library, Philadelphia. Samuel Harrison Smith, "Remarks on Education" Essay presented to the American Philosophical Society, 1798. *Early American Imprints*, No. 34558, p. 66.

[18] B. Edward McClellan, "Public Education and Social Harmony: The Roots of an American Dream," *Educational Theory* 35 (Winter 1985), p. 34.

[19] Carl F. Kaestle, *Pillars of the Republic, Common Schools and American Society, 1780–1860* (New York: Hill and Wang, 1983) p. 79.

It is believed that the most effectual means of preventing [tyranny] would be, to illuminate, as far as practicable, the minds of the people at large, and more especially to give them knowledge of the facts, which history exhibiteth, that, possessed thereby of the experience of other ages and countries, they may be enabled to know amibition under all its shapes, and prompt to exert their natural powers to defeat its purposes.[20]

It was a similar message which Thomas Cooper, educator and future president of the University of South Carolina, gave in his *Lectures on the Elements of Political Economy* (1826). "There is no remedy," said Cooper, "against mistake or imposition of any kind, political, clerical, medical, or legal, but knowledge." And, continued Cooper, "there is no method of attaching the mass of the people to republican institutions, or of inducing them to prefer common sense to mystery, but by giving them information and enabling them to think and reflect."[21] Nothing was to be left to chance in these warnings for the safety of the young republic. Education was both a matter of public enlightenment and proper socialization; its conduct was to be purposeful and systematic. The civic model for literacy was accompanied by a fervent evangelical Protestant tradition. Republican politics and evangelical Protestantism were not incompatible. Smith has noted that leading citizens in the mid-nineteenth century "assumed that Americanism and Protestantism were synonymous and that education and Protestantism were allies."[22] The long tradition of biblical literacy to which nineteenth-century reforms were heir persisted as a "way of doing literacy," and its purposes were not forgotten as educational reformers attempted to promulgate their visions of a moral republic. For eighteenth-century evangelicals, "America was the center of God's interest in the world." Cowing has observed that these "new lights" tended "to ignore religious and political boundries and press for a continental union." The result was a "deep and pious nationalism" on the eve of the War for Independence.[23]

The aim of Bible literacy was a conspicuous feature of colonial New Englanders' attempts to educate their young. Bible literacy and its correlates in hornbook and primer aimed to catechize and shape the behaviors of children in a way that would be "rewarded by Church and God alike."[24] Family and school were allied in this defense against the "Ould Deluder Satan." The purpose of biblical literacy was fundamentally conservative in both aim and method. Interpretation of biblical passages was doctrinaire, and the method of recitation used to teach reading emphasized memorization. Resnick and Resnick have observed that "the earliest mass-literacy effort, Protestant-religious instruction, was intended to develop not a generalized capacity to read but only the mastery of a very

[20] Thomas Jefferson, "A Bill for the More General Diffusion of Knowledge," in Wilson Smith, ed., *Theories of Education in Early America, 1655–1819* (New York: Bobbs-Merrill, 1973), p. 233.
[21] Thomas Cooper, "Lectures on the Elements of Political Economy," in Rush Welter, ed., *American Writings on Popular Education, The Nineteenth Century* (New York: Bobbs-Merrill, 1971), p. 15.
[22] Timothy L. Smith, "Protestant Schooling and American Nationality, 1800–1850," *Journal of American History* 53 (March 1967), p. 680.
[23] Cedric B. Cowing, *The Great Awakening and the American Revolution: Colonial Thought in the Eighteenth Century* (Chicago: Rand McNally, 1971), p. 203.
[24] Soltow and Stevens, *Rise of Literacy*, p. 29.

limited set of prescribed texts."[25] The aim of literacy, then, was not enlightenment in a general sense but, rather, a particular way of viewing the world.

Religious teaching was widespread in colonial America. American evangelical Protestants had learned their lessons well from their English counterparts. The press had historically been a powerful weapon in bringing about church reform and in saving the spiritually unwashed. On the basis of his work with Welsh peasants, Griffith Jones, an eighteenth-century clergyman of the Anglican Church, concluded that preaching and catechising without basic literary could not succeed. Hannah More, author of the "Cheap Repository Tracts," conceived of the uses of literacy in a broader way. More, social reformer and educator of the poor, knew Bible literacy could allow the poor to do their religious duty. In addition, however, it would also help them to acquire the habits of industry and thrift, and a sense of their place in the social order.[26]

Tracts had served a proselytizing purpose since the Reformation. In England, the tract tradition was well established by the end of the eighteenth century. American evangelicals drew heavily upon the English experience.[27] Devotional literature was circulated widely, and American printers and book sellers imported many titles from England. Lay readers in England were accustomed to cheap books on religious subjects, and the market for these was realized by late eighteenth- and early nineteenth-century printers in America.

Sacred literature could become popular literature, as the printing of Joseph Alleine's *Alarm for the Unconverted* (1767) reminds us. One impression of the book was 30,000 copies, and 70,000 were sold in a few years. Of course, psalm books, primers, catechisms, and Bibles were steady sellers also. Reading aloud from devotional literature was common and, for a responsible parent, a duty. Favorite passages were read repeatedly and children learned these by heart. This was a habit born not only of the nature of religious instruction, but of scarcity. Hall has observed that "the religious context, the scarcity of print, the habit of repetition were [all] cumulatively involved in the pace and quality of reading as a style." Hall continues, "Reading in early New England was an act that took place slowly and with unusual intensity, in contrast to the faster pace and casualness of mid-nineteenth century reading."[28]

In practice and in ideology the roots of nineteenth-century literacy campaigns were found in the civil, intellectual, and religious precedents of the previous century. Scientific enlightenment, republicanism, and evangelical Protestantism were fertile grounds for efforts to generalize the impact of literacy in nineteenth-century United States. Most of the major expectations for literacy may be found in these ideological roots, also. By midcentury, technological

[25] Daniel P. Resnick and Lauren Resnick, "The Nature of Literacy: An Historical Explanation," *Harvard Educational Review* 47 (1977), p. 383.
[26] John McLeish, *Evangelical Religion and Popular Education* (London: Methuen & Co. 1969), pp. 19–20, 55–56.
[27] Richard D. Altick, *The English Common Reader: A Social History of the Mass Reading Public, 1800–1900* (Chicago: University of Chicago Press, 1957), pp. 73–76; T. Scott Miyakawa, *Protestants and Pioneers* (Chicago: University of Chicago Press, 1964), p. 110.
[28] Hall *et al.*, *Printing and Society*, p. 23, 29.

innovations in printing, internal improvements, and adequate capitalization of the printing trade had helped to clear away obstacles to the advance of literacy. Printing technology, internal improvements, and the skills that came with having to manage large-scale organizations changed the way in which nineteenth-century religious proselytizers carried out their mission. They did not, of course, alter the mission. This not only survived the pressures of secularization, but seemed to grow stronger with a new frontier to civilize and a new nation of immigrants to Americanize.

TECHNOLOGY AND THE MASS MARKET

American imprint production grew steadily in the two-hundred year period from 1650 to 1850. The number of imprints increased more rapidly than the population. The per capita growth from 1660 to 1831 "was about .7 percent a year—a substantial change."[29] The American book trade was "extraordinarily decentralized" through the first half of the nineteenth century, and, in this respect, suffered from an inability to achieve economies of large-scale production. In Massachusetts alone "one or more editions of the Bible or New Testament were printed at twenty-four separate locations."[30] By 1850, however, the book trade was undergoing rapid change in its capital structure. The process had begun by 1830 with the formation of Carey, Lea in Philadelphia and Harpers in New York. The transformation was complete by the opening of the Civil War, and the "village printer-bookseller was rapidly becoming a figure of the past."[31]

By 1840, newspaper production was increasing rapidly, and the number of men employed in printing and binding rose accordingly. Generally, the number of employees engaged in printing in the various states also showed an inverse relationship to illiteracy. This inverse relationship between illiteracy and printing activity was on the order of 5:1, so that "a state with roughly five times the newspaper production of another could expect to have but one-fifth the illiteracy."[32]

It is important to note at this point that imprint production and the spread of literacy are not necessarily linked in a simple causal relationship. When a general commitment to mass literacy is lacking and readership is confined to a select few, it would be expected that printers would produce in limited quantities. Where a *potential* mass market exists, however, entreprenurial activity may be expected to be strong, and the increased availability of reading materials "can serve as an inducement for illiterates to learn to read."[33]

Technological breakthroughs in printing gradually brought economies of scale, and thereby contributed to lower costs for the consumer. It is interesting

---

[29] Soltow and Stevens, *Rise of Literacy*, p. 40.
[30] Hall *et al.*, *Printing and Society*, p. 7.
[31] Ibid., p. 10.
[32] Soltow and Stevens, *Rise of Literacy*, p. 166.
[33] Ibid., pp. 164–166.

that testimonials give evidence that early nineteenth-century advocates of expanded literacy associated low prices with success in promoting greater public enlightenment. When addressing the Phi Beta Kappa Society of Cambridge in 1826, Joseph Story "declared that the cause of early nineteenth-century Americans' great interest in reading was 'to be found in the freedom of the press, or rather in co-operating with the cheapness of the press'."[34] A group of Boston citizens likewise found a causal relationship between the cost of producing printed materials and a free nation's capability to survive in the face of plutocrats:

> Without the means of transmitting knowledge with *ease*, and *rapidity*, and *cheapness*, a nation, however free in name, must become the blind followers of the wealthy and the well-informed, or the tools of the designing. Every means, therefore, which renders the access to knowledge more difficult or more expensive directly *increases the power of the few, and diminishes the influence of the many*, and thus tends to weaken the foundations of our Government.[35]

Inexpensive editions of pulp literature were common in eighteenth-century England, and English imports sold well in America also. There were, however, serious attempts to link together the production of cheap printed material with the aim of public enlightenment. The production and dissemination of inexpensive, educational printed materials for mass consumption had been a concern of Webster in the late eighteenth century. Webster, of course, had sought a mass market for his *Speller* and attempted to combine his entreprenurial zeal with a commitment to the reform and standardization of the English language. His efforts at orthographic reform were a marvelous interplay of patriotic, moral, and technical considerations. A uniform, "federal language" that would facilitate "the acquisition of our vernacular tongue" and correct a "vicious pronunciation which prevailed extensively among the common people of this country" was the avowed aim of Webster.[36] Monaghan has noted that Webster was involved with the business aspects of his books throughout his life, and that he had a "keen appreciation of the factors that enhanced or detracted from a book's sales."[37] Webster's books were not always the cheapest (Dilworth's speller sold for ten cents and Webster's for fourteen in 1790), but he was a price-conscious entrepreneur and price adjustments were part of his strategy.[38]

What was desirable in the way of inexpensive printed materials was not, of course, always a reality in fact. An adult buyer of books in the early nineteenth century would have made a difficult choice in deciding to purchase a "cheap" book for $1.00. He would have received poorly bound and printed merchandise for an amount which could have bought five loaves of bread, twelve pounds of

---

[34] Ibid., p. 63. Joseph Story, "A Discourse Pronounced at Cambridge, before the Phi Beta Kappa Society, Aug., 1826," in E. B. Williston, ed., *Eloquence of the United States* 5 (Middletown, Conn.: E. and H. Clark, 1827), pp. 419–420.

[35] "Memorial of a Number of Citizens of Boston to the Senate and House of Representatives, 13 Feb., 1832," in *American State Papers*, class VII (Washington: G.P.O., 1834), p. 341.

[36] Jennifer E. Monaghan, *A Common Heritage, Noah Webster's Blue-Back Speller* (Hamden, Conn.: Shoe String Press, 1983), pp. 38–39.

[37] Ibid., p. 73.

[38] Ibid., pp. 97–99.

beef, or a third of a gallon of brandy. Even the amount spent on a "cheap" book at eighteen and a third cents could have been used to buy two dozen eggs or twenty quarts of milk. By 1850, however, the options were somewhat better. Children's books could be bought at prices from 1 to 12½ cents, and spellers cost about 8½ cents. McGuffey's *First Reader* was two cents, the *Second Reader*, thirteen cents, the *Third Reader*, twenty cents, and the *Fifth Reader*, fifty cents. Thus a family that was willing to pass the books around could supply its children with a set of *Readers* and a speller for ninety-eight cents.[39]

The Religious Press

School books were the major way, of course, to bring inexpensive printed materials within the reach of most children. For adults, almanacs, calendars, broadsides, registers, and gazeteers were all part of the mass literacy tradition established in the eighteenth century. Perhaps the single greatest effort to bring the reading habit to the mass public, children and adults alike, however, was the religious press. The evangelical, Protestant press made advances in the production and distribution of print which, in many ways, outshone anything done by the commercial press.

The great success of the religious press in the 1830s was preceded by a period of uncertainty and difficulty in the late eighteenth century, however. Nord has pointed out that "it was the will to print, not the way to print, that first led American evangelicals into the business of mass media." For Christian Federalists, as Nord calls them, the late eighteenth and first decade of the nineteenth century was a dismal period. Orthodoxy was "under assault," and the ties between government, religion, and the moral order of society were threatened.[40]

The evangelical response to secularism and the discontent that threatened orthodoxy was local and denominational in inspiration and organization. In these two dimensions of the evangelical response we find both the strengths and weaknesses of the movement. Both denominationalism and localism were obstacles to the development of a centralized effort to disseminate inexpensive printed materials. Both, however, were the bases for the communitarian spirit that made a concerted effort possible. Within seven years of the founding of the first American tract society in New Haven (1807), and within six years of the first Bible society in Philadelphia (1808), there were "more than 100 Bible societies" formed and "dozens of tract societies" organized. There was, as Nord has pointed out, very "little communication or coordination among them," however.[41]

The Religious Tract Society of London (1799) and the British Foreign Bible Society (1804) provided the models for coordinating large-scale mass media efforts. The tract society, also, was the "source of nearly all the tracts that were

---

[39] John Tebbel, *A History of Book Publishing in the United States*, Vol. I (New York: R. R. Bowker, 1972), pp. 217, 533, 552.

[40] David Paul Nord, "The Evangelical Origins of Mass Media in America, 1815–1835," *Journalism Monographs* 98 (May 1984), p. 3.

[41] Ibid., p. 4.

reprinted and circulated by the early tract societies of America." The Bible society provided donations of Bibles and New Testaments and cash contributions to the fledgling societies of America.[42] The market, however, was far greater than imports could satisfy.

New York City proved to be the place where technological innovation and ease of transportation came together to solve the problem of mass media. As Nord has observed: "The founders of the Tract Society chose New York for the same reasons that other businesses did. New York was the leader in technology, transportation, and money." It was likewise with the American Bible Society. Stereotyping, the steam power press, and machine paper-making were the technological saviors of the American evangelical movement.[43] Centralization, including mergers of local societies and consolidation of ownership of stereotype plates, was the organizational foundation for spreading the Word. By the late 1820s, the evangelical Protestant movement stood ready to place a tract in the hands of every American, and to conquer the old American West.[44]

The staging for the expansion of literacy in the middle years of the nineteenth century had been set by the early 1830s. Organizational precedents had been set, technological improvements were in place, and the ideological roots were firm. What remained was to develop the public and commercial strategies for the expansion of literacy.

For the evangelicals, it was a matter of extending previous goals and refining the techniques of mass distribution. The religious press continued to dominate the book trade through the early 1830s. Six million books had been published by the American Sunday-School Union by 1830. Among their offerings were the popular children's magazines titled *Youth's Friend, Infant's Magazine, Child's Companion,* and *Sunday School Banner.* The efforts of S. V. S. Wilder, first president of the American Tract Society, became legendary as he mounted a giant merchandising campaign. His "Tract of the Month" program, which gave readers book dividends, was but one of his innovations. His corps of field agents represented "one of the most ambitious, aggressive, and successful promotion enterprises ever realized by an American publisher."[45]

In 1829, under the leadership of Arthur Tappan, the New York Tract Society developed the "Systematic Monthly Distribution Plan," the aim of which was to "place in the hands of every city resident at least one tract, the same tract, each month." Other cities emulated the plan, as did the New England Tract Society (to become the American Tract Society in 1825) instituted in Boston in 1814. Collectively, the goal was to supply *every* American with at least one religious book or tract. The goal was not attained, though not because of the sheer

---

[42]Ibid., p. 5.

[43]Stereotyping is a printing process whereby a facsimile page of type is produced from a "mold from a page composed of moveable type and then casting a solid metal 'plate' in that mold." The stereotype plate is then used "in a printing press, in place of moveable type." The advantage of this, explains Nord, is that the printer does not have to keep his "capital locked up in standing type during a long press run." (Nord, "Evangelical Origins," p. 7).

[44]Ibid., pp. 7–8, 13–16.

[45]Tebbel, *History of Book Publishing,* Vol. I, p. 514.

quantity printed—distribution turned out to be the problem. Between 1829 and 1831, the Society's production never fell below five million tracts annually, and it "annually printed at least five pages for every man, woman, and child in America."[46] This strategy of the "mass media" was taken westward with enthusiasm, as well. Here, for example, the Methodist Book Concern in Ohio organized a district system for distribution. The "warehousing" of periodicals, books, and tracts helped to keep a steady supply for the sparsely settled regions of the West.

THE SECULAR PERIODICAL PRESS AND EDUCATIONAL REFORM

The religious press taught American publishers a great deal about how to create and supply a mass market. They were not the only practioners of mass media techniques, however. Their secular equivalent may be found in the entrepreneurship of newspaper editors, in the efforts of the Anti-Slavery Society, and in attempts by agricultural reformers to bring experimental methods to American farmers. The agricultural press cannot be dealt with at length here; however, even scattered circulation records indicate impressive figures. Demaree, for example, estimates 350,000 circulation for agricultural periodicals in 1860.[47] Much of the technical information in these periodicals was difficult to read, and it is questionable whether the majority of subscribers could read the technical essays. General essays on farming and the essays giving moral advice, however, were easier to read, and probably found a larger audience.

Aside from the religious press, the most entrepreneurial of the many crusaders for expanded literacy were newspaper editors. Their self-serving essays on the need for more newspapers generally give an immodest portrait of them. Yet, their concern with general public enlightenment also identified them as mainstream Americans. Their advocacy of expanded common schooling, moreover, made them an important part of educational reform and the crusade for literacy. They were missionaries and entrepreneurs, all in one. Leaving the latter aside, "newspaper editors taught their subscribers, and those who listened to their subscribers read aloud, the value of literacy itself."[48]

Beyond their general belief in the value—and values—of literacy, printers and editors of newspapers were active proponents of better schooling. The newspaper was, as it is today, a major instrument for the control and molding of public opinion. In the nineteenth century, it functioned as a vehicle for raising public consciousness to critical educational issues, as a device for demanding accountability from legislators, citizens, and school officials, and as one of several instruments to build "systems" of public schooling.

The number of newspapers per person increased rapidly from 1810 to 1850 in the United States. In 1810 there were 3.81 papers per person; this rose

---

[46] Nord, "Evangelical Origins," pp. 20–21.
[47] Demaree, *American Agricultural Press*, p. 18.
[48] Soltow and Stevens, *Rise of Literacy*, p. 63.

to 13.80 in 1840, and in 1850 to 21.81 papers per person.[49] The increasing consumption and popularity of newspapers in the United States during the first half of the nineteenth century is clear and is what we would expect, along with the steady growth of books, pamphlets, and periodicals from the colonial period to the mid-nineteenth century. Moreover, the fact that newspapers were capable of penetrating sparsely settled areas made them especially valuable in winning over residents of these regions to the common school cause.[50] As Louis Wright has noted, the country editor "was usually the advocate of schools, libraries, lecture programs and other means of bringing literacy and enlightenment to the people."[51]

The state of Ohio offers an excellent example of the way in which educational reformers used the press to mold public opinion in support of free common schooling. The challenge in Ohio was probably similar to other states where ethnic diversity and regional variations in cultural heritage were potential obstacles to legislative backing of common school reform. Finding a way to act cohesively was a formidable task in a state where large constituencies of German and Irish vied for political power, where distinct settlement patterns of Virginians and New Englanders formed the basis for factional politics in the state legislature, and where great differences in rate and kind (urban/rural) of economic development resulted in differing capabilities to support public schooling.

In Ohio, educational reformers recognized that the press was a needed mechanism to carry out their reforms. The Western Literary Institute, located in Cincinnati and a leading educational reform group of its day, made certain its deliberations and reform sentiments made their way to newspapers. As the *Minutes* of this organization demonstrate, nothing was left to chance. In its October, 1834 meeting it was "resolved, that the Report of the Executive Committee of the Institute be accepted and published in one or more of the city papers." In 1838, the *Minutes* show that in the matter of reading reports, it was the duty of the Committee of Arrangements of the Institute "to announce the same in the State Assembly, and through the daily press."[52] This attention to mundane matters paid off in the form of free publicity for reform efforts, and in the actual sponsorship of such organizations by sympathetic newspaper editors.

At another level, Samuel Lewis, nominee for Ohio's new office of State Superintendent in 1837, also recognized the press as an essential vehicle for educational reform. The presumption that "popular sentiment [was] in favor of common schools" did not deter him from making every effort to publicize the common school cause. In the absence of systematic schooling itself, the newspaper's role was even more essential as an instrument for establishing "good" public relations between school and community. In his numerous addresses to groups of teachers, ministerial associations, school officers, and parents, Lewis

---

[49] Ibid., p. 76.
[50] Ibid., pp. 76–77.
[51] Louis B. Wright, *Culture on the Moving Frontier* (Bloomington, Ind.: Indiana University Press, 1955), p. 236.
[52] *Transactions of the Fourth Annual Meeting of the Western Literary Institute*, Oct. 6, 1834. (Cincinnati, 1835), p. 6; *Transactions*, Oct. 6, 1838.

"pressed the advantage of education to their material interests," but he recognized, at the same time, that a much larger audience awaited him. Thus Lewis was willing to seek out newspaper editors and to use their expertise. In an 1839 circular to county auditors, Lewis announced that communications with school officials would be made "chiefly by means of circulars and communications to . . . newspapers." He was certain, notes his biographer, "that Editors would insert an article once a week for the good of Education, and he solicited county auditors [themselves] to prepare articles for the local papers."[53]

In their promotion of an expanded system of common schooling, local newspaper editors and printers had more at stake than a sense of social duty. Expanded schooling meant increased trade for most, since it was common practice for the local newspaper printer to supply and print schoolbooks. Lists of available textbooks were commonly printed and, at times, particular texts were recommended.

When the McGuffeys first made their appearance, the editor of the *Zanesville Gazette* (Ohio) encouraged parents and teachers to examine the new series.[54] When it came to the publication of primers, spellers, and first readers, local editors who were both publishers and printers were willing to recombine selections from previously published material into new editions to cater to regional tastes. It is likely that the relationship between local newspapermen and the schools in their respective communities was symbiotic, since the schools *themselves* depended heavily upon newspapers to legitimize their activities. All of this, of course, attests that common school reform was an intensely political process. That is, the strategies used to bring statewide systems of public schooling to fruition were manipulative in nature, and attempted to mold a public opinion favorable to educational reform.

It is widely acknowledged that newspapers in the first half of the nineteenth century were intensely partisan and political in content. Yet there is abundant evidence from Ohio that dailies, weeklies, and triweeklies also gave an excellent general accounting of critical educational issues, including the concerns of female education, moral education, the role of education in good citizenship, and parent–child relations with respect to education.[55]

The fact that the fortunes of local educational systems were inevitably tied to state legislative action did not escape editorial observers of the period. The targets of reform-minded editors were therefore often state officials. The reformist climate generated by the press, in addition to the initiative of reformist legislators, made it possible to enact legislation such as that of 1821 in Ohio, which provided for the establishment of township school districts, the organization of school committees, the hiring of teachers, and voluntary local taxation. It was the same with an 1825 law establishing a school fund by the sale of school lands.

---

[53] William G. Lewis, *Biography of Samuel Lewis* (Cincinnati: R. P. Thompson, 1857), pp. 179, 212, 244–245.

[54] *Zanesville Gazette*, Zanesville, Ohio, Nov. 16, 1836, 3:2.

[55] A survey of approximately eight thousand issues of thirty Ohio newspapers. Papers were distributed throughout northern, southern, eastern, western, and central Ohio.

Once reform had been achieved at the state level, the press encouraged compliance and urged local communities to make the most of the opportunities. Editors commonly reprinted or quoted extensively from governors' messages, legislative enactments, or other official reports, a practice which undoubtedly had the effect of reinforcing, for the local populace, the legitimacy of the public common school. A quotation from a state official's report could be a way of swaying the uncommitted to the reformist cause, a device for urging compliance to state regulations, and a statement of priorities for those who might wish to spend state monies for improvements other than education. Thus, the following excerpt from the County Examiner's *Report*, as found in the *Athens Mirror and Literary Gazette* in 1826, helped define the issue of educational reform as one of spending priorities:"We are happy, nay we say more, we feel *rapture* of the heart, to find our system of elementary education *taking* with the people. . . . Important as the canal is, it is not more so, in our estimation than its sister law for the improvement of the mind."[56]

Having helped to win the battle for extended common schooling, editors turned their attention in the 1830s to issues of equal opportunity and teacher quality. The approach of editors to the issues of the 1830s was decidely an individual matter. In the southwestern section of the state, in the city of Xenia, Ohio, the editor of the *Greene County Gazette* noted in his first issue of December 24, 1835 that "our system of Common Schools is not, as yet, fairly carried into operation in this county, but the work is progressing; and we confidently hope that in a short time each neighborhood will feel and recognize and appreciate the glorious truth, that 'the schoolmaster is abroad'."[57]

In the east central city of Zanesville, Ohio, one of the most impressive press coverages of education occurred following the passage of the law creating the State Superintendent of Common Schools in 1837. Zanesville's proximity to the State Capitol of Columbus made for easy access to reformist sentiment at the state level, including the office of the State Superintendency. Yet the extent of coverage indicates editorial initiative as well.

The first annual *Report* of State Superintendent Lewis, it was noted in the *Zanesville Aurora*, "exemplified not only the wisdom of the Legislature, which created the office, but their judgment in selecting an individual to carry into effect the objects of the law." "The question is," continued the column, "will the present Legislature carry out . . . the intentions of the last, and add such a stimulus to the cause of *universal* education, as will bring the means of intelligence to the door of every child in the State, whatever may be the conditions of life."[58]

From July, 1837 to April, 1838 the *Zanesville Gazette* carried seven front page stories covering twelve full columns on educational matters—all this in addition to the usual second or third page coverage. During the month of July, readers of the paper were treated to an address by William Ellery Channing on the nature of education and the obligations of philanthropy to effect social

[56]*Athens Mirror and Literary Gazette*, Athens, Ohio, May 20, 1826, 2:5.
[57]*The Greene County Gazette*, Xenia, Ohio, Dec. 24, 1835, 3:5.
[58]*Zanesville Aurora*, Zanesville, Ohio, Feb. 2, 1838, 1:4.

progress without government intervention. In the same month, the paper carried a two-column front page story on the duties of sabbath school teachers, particularly as they related to providing a proper moral and civil education. During the autumn of 1837 and the winter of 1838, readers received a full slate of material relating to education, including advice to parents from the *Common School Advocate*, a Cincinnati publication, the *Proceedings* of the Muskingum Practical School Teachers Lyceum, an address on common schools given before the same Lyceum, and a plea to the public to elect as township clerks and treasurers those "friendly to the advancement of Common schools, qualified to discharge the important duties that will devolve upon them."[59]

The panoply of periodic literature was designed to fix in the minds of the unconverted the necessity for better and expanded common schooling. The crusade of the press in behalf of common schooling was also important to the overall success of common-school reformers who orchestrated legislative support. Legislators themselves were addressed in reports and testimonials designed to show that increased and expanded literacy and schooling were necessary for the economic, political, and moral welfare of the nation. The power of the press was exercised unabashedly, and reformers missed few rhetorical devices in their efforts to persuade Americans that more and better schooling was to their benefit.

EXTENDING THE CAUSE

The triumphs of common school reformers from 1830 to 1850 have become legendary in the history of American education. Their exploits, however, have a long list of supporting actors. Their cause, like the cause of literacy, was also part of a larger commitment to a republican constitutional ideal and a social vision which posited a spiritual and moral consensus while acknowledging a plurality of secular interests. Their view of the common school was a direct outgrowth of their social vision, and their institutionalization of the literacy process helped to shape the uses and purposes of literacy.

By the 1830s the ideological and technological groundwork for extending literacy to all Americans had been laid. It was the major task and accomplishment of mid-nineteenth-century common school reformers to convince the American public and those who controlled state funds that the primary responsibility for a literate nation lay with public schools. The diversity of means for offering education made this a difficult task. Family, church, private schooling, and public schooling were competitors for the loyalties of Americans. Thus, common school reformers were obliged to market the ideal of mass public schooling by (1) assuring parents, churchmen, and political leaders that no basic conflicts existed among them, and (2) that the individual and social benefits of public schooling outweighed the costs. The first goal was accomplished by an appeal to the ideal of a moral and civic consensus, the second by an appeal to the economic utility of schooling.

[59] *Zanesville Gazette*, Zanesville, Ohio, Nov. 16, 1836, 3:2; July 5, 1837, 1:3; July 26, 1837, 1:1–2; Feb. 28, 1838, 2:5.

Pedagogically, the aim of the common school was to teach the "fundamentals." Politically and socially, the aim was to teach the common elements of American culture, as conceived broadly by educational reformers. This, in effect, constituted a moral education built upon the community of values perceived by nineteenth-century educational reformers. Michael Katz has argued that moral education in the mid-nineteenth century was "a kind of intellectual totalitarianism" in which "relativism was inconceivable." The imposition of educational reforms by the "prominent of the community" was guided by their own perceptions of social need. Those perceptions shaped the objectives of reform, says Katz, and "the goals of that reform represented the imposition of upper-and middle-class fears and perceptions of social deficiencies." Finally, argues Katz, the "content of a reformed education represented an imposition of the values of communal leaders upon the rest of society."[60]

By 1840, a developing American pluralism was perceived as a threat to cultural unity. The polarization of Protestant and Catholic, foreigner and native, strained the belief in an essentially homogeneous and consensus-based social order. The public school offered a mechanism to overcome religious and ethnic diversity and to transcend the emerging tensions in the American social order.

The rhetoric of national unity that persisted in mid-nineteenth century educational reform was closely linked to the moral utility of public schooling. Thus, the aim of moral utility was not intended to destroy diversity, but rather to define its limits. The argument for restriction was broadly construed, but applied especially to criminal deviancy. Reformers of the period observed that inmates of penitentiaries had a proportionately greater incidence of illiteracy. They assumed, as Graff has pointed out in *The Literacy Myth*, a causal model linking illiteracy to the deviant traits of idleness, intemperance, and improvidence. These, in turn, led to poverty and criminality.[61] The public school, as an instrument of social policy, was to be, as Horace Mann described it, the "balance wheel" of the social machinery.

The argument for the utility of a common school education also capitalized on a tradition of the value of useful knowledge. Broad appeals for public enlightenment had often rested upon the presumption that useful knowledge was the most important knowledge. Schoolbooks themselves conveyed the importance of "useful" knowledge. Such knowledge, says Ruth Elson, was "presumed to be uniquely characteristic of American education."[62] Republican government itself necessitated the teaching of useful knowledge. Inidividual success also was related to the acquisition of useful knowledge, as was literacy in general. The child who used Crandall's *Columbian Spelling Book* (1820) was advised to love his book more than play, "for he who will love his book, and try to learn to read in it, may come to be a rich man; but if you love play most, you will be poor."[63]

Both character training and economic utility were to result from the teaching of useful knowledge. Elson suggests that "The 'useful knowledge' offered

[60] Michael B. Katz, *The Irony of Early School Reform* (Boston; Beacon Press, 1968), pp. 130–131.
[61] Graff, *Literacy Myth*, p. 240.
[62] Ruth M. Elson, *Guardians of Tradition, American Schoolbooks of the Nineteenth Century* (Lincoln, Neb.: Nebraska University Press, 1964), p. 222.
[63] Daniel Crandall, *The Columbian Spelling Book* (Cooperstown, 1820), p. 38.

in the school was useful to success in the material world, but it was also expected to produce those qualities of character that we associate both with Puritanism and with the self-made man: thrift, hard work, and the rejection of frivolity."[64] Parallel to, but compatible with, the aim of moral utility was the claim of economic utility. More than any other common school advocate, it was Mann who articulated this goal of the common school. His arguments, contained in a series of *Annual Reports* published while he was Secretary of the Massachusetts Board of Education from 1837 to 1848, were eloquent testimony to the meritocratic ideal and the value of education in a capitalist economy. Mann's view was remarkably similar to what economists and educators today call "human capital theory."

Vinovskis has argued that Mann addressed the economic productivity of education in his *Fifth Annual Report* (1842) "because he saw this as a necessary tactic to win additional support at a time when the Board of Education was facing an increasingly hostile legislature." His methods of calculation were not reliable, nor was his sampling, yet he did attempt to quantify "what had hitherto been mere speculation."[65] In his *Fifth Annual Report* of 1842, Mann argued for a utilitarian view of the educational enterprise. The view that education is a "dispenser of private competence, and the promoter of national wealth" had "intrinsic merit." Mann was convinced that he had "novel and striking evidence to prove that education is convertible into houses and lands, as well as into power and virtue."[66]

Mann's correspondence with manufacturers and his observations of agricultural workers led him to conclude that individual productivity increased with education. Two of the correspondents made their own calculations of the economic productivity of schooling in terms of increased wage rates. Mann then took these calculations and made an average approximation. Mann compared the extremes of illiteracy ("those who make their marks") and literacy. Different levels of literacy did not enter into the formula.[67] Mann determined that the result was both increased productivity in the aggregate and greater opportunity for individual economic mobility. As Mann said of the latter, "Individuals who, without the aid of knowledge, would have been condemned to perpetual inferiority of condition, and subjected to all the evils of want and poverty, rise to competence and independence, by the uplifting power of education."[68] Where opportunity for upward economic mobility was present in the sense of an absence of "extrinsic circumstances" that "bind a man down to a fixed position," education paid off for the individual

> just as easily and certainly as particles of water of different degrees of temperature glide by each other,—there it is found as an almost invariable fact,—other things being

[64] Elson, *Guardians of Tradition*, p. 226.
[65] Maris A. Vinovskis, "Horace Mann on The Economic Productivity of Education," *New England Quarterly* 43 (Dec., 1970), pp. 569–571.
[66] Secretary of the Board, *Fifth Annual Report of the Secretary of the Board of Education, Massachusetts* (Boston, 1842), p. 82.
[67] Vinovskis, *Horace Mann on the Economic Productivity of Education*, p. 566.
[68] Secretary of the Board, *Fifth Annual Report*, p. 85.

equal,—that those who have been blessed with a good Common School education, rise to a higher and higher point, in the kinds of labor performed, and also in the rate of wages paid, while the ignorant sink, like dregs, and are always found at the bottom.[69]

In his *Report* of 1842, Mann explained the economic utility of education in a general sense, observing of the facts at his disposal that "They seem to prove incontestably that education is not only a moral renovator, and a multiplier of intellectual power, but that it is also the most prolific parent of material riches." In one of his eminently quotable sentences, Mann announced in the same *Report* that "Intelligence is the great money-maker,—not by extortion, but by production." As part of his theory of the political economy of education, Mann concluded that education has "a right, therefore, not only to be included in the grand inventory of a nation's resources, but to be placed at the very head of that inventory."[70]

The international, competitive significance of education was not lost on the educational reformers in nineteenth-century United States. Once again we may look to Mann's articulation of this point. Attempting to gain a competitive edge against the already established giants of western Europe was no easy task. A wealthy nation depended upon intelligence (education) said Mann in this Twelfth *Annual Report* (1848). The greater the number educated, the faster would a nation progress and "the more will it outstrip and outshine its less educated neighbors." To illustrate the point, Mann used the following example: "The advance-guard of education and intelligence will gather the virgin wealth of whatever region they explore as the reward of their knowledge, just as the Portuguese reaped the great harvest of the riches of India as their reward for discovering the new route to India."[71]

Mann was obviously cognizant of the theories of political economy of his time when he explained the basis for his assertion that education was an important national resource. Education, he said, created property. Moreover, it was more than a commodity: "it rather resembles fixed capital yielding constant and high revenues." Mann then went on to list the advantages of education from an economic standpoint. It was, he said, immune from "common casualities," so it had no costs for insurance or defense; it was free from "fluctuations in trade," and "above the reach of changes in administration." From the standpoint of national wealth, said Mann, education "is more powerful in the production and gainful employment of the total wealth of a country, than all other things mentioned in the books of the political economist."[72] In short, Mann was arguing that education was a good investment from both an individual and collective standpoint.

Mann did not use the language of modern human capital theory, and the idea that man was a commodity or an object of investment would have been repugnant to him. The skills and knowledge imported by education, however,

[69] Ibid., p. 86.
[70] Ibid., pp. 100–101; 107.
[71] Secretary of the Board, *Twelfth Annual Report of the Board of Education, Massachusetts* (Boston, 1849), p. 71.
[72] Secretary of the Board, *Fifth Annual Report*, p. 101.

were clearly thought of as capital for future development. His argument found a receptive audience. The *Fifth Report* received national attention as evidence of the need for school reform. The *Report* was distributed overseas and translated into German. The New York legislature ordered the printing of 18,000 copies.[73] The argument for the economic payoff for literacy and schooling was a welcome addition to the arsenal of common school reformers and their sympathizers, facing budgetary restraints in hard times.

The rhetoric of moral and political utility continued to be prevalent in mid-century arguments for expanded common schooling. By the opening of the Civil War, however, claims for the economic utility of the school were occurring with greater frequency.[74] In the latter nineteenth century economic utility would eventually emerge as the major claimant for the utility of public schooling. Analytic distinctions among the various claims for common schooling should not obscure the fact that the multiple expectations for the common school were not so much rivals as complementary elements of an ideological amalgam that shaped the schooling experience. Seldom did advocates of expanded common schooling dissect the network of beliefs moving them to action. Kaestle has observed that the various tenets of a "native Protestant ideology" were linked as a series of propositions. These described the nature and necessity of republican government and included its essential Christian character. Within this were stated the priorities of private property, material and social progress, individual enterprise and self-help, and the importance of individual morality to the establishment of a larger social morality.[75] The aims of common schooling and their successful institutionalization affected, in turn, the meaning(s) of literacy as acquired through schooling.

In short, schooling and its product—basic literacy—were seen as a means to enhance personal and national wealth, and to assure social and political stability by inculcating traditional morality and civic virtues associated with republican government. The larger meanings of literacy, though, did not transcend the ideological boundaries established by a republican constitutional ideal and the emergence of industrial capitalism.

THE RESULTS

By 1850, common-school reformers had successfully established the common school as the major institution for transmitting basic literacy. The school had become, as well, an institution comparable in importance to the family for socializing the young to the secular paths for economic success and for the basic morality thought necessary to the survival of the republic. In the North, the

[73] Vinovskis, "Horace Mann," p. 569.
[74] See Katz, *The Irony of Early School Reform* (pp. 28–29) for the arguments made by the school committee of Brookline, Massachusetts. Agricultural reformers continued to promote agricultural education and literacy, on the assumption that greater knowledge was the way to greater productivity.
[75] Kaestle, *Pillars of the Republic*, p. 102.

next twenty years were devoted to consolidating the gains of the previous generation, overcoming the upheaval of the Civil War, carpetbagging the reforms of the North, and building the foundation for expanded secondary education during the last three decades of the nineteenth century.

Common school reformers looked back with pride on their efforts. Yet some caution must be exercised in accepting their optimism at face value. School attendance remained a problem and, like literacy in general, was related to factors of age, region, ethnicity, nativity, and wealth. Parental wealth was not a factor in school attendance up to age nine; beyond that, it was. Nativity of parents and grandparents continued to influence the prospects of school attendance for children ten and above. Region and urbanity continued to have a dramatic impact on school attendance and literacy rates. The minimal development of the common school in the antebellum South, and the devastation of the War itself, were to influence literacy rates in that region for the next century. Intergenerational illiteracy persisted, especially where the relative lack of schooling effectively eliminated changes that might break the illiteracy cycle.[76]

The most crucial question left after reviewing the anatomy of the literacy campaigns in the first half of the nineteenth century is whether they were successful. The overall answer is affirmative, if our standards are those of school attendance at the elementary level, and a rise in literacy rates as measured by signatory rates and self-reported Census data on the ability to read and write. If our criteria are the reduction of crime and poverty and the altering of structural inequalities in American society, then the answer is negative. There were proportionately fewer illiterates in 1870. There was a decline in illiteracy rates between 1820 and 1870 on the order of seventeen percent overall. By 1860, a large majority (78%) of children between ages ten to fourteen in the North were enrolled in school. In the South this figure was fifty-seven percent. The proportions dropped sharply, however, between ages fifteen and nineteen: fifty percent in the North, and forty-two percent in the South in 1860.[77]

By 1870, the limits of reform had also become evident, as had the problems associated with institutionalizing the achievement of literacy in the common school. The triumph of the common school had effectively reduced the alternatives available for achieving basic literacy. In so doing, access to schooling became all important—being increasingly associated with the opportunity to vote—as did school attendance and upward economic mobility. School reformers had argued that education and literacy resulted in more intelligent voting and allowed greater opportunity for economic advancement. Yet, wide local variations persisted in the opportunity to attend school and left these expectations unfulfilled. Even if opportunities had been equal, however, the equation between intelligent voting and education would have been more an article of faith than a verifiable relationship.

Sparsely populated regions often lacked an adequate tax base to fund schools; even when a school could be built and a teacher hired, the duration of

[76]Soltow and Stevens, *Rise of Literacy*, pp. 128–129, 146–147, 159, 184–188.
[77]Ibid., pp. 119, 198.

schooling was problematic. Optimism often faded to realism as funds ran out and/or teachers found better jobs. Literacy rates themselves continued to reflect population density, economic development, and opportunity to attend school. County wealth per capita in 1850 was a more sensitive indicator of literacy rates than was population density. A very stable and inverse linear relationship existed between male illiteracy and indices of economic development in 1870. Thus, when the proportion of improved acreage, cash value per acre, and capital employed in manufacturing per adult male declined, illiteracy increased. The number of schools and school attendance were also both related to levels of literacy. In fact, the relationship between school attendance and literacy was stronger in 1870 than in 1840.[78]

Claims for the individual economic utility of literacy and schooling were given some credence by differential wage rates. The claims, however, should be qualified, when examining accumulated wealth during an individual's life cycle. Illiterate white males were not distributed evenly over the entire wealth range in 1860 and 1870. Rather, there were more illiterates at the lower end of the wealth distribution. The top twenty percent of wealth holders in 1860, for example, had eight percent of the illiterates. Thirty-six percent of the illiterates were above the median wealth value in the same year. The same type of distribution is found in 1870, though not quite as strong. Wealth–literacy correlations were stronger in urban areas than in rural ones, and suggest that literacy itself may have been more important in commercial and business activity than in farming. Within the context of wealth, age and illiteracy were related also. The young (and probably physically stronger) illiterate males were able to achieve greater wealth on the average than men over forty. About forty percent of illiterate white males in 1860 and 1870 could still "obtain a fair . . . standard of living" and rise above the median wealth line. For older individuals (probably those whose physical strength had declined), it required more literacy skills to remain at or rise above the median wealth level.[79]

By 1870, the problems of school attendance, meritocracy, and the economic value of literacy were virtually inseparable. The problem of literacy had become a school problem—one of both quality and quantity. The common school had been promoted as both a panacea for national ills and a channel for individual success. The value of schooling and the value of illiteracy had themselves become part of the foundation for the larger task of defining opportunity and assuring that it was available to all children. Gradually, this burden and the burden of rising expectations was shifted to secondary schooling, where it met the same intractable demographic and economic limitations. That, however, became a problem for succeeding generations, who sought the solution in an ideology of equal opportunity.

[78] Ibid., pp. 171–175.
[79] Ibid., pp. 176–80, 201.

CHAPTER 6

Russian Literacy Campaigns

1861–1939

BEN EKLOF

Irony, no stranger to history, informs the story of Russian national literacy. This
story begins with the Emancipation of the serfs in 1861, with the hopes born in
the period of Great Reforms, and the village schools built on these hopes. The
story continues with elite intervention in the 1890s, prompted both by the faith
that education was the key to progress and by the fear of "wild" popular literacy.
It ends with widespread popular resistance in the thirties to a school system
forcibly imposed by an authoritarian, interventionist regime bent upon destroy-
ing all vestiges of popular autonomy. A campaign that began in the largely self-
governing peasant commune ended with the imposition of a ruthlessly centralized political order and the very destruction of that commune, the hearth of
traditional Russian popular culture.

The pages that follow document this story, but only in the broadest of
strokes. The focus is upon village culture and village schools, because rural life
dominated Russian culture (and even Russian cities) well into the 1920s. The focus
is upon Russian schools, for treatment of minority regions would require another
article and command of languages not in my possession. This imposes a certain
false uniformity upon what was, in fact, an unusually variegated reality, but it
permits treatment of the main events in the heartland of the Russian Empire.

LITERACY IN TSARIST RUSSIA

The modern impulse to literacy in Russia began with the Great Reforms
(1861–1874). Before the serfs received their juridical freedom, primary schooling was virtually unavailable for most of the peasant population, which comprised
some eighty percent of the Empire. Literacy was a rarity, and even a sizeable
proportion of the nobility could not read or write. Since Peter first established
cypher schools, the Tsarist government had been interested in sponsoring,
organizing, and controlling education. But its efforts had been concentrated on

BEN EKLOF • Department of History, Indiana University, Bloomington, Indiana 47405.

university, secondary, and specialized education, leaving the first years of schooling to private tutors, the whim of serf owners, or the occasional enterprise of municipal government, factory, or village commune.[1]

The Emancipation (1861) set in motion several forces encouraging the spread of literacy and numeracy. An Education Statute (1864) provided a structure for primary education throughout the Empire. Like an earlier (1804) Statute, it left funding to local sources. This time, however, newly established zemstvos (local institutions of partial self-government), set up to fill the vacuum created by the dissolution of serfdom and to provide basic social services to the countryside, stepped in to fill the void. During the next fifty years, the zemstvos, together with their municipal equivalent, dumas (established in 1870) and local organizations of the Orthodox Church, played a major role in establishing, operating, and funding primary education. On the eve of World War I, there were as many as fifty-seven different types of primary school in the Russian Empire, but the two most important were the church parish and zemstvo schools. Beginning in the 1890s, the central treasury began to provide large subsidies to both church and zemstvo schools. In 1908, a School Bill was passed by the Duma, which set up a special school construction fund for grants to local zemstvos. To receive subsidies, the zemstvo had to submit a plan to make schooling universally available within ten years. Among the conditions for financial aid were that each teacher be responsible for no more than fifty pupils, that school buildings be constructed according to approved blueprints, and that all school expenses be assumed by the zemstvo rather than the peasant community. (Zemstvo schools imposed no tuition fees, but salaries and building maintenance were often the responsibility of the peasant commune.) Thus, between 1864 and 1914 the essential legislation was drawn up, and funds set aside, to make the Russian Empire a literate nation.[2]

Basic education was also stimulated by the military reforms following upon the Emancipation. Universal conscription introduced in 1874 brought male youths into the armed services, which provided reduced terms for those who could present a certificate of primary education, certifying the ability to read with comprehension (retell a passage from an unfamiliar book), write, and count (perform the four functions). The army also provided direct instruction to recruits. Although army literacy schools more often existed on paper than in the barracks, some historians assert that, in the last quarter of the nineteenth century, they

---

[1][I have relied where possible on English-language sources, or translations of Russian-language works—Author] On the bias toward higher education in Tsarist and Soviet policy, see Michael Kaser, "Education in Tsarist and Soviet Development," in C. Abramsky, ed., *Essays in honor of E. H. Carr* (London, 1974), pp. 229–254. The best English-language history of Russian education remains Thomas Darlington, *Education in Russia* (Great Britain: Board of Education. Special Reports on Education. Number 23. London, 1909). For a more recent brief study see James C. McClelland, *Autocrats and Academics: Education, Society and Culture in Tsarist Russia* (Chicago, 1979). For a fuller listing of sources, see the bibliography in Ben Eklof, *Russian Peasant Schools: A Social and Cultural History, 1861–1914* (Berkeley, Ca., 1986).

[2]See A. V. Ososkov, *Nachalnoe obrazovanie v dorevoliutsionnoi Rossii, 1861–1917* (Moscow, 1982), E. N. Medynskii *Istoriia russkoi pedagogiki* (Moscow, 1938); and N. V. Chekhov, *Narodnoe obrazovanie v Rossii* (Moscow, 1912).

taught millions of peasants how to read and write.[3] Another important consequence of the military reforms was to indirectly control the curriculum of the
primary schools, which worked to prepare pupils to qualify for the reduced term
benefits.

The central government supervised education through local school boards
established in 1864 and through a standardized curriculum (set out in broad
terms in 1864 and in detail in a Model Program published in 1897). The 1908
school bill was accompanied by legislation further centralizing state control:
teachers were incorporated into the state bureaucracy, and the powers of inspectors increased. Yet, despite standardization and control exerted through school
boards run by government appointed directors, there was much freedom and
variety. Because a single province was often larger than the whole of Ireland or
the state of Texas, the meager forces mustered by the Ministry of Education to
watch over the schools—ordinarily one director and two inspectors—could do
little or nothing by way of direct supervision. No compulsory schooling law was
ever passed in Tsarist Russia (many educators were fearful that the government's
traditionally harsh approaches when dealing with the population would boom-
erang). For this reason, the peasants also exerted a negative control over
curriculum—when they didn't like it they could simply exercise their exit option
and withdraw their children from the schools.[4] The British school inspector
Darlington observed early in this century:

> the amount of control which the state is able to exercise over teaching in primary
> schools is limited. . . . It is one of the paradoxes of Russian life that in spite of the
> elaborate bureaucratic machinery created by the state . . . the schools are in fact, less
> strictly supervised from the educational point of view by the officials of the central
> government than in England.[5]

The Emancipation also released a wave of popular initiative. Spurred on
by the new opportunities created by personal release from bondage, millions of
peasants set up informal village schools (*volnye shkoly*) taught by itinerant literates,
local priests, or retired soldiers, and funded either by payments from individual
households or by the entire commune. The popularity of these schools has been
documented, even though until 1882 they were illegal, and lived a furtive existence. In fact, as late as the turn of the century, local studies in factories and
villages continued to show that a large proportion of the literate population had
first learned how to read and write outside the formal school network.

Elsewhere, I have argued that the massive expansion of formal schooling
that took place in the fifty years after the Emancipation was in part a process
of formalization, of registration of already existing informal peasant *volnye shkoly*.
As one educator noted:

[3]On this, see John Bushnell, "Peasants in Uniform: The Tsarist Army as a Peasant Society," *Journal
of Social History*, Vol. 13, No. 4 (Winter 1980), pp. 565–566, 573. Darlington, *Education in Russia*,
p. 192.
[4]For more detail, see my *Russian Peasant Schools*, chapter 5 ("Control of the Schools"). A teacher
discussed the use of the exit option to control curriculum in N. Bratchikov, "Uchebno-vospitatelnaia
chast v nachalnoi shkole," *Russkaia shkola*, vol. 20, no. 1 (Jan. 1909), p. 115.
[5]Darlington, *Education in Russia*, p. 303.

> Much more important [than official schools] was the independent initiative of the
> peasant population, expressed in the opening of thousands of literacy schools in the
> sixties. Despite the extremely impoverished circumstances of these schools, the barely
> literate teachers . . . and the complete absence of textbooks or amenities . . . these schools
> turned out to have the greatest vitality, and formed the cornerstone of the zemstvo
> schools, into which they were transformed in the seventies and eighties.[6]

This argument receives confirmation in statistical evidence showing that
literacy began to rise before large-scale elite intervention, which began in the
1890s. Other data show that official schools began to open before funding was
forthcoming, suggesting that elite activities began as an attempt to control and
guide already existing schools, rather than to sponsor new ones.[7]

In brief, it can be said that Russia's first literacy campaign took place in
three stages. It began with peasant initiative in the 1860s. The second stage was
marked by local zemstvo, duma, and private elite attempts to build upon existing
volnye shkoly. The third was the national literacy campaign, which began with a
mounting level of concern about Russia's backwardness and growing social disorders in the Empire in the 1890s; this campaign led to joint efforts by the
public and the central government to draw up plans and find funds to build
schools, and culminated in the 1908 School Bill. Even with the complete formalization of schooling and appropriation of funding by central authorities,
popular pressure continued to play a role after 1890. First, literacy continued
to outstrip schooling, prompting widespread fear in educated circles about the
untoward consequences of "unschooled literacy." Second, peasant demand for
basic schooling remained partially unsatisfied; as late as 1911 as many as a million
children were denied access to school because of lack of space.[8] For every three
children newly entering a school, one was turned away.

What were the results of the first Russian literacy campaign? There was
an increase in primary schools, rural and urban, from eight thousand in 1856
to 25,000 in 1879, to 87,000 in 1896, and to 100,749 in 1911. The increase in
pupils was from 450,000 to 1,100,000, to 3,800,000, and to 6,600,000, respectively (7,788,000 in 1915). Annual school openings suggest the tempo of change
(subject to the reservations above): from 766 openings per year between 1864
and 1868 to 952 between 1874 and 1878, to 2338 each year between 1894 and
1898 and, beginning in 1909, to 5,036 new schools opened every year.[9]

---

[6]N. V. Chekhov, *Tipy russkoi shkoly v ikh istoricheskom razvitii* (Moscow, 1923), p. 35. For the argument
on formalization and peasant initiative, see Ben Eklof, "Peasant Sloth Reconsidered: Strategies of
Education and Learning in Rural Russia before the Revolution," *Journal of Social History*, Vol. 14,
no. 3 (Fall, 1981), pp. 355–385, and by the same author, "The Myth of the Zemstvo School: The
Sources of the Expansion of Rural Education in Imperial Russia: 1864–1914," *History of Education
Quarterly* (Winter, 1984), pp. 561–184.

[7]Eklof, "Myth of the Zemstvo School," pp. 568–575.

[8]The exact figure was 999,852, out of an estimated school-age population of 12,000,000. See Ibid.,
p. 581.

[9]A. I. Piskunov, *et al.*, *Ocherki istorii shkol i pedagogicheskoi mysli narodov SSSR* (Moscow, 1975), p. 518;
A. Chekini, "Nachalnoe narodnoe obrazovanie, *Novyi entsiklopedicheskii slovar Brokgausa-Efrona*, Vol. 28,
pp. i–iv.

Moreover, in most of European Russia, zemstvos had signed agreements with the central government to make primary schooling universally accessible within the next decade. By 1914, ninety-one percent of all district zemstvos had concluded agreements with the Ministry of Education. Of 441 districts, three percent had already completed the network of local schools, by design located within three versts of all households; sixty-five percent were within five years, thirty percent within ten years, and only eight percent more than ten years from their goal.[10]

What remained was a "mopping up" operation, to borrow Robert Altick's phrase. To be sure, the official goal of 1922 was unduly optimistic. Recent studies of literacy and schooling in developing countries indicate that the midway point, when approximately one half of all children are enrolled, usually marks a barrier, after which schooling must reach out to isolated villages and will require smaller schools and higher unit costs.[11] This is precisely where Russia was in 1914. Moreover, the pattern of expansion, from heartland to minority borderland, spelled future trouble. The spread of official schools had, since 1880, been associated with the forcible suppression of local languages and religions in favor of Russian and Orthodoxy. In advanced, highly literate areas such as the Baltic and Poland, resistance to russification had even led to a decline of schooling in the last quarter of the nineteenth century. Central Asia had the lowest literacy levels; there the population was largely Muslim. If the large-scale revolt against Russian rule (precipitated by conscription measures) in 1916 is any indication, progress would have been difficult indeed, unless literacy had suddenly been decoupled from the forcible integration of minorities—hardly likely, given the past record of the Tsarist regime. All reservations aside, the Tsarist government had placed universal literacy on the agenda.

Yet, critics of the Tsarist government, Soviet historians, and many Western historians as well, have concluded that a massive "educational failure" was one of the contributing factors to the collapse of the Tsarist Empire and the Russian Revolution. Widespread illiteracy not only doomed the Romanov autocracy, it added to the violent nature of the events of 1914–1921, and it eliminated the prospect of democratic institutions being established in 1917.[12]

---

[10] Nicholas Hans, *History of Russian Educational Policy, 1701–1917* (New York, 1964), pp. 213–214, A. Chekini, "Nachalnoe narodnoe obrazovanie," pp. 143–146; P. F. Kapterev, *Novye dvizheniia v oblasti narodnogo obrazovaniia i srednei shkoly* (Moscow, 1913), pp. 45–47. Chekhov, *Narodnoe obrazovanie*, p. 219, includes a much-cited table depicting how close each education district was to achieving universally accessible education in 1911.

[11] Richard D. Altick, *The English Common Reader: A Social History of the Mass Reading Public, 1800–1900* (Chicago, 1957). H. W. Phillips, *Basic Education—A World Challenge* (London, 1975), p. 30.

[12] Exceptions can be noted: Paul Ignatiev, *et al.*, *Russian Schools and Universities in the World War* (New Haven, Conn., 1929); Nicholas Timasheff, *The Great Retreat* (New York, 1946); Allen Sinel, *The Classroom and the Chancellery* (Cambridge, Mass., 1973), esp. pp. 214–252; and the works by Lapidus, Fitzpatrick, and Kenez, cited below. In private, Soviet historians will often concede that the notion of Tsarist educational failure is overdrawn. For one example, see A. I. Piskunov and E. D. Dneprov, "A Short History of the Soviet School and Soviet Pedagogy over Sixty Years," *Soviet Education*, Vol. 20, no. 4–5 (Feb.–March, 1978), pp. 9–10.

Table 1. Russian Literacy, 1897[a]

Region	Men	Women	All
Russian Empire	29.3	13.1	21.1
European Russia	32.6	13.7	22.9
Caucasus	13.2	6.0	12.4
Central Asia	7.9	2.2	5.3
Siberia	19.2	5.1	12.3

[a]Figures are percentages.

Table 2. Russian Literacy, 1897: by Age [a]

Age	Men	Women	All
10–19	45.1	21.8	33.5
20–29	45.3	19.5	32.3
30–39	39.5	15.7	27.6

[a]Figures are percentages.

The evidence of failure is based upon the abjectly low literacy levels recorded in the 1897 all-Russian census. According to the census, only one in five subjects of the Russian Empire could sign his own name (Table 1).[13]

Soviet historians then compare the results of the 1897 census with the 1926 census to show the significant gains posted by the Revolution. This information is supplemented by a chart originating in the 1911 School Census, and reprinted in a well-known article by Rashin, which demonstrates that only 23.8% of children aged seven to fourteen (33.3% of boys and 14.2% of girls) were attending primary school. Scattered zemstvo studies of the countryside also showed that as late as 1910–1914 only fourteen to forty-one percent of the population could read or write.[14] According to one Soviet historian, virtually nothing was achieved between 1897 and 1914. Another cites estimates published in 1906 (before the School Bill) that it would take 180 years to achieve universal male literacy and over two hundred before all women could read and write.[15]

But such conclusions must be treated with extreme caution, if only because Soviet historians have a vested interest in demonstrating how backward the Russian Empire was—thereby highlighting progress made since 1917. Consider, for example, the literacy of new recruits in the armed forces. In 1870 two-fifths of recruits could read; in 1900 four in ten were literate, and by 1913 fully two-thirds could read before induction into the services.[16] As Roger Pethybridge has

---

[13]A. G. Rashin, "Gramotnost i narodnoe obrazovanie v Rossii v XIX i nachale XX vekakh," *Istoricheskie zapiski*, no. 37 (1951), p. 48.

[14]Ibid., pp. 69, 37.

[15]Piskunov and Dneprov, "Short History," pp. 9–10; L. M. Zak *et al.*, *Stroitelstvo sotsializma v SSSR: istoriograficheskii ocherk* (Moscow, 1971), p. 171. See also Roger Pethybridge, *The Social Prelude to Stalinism* (London, 1974), who asserts that "not much was done on an official basis between the census of 1897 and 1917 to improve the situation of the illiterates" (p. 140).

[16]Rashin, "Gramotnost," p. 37.

Table 3. Russian Primary Education, January 1, 1915

Data	European Russia	Russian Empire
Number of 8- to 11-year-olds in population	11,171,283	15,253,758
Number of children in school	6,490,174	7,788,453
Percent of all 8- to 11-year-olds in school	58	51
Number of teachers	156,632	186,859
Number considered necessary	223,425	305,075

observed: "some element of mystery still surrounds the apparent discrepancy between these figures and the much less optimistic scattered evidence from other sources."[17] Moreover, it is only logical that a literacy campaign which directed its scarce resources to the new generation, and paid far less attention to adult literacy, would only gradually produce large-scale results visible in a general census. Thus, while only one in five were literate in 1897, the levels were higher for the younger-age cohorts (Table 2).[18]

Nicholas Timasheff estimates that by 1914, the literacy level in Russia had risen to forty-one percent. Moreover, he shows that in the 1926 Census, the most literate group was that aged twenty-five to thirty. These were people born between 1901 and 1906, and entering school between 1909 and 1914. In his words, the facts confirm the proposition that "in 1914 a climax was reached, to be followed by a period of decline and to be surpassed only in the late twenties."[19]

Educational enrollments must also be reconsidered. In Russia the index of education (percentage of entire population enrolled in elementary schools) rose from 1.16 in 1880 to 4.93 in 1911. According to the 1911 School Census, forty-four percent of all children in the Russian Empire were in school. According to estimates, by 1914 this figure had risen to fifty-one percent (or fifty-eight percent in European Russia) (Table 3).[20]

The difference between the enrollment levels of fifty-one percent and twenty-three percent stems from the fact that Rashin and others used an age cohort of seven to fourteen, while the proper age cohort for three- to four-year schools was eight to eleven. So, by 1914, not one quarter but one half of Russia's children were receiving schooling. In European Russia, the figure was sixty percent. This conformed with the declared strategy of the Russian government: to achieve universal education in the heartland first, and then to concentrate efforts in the minority regions.

But even these figures considerably understate the degree of contact between school and population. The average length of schooling was in fact 2.5 years for most Russian children, but the schoolage cohort used above was four years (eight

[17] Pethybridge, *Social Prelude to Stalinism*, p. 161.
[18] Rashin, "Gramotnost," p. 49.
[19] Timasheff, *The Great Retreat*, pp. 34, 313–314.
[20] Jeffrey Brooks, "The Zemstvo and Education," in *The Zemstvo in Russia*, ed. Terence Emmons and Wayne Vucinich (Cambridge, 1982), p. 270.

to eleven) in term. It takes only a moment's reflection to grasp that of the fifty percent of children not in school the day of the School Census, a large proportion had not yet begun their schooling, or had already completed it. Local studies confirmed this fact. In Moscow province in the 1890s, as many as ninety percent of all children were either enrolled, already "schooled" (*obuchavshikhsia*) or "not yet enrolled." Among the latter category, most children were ages eight to nine. Literacy and enrollment levels were extremely high in the eleven- and twelve-year-old group.[21]

Finally, it should be noted that the quality of literacy achieved by Tsarist schools was surprisingly good. I have documented this at length elsewhere; suffice it to say that retention studies of many thousands of former pupils carried out between 1880 and 1911 in various areas of the country, and testing the level of reading, writing, and counting skills of graduates five to ten years after leaving school, showed remarkably high levels of retention of basic skills. Regressive illiteracy was the exception. Most former pupils continued to use, or even build upon, the reading and writing abilities they had achieved while enrolled.[22]

REVOLUTION AND CIVIL WAR 1917–1921

The Bolshevik Revolution of October 1917 took place in the city of St. Petersburg. It spread from there to provincial cities and those outlying regions of the Russian Empire that had not seceded or been occupied by foreign powers. Before Bolshevik authority had been fully consolidated, a civil war erupted in the summer of 1918 that lasted three years and cost eight million lives. All told, in the years of war, famine, and revolution, the loss of life may have been as high as thirty million.[23]

During this period (1917–1921), the young Soviet republic launched a "remarkable literacy drive" bearing what has been called "an uncanny similarity" with literacy drives introduced later in the century in Cuba and Nicaragua.[24] In conditions of civil war and dire scarcity, foreign currency was allocated to publish millions of basic textbooks. School conferences and conventions on combatting illiteracy were summoned in the nation's cities, and the institutional

---

[21] For a more detailed discussion of this issue see Eklof, "Myth of the Zemstvo School," pp. 576–579.

[22] See Ben Eklof, "Schooling and Literacy in Late Imperial Russia," in Daniel Resnick, ed., *Literacy in Historical Perspective* (Washington, D.C., 1983), esp. pp. 119–121. The retention tests were summarized in E. A. Zviagintsev, *Narodnaia zhizn i selskaia shkola*, 2 vols. (Moscow, 1912), vol. 1, pp. 1–21.

[23] See Frank Lorimer, *The Population of the Soviet Union: History and Prospects* (Geneva, 1946). See also Barbara Anderson and Brian Silver, "Demographic Analysis and Population Catastrophes in the USSR," *Michigan Working Papers in Soviet and East European Studies* (Ann Arbor, Michigan, 1985), pp. 1–28.

[24] Peter Kenez, "Liquidating Illiteracy in Revolutionary Russia," *Russian History*, Vol. 9, Pts. 2–3 (1982), p. 173.

framework was established to set up thousands of *likpunkty* ("liquidation points") to provide crash six to ten week literacy courses.[25]

The Bolshevik Party entrusted the literacy campaign to the Narkompros (i.e., the People's Commissariat of Enlightenment—the equivalent of a ministry of education) under A. V. Lunacharskii. (A leading figure in the Ministry was Nadezhda Krupskaia, Lenin's wife and a former schoolteacher.) In October, 1918 "Regulations on the Unified Labor School" combined the bewildering network of primary schools surviving from Tsarist times into a homogenous system divided into two levels: primary five-year (eight to thirteen) and secondary four-year (fourteen to seventeen).[26] On December 26, 1919, the government issued a famous Decree on Illiteracy, requiring all illiterates aged eight to fifty to study, empowering local organs of Narkompros to draft literate citizens to teach, and making it a criminal offense to refuse to teach or study.[27] In June, 1920, the All-Russian Extraordinary Commission for the Eradication of Illiteracy (VChK/1b) was created and given the power to issue regulations with the force of law.[28] Finally, during the Civil War, compulsory education was instituted in the newly-created Red Army.

Peter Kenez has called the early literacy drive a success, particularly in teaching the soldiers of the Red Army, but also in spreading Bolshevik ideology and mobilizing the population.[29] Yet, he concedes that in the first two years after the Revolution, "the war against illiteracy was largely fought with words."[30] At the time, Soviet educators claimed that between 120,000 and 200,000 teachers had been mobilized to instruct illiterates, and that as many as seven million adults were made literate between 1917 and 1920. However, Soviet historians today admit these estimates are grossly overstated.[31] Even Lunacharsky's claim that three million had passed through the twelve thousand likpunkty existing in 1920 was later rejected.[32] Many poor peasants, soldiers, workers, and especially women undoubtably first learned how to make out the letters of the alphabet during this time, in one of the 6.5 million textbooks printed by the Bolsheviks, and encountered the stirring first words of the reader compiled by Dora El'kina, "*My ne raby, ne raby my*" ("We are not slaves, slaves we are not!"). But given the chaos of the time, the tenuous hold of the Bolsheviks over large stretches of the country, and the lack of even a rudimentary administrative network to extend its authority, generally speaking, "educational policy was formulated in a vacuum."[33] Ten years after the Decree on Illiteracy, Krupskaia complained that not a single article in it had been implemented. Moreover, most sources agree that much of

[25] Ibid.

[26] Piskunov and Dneprov, "Short History," p. 23.

[27] Kenez, "Liquidating Illiteracy," pp. 180–181.

[28] Ibid., p. 184; Piskunov and Dneprov, "Short History," p. 26.

[29] Kenez, "Liquidating Illiteracy," p. 185.

[30] Ibid., p. 178.

[31] V. A. Kumanev, *Sotsializm-i-vsenarodnaia gramotnost* (Moscow, 1967), p. 98.

[32] Ibid., pp. 98–99; see also the same author's *Revoliutsiia i prosveshchenie mass* (Moscow, 1973), p. 142.

[33] Gail W. Lapidus, "Socialism and Modernity: *Education, Industrialization and Social Change in the USSR*," in Paul Cocks, Robert Daniels and Nancy W. Heer, eds., *The Dynamics of Soviet Politics* (Cambridge, Mass., 1976), p. 200.

the educational capital accumulated before 1914 was dissipated during this period.[34] Teachers were drafted in large numbers during World War I, and many others fled the countryside to escape the epidemic of rape and murder accompanying the widespread peasant disorders and civil war.[35] After the Bolshevik Revolution, the socialist but anti-Bolshevik All-Russian Teachers' Union went on strike (to protest the October coup and in favor of democratic elections), and more teachers left the profession. As Gail Lapidus observed, "war and civil war gave primacy to military and economic needs, and generated an atmosphere inhospitable to substantial educational benefits."[36] As school buildings were turned into military barracks, a new generation of children emerged illiterate. Whatever the number of adults taught in *likpunkty*, it was certainly fewer than the number of children bypassed by the collapsing primary school children.[37]

But the Civil War did leave a lasting imprint on the Soviet system. The culture and institutions emerging out of this period were ineffably marked by the militarization, brutality, siege mentality, and habits of command and compulsion marking the "War Communism" model. Literacy became the "Third Front," after the War and the Economy. The Red Army loomed large in adult literacy efforts. Fittingly, the new committee established to coordinate literacy efforts was called the *gramCheka* (Cheka being the initials of the secret police, and *gram* an abbreviation for literacy). The campaign mentality, largely dormant in the twenties, was to resurface with a vengeance in the Stalinist cultural assault of the thirties.

NEW ECONOMIC POLICY (NEP) 1921–1927

In 1921, Russia, though finally at peace, faced a terrible famine that ultimately claimed another five million lives. The new Soviet land "stood alone, bled white, starving, shivering with cold, consumed by disease, and overcome with gloom."[38] Confronted with internal discontent, strikes, even rioting, the leadership introduced the New Economic Policy, abandoning centralized control and force in favor of the marketplace and material incentives. A mixed economy emerged, with Bloshevik control over the "commanding heights" (transportation, strategic industries, banking). Although a one-party system was retained and outright opposition ruthlessly crushed, cultural pluralism reigned, modernism

---

[34] See, for example, Sheila Fitzpatrick, *Education and Social Mobility in the Soviet Union, 1921–1934*, p. 169; Lapidus, "Socialism and Modernity," p. 200.

[35] See Kumanev, *Sotsializm*, pp. 1–99 for this period. Also the pioneering work by Sheila Fitzpatrick, *The Comissariat of Enlightenment: Soviet Organization of Education and the Arts under Lunacharsky, October 1917–1921* (Cambridge, England, 1970).

[36] Lapidus, "Socialism and Modernity," p. 200.

[37] For an argument that the number of schools increased between 1911 and 1920, see, V. A. Kozlov, *Kulturnaia revoliutsiia i krestianstvo, 1921–1927* (Moscow, 1983), p. 28. See also N. P. Kuzin, *et al.*, *Ocherki istorii shkoly i pedagogicheskoi mysli narodov SSSR, 1917–1941* (Moscow, 1980) pp. 51–53.

[38] Isaac Deutscher, cited in Michael Kort, *The Soviet Colossus* (New York, 1985), p. 125.

flourished in the arts, progressivism dominated social and criminal legislation, and experimentalism was the rule in education. Literacy in the countryside was given a big boost as the Red Army demobilized, from 5.5 million to .8 million men in 1922, and millions of literate veterans returned to their villages.[39]

On the eve of NEP, conditions in the schools were truly atrocious. For example in 1920 Narkompros received the following six-month allotment: one pencil per sixty pupils; one pen per twenty-two pupils; one notebook for every two pupils.[40] In some provinces, pupils had been using charcoal instead of pencils for some time. In others, twigs were sharpened and dipped into a mixture of soot and water. Erzatz ink was devised from cranberries, alder cones, or beets. In several provinces, paper was taken from local archives; in others, teachers resorted to stripping bark from birch trees; in still others, children wrote with coal on newly whitewashed school walls. One village found a supply of wrappers for caramel candies and expropriated them for writing paper for the local school.[41] In many areas, instruction took place by candlelight or even lighted twigs. In 1921, the literacy Cheka prepared a brochure for short-term literacy courses including a chapter entitled "How to get by without paper, pencils, or pens." At the same time, the Elabuga district (Viatka province) *likbez* committee reported: "The main reasons delaying the liquidation of illiteracy are the typhus epidemic raging throughout the district, the road corvee, and the dire shortages of readers and paper."[42] In other words, everyone was out engaged in compulsory labor rebuilding the country; disease was rampant, and teaching materials were non-existent. The level of human suffering was virtually unimaginable, and, according to Pethybridge, as paper shortages also struck the printing industry, "for a time Russia slipped back at least half a century into a predominately oral tradition."[43]

NEP brought about massive economic retrenchment and a sharp contraction of the central budget. The burden of support for primary education was shifted to local communities, fees were introduced at all levels, and expenditures per pupil fell far below prewar level. As a result, schools closed all over the country, and *likbezy* dissolved (in one district in Siberia they declined in one year from 424 to six); throughout the country the average number of liquidation points dropped from 105 to six, and the number of literacy schools by twenty-two percent. By most accounts, the nadir was reached in 1923, after which education conditions stabilized.[44]

Internally, the schools were beset by confusion about methods, mission, and organization. From at least 1918, a debate raged in education circles about the value of textbooks, the authority of the teacher in the classroom, the

---

[39] Kozlov, *Kulturnaia revoliutsiia*, p. 47.
[40] Piskunov and Dneprov, "Short History," p. 23.
[41] Kumanev, *Sotsializm*, pp. 73–74, 151.
[42] Ibid., pp. 104, 113.
[43] Pethybridge, *Social Prelude to Stalinism*, p. 157.
[44] Lapidus, "Socialism and Modernity," p. 205; Kumanev, *Sotsializm*, pp. 105–107; Piskunov and Dneprov, "Short History," p. 29.

organization and presentation of knowledge, and the relationship between school and society.[45] According to Gail Lapidus, the Bolshevik vision of education "differed radically from its Tsarist predecessor in clientele, curricula and values," but drew heavily from Russian and foreign progressive thought "for lack of a distinctively Marxist educational theory."[46] The objectives of the educational reform movement in prerevolutionary Russia had been: the democratization of education and equal educational opportunity for all classes; the autonomy of education (freedom from church and state); an education "both secular and depoliticized"; local control, rather than centralization; replacement of rote learning, of excessive reliance on homework, bells and discipline by "learning to live," encouraging creativity and independence, as well as the critical faculties. Lapidus notes that the new rulers added two distinctive elements: they "denied the very possibility of an autonomous educational system; and they insisted that education be linked with productive labor."[47] It is striking that

> The vision of socialism underlying this broad educational program was an amalgam of several distinct and partly conflicting elements. It combined a libertarian and humanist ideal of the free, fully developed and creative individual with a commitment to the revolutionary mission of the proletariat as a class. These goals were uneasily joined to a definition of modernity that emphasized scientific and technological progress and took industrial, mechanized America to be the image of the Russian future.[48]

Lenin's views on education were complex, and still await full elucidation. But it is clear that he opposed too rigid a marriage of politics and culture. By upbringing and taste he was a cultural conservative. Brought up in a cultured family, the son of a dedicated school inspector who tried to bring literacy to the primitive Simbirsk countryside, Lenin valued enlightenment and classical culture. He had little use for modernism and was impatient with cultural radicals who advocated jettisoning the riches of civilization and creating *ex nihilo* a new proletarian culture. Confronted with the awesome task of rebuilding Russia after the Civil War, Lenin advocated gradualism, persuasion, and material amelioration in opposition to those pushing for an abrupt, forced march to socialism. He saw the danger of overpoliticizing the literacy campaign, and advocated quality over speed in spreading education. In his words, "As long as there is such a thing in the country as illiteracy it is hard to talk about political education." Later, he noted: "The illiterate person stands outside politics. First it is necessary to teach him the alphabet. Without it there are only rumors, fairy tales, prejudices, but not politics."[49]

Under the stewardship of A. Lunacharsky (1917–1928), Narkompros sought to balance conflicting pressures, promote both progressivism and basic literacy,

[45] Piskunov and Dneprov, "Short History," pp. 16–20; pp. 50–55.
[46] Lapidus, "Socialism and Modernity," pp. 196–197. See also her "Educational Strategies and Cultural Revolution: The Politics of Soviet Development," in Sheila Fitzpatrick, ed., *Cultural Revolution in Russia, 1928–1941* (Bloomington, Ind., 1978), pp. 78–104.
[47] Lapidus, "Socialism and Modernity," p. 197.
[48] Ibid., p. 198.
[49] Cited in Kenez, "Liquidating Illiteracy," p. 175.

and provide a modicum of technical training to youth. At the same time, Luna-charsky tried to resist discrimination against the children of formerly privileged families (such discrimination was one of the uglier sides of Soviet education in the twenties).[50]

Throughout the twenties, successive waves of experimentalism swept the schools. Educators rejected textbooks, exams and promotion, traditional curri-cula, and the "frontal approach" to teaching. Yet, according to official investi-gations, prerevolutionary methods and syllabi retained popularity. Parents and teachers preferred the traditional content and ambience: "lessons, bells and books." Larry Holmes notes that at no time did a majority of teachers respond as Narkompros wished.[51] This inertia probably provided an element of much-needed stability. But the attempt to introduce untested approaches at a time when the Soviet school system, beset by extreme material needs and faced by acute shortages, was barely able to survive, surely wreaked havoc in the literacy campaign. The confusion reigning in the schools in 1918[52] can hardly have improved substantially in the twenties, given these conditions and the conflicting pressures on the schools.

Organizationally, the literacy campaign made strides in the twenties. In 1923, the Down with Illiteracy Society (ODB) was set up to draw in volunteers and coordinate efforts to establish literacy schools for adults. In the same year, Soviet educators worked out a plan for the elimination of illiteracy for all citizens aged eighteen to thirty-five by 1927. In 1924, government agencies developed plans for compulsory universal education that were soon ratified. Finally, in August 1925, a decree mandated instituting universal compulsory education over the next ten years.[53]

What, in fact was achieved during NEP? In the early twenties, many Rus-sians still spoke of their country's "Asiatic lack of culture." In 1921, Lenin wrote in disgust of a country vast enough to house several major civilizations, yet dominated by "patriarchy," "semi-barbarity—even total barbarity." This view was overstated, yet the despair over the distance left to cover and over slippage due to war, disorder, and reduced budgets is understandable.[54] But one recent Soviet study asserts that 1923–1924 represented the turning point. From that time, the country's school network and pupil enrollment grew steadily. In this view, the evidence for change is in data showing an increase in literacy in the period 1920–1926 from thirty-two percent to fifty-five percent; an increase in school enroll-ment between 1914 and 1927 of thirty percent, and the achievement of a seventy

[50]Lapidus, "Educational Strategies," pp. 82–83. As she notes, in a context of scarcity, utopian visions had to be curtailed, and *allocation* rather than *expansion* of educational opportunity become the crucial issue.
[51]Larry Holmes, "Soviet Schoolteachers and Moscow: Educational Policy and Classroom Practice, 1921–1931," Kennan Institute for Advanced Studies: *Occasional Paper*, Number 193 (1984), pp. 9, 25–26.
[52]Piskunov and Dneprov, "Short History," p. 16.
[53]Ibid., p. 30; Kumanev, *Sotsializm*, pp. 110–148; Piskunov and Dneprov "Short History," pp. 26–30.
[54]Piskunov and Dneprov, "Short History," p. 29; Moshe Lewin, *The Making of the Soviet System: Essays in the Sovial History of Interwar Russia* (New York, 1985).

percent enrolled-eligible ratio for school-age children by 1927 (compared with fifty-one percent in 1914.[55] In addition, the Central Statistical Agency estimated that between 1921 and 1927 no fewer than 7.5 million adults had acquired (read: been instructed in) literacy. For the first decade following the Revolution, the total instructed was ten million.[56]

However, few specialists accept this analysis. Census data from 1920 and 1926 are not fully compatible; Pethybridge estimates that illiteracy had declined by 17.3% from 1897, but only by 7.7% from 1920. Fizpatrick notes that the literacy level of fifty-one percent in 1926 was only a twelve percent increase from 1914, and "that it is doubtful that the Soviet literacy campaign had added much to the natural increase in literacy" stemming from the expansion of mass education before 1914.[57] Lapidus agrees that 1923 was a turning point, but asserts that recovery was slow, and that prewar enrollment levels were achieved only by 1927.[58] Fitzpatrick astutely notes that the two million increase in primary school enrollments since 1914 does not support the claim that education was virtually universal for the eight-to-eleven age group, because one third (34.5%) of all pupils were above the normal age for grades one to four and were adolescents earlier deprived of education. She estimates that about fifty to sixty percent of all school-age children were enrolled; not a substantial improvement, given the unusually small size of the age group (born between 1916 and 1919).

Fitzpatrick concludes that

> despite the claims that were sometimes made for Soviet achievement in mass education during the first ten years, the achievements were largely based on pre-war investment and the expansion of literacy among young males as a result of military service (but war was also disruptive of the education of those of primary school age). During NEP, the Soviet growth rate in primary education was almost certainly lower than that which would have been predicted for the Tsarist regime on the basis of the very rapid growth of the immediate pre-war years.[59]

In fact, Nadezhda Krupskaia noted in 1927 that all that had been done to that point had been to "build a raft" keeping the level of literacy afloat, but making no progress upstream. Because of the emphasis upon adult literacy, primary education for children had suffered. The number of children age eight to eleven who remained uninstructed was about the same as the number of adults enrolled in literacy courses. This meant, in effect, a net decline in quality, for formal schooling, whatever its shortcomings, was undoubtably better than the education received two or three hours a week after work over six months in adult courses.[60] Moreover, studies showed that regressive illiteracy was disturbingly common.[61] Libraries, both private and public, had been wiped out in

[55] Piskunov and Dneprov, "Short History," p. 30; N. A. Konstantinov, et al., Istoriia pedagogiki (Fifth edition: Moscow, 1982), pp. 350–352.

[56] Of whom 5.5 million were in the RSFSR: Kumanev, Revoliutsiia i prosveshchenie, p. 196.

[57] Pethybridge, Social Prelude to Stalinism, p. 155; Fitzpatrick, Education and Social Mobility, p. 169. See also Kumanev, Sotsializm, pp. 156–163.

[58] Lapidus, "Socialism and Modernity," pp. 202–205.

[59] Fitzpatrick, Education and Social Mobility, p. 169; see also Kenez, "Liquidating Illiteracy," p. 177.

[60] Kozlov, Kulturnaia revoliutsiia, pp. 47–48.

[61] Kumanev, Revoliutsiia i prosveshchenie, p. 198.

the turmoil of war and revolution. Where they remained, book selection was inadequate. In the villages, only twelve percent of literates drew books from libraries.[62] Jeff Brooks reports:

> Because of (the limited quantity and lack of appeal of) popular printed matter, it is most likely that common Russians read less in the decade after the revolution. . . . In this respect the first decade of Soviet power was a reversal of pre-revolutionary trends . . . a number of investigators reported an increase in superstition among rural people, outbreaks of wild rumors, and confusion about who ruled the country. Literacy itself may have lost some value to people who could find nothing they wanted to read.[63]

Most disquieting was the waning of energy among the ranks of literacy workers. As early as 1924, Lunacharsky complained that "the society for the liquidation of illiteracy passes wonderful resolutions, but the concrete results of its work are despicable."[64] The Smolensk Party archives, the only ones available to Western scholars, indicate a slackening of efforts as early as 1926. The discouraging results of the 1926 Census seem to have further dampened enthusiasm.[65] At that time it was calculated that the achievement of universal literacy would take at least twenty-five more years.[66] Kumanev describes a widespread retreat in the literacy campaign in 1927–1928, manifested by the drying up of funds, closing of *likbez* centers, and attrition of personnel. Trade unions, local party organizations, and local soviets turned away from the literacy campaign.[67] Even more depressing, local studies conducted in 1927–1928 showed illiteracy on the rise in many areas,[68] even in regions with traditionally high levels.[69] Lapidus points out that "popular frustration with the inadequate resources provided for rural education was widespread and was expressed by the creation of schools outside the official network."[70] On the eve of Stalin's "Great Transformation," it seemed, Russia was edging back into illiteracy, had lost the habit of reading, and was reverting to the establishment of *volnye shkoly*! This is of course, overstated, but in 1927–1928 Russia was experiencing a war scare, a severe shortfall of grain collections, and sharp concern over a declining rate of industrial growth as well as increasing social tensions. The faltering literacy campaign, given Bolshevik belief in the need for a "cultural revolution" can only have heightened apprehension about the fate of the country and contributed to the growing sense of crisis in ruling circles.

---

[62] Kozlov, *Kulturnaia Revoliutsiia*, pp. 45–46, 49; Kumanev, *Revoliutsiia i prosveshchenie*, p. 198.

[63] Jeffrey Brooks, "Discontinuity in the Spread of Print Culture, 1917–1927," Kennan Institute for Advanced Russia Studies, *Occasional Paper*, Number 138 (Washington, D.C., 1981), pp. 32–33.

[64] Pethybridge, *Social Prelude to Stalinism*, p. 152.

[65] Ibid., p. 158.

[66] Kumanev, *Sotsializm*, p. 175.

[67] Ibid., p. 172.

[68] Ibid., pp. 164–5; Pethybridge, *Social Prelude to Stalinism*, p. 165. 1928 figures showed that in the age group 16–35, there were sixteen million illiterates and thirty to forty million semiliterates. According to another calculation, among *peasants* 16–35, there were seventeen million illiterates (in a population of 114 million over the age of 10). On this, see also Timasheff, *The Great Retreat*, pp. 312–314.

[69] Fitzpatrick, *Education and Social Mobility*, p. 169.

[70] Lapidus, "Socialism and Modernity," p. 206.

STALINIST LITERACY

The literacy drive launched with the Sixteenth Party Congress (in 1930) reached for both full adult literacy and universal primary enrollment. In the dry phraseology of an official Soviet textbook, "this marked the beginning of a decisive stage in the universal compulsory education program."[71] In fact, this era bore the earmarks of the earlier civil war campaign, with its strident militancy, regimentation, and emphasis upon coercion. But unlike the civil war campaign, Stalin's war against illiteracy was accompanied by massive industrialization, urbanization at a rate unprecedented in history, and forced collectivization.[72] Industrialization compressed a century of Western economic development in one brief decade. Urbanization uprooted millions of workers and produced a vast floating population migrating from spot to spot in search of better conditions.[73] Collectivization utterly transformed the age-old way of life of the peasantry in the space of seven short weeks, was carried out with utter brutality (prompting a man-made famine in the Ukraine costing perhaps five million lives), and left permanent scars in the Russian village. The socioeconomic revolution resulting from these events was also accompanied by a sharp reversal of the egalitarianism, progressive experimentalism, and child-centered education of the twenties. Stalinist consolidation produced "a dramatic shift in the values and ethos of the educational system."[74]

This may be because the main goal of the literacy drive was now economic rather than cultural.[75] It has often been argued that there is a basic conflict between the goals of revolution and development, between socialism and modernity. By installing an authoritarian, streamed, vocationally-oriented rote education, Stalin chose development and modernity over revolutionary egalitarianism, and functionally adapted the schools to the new order.[76] But Lapidus disputes this interpretation. Just as the real contribution of collectivization and forced draft industrialization to Russia's development has been challenged by critics (could it have been done as well or better at less cost?; did the losses in waste and deliberate destruction actually exceed the gains?) so it can be argued that many elements of Stalin's educational campaign were dysfunctional, actually

---

[71] Piskunov and Dneprov, "Short History," p. 31.

[72] This point is emphasized in Lapidus, "Educational Strategies and Cultural Revolution," p. 80.

[73] This is well described in Lewin, *The Making of the Soviet System*, pp. 221–222. It has often been noted that literacy finds optimum conditions when the population is twenty-five percent urban. Russia reached that level in the 1930s. In 1914, she was roughly fourteen percent urban, after which a massive process of deurbanisation took place. See Daniel Lerner, *The Passing of Traditional Society* (New York, 1962), p. 59 and Pethybridge, *Social Prelude to Stalinism*, p. 138.

[74] Lapidus, "Socialism and Modernity," p. 216. Lapidus lists the following changes in the educational system: an end to preferential access for children of peasant and working class background; a new emphasis upon individual achievement, grades and exams; streaming; the stabilization of curriculum; and an end to experimentation and diversity.

[75] Pethybridge, *Social Prelude to Stalinism*, p. 156.

[76] See, for example, J. P. Nettl, *The Soviet Achievement* (London, 1967), p. 134. Timasheff, *The Great Retreat*, argues that social and cultural developments of the thirties were a throwback to Tsarist patterns.

hindering Russia's growth.[77] Stalin reversed Lenin's emphasis upon quality over speed. In doing so he achieved "a sharp rise in the literacy rate at the expense of true education."[78]

Briefly, the events proceeded as follows. Target figures set for the first Five Year Plan provided for 18.2 million illiterates or semiliterates aged fifteen to thirty-five to receive instruction by 1932–1933. A special resolution of the Party Central Committee (May 17, 1927) called for all factory workers to be literate in one year, and all collective and state farmers within two years. In September 1930, a reorganized Agency to Combat Illiteracy was given central control over all participating agencies in the literacy drive. A decree of the Central Committee (July 25, 1930) followed the Sixteenth Party Congress (which called for both full adult literacy and universal primary schooling), making four-year schooling compulsory for all children, *effective in the fall of 1931*. Finally, an order of the RSFSR Council of People's Commissars (August 15, 1931) stipulated that all illiterates aged sixteen to fifty were required to take instruction. According to Pethybridge, "the exact numbers will never be known, but it is certain that 1929–1933 mark the greatest achievement in the whole of the literacy campaign under Soviet rule."[79]

It bears repeating that the Stalinist literacy drive came at a time of mounting social and political tensions, and included a strong dose of coercion. Sheila Fitzpatrick observes:

> Soviet literacy campaigns had been associated with coercion since the Civil War; they had been headed in the early 1920s by an anti-illiteracy "Cheka" and even during NEP it had been necessary to remind provincial authorities that attendance at literacy schools was voluntary.[80]

The Komsomol (Young Communist League) provided most of the three million or so new recruits to the literacy campaign. The language used is revealing: the new instructors were called *kultarmeitsy* (cultural soldiers) and were organized into *kultbrigady* to carry out the cultural campaign (*kultpokhod*). Indeed, the "Komsomol organized the drive against illiteracy as if it really were a military campaign. . . . The Komsomol seemed constantly on the brink of treating the village as occupied territory, and the illiterate population as the enemy.[81] Liquidators of illiteracy arrived in the villages to staff liquidation points, at the very same time that Stalin was calling for the "liquidation of the kulaks" as a class. By driving a wedge into the village, confiscating the property of, and deporting, "wealthy" peasants, Stalin hoped to drum up support for collectivization among the poorer peasants. The campaign was simultaneously linked with a major assault against religion.

---

[77] Lapidus, "Socialism and Modernity," pp. 218–220. For a concise discussion of the costs and benefits of Stalinist individualization, see Kort, *The Soviet Colossus*, pp. 230–231 or, more favorably, Alec Nove, *Stalinism and After* (London, 1975), pp. 72–78 and pp. 109–113.

[78] Pethybridge, *Social Prelude to Stalinism*, p. 176; see also Kumanev, *Sotsializm*, pp. 179–206.

[79] Pethybridge, *Social Prelude to Stalinism*, p. 176.

[80] Fitzpatrick, *Education and Social Mobility*, p. 162.

[81] Ibid., p. 161.

Unsurprisingly, many peasants balked. Village solidarity far exceeded tensions caused by what were minor differences in wealth and property, and the collectivization campaign resulted in fierce resistance, as well as the slaughter of vast numbers of livestock. Peasants saw their well-being and entire way of life threatened. In this climate, what could they have thought of the wave of *kultarmeitsy* inundating the villages? Rumors spread that those driven to the *likpunkty* would be sent off to war and (in the case of girls) be sold off to China, or that pupils would be branded with the mark of Antichrist. Violence often erupted, and the most vulnerable target was the teacher, already subject to abuse of all kinds from local officials. Apparently up to forty percent or more of all literacy workers were attacked in a period of nine months in 1929 alone.[82] Schools were set on fire with teachers inside, beatings and murders occurred, and acid was thrown in the face of one teacher.[83] Fitzpatrick explicitly links the violence against teachers in 1930 to the entire onslaught against the village "as the peasants reacted to forced collectivization, the expropriation of the kulaks, and the closing of churches."[84] In her view, the antischool violence was more an expression of general grievance against the Soviet regime. Peasants had frequently complained against the lack of access to schooling during the NEP. But they had also expected that with compulsory schooling would come free textbooks, writing materials, even hot lunches, shoes and clothing for their children.[85] Moreover, they had certainly not anticipated the context in which compulsory schooling was introduced—one which surpassed the worst nightmares of those Tsarist educators who had argued against compulsory education, fearing that Russia's statist tradition and frequent resort to forced labor for state projects would result in heavy-handed measures, abuse of the peasantry, and resistance—all in time-honored fashion.

It is vital to note that collectivization of the peasantry spelled an end to a decade during which the peasant commune had enjoyed genuine self-government. Freed for the first time from the grasp of noble landowners, the peasant also seldom saw a representative of the Party or the government between 1921 and 1929. If one examines Russian history from the time of Peter the Great, the NEP period immediately stands out as one of unique peasant autonomy. It has, indeed, been pointed out that the 1917 Revolution was overwhelmingly the victory of the self-governing peasant commune, the culmination of centuries of peasant utopian hopes and stubborn clinging to a way of life and form of self organization. All the more bitter Stalin's onslaught against the peasant commune. All the more significant, and unfortunate, the coincidence of the literacy drive with the collectivization campaign.

Given the turmoil and brutality, it is remarkable that anything was achieved. Yet, most sources agree that there was a spectacular increase in both primary

[82] Kumanev, *Sotsializm*, p.224.

[83] Fitzpatrick, *Education and Social Mobility*, pp. 161, 163, 171. To make matters worse, teachers were also forcibly dekulakized (stripped of their possessions), and either deported or forced to register with the commune—which deprived them of the right to leave the village, among other disabilities.

[84] Ibid., p. 163. See also Levin, *The Making of the Soviet System*, pp. 91–190.

[85] Fitzpatrick, *Education and Social Mobility*, p. 171.

school enrollments and adult literacy during the first two five-year plans (1929–1938). It was officially, and perhaps accurately, claimed that by 1931–1932 ninety-five percent of all children eight to eleven were enrolled in primary school. Another three million adolescents who had slipped by the school net were also enrolled in special retrieval courses, or in regular schools. Total enrollments in grades one to seven increased from eleven million in 1927–1928 to 21,000,000 in 1932–1933, and eight million of that increase occurred in grades one to four in rural schools.[86] A Soviet study justly boasts, "By 1933, universal elementary education had been instituted throughout the entire Soviet Union."[87] Only five years earlier, the most optimistic estimates had put this goal at least a quarter century away. The *increase* of 8 million in rural schools exceeded the *entire* primary school enrollment in the Russian Empire in 1914.

Figures concerning all types of schools are also noteworthy. All schools numbered 106,000 in 1914, but 199,000 in 1940. Enrollments rose from 8 million to 35.5 million (more than fourfold). Universities increased from 105 to 817, with enrollments rising from 127,000 to 811,000. Between 1928 and 1939, the Soviet system produced 700,000 alumni and 1.5 million technicians with a secondary education.[88]

The results of the *adult* literacy campaign were even more impressive. Gosplan statisticians claimed that by the end of the First Five-Year Plan, literacy had risen in the USSR to ninety percent after 45 million adults had passed through literacy schools.[89] Other estimates put the number instructed variously at 38 million illiterates, or 29 million illiterates and 17.7 million semiliterates.[90] Fitzpatrick calls these figures "sheer wishful thinking," however, for even if true, such attendance at crash literacy schools "was not a guarantee of permanent or even temporary literacy."[91] The 1939 census showed that 81.2% of the population was literate, and 89.1% of those nine to forty-nine years of age could read or write. (By comparing the results of the 1926 and 1939 censuses, and assuming a steady rise since that date, Fitzpatrick has estimated that literacy in 1932 was actually about sixty-eight percent.) Using data made available in 1940, we learn that the number of adults instructed remained approximately equal during the First and Second Five-Year Plans, and that the average number taught each year was four to five times higher in the decade beginning 1927 than in the previous ten years.[92] There is good reason to conclude that in twenty-two years (1917–39), the Soviet Union had accomplished what it took Britain, France and Germany at least a hundred years to do,[93] and that most of the progress took place

---

[86] Ibid., p. 175.

[87] Piskunov and Dneprov, "Short History," p. 31.

[88] Lewin, *Making of the Soviet System*, p. 39.

[89] Fitzpatrick, *Education and Social Mobiligy*, p. 175.

[90] Kumanev, *Sotsializm*, 265; Pethybridge, *Social Prelude to Stalinism*, p. 166.

[91] Fitzpatrick, *Education and Social Mobility*, p. 175.

[92] Ibid., p. 176; Pethybridge gives slightly different figures: *Social Prelude to Stalinism*, p. 167. For the most thorough treatment of the 1939 census and literacy in general, see I. M. Bogdanov, *Gramotnost i obrazovanie v dorevoliutsionnoi Rossii i v SSSR* (Moscow, 1964).

[93] Pethybridge, *Social Prelude to Stalinism*, p. 167.

in the space of a single decade. An authoritative Soviet encyclopedia summarizes the progress in literacy since the turn of the century in Table 4.[94]

But the quality of the education provided and of the literacy achieved is another matter. Despite a doubling of the number of teachers (an increase of 230,000) between 1927 and 1932, and a slight improvement in teacher–pupil ratios, the *kultpokhod* and collectivization undoubtably affected teaching personnel. Thousands fled the countryside to avoid being forcibly registered in communes; many others were dekulakized, and stripped of their possessions or even deported.[95] Volunteers in the literacy campaign "often knew little more than their pupils,"[96] so the results of instruction must have been limited. Seventy-one percent of all teachers also worked in literacy schools for adults, but this was an unpaid extra duty on top of a work load generally exceeding sixty hours a week. The net result of this "volunteer" activity was probably that teaching suffered in the primary school, and that the contribution to adult literacy was perfunctory.

The haste, brutality, obsession with numbers, and indifference to quality that characterized Stalinist "storming" in other endeavors must have left their mark in schooling as well. Though investments in education increased, all sectors except heavy industry had to make do with only limited resources and excessive demands for results. For example, schools were shockingly overcrowded, and as late as 1938, the shift system remained in operation in almost half of all rural and three quarters of all urban schools.

What is more, the *kultpokhod* also signalled the transition from a child-centered, experimental approach, with at least a modicum of self-government,

Table 4. Literacy in the Russian Empire and in the Soviet Union, 1897–1939 (Population Aged 9–49)[a]

	1897	1926	1939
	Urban		
Men	66.1	88.0	97.1
Women	45.7	73.9	90.7
All	57.0	80.9	93.8
	Rural		
Men	35.5	67.3	91.6
Women	12.5	35.4	76.8
All	23.8	50.6	84.0
	Total		
Men	40.3	71.5	93.5
Women	16.6	42.7	81.6
All	28.4	56.6	87.4

[a] Figures are percentages.

[94] I. M. Bogdanov, "Gramotnost," in *Pedagogicheskaia entsiklopediia* (4 vols., Moscow, 1964); Vol. 1, p. 612.
[95] Fitzpatrick, *Education and Social Mobility*, p. 174.
[96] Ibid., p. 173. See also Kumanev, *Sotsializm*, p. 200.

to the rote, "frontal" instruction that has characterized the Soviet schools ever since. Stalin's schools were designed to teach the rudiments to as many children and adults as possible, and to provide "political literacy" as well—but of a Stalinist type. It may well be that rote learning (decoding) has to precede independent thought (encoding), but the latter never came, at least under Stalin:

> The fastest process of crude elementary education the world has ever seen coincided in time with the imposition of one of the most efficient systems of censorship known in the history of man since he became a language-using animal . . . it has never been pointed out that censorship was tightened up at the very moment when, for the first time in its history nearly the whole Russian population was on the brink of being able to make independent, though perhaps naïve, judgements on political affairs based on reading. . . . ensuring that literacy would not come to be synonomous with independence of mind at a crucial and unstable stage of Soviet history.

Stalin perpetuated, not only his own power, but also the relationship between dominant and subordinate cultures, between party and masses, for decades to come.[97]

The Soviet Union has changed immeasurably since the death of Stalin. Its human capital resources are impressive, and the education system has continued to expand from decade to decade. With the spread of university and technical education, a nation has emerged far more sophisticated, skeptical, pluralistic, and demanding than the generation of newly literate, uprooted and traumatized peasants who bore the brunt of Stalinist development. It has been argued that in the thirties the population carried into the public arena old village beliefs in, for example, the "evil eye," demonology (*nechistaia sila*), and mysterious forces (*nevedomaia sila*)[98] Stalin tapped this demonology to make his purges more palatable ("enemies are everywhere"). Today, given the sophistication and level of education of the Soviet population, it is unlikely that these events could be repeated.

Yet, it must be added that the events of the thirties left a distinctive imprint. Earlier, we noted that the literacy campaign was accompanied by unprecedented urbanization. But Moshe Lewin has argued that this urbanization also led to a "ruralization" of the cities, to the imposition of peasant mores and the swamping of urban culture. As late as 1939, seventy-eight percent of city dwellers (ten years or older) had no education or no more than elementary schooling. Time budget studies showed that the time workers devoted to "culture" fell in this period. Thus, between 1923 and 1939, the average time workers alloted weekly to newspapers fell from 2.3 to 1.8 hours, and to books and periodicals from 2.1 to 1.0 hours.[99]

Even today, the legacy of ruralization can be felt. Using (inflated) figures for book output, Soviet propagandists boast that their nation is the most "well-read" nation in the world. Anyone who has spent time in the Soviet Union can affirm the high level of respect for the written word (encouraged, ironically,

---

[97] Pethybridge, *Social Prelude to Stalinism*, pp. 176, 179.
[98] On this, see Lewin, *The Making of the Soviet System*, pp. 67, 269–270.
[99] Ibid., p. 39.

by censorship—what is forbidden *must* be important—and by the difficulty of obtaining good books). But Soviet sociologists have also discovered in recent years that a large percentage of the population turns infrequently to the printed word, and then largely for escape. Soviet ideology posits that the new Soviet Man should read regularly, make use of a variety of sources, and should have a firm, continuing interest in either sociopolitical, scientific works, or good literature. In fact, one-tenth of the population never reads newspapers, one fourth never read journals, and one-fifth "hardly ever" read books of any kind.[100] Reading is turned to most often for entertainment: potboilers, mysteries, science fiction, and adventure stories are very popular in the USSR, despite low press runs and limited access.

A study of five villages in the mid-sixties discovered that thirty-two percent of the population (forty-one percent of women and seventeen percent of men) never read books. In the seventies, studies showed that seven percent of families had no readers at all. Although readers were differentiated by occupation and income, most were interested primarily in "undemanding" fiction; few read for utilitarian purposes (whether to improve performance at work or to keep up with general achievements in science and technology). Library subscribers took out books on politics in far smaller numbers than their availability. Books checked out were concentrated in the areas of travel, biography, and history (primarily on World War II: military memoirs, spy documentaries, regimental histories). One study noted that "readers in small towns found foreign names and concepts difficult to grasp, and some claimed to be discouraged by the different world-view of non-socialist authors."[101] The point here is not to disparage Soviet literacy or Soviet readers, but only to note that reading trends observed in the western world have their parallel in the USSR, and that a substantial proportion of the public makes only limited use of the printed word. When people read, it is less often for self-improvement.

Most striking is the continued political passivity, or aggressively apolitical state of the population. To the degree that the Soviet people became aware of the outside world in the thirties, its concepts were shaped by the exclusive, dogmatic, yet infinitely malleable doctrine of Stalinism. The population learned to decode but not to encode thoughts. Under Stalin, people learned how to read and write, but seldom to learn from reading. One of the major criticisms by Soviet educators of their own schools in the sixties was the inability of students to reason independently, to deal with conflicting views of reality, or to devise scientific experiments on their own.

The expansion of the secondary and tertiary system under Stalin was also deceptive. Fitzpatrick notes that "on paper, many forms of education . . . were characterized by extreme specialization . . . in practice this seems usually to have

---

[100]On this see Jenny Brine, "Reading as a Leisure Pursuit," in Jenny Brine, Maureen Perrie and Andrew Holt, eds., *Home, School and Leisure in the Soviet Union* (London, 1980), pp. 239–269, esp. p. 245. Of those with a primary education (the thirties generation), two-thirds of men and four-fifths of all women do not read books regularly.

[101]Ibid., pp. 252–260.

been a euphemism for training at an extremely low level."[102] Lewin suggests that medical personnel, engineers, and technicians, as well as trade employees, were poorly educated and trained (eighty-three percent of trade employees and sixty-eight percent of medical personnel had only a *primary* education): "a very rude and crude mass indeed, from which the population suffered endless miseries, and still does to a large extent today."[103] Half of all officials (three million) had no professional education whatsoever: "they were poorly trained . . . clogging factories and other offices, and notorious for their bad performance."[104] Among the two million top leaders (*rukovoditeli*), sixty-eight percent had only a primary education. Of course, these figures speak of a revolution in social mobility of enormous dimensions, but hardly of a *cultural* revolution in the sense of a genuine transformation of valves, tastes, and cognitive orientations. Once again, Lewin has best described the overall impact of the Stalinist emphasis on speed over quality:

> Even the leaders were products of a revolution, but not of a cultural one. The population and the cadres had reached some halfway point, as a result of the policies and the industrial effort pursued by the regime . . . instead of the term "cultural revolution" it is more appropriate to use something else—"acculturation"—perhaps, to express the reality of a still poorly educated population coming out from deep illiteracy, producing a growing mass of trained people who formed, nevertheless, only a quasi-intelligentsia at best.[105]

The lesson of the Soviet literacy drive is not a happy one. The Soviet literacy campaign, massive and rapid as it was, could never have been carried out without the growth and consolidation which had occurred in the fifty years following the Emancipation and preceding the Revolution of 1917. Between 1917 and 1929 literacy at best remained stable, despite much effort at improvement. Benefits from the Stalinist campaign of the thirties there surely were, but the costs were also high, and the wastage extreme. It is fitting to recall the words of the famous revolutionary Nikolai Chernyshevsky that the wealth of a nation can bring poverty to a people. Chernyshevsky was rejecting the positivist dogma of inevitable progress; he saw that accumulation of wealth at the national level does not automatically bring with it improvements in living standards: Nor, by analogy, does the coming of literacy bring with it increments of individual freedom, particularly when the state is the bearer of the written word. Whatever it brought in economic and political gains, the Soviet literacy campaign did not bring personal emancipation.

[102] Fitzpatrick, *Education and Social Mobility*, p. 180.
[103] Lewin, *The Making of the Soviet System*, p. 40.
[104] Ibid.
[105] Ibid., p. 41.

CHAPTER 7

Literacy Movements in Modern China

CHARLES W. HAYFORD

> *Surely it is good to be able to read. The old people told us about*
> *what happened, what they learned when they went to the market*
> *places. The young people read to us from the newspapers.*
> —*Ning Lao Taitai, "Old Mrs. Ning"*

On October 1, 1949, a few years after Mrs. Ning made this remark, Mao Zedong stood on the Gate of Heavenly Peace in Beijing and announced that China had "stood up": "The era in which the Chinese people were regarded as uncivilized is now ended. We shall emerge in the world as a nation with advanced culture." Mrs. Ning just wanted to know what happened.[1]

The contrast between these two voices tells us a great deal about the contrast between the varied aspirations of China's common people on the one hand, and the cultural goals of modernizing intellectuals and the engineering zeal of political reformers, on the other. A survey in the 1930s showed villagers with practical reasons for valuing the arts of reading and writing: about a quarter of the villagers said that literacy was most important to keep accounts (27%), or to read and write letters (26%); another goodly number mentioned to avoid being cheated

---

[1] This chapter is drawn from a piece of ongoing research done in collaboration with a group of former colleagues and friends at the Chinese University of Hong Kong. The group, to whom I give my grateful thanks, includes Thomas H. C. Lee, David Faure, Bernard Luk, Alice Ng and Tam Yueh-him, who are preparing a volume tentatively titled *The Changing Significance of Literacy in China, 1960–1937*. This research-in-progress is reported in "Oral History Research (Hong Kong History, Customs, Culture)," Chinese University of Hong Kong *Bulletin* 4 (1984), pp. 14–21. They have not seen the present article, however. That volume will include many more extensive references to Chinese and Japanese language sources, which have therefore been avoided in the present essay. Readers who wish such references should consult my own *Y. C. James Yen and Rural Reconstruction in China* (Columbia University Press, forthcoming); Evelyn Sakakida Rawski, *Education and Popular Literacy in Ch'ing [Qing] China* (Ann Arbor: University of Michigan Press, 1979); Sally Borthwick, *Education and Social Change in China: The Beginnings of the Modern Era* (Stanford: Hoover Institution, 1983); John DeFrancis *The Chinese Language: Fact and Fantasy* (Honolulu: University of Hawaii Press, 1984).

CHARLES W. HAYFORD • Department of History, Northwestern University, Evanston, Illinois 60201.

(10%), and only a few (6%) added to read newspapers and books.[2] The educated and political elites had much more abstract aims; they led or coerced the "unenlightened" through various campaigns, movements, and reforms, in order to mobilize them as citizens of the nation to be. All valued literacy (but for quite different reasons), all inherited positions within China's quite particular history, all faced the problem of dealing with China's system of writing, and all freely manipulated values, techniques, and institutions.

LITERACY AND SOCIETY IN LATE IMPERIAL CHINA

Looking back on imperial times, modern Chinese reformers and Western scholars have agreed with traditional Confucians on at least one thing—the centrality of "culture" (*wenhua*). Instead of crediting it with China's strengths, however, moderns have blamed it for China's shortcomings. The young Mao Zedong, freshly graduated from normal school in the 1920s, was typical in lamenting that "in China, culture has always been the exclusive preserve of the landlords, and the peasants have had no access to it. . . . Ninety percent of the people had no education."[3] Western scholars for many years went along with this equation of education, literacy, and stagnation:

> The Chinese writing system was not a convenient device lying ready at hand for every schoolboy to pick up and use as he prepared to meet life's problems. It was itself one of life's problems. If little Lao-san could not find time for long-continued study of it, he was forever barred from social advancement. Thus the Chinese written language, rather than an open door through which China's peasantry could find truth and light, was a heavy barrier pressing against any upward advance and requiring real effort to overcome—a hindrance, not a help, to learning.[4]

Reformist modernizers tended to be strongly feminist, and the unblushing sexism of traditional education was still another sign of its hopeless feudalism in their eyes, for women were almost never allowed in schools. As Alexander Woodside has pointed out, China did not have the religious rivalries encased in national competitions that motivated the growths of literacy rates in Europe; there was no competitive need to make the flock literate to mobilize the people before the twentieth century.[5]

Recent scholarship, while not rejecting this line of observation, has modified it considerably. Evelyn Sakakida Rawski's 1979 book, *Education and Popular*

[2] Ida Pruitt, *Daughter of Han* (New Haven: Yale University Press, 1945; Stanford, 1967), p. 244; Gan Yuyuan *Xiangcun minzhong jiaoyu* (Shanghai: Commercial Press, 1934), pp. 47–49, quoted in Rawski, *Education and Popular Literacy*, p. 21.

[3] "Report from the Hunan Countryside . . ." *Selected Works of Mao Tse-tung* I:54 (Peking: Foreign Language Press, 1967). I have amended the translation slightly: the terms which appear in English as "culture" and "education" are both *wenhua* in the original.

[4] John King Fairbank, *The United States and China* (Cambridge, Mass.: Harvard University Press, 1981), p. 43.

[5] Alexander Woodside, "Some Mid-Qing Theorists of Popular Schools: Their Innovations, Inhibitions, and Attitudes Toward the Poor," *Modern China* 9.1 (January 1983), p. 20.

Literacy in Ch'ing [Qing] China, marked a major reevaluation of literacy and its uses in late imperial China. Earlier estimates of overall literacy rates ranged as low as one to two percent, for they defined literacy as the ability to read classical prose and write classical compositions. Observers of China were struck with Japan's relatively faster economic development, assumed China's rate of literacy to be low, and then used it to "explain" China's poor performance. Using new research materials and a more realistic definition of literacy afforded by comparative studies, and assuming China's early modern economic performance to be in fact comparable to Japan's, Rawski argued that "information from the mid- and late nineteenth century suggests that 30 to 45 percent of the men and from 2 to 10 percent of the women in China knew how to read and write." Conceding that literacy could mean the knowledge of only a few hundred characters, she concluded that "there was an average of almost one literate person per family." Literacy, she argues, could not have been the bottleneck for China's presumed failure to modernize swiftly and cleanly.[6]

This revised view has many implications. The traditional school "system" turns out to have been far more complex and effective, in its own terms, than modernizing critics gave it credit for, though scarcely a system in the sense of having an overall plan or unitary objective. At the top (at least in its own view), was the imperially dominated structure, leading to national examinations for entrance into the government bureaucracy.[7] The imperial bureaucracy effectively controlled middle-level education simply by setting the questions and standards used on the exams, but took no responsibility for lower level education.

Yet, there were many more elementary school students than can be explained by ambition to take the civil service examinations. A family could send little Lao-san to school in hopes that he would become Prime Minister or at least defend the village in law suits; they could also send him in for a quick shot of discipline from the teacher's bamboo, a few useful characters, and the prestige of keeping up with the Zhangs. The New Territories of Hong Kong, as described by an oral history team at The Chinese University of Hong Kong, offer a clear example, especially telling since after 1898 the residents were under British rule and could not sit for the examinations. Nearly seventy-five percent of males between the ages of seven and fourteen attended school, with an average stay of four years. Villages maintained the schools out of a "profound reverence for learning," or "face"—the two motivations being perhaps closer than we would like to think.

Nowhere in China were the costs terribly high. Schools (or perhaps more accurately "classes") could be set up by anyone with a few coppers to hire a tutor. Villages, families, clans, and beneficent individuals did just that. In a time when the nationalized standards of professional education and licensing were not yet implemented even in the West, every educated Chinese male was a potential

---

[6]Rawski, *Education and Popular Literacy,* p. 140.
[7]The most sophisticated study is Ho Ping-ti, *The Ladder of Success in Imperial China: Aspects of Social Mobility* (New York: Columbia University Press, 1962). See also Miyazaki Ichisada, *China's Examination Hell: The Civil Service Examinations of Imperial China* (Tokyo, 1963; tr. Conrad Shirokauer, New Haven: Yale University Press, 1976).

teacher.[8] The common texts, after all, had been in print for centuries and were widely available. Little equipment was needed: before students started returning from Japan or Columbia Teachers College, nobody felt the lack of blackboards, maps, or desks, much less of slides (either to look at or play on), laboratories, indoor heat, light, or flush toilets. Students followed individual programs and calendars, progressing as fast or slow as seemed right, taking time off for holidays, harvests, or family needs as allowed. With the basics so cheap, there was no need to send students away from home to board in expensive cities. Essentially the same cheap, flexible setup could be used to teach martial arts, medicine, geomancy, or a wide range of other skills. In short, it would be hard to beat the traditional school for economy and adaptibility.[9]

We do not yet adequately understand the varieties of schools in late imperial China; they differ geographically, socially, and across time. Sally Borthwick's study of educational reform in early twentieth-century China sees two tracks of elite-sponsored education. One track focused on improving customs and reforming manners among the masses, and operated through imperially sponsored but locally organized morality lectures. The other, more formal, system provided the elite with the training for entry into politics, and operated through the local schools feeding into the examinations. Alexander Woodside, in a key study of Qing educational reformers, argues that the elite-sponsored popular schools aimed to control local society through education, rather than spreading economically useful skills. Woodside thus speaks of the "antiquarian immobility" of even the most reform-minded of the Qing schools, which made them "ritualized shrines" unwilling to bend to the economic needs of poor and common people.[10] We may still suspect that education also took place outside this elite-sponsored system. In contrast to Confucian stiffness, the run of villagers and city dwellers shifted for themselves; education must have included training in various and discrete individual skills, ranging from arithmetic or reading to herbal medicine and religious rituals.

In this context, as Rawski explains, there was not any one skill corresponding to the idea "literacy" so much as there was a series of specific literacies and situations in which reading or writing was used—and therefore no meaningful, unitary "literacy rate."[11] Some occupations demanded control of a certain number of characters, though not a general competence in reading. Apothecaries,

---

[8] A well-informed observer in the late nineteenth-century said that it is "far from being the fact that every Chinese village has its school, but it is doubtless true that every village would like to have one, for there is the most profound reverence for 'instruction'." Arthur H. Smith, *Village Life in China* (New York: Fleming H. Revell, 1893), p. 73.

[9] A survey taken in the 1920s found that in the 453 villages of a rather typical county on the North China plain, 451 had village schools. See Hayford, *Yen and Rural Reconstruction*, Chapter Four, "Reform and Uplift in Ting Hsien: Officials, Gentry, and Intellectuals, 1890–1929."

[10] Borthwick, *Education and Social Change in China*, p. 4. Alexander Woodside, "Some Mid-Qing Theorists of Popular Schools," p. 32.

[11] There has been dissatisfaction with recent efforts to define literacy. The concept of "functional literacy," as used in the world debates since the Second World War, writes a skeptical British sociologist, is a "wooly and elusive notion," and "in lieu of a comprehensive and coherent account of the role of literacy and illiteracy in society, we have nothing more than a jumble of ad hoc and

to take an extreme example, had to know the otherwise abstruse characters used to write the names of medicinal herbs, while a merchant's purposes might be met by knowing numbers and enough characters to keep records and write orders. The use of the abacus, by the way, was taught in a number of popular handbooks providing mnemonic rhymes for the complex rules needed to add and multiply.[12]

Our modern expectation is that we must be literate in order to know what is going on. But local society in imperial China had access to empire-wide information and historical culture through such specialists as teachers, priests, doctors, story tellers, and dramatic troupes, all of whom orally spread material drawn from written texts to audiences not necessarily literate. We also should remember that in China, the classical language was a political and cultural tool to unite the empire. Our very terminology reflects the success of the effort: in Europe we speak of French, Italian, and Spanish as "languages"; in China, Cantonese, Shanghai, and Fukien are called "dialects." In any case, there was a constant interplay between the written classical or bureaucratic language and the village patois. A villager might well sing a verse based on a Tang dynasty poem, have a classical couplet pasted over the family door at New Year, apply a pithy classical proverb, and be able to follow a complex historical or romantic play, all of which drew on a common well of story and allusion. True, villagers could not freely read elite texts, which used classical forms and vocabulary as well as thick and abstruse allusion, but the difficulty was more a matter of style and usage (or of pronunciation) than of basic linguistic structure. Popular almanacs, tawdry editions of saintly stories, and even, in the wealthier cities, popular fiction, attest to the fact that literacy for fun and profit was well established,[13] and that its impact was magnified by being directly tied into a larger oral network.

THE WRITING SYSTEM AND THE TRANSMISSION OF LITERACY

In order to understand how specific literacies were related and how they were taught, we must pause to look at the nature of the Chinese writing system. Traditional Chinese methods of literacy instruction would eventually send shudders up the progressive spines of American educationalists, but once we cease to assume abysmal medieval rates of literacy, we can argue that traditional teaching techniques were adapted to teaching a nonalphabetic system.

---

largely mistaken assumptions about literacy's economic, social, and political dimensions." Kenneth Levine, "Functional Literacy: Fond Illusions and False Economies," *Harvard Educational Review* 52.3 (August 1982), p. 249.

[12] Lam Lay-young, "The *Jih yung suan fa*: An Elementary Accounting Textbook of the Thirteenth Century," in Nathan Sivin, ed., *Science and Technology in East Asia* (New York: Science History Publications, 1977).

[13] For a more detailed discussion of these points, see the various articles in David Johnson, Andrew J. Nathan, and Evelyn Rawski, ed., *Popular Culture in Late Imperial China* (Berkeley: University of California Press, 1985).

Though nobody can know the exact number of characters in the Chinese language (they are continually coming into existence or passing out of use), the estimate of 40,000 is close enough. Of these, perhaps 7,000 are used commonly enough today to be in the basic newspaper font; a knowledge of 3,000 constitutes unchallengable literacy; while the possessor of a mere 1,500 can be called literate without provoking instant ridicule. Although the popular Western understanding (fed, to be sure, by Chinese misunderstanding) has it that the writing system is pictographic or ideographic, less than three percent of the characters fall into these categories. Chinese characters are not random strokes in unique picture formations, but are most often composed of meaningful elements. The Chinese spoken language has used relatively few distinct syllables, resulting in a large number of words using the same sound—homophones such as *ma* "horse" and *ma* "mother." A phonetic system of writing would not have been able to deal easily with this source of confusion; China's nonalphabetic orthography took advantage of it. The vast majority of Chinese characters are compound, made up of first a phonetic element (which was in ancient times often used at the whim of the scribe to write any one of a number of words with the same sound) and then a semantic element, carrying an indication of the word's area of meaning, added in later years to resolve that homophonic confusion. The task facing any pedagogy is to find some reasonable order in which to teach characters, first introducing those leading to the retention of those that follow.[14]

In dynastic China, the most common first step for a beginning student was to memorize the so-called "Three-Hundred-Thousand" (*San-bai-qian*), a family of three literacy primers, each of which appeared in many variations and adaptations. The most famous, and usually the first, of these was the *Qianzi wen* (Thousand-Character Classic), written in the sixth century A.D. The piece is a *tour de force*, using a thousand characters in rhymed couplets without repetition. The equally renown *Sanzi jing* (Three Character Classic) is a composition of three-character lines, which form a more coherent moral and historical exposition than the tortured syntax of the Thousand-Character Classic could afford. Finally, the student memorized the *Bai jia xing* (One Hundred Family Surnames), which actually contained some four hundred family surnames. Allowing for overlap in vocabulary and for variation among the different versions of each text, a person who had memorized these basic primers had a command of roughly three thousand characters, and was then ready to move on to the task of writing and to read materials where content was important. As Evelyn Rawski puts it, the *San-bai-qian* constituted a "crash course" for learning a set number of characters within a short time.[15]

---

[14] For an incisive discussion of the writing system and its relation to the language, see DeFrancis, *The Chinese Language*, pp. 70–130, "Rethinking Chinese Characters." For breakdown of characters, see Table 3 on p. 84, "Structural Classification of Characters."

[15] Rawski, *Education and Popular Literacy*, pp. 45–52. An analysis of a crucial transitional period is given in Thomas H. C. Lee's important article, "Life in the Schools of Sung China," *Journal of Asian Studies* 37.1 (November 1977), pp. 45–60. See also Francis W. Paar, ed., *Ch'ien Tzu Wen [Qianzi wen]: The Thousand Character Classic, A Primer* (NY: Frederick Ungar, 1963), and Herbert Giles, tr.,

At this point, the structure of the majority of Chinese characters (phonetic plus semantic) comes into play. John DeFrancis argues that this memorized body of material gave the student an awkward and unplanned syllabary with which it was then possible to "spell out" many further characters. That is, the reader guessed from the phonetic element common to the two characters how the unknown character might be pronounced, and then guessed the particular word from the context. Since the reader might well be already familiar with the plot or context of the new material, reading some kinds of new materials (especially vernacular novels, say) could be reasonably easy. Specialized literacies in other areas could be picked up under the supervision of a mentor. After two or three years of instruction, many left school and promptly forgot what they had sweated to learn. Only the very few village boys remaining in school (and there were few girls) went on to learn composition or even to read to the point of full literacy.

In short, literacies were various, particular, delimited, but not highly restricted. It would be hard to argue that orthography, or schools, or pedagogy constituted a clogged bottleneck, in the sense that its unplugging would release a gurgle of further free change. Reformers did have a case, however, for curing the system of its vicious sexism. Twentieth-century indictments of these elements are only partly rational in economic or instrumental terms; they are also symbolic, cultural, and moral.

STRENGTHEN THE COUNTRY, UPLIFT THE PEOPLE

China's modern political leaders and intellectuals felt the pull of nationalism quite personally. Their sense of Darwinian international rivalry led them to value cultural unity and a strong state, traditional Confucian concerns in any case. One group (or perhaps better "impulse") saw the bureaucratic machinery of the centralized nation-state as the best instrument for promoting China's interests; extending cultural and political control of the government down to the people was their aim. Another group or "impulse" saw cultural reform as more basic than political machinery; they worked to build (or rebuild, as they saw it) a national moral community from which a strong state would emerge. In either case, spreading literacy was crucial.

Over the course of the twentieth century, there has been a broad, continuous, three-pronged literacy movement. The three strategies have been (1) to reform the language, reform the orthography, or both; (2) to reform and expand the formal school system; and (3) to create new techniques for nonschool ("social") education for both children and adults to supplement the inadequate formal system. Social education also had the advantage of leaving people in place, not removing them from their original community, and not involving the expenditure of money for separate buildings and institutions.

San Tzu Ching [Sanzi jing]: Elementary Chinese (Reprint, NY: Frederick Ungar, 1963). Incidentally, a check in my local Chinatown bookstore shows all three books stocked in current editions.

Concerted attack on educational problems came early in the century. In the early 1900s, officials of the Manchu court enthusiastically promoted a two-tiered national school system modelled on Meiji Japan. In this system, higher education provided technical training for the few, while a broader primary education inculcated the virtues of citizenship through simple vocational literacy. Normal schools, professional education associations, government supervision of teaching standards and texts were set up, in short, the whole apparatus (though on an inadequate scale) of a professionalized school system, consciously attempting to set up the machinery of a nation-state.

Some officials emphasized political benefits. A governor of Shantung eagerly pointed out that "the more the knowledge of the people increases, the easier it will be for government orders to be implemented." Others focused on cultural uplift. One reformer complained that commoners resorted to "low and vulgar amusements" that education could wipe out.

The more radical of the government's critics also called for new education to create new citizens. One wrote in 1903 that Chinese were "men of conscience and very patriotic," and asked why it was that "we don't lift a hand in protest or cry out when the Japanese and Russians start quarrelling over who will get Manchuria." The answer: "It's because we're illiterate," and the magazines and newspapers have no effect: "It's like playing the lute for a cow." He complained that the classical language used in the newspapers formed a barrier to civic communication. When "we common people" see all that " 'Yea verily,' 'According to the *Book of Odes*,' and 'The Master says . . .', we don't feel like reading all those peculiar essays and terms."[16]

In the late nineteenth century many educated people had turned their hands to publishing books and newspapers for "new readers" (including women), using a simpler vocabulary and grammar.[17] This new and simpler classical style, still a far cry from a written colloquial, reached a new city audience whose interests were less puritanical and political than those of the Confucian literati.[18] Language reform and reengineering of the writing system were also promoted, to the point where orthographic tinkering became a favored indoor sport. On their own, prominent literati drew up any number of schemes for phonetic writing to replace characters. Many considered this on the far side of radical, but General Yuan Shikai, the military prop of the Manchus and not known for his intellectual daring, supported an alphabetic scheme.[19]

Formal adult education classes were begun. In 1906, the Manchu court

---

[16]Lin Hsieh, from the *Zhongguo pai-hua pao* (the China vernacular press), translated in Mason Gentzler, ed., *Changing China* (New York: Praeger, 1977), pp. 136–137.

[17]Charlotte Beahan, "Nationalism and Feminism in Modern China," *Modern China* 1.4 (October 1975), p. 387.

[18]Leo Oufan Lee and Andrew J. Nathan, "The Beginnings of Mass Culture: Journalism and Fiction in the Late Ch'ing and Beyond," in Johnson *et al.*, eds., *Popular Culture in Late Imperial China*.

[19]The most thorough discussion of this period is John Paul Bailey, "Popular Education in China, 1904–1919: New Ideas and Developments" (unpublished PhD thesis, University of British Columbia, 1982). See also: John DeFrancis, *Nationalism and Language Reform in China* (Princeton: Princeton University Press, 1950).

promulgated regulations for half-day schools and in 1908 established in the
capital a series of Language Made Easy Schools intended for adults who had
left school or had not the money to begin. The classes were to be held in existing
school buildings and limited to two or three hours a day. Students used specially
written literacy or accounting texts in a one-to-three year course.

The aim of all these activities was nation building, or, more specifically,
republic building. One Chinese participant remembered slightly later that "for
the ten years before the founding of the Republic in 1911, everybody understood
that the base of constitutional government was local self-rule, which in turn was
based on the spread of education." Thus officials at court, radical reformers
and revolutionaries in exile, and reform officials in the provinces all agreed, for
differing reasons, on the centrality of education. The three techniques of orthographic reform, school expansion, and adult education were all initiated during
these late Manchu reforms.[20]

With the fall of the empire in 1911, there was an advent of enthusiasm
and hope, which soon gave way under the press of President Yuan Shikai's
ambition for a centralized nation-state. Yuan continued support for the unfin-
ished two-tiered education system of general-citizenship schooling for the masses
and technical education for an elite.[21] With Yuan's death and the discrediting
of the central government, hope for central funding or leadership was lost. To
be sure, private elites and local officials tried to fill the educational gap. From
1915, a "Common Education Society" in Beijing edited and published over eight
hundred volumes of fiction, three hundred of drama, and continued to maintain
a Model Lecture Bureau. The Beijing Police Department, still largely run by
Manchus, took general social welfare as its bailiwick and ran literacy schools for
indigents and convicts.

Public lecturing was popular among the educated, continuing the Ming
and Qing tradition of exhortation, but substituting modern public morality and
science for imperial Confucian homilies. For instance, one expedition organized
by the progressive Jiangsu Provincial Government spoke in 350 places to an
estimated total of 160,000. In 1919, the Agricultural Bureau sent out its first
team of skirmishing lecturers in a railroad tour along the Beijing–Hankow rail-
way; farmers were rounded up at the railroad stations for the arrival of the
train, and could inspect demonstrations, see lantern-slides, and hear lectures
that were "worded in a simple manner so that illiterate countrymen can understand them without difficulty."[22]

---

[20] Marianne Bastid, *Aspects de la reforme de l'enseignment en Chine au début du 20e siècle* (Paris, 1971),
pp. 58–60; Gao Chien-ssu, "Sanshiwu nien lai ti Zhongguo zhi minzhong jiaoyu" (*The Last Thirty-
Five Years in China's Mass Education*), in *Zuijin sanshiwunian zhi Zhongguo jiaoyu* (*The last thirty-five
years in Chinese education* (Shanghai, 1931; reprinted Hong Kong, 1969), p. 166.

[21] Ernest P. Young, *The Presidency of Yuan Shih-k'ai: Liberalism and Dictatorship in Early Republican China*
(University of Michigan Press, Ann Arbor, 1977), pp. 195–199; Bailey, *Popular Education*, pp. 176–
178.

[22] Chuang Tse-hsuan, "Zhongguo Zhi Chengizen jiaoyu" ("China's Adult Education"), *Xin jiaoyu* (*The
New Education*) 4.3 (March 1922), reprinted in Shu Hsin-ch'eng, ed., *Zhongguo xin jiaoyu gaikuang*
(*The General Situation of China's New Education*; Shanghai, 1928), pp. 192–193, 196; Hollington K.

An ambitious program had envisioned building one library for each of China's nearly two thousand counties, but no more than two hundred were ever built. This was no small number, but procedures for borrowing books, selection of titles, and even hours of opening and closing made them nearly impossible for the ordinary working person to use.[23]

NEW CULTURE, BUILDING THE NATION, AND POPULAR EDUCATION

On May 4, 1919, while Woodrow Wilson preached his democratic nationalism to the Allies in Paris, a group of students in Beijing stormed government offices and attacked government officials for allowing the Japanese to take over the German colonies in China. In the following days of demonstrations, arrests, and publicity a new generation crystallized. They took upon themselves the task of transforming Chinese culture in order to build a nation, iconoclastically attacking everything old as feudal, patriarchally imperial, and oppressive, while welcoming the new, the scientific, the democratic. They felt that the constitutional Republic had failed because of popular ignorance, but their concept of the Chinese nation was based on the "people," rejecting the definition of the nation as formed by and around the state and its bureaucracy.

This patriotic and modernizing populism, embodied most clearly in a self-proclaimed "New Culture" Movement, still implicitly accepted the Confucian melding of politics, society, and culture, and took language and education as central to its mission. In the period of initial enthusiasm in the early 1920s, perhaps no other activity was as widespread as this popular or mass education movement, and no issue raised as much basic controversy as that over the nature of the Chinese language, particularly the movement to promote the educated vernacular (*baihua*) as the written medium.

At the radical fringe, some turned again to orthographic abolitionism, calling for an end to Chinese characters. Still, none seem to have gone as far as the Meiji Japan reformer who proposed using English instead of uncivilized and inadequate Japanese. (Esperanto, however, was widely admired.) An undergraduate leader at Peking University denounced the "deeply rooted barbaric character" of the Chinese language: "the invention of ideograms being a matter of barbaric antiquity, it cannot be helped that the language has remained barbaric. Cannot one be ashamed of its being in continuous use in modern times?" He elsewhere agreed with a prominent anarchist that the "Six Classics and Three

---

Tong, "The First Agricultural Education Train in China," *Millard's Review* 6.3 (September 21, 1918), reprinted in C. F. Remer, ed., *Readings in Economics for China* (Shanghai, 1922), pp. 557–561.

[23]Sidney Gamble, *Peking: A Social Survey* (New York: George H. Doran, 1921), pp. 147–156, has information on the libraries in Beijing which were meant to be emulated in the rest of the country. A recent story reported that by the end of 1985, eighty percent of the counties will have their own public libraries. "New Library Services See Nationwide Craze," *China Daily*, October 24, 1985, p. 1.

Histories should be used to paper windows or as tinder to burn the Er Ya and the Shuo Wen" (two famous dictionaries). Conservatives defended the beauty of the script and the moral value of the old literature: "Ha! Ha!" he sneered, "This really makes me die laughing," and speculated that they would next argue that bound feet should be preserved as national treasures![24] Not surprisingly, he called for the propagation of a scientifically designed phonetic script to save the nation.

A national conference of linguists met in 1926 and adopted a National Phonetic script (*Gwoyeu Romatzyh*) that elegantly represented both the sound and the tone of a syllable, using only the symbols on an ordinary English typewriter or common news font. But the major flaw in phonetic writing became apparent. For those whose native speech was some form of Mandarin, use of a national phonetic system was relatively easy. They had only to learn the principles of writing and the particular symbols of the system confronting them. On the other hand, those who did not already speak standard Mandarin had first to learn it before they could deploy any national phonetic system. As John DeFrancis puts it, for a speaker of such regional languages as Cantonese, Shanghai, Fukienese, and Swatow, this was "a task more or less akin to an English speaker having to learn Dutch for literacy," though he concedes that "given a few centuries it may succeed."[25]

Other problems with phonetic alphabets emerged. New learners and their families or bosses wanted the real thing; there was nothing either useful or titilating to read in romanization. Many local leaders opposed even the vernacular style as too radical, and to propose romanization to them would have risked decapitation.

For the most part, however, the eager New Culture radicals did not want to dilute their culture but to spread it. They generally accepted traditional Chinese characters, but created a new written colloquial style. They took written colloquial usage both from China's past, particularly from popular novels, and abroad, particularly Japan, which had written many new concepts with new combinations of Chinese characters. The new vernacular was thus largely a literary construct, based grammatically on spoken Northern Chinese but using a vocabulary accessible only to those with a modern education. Paradoxically, the emphasis on writing the vernacular set back the phonetic cause; most creativity went towards a new written national dialect, rather than writing local dialects. This vernacular was quite a break with established practice, and was billed as a Chinese Renaissance, but was not of much help in spreading literacy to the masses.[26]

Young energy did go into evening schools and lectures. At Peking University, students formed a night school for their janitors, proclaiming that a

---

[24]Fu Sinian (later an eminent linguist and supporter of the Guomindang), quoted in C. T. Hsia, *Modern Chinese Fiction* (New Haven: Yale University Press, 1963), p. 10; John DeFrancis, *Nationalism and Language Reform*, p. 70.

[25]DeFrancis, *The Chinese Language*, pp. 191, 245.

[26]John DeFrancis, "China's Literary Renaissance: A Reassessment," *Bulletin of Concerned Asian Scholars* 17.4 (December 1985), pp. 52–63.

"republic takes popular education for its foundation." Students at nearby Beijing Normal University formed a similar group, and other institutions in the capital did likewise. They had a lot to learn about the needs and habits of their conscripted audience and students. On school holidays and weekends, teams of students travelled to factories and were surprised to find that workers also had the day off. On a beginning trip to a village, described in deflating detail in the *Peking University Daily*, the young scholars discovered that the university's spring vacation was precisely the busiest season for a working farmer, and only old women and children could spare time to be exhorted. Even these few became so bored that they left before the second lecture. In another village, the young teachers set up their flag and record player, to be greeted by perhaps half a dozen people, again mostly children. On another occasion the local police led them away for appearing without license or permission. (The next time their visit was sponsored by the county library, and local officials turned out an audience of more than five hundred.) They lectured on such topics as "Democracy," "Freedom," "Emperors and Presidents," The Chinese Republic," "The Elimination of Superstition," and "The Spirit Expected of a Citizen of the Republic."

In Shanghai, Beijing's upstart commercial rival for leadership of new and young China, popular education was also at the boil. A coalition of eleven groups formed a Popular Education Association. These eleven included the YMCA, YWCA, the China Continuation Committee (a Christian umbrella), but also a number of long-standing and prestigious government groups, such as the Jiangsu Provincial Education Association, and private groups such as the Vocational Education Association, the World Chinese Student's Association, the Western Returned Student Association, and the Shanghai Students' Union. Part of the aim had been to form free schools for poor children, but in the event most of the activity was confined to lecturing. Still, one Christian colleague of Sun Yat-sen's congratulated the group for having successfully avoided "those destructive tendencies which come from unbridled impulsiveness and enthusiasm, and which have made Russia a country of lawless and brutal Bolshevism."[27]

Across the country, especially in provincial educational centers such as Wuhan in Hubei, Chengdu in Sichuan, and Changsha in Hunan, students grasped the idea of public lecturing, literacy classes for workers, and free schools for poor children. Paul Monroe, a prominent educator from Columbia Teacher's College, found that "in 1921, when I visited government and private schools in ten of the provinces, scarcely a school was found, even among those of an elementary character, that was not conducting a free school for poor children, taught and supported by teachers or pupils or both."[28]

The achievement of mass education, however, was mixed. The late Qing bureaucratic reform effort, continued under Yuan Shikai, quailed in the face of China's fissiparous immensity. The New Culture students tried to take illiteracy

[27]T. H. Lee, "The Popular Education Movement in China," *Chinese Recorder* 51.1 (January 1920), pp. 44–49; Joseph Chen, *The May Fourth Movement in Shanghai* (Leiden: E. J. Brill, 1971), pp. 82, 88.
[28]Paul Monroe, *China: A Nation in Evolution* (New York: Macmillan, 1927), p. 284.

by storm, by a sort of educational human wave attack, but had also seen their considerable accomplishment shrink to disappointment in the face of seemingly limitless shoals of illiteracy and ignorance.

NEW CULTURE AND THE LITERACY CAMPAIGN

The time was ripe for the invention of the national literacy campaign, a breakthrough which affected all literacy work in China from that time on.

The most basic element in the new literacy campaign was still the nationalistic cultural populism of educated young Chinese, but the organizational form drew from other sources both in traditional China and abroad. In the early years of the century, the Chinese YMCA had conducted a vastly popular series of city "campaigns" that promoted health and scientific knowledge, often cosponsored by local governments and weighty citizens. Typically, the opening of the campaign was a city-wide parade which used the brass band and banners of an American college homecoming weekend to draw a crowd. Most important was to first assemble a committee of "kingpins" or "pinnacle group" that would handle local connections and broad planning. (This use of the word "kingpin," as in bowling, is a nice metaphor for the social vision of the Y at this point: local elites were the key element in society, and if they could be bowled over, the rest would follow.) Once set up, this campaign structure could make good use of the latest in American public relations and advertising—promoting health and science for an audience-public was not so different from selling middle class consumer products. Thus the term "campaign" (*yundong*) didn't have so much a military implication as a commercial one.[29]

The patriotic appeal of literacy, the organizational tools of the YMCA health campaign, and the creative enthusiasm of young China came together under the leadership of Y. C. James Yen, a young Chinese Yale graduate who had learned the value and necessity of literacy by teaching it to so-called "coolies" recruited by the Allies to labor in France during The Great War.[30] When Yen returned to Shanghai in 1920, he was called upon by the Chinese National YMCA to head an independent national literacy program.

The first to invite Yen to set up a city literacy program was the Y in Changsha, one of the many provincial capitals seething with cultural and political

---

[29]Shirley Godley Garrett, *Social Reformers in Urban China: The Chinese Y.M.C.A. 1896–1926* (Cambridge, Mass.: Harvard University Press, 1970) gives a lively and analytical description of these activities. John Hersey's *The Call* (New York: Alfred Knopf, 1985) is a fictionalized but basically accurate account of these campaigns. James Yen appears in the novel as "Johnny Wu." This campaign technique had an influence outside China, when the concept was taken up as a model by UNESCO in its early years after the Second World War. The first of the UNESCO Monographs on Fundamental Education noted that "it was against the background of James Yen's statement, and not as the result of pure theory, that the UNESCO delgates adopted the term 'fundamental education.' " *Fundamental Education: A Description and a Program* (Paris: UNESCO, 1949), p. 9.
[30]See my *Yen and Rural Reconstruction*, Chapter 1.

change. Changsha put together a general committee of some seventy business-
men, college presidents, editors, officials, guild leaders, pastors, teachers, and
students. Many of these people were members of the well-established Strengthen
Education Society of which Mao Zedong, as a primary school principal, was a
member. They formed committees on finance, recruiting, finding classrooms,
and publicity. Colorful posters plastered the city, graphically arguing the evils
of illiteracy for both the individual and the nation: "An illiterate man is a blind
man," "An illiterate nation is a weak nation," "China's salvation? Popular education!" and "Can you endure to see three-quarters of China go blind?"[31] Volunteers in groups of four canvassed the town, house by house, shop by shop,
waving their literacy banners as they went. The greatest number of illiterate
recruits were laborers, small business apprentices, or workers of one sort or
another, but there were three pig buyers, eleven scavengers, ten policemen, and
two beggars. The eighty volunteer instructors were given a brief training course
in the specific techniques for teaching adult and young illiterates, such as games
and group singing. Classes were held in more than sixty schools, churches, guild
halls, temples, union club houses, private homes, and even the police station.

The literacy text was the newly assembled *Peoples Thousand Character Primer*
(*Pingmin qianzi ko*) published by the Chinese National Y. Using the title of the
traditional primer, the new text was a pedagogical breakthrough. The old style
literacy primer had introduced characters chosen by instinct, in an order dictated
by whim—one popular text simply introduced the characters written more simply
first, regardless of whether they were common or useful. To provide a scientific
selection of basic characters, an American trained professor at Nanking University made an actual count of frequency in selected texts, on street signs,
standard contracts, and notices. The selected characters (in fact 1,200 of them)
were divided into four separate books, each of which took a month to finish.
Lessons focused on immediately relevant topics, such as how to write a letter or
fill out simple forms, rather than Confucian philosophy. There was a highly
moral message, to be sure, but it concerned washing hands, respecting elders,
and saluting the nation's flag.

The lessons were well paced to reinforce learning. Before the pupil's initial
enthusiasm had worn off, the class had finished the first book and could "graduate" to the next volume. After finishing each volume, the pupil received a stripe
on a simple badge, which formed the Chinese flag when all four stripes had
been earned. At the end of four months there was a mass final exam, followed
by a grand graduation ceremony for those who passed. The newly minted literate
would presumably join the public of active, informed, and scientific citizens.[32]

The Y's use of modern publicity, pedagogy, and psychology had combined
with cheap, small scale and flexible Chinese popular school organization to produce the campaign. Almost immediately, cities across the country organized
literacy campaigns on the Y model, and quite a number called James Yen in to

---

[31] Yen, "The Campaign Against Illiteracy," *China Mission Year Book*, 1923, pp. 205–215. For Mao's
participation, see Linda Shaffer, *Mao and the Workers: The Hunan Labor Movement, 1920–1923* (White
Plains: M. E. Sharpe, 1982), p. 59.
[32] Yen, "The Campaign Against Illiteracy."

organize. In the fall of 1923, Mao Zedong and his party comrades joined the YMCA's second Changsha literacy campaign as volunteer teachers. Naturally they were not satisfied with the content of the YMCA Thousand Character Primer and commissioned their own adaptation, which introduced a vague socialism and the thought of Marx. Soon a leading CCP labor organizer in Shanghai wrote excitedly that "comrades all over the country are using the *Thousand Character Primer*."[33]

The Changsha campaign also attracted Tao Xingzhi, a recently returned student of John Dewey's at Columbia Teachers College. Tao wrote excitedly to his friends that the new literacy campaign was the answer to China's weakness; "wherever I set my foot," he vowed, "will be a place touched by Mass Education." He proselytized his scholarly friends to set up family literacy circles for their wives, servants, and sisters, and lobbied local governments to promote literacy.[34] In August of 1923, Tao and Yen organized a National Association of Mass Education Movements (MEM), which Yen headed until its dissolution in 1951. At the height of its literacy campaign in the 1920s, Yen estimated that the MEM had five million students and more than 100,000 volunteer teachers.

Tao went on to become the nation's leading promoter of rural teacher's education. At his village-based normal school outside Nanjing, he produced a number of innovative techniques such as the "little teacher," who taught his or her family what had just been learned in school, and the "each one teach one" technique of organized teaching networks. This non- (or even anti-) professional pedagogy was quite influential. The national authorities closed down Tao's rural school in 1930, but provincial governments, goaded by independent reformers like Yen and Tao, established their own schools for primary and adult education training. By the end of the 1920s, when the Nationalist Government of Chiang Kai-shek sought to regulate and control all educational activity, the Mass Education Movement had produced millions of graduates.[35]

VILLAGES AND THE MOVE BEYOND LITERACY

When the literacy movement found its way to the villages, it was transformed. In the years 1925–1926, James Yen's MEM set up another rural literacy experiment, this time in Ting Hsien (Dingxian) Hebei, at the foot of the Wutai Mountains in the central plains south of Beijing. In the same years Mao Zedong

[33] Shaffer, *Mao and the Workers* pp. 57–61, 86–88. Yun Daiying, quoted in Hayford, *Yen and Rural Reconstruction*; "Textbooks of China's Early Labor Movement," *China Reconstructs* 24.1 (January 1975), pp. 33–35. See also Cyrus Peake *Nationalism and Education in Modern China* (New York: Columbia University Press, 1932), Appendix I, pp. 159–193, "A Digest of Textbooks used in the Mass Education Movement and the Most Popular Textbooks Used in the Primary and Middle Schools of China from 1905 to 1929." The *Thousand Character Primer* was translated for students of Chinese by Walter Simon of the School of Oriental and African Languages as *1200 Basic Chinese Characters* (London: Lund, 1944, Humphries, 1957).

[34] Barry Keenan, *John Dewey in China* (Cambridge, Mass.: East Asian Research Center, 1979).

[35] See, for instance, Lee Byung Joo, *Rural Reconstruction Movement in Jiangsu Province, 1917–1937: Educators Turn to Rural Reform* (PhD thesis, University of Hawaii, 1978; University Microfilm 780428-02050).

toured his native Hunan and found a situation that shook his preconceptions. Armed in part with his experience in the Changsha Mass Education Movement, Mao saw a new countryside:

> See how the peasants who hitherto detested the schools are today zealously setting up evening classes! They always despised the "foreign" style school. . . . The texts used in the rural primary schools were entirely about urban things and unsuited to rural needs. . . . Hence the peasants preferred the old-style schools ("Chinese classes" they called them) to the modern schools (which they called "foreign classes") and the old-style teachers to the ones in the primary schools.[36]

Yen and the Mass Education Movement thought along parallel lines. They ridiculed China's "two dead educations," one the traditional Confucian education, the other the Western "new" education that had no more relevance to the village than classics from Mars. Instead, they began to rethink the task of producing schools that would combine the cultural Chinese qualities of the traditional village school with the scientific qualities of the modern school. Mao and Yen differed quite considerably as to the particulars, but agreed on the nature of the general task, that is, to produce a Chinese modern system that would serve the people, regenerate Chinese culture, and become the basis for a proud new nation.

Organizationally, the MEM abandoned the independent literacy campaign. Yen has often told of the villager who thanked him effusively for teaching him to read, but added, "Dr. Yen, my stomach is just as empty as my illiterate neighbor's." In response, the MEM created a coordinated program in education, health, economics, and politics, and called the result Rural Reconstruction. This approach was an influence on, and a forerunner of, Community Development practiced in Asia and Africa in the 1950s and 1960s. The MEM did not want to impose bureaucratic control on the village by extending the government schools into the countryside. Instead, Yen and his colleagues decided to build upon the tradition of the local school, self-supported and self-centered. They called it a *minban xuexiao*, "Peoples' School" or "managed by the people." The new Peoples' Schools developed many innovative techniques to make use of nonprofessional teachers and to substitute village organization for the introduction of outside teachers.

The MEM returned to the question of language, literacy, and orthographic reform, but this time from the vantage point of the village. The Peoples Schools taught still another phonetic syllabary (*zhuyin fu hao*), and after 1932, the MEM's local publications adopted a mixture of National Phonetic and traditional characters, a device which allowed villagers to write much of the contents of the weekly newspaper and to keep diaries. Unknown characters were simply written in the phonetic, resulting in a readable macaronic style.

Energy went into creating a literacy environment. Economic reforms, social progress, health information, and political ferment were brought together in a web of organization in which literacy had immediate use and national relevance. Literacy was used not just to read more literacy texts but to open new worlds.

---

[36] *Selected Works of Mao Tse-tung*, I:54 (Peking: Foreign Languages Press, 1967).

Portable libraries were hauled by donkey carts to the villages; a radio network was built, with each village supplying an "explainer" to clarify the news; villagers wrote wall newspapers and on blackboards to spread the latest national news; they formed singing groups, modernized village plays, and staged art fairs; and, underlying the enterprise, they promoted a coordinated economic program of buying and marketing cooperatives, agricultural improvement, and the reorganization of village handicrafts. Women were organized, mobilized, and educated. This Ting Hsien Experiment burgeoned, only to be stifled by the Japanese military and their North China puppets in the invasion of 1937.

THE CCP'S REVOLUTIONARY LITERACY BEFORE 1949

With the creation of the Red Army in the late 1920s came the establishment of an independent Soviet in the scrawny mountains of Jiangxi.[37] Radical social reform based on land revolution was the central policy, but the Party quickly turned attention to schools, culture, and literacy. Mao's old Changsha teacher, Xu Teli, became the Soviet Commissioner of Education.

Deeply influenced by the Russian example, Xu and the fledgling Chinese Soviet drew up ambitious plans to reduce illiteracy to zero. Lenin Schools (the very name reflecting sympathy for Soviet Russia) were set up for elementary students, night schools for illiterates under the age of thirty, and adult literacy classes for all others in their work units. Tao Xingzhi's teachings were very influential; Xu Teli for a time called himself Xu Shitao, that is, Xu "study-Tao." As Commissioner of Education, he promoted local reading circles modelled on Tao's: "Let the husband teach his wife, the son teach his father, the secretary teach his boss, and those who know more teach those who know less." Village literacy teachers painted familiar objects with their characters—doors, trees, chairs, and pigs were turned into living primers. Special emphasis was placed on literacy in the army and on teaching the cadres (party designated activists) to read.

Still, by the time the Jiangxi Soviet had to be evacuated for the Long March in 1934, the development of mass education was low and very uneven. In Xinguo County, the center of educational activity, the CCP claimed to have wiped out illiteracy in the school-age population, but even these estimates were inflated by eagerness to win political competitions, and the standards were in any case quite low. Mao himself reported that some students in literacy classes knew only forty or fifty characters. In spite of all, however, the period saw the foundation of a revolutionary literacy approach. Mao trumpeted the success of enrolling peasants in classes at all and in mobilizing their support. He was especially proud of

[37]The material in these three paragraphs is drawn from Lu-tao Sophia Wang [Kang], *Teaching Peasants to Read: The Earliest Communist Mass Education Efforts in China, 1931–1934* (unpublished MA Thesis, University of Iowa, February 1975). See also, H. S. Wang, "A Study of Chinese Communist Education During the Kiangsi Period," *Issues and Studies* 9.7 (November 1973), 9.8 (December 1973), 9.9 (January 1974). "Hsü T'e-li," *Biographical Dictionary of Republican China* (New York: Columbia University Press, 1968), Vol. II, pp. 146–148.

mobilizing village women, who were only gradually becoming recognized as an object of mobilization and source of revolutionary energy.

In Mao's approach, political mobilization and general communication were more important than general literacy. Large numbers of villagers were brought to political awareness, what might be called political literacy, even though they remained unable to read books, magazines, or newspapers. Talks, songs, plays, and face-to-face persuasion developed from the political network reaching down toward (but not yet reliably into) the village. All of this built on the village tradition of communications, not on the formal school network.

When the Long March reached the area near Yan'an in 1935, Mao opened a new phase of the revolution, in which the war with Japan overshadowed the class struggle. He welcomed students and intellectuals to join a United Front, a multiclass coalition to attack the problems of the village and defend the nation. Literacy was not in the forefront during this dangerous and opportune period, but still played a role.

In the early 1930s, CCP leaders trained in Moscow had introduced a phonetic alphabet using roman letters developed in the Soviet Oriental Institute of Leningrad. This *Sin Wenz* or "New Writing," from which the present *pinyin* system differs only slightly, was much more linguistically sophisticated than earlier alphabets, with the major exception that it did not indicate tones. Still, it appealed to the old New Culture leaders and new influx of educated youth, who felt Chinese characters to be a feudal stink in the nose of the righteous.[38] The important CCP leaders agreed with the orthographic reforms. By 1940, several thousand members attended a Border Region *Sin Wenz* Society convention. Chairman Mao and General Zhu De, head of the army, both contributed their calligraphy (in characters!) for the masthead of the Sin Wenz Society's new journal. Outside the CCP, other prominent supporters included Sun Yat-sen's son, Cai Yuanpei, the country's most prestigious educator, Tao Xingzhi, and Lu Xun, China's best-known writer. Over thirty journals soon appeared, plus large numbers of translations, biographies (including Lincoln, Franklin, Edison, Ford, and Charlie Chaplin), some contemporary Chinese literature, and a spectrum of textbooks. In 1940, the movement reached an apex when Mao's Border Region Government declared that the *Sin Wenz* had the same legal status as traditional characters in government and public documents. Many educators and political leaders looked forward to the day when they would be universally accepted and completely replace characters.[39]

In the heady atmosphere of hope and energy during the early war years, the first Border Region Representative Assembly announced that illiteracy might be wiped out within five or six years by extending the school system and promoting literacy classes. Reports to the Assembly in 1939 claimed that there were over six thousand literacy and other social education groups, and by 1940 the number of elementary schools had grown from a reported 120 in 1937 to 1,341. The wartime social and political mobilization not only brought organization of

---

[38] DeFrancis, *The Chinese Language*, pp. 246–247.
[39] DeFrancis, *The Chinese Language*, pp. 247–255.

literacy classes, but a push to bring new types of literacy to the masses. In each of the Base Areas, separated by Japanese occupation troops, there was a characteristic emphasis on what Roy Hofheinz, Jr. has usefully called "literary mobilization," that is, local publication of pamphlets, magazines, journals, and newspapers. In a few places there were printing presses with moveable lead type, but most printing was by the "oil press," a cheap and long established mimeo technique.[40] The CCP and its local allies in the wartime United Front found and published local writers who would produce a "peoples' literature" to be read by the people in their own dialect. Mobilization was not limited to written culture. For instance, the "rice-sprout song" (*yangge*) was taken up from its original form as a village New Year dance and promoted as the symbol and celebration of a new democratic peoples' culture.[41]

Yet, the path was far from smooth. Peter Seybolt, the most careful student of education in the Yan'an period, notes that "in its own assessment, the Party made more mistakes in mass education than in any other endeavour."[42] New recruits, mostly young intellectuals with little experience among the pigs and peasants, had a rough time in carrying out the ambitious plans made in earlier, happier, safer circumstances. Gruesome military pressure from the Japanese exacerbated what would have been awesome problems in any case. Their first impulse, to expand and improve the formal school system, carried them through an initial period of enthusiasm, but soon broke against the craggy realities of a poor, inward, and suspicious area of China. The Border Region Government was gasping for survival and had no way to subsidize local education; even training and ideological uplift for party and army members required a major effort and creative adaptation.[43] The phonetic *Sin Wenz* movement foundered. Once again, reformers learned that a phonetic system could not gain wide acceptance when China contained such a variety of spoken languages. Phonetic reformers adapted their scheme to write Cantonese, Hakka, Shanghai, and Fukien dialects; for their troubles, nationalists accused them of mounting a "cultural movement of traitors." Dialect phonetic writing, the attackers charged, would deny China the "capitalist unity" it required before it could move on to socialism, and, by dividing the country into regions, opened the way for Japanese divide and conquer tactics.[44] Villagers—who traditionally sent their sons to school for short periods of moral stiffening and a few useful characters—were slow to see

---

[40] Roy M. Hofheinz, Jr., "The Ecology of Chinese Communist Success: Rural Influence Patterns, 1923–1945," in A. Doak Barnett, ed., *Chinese Communist Politics in Action* (Seattle: University of Washington Press, 1969), pp. 40–43.

[41] David Holm, "Folk Art as Propaganda: The *Yangge* Movement in Yan'an," in Bonnie S. McDougall, ed., *Popular Literature and Performing Arts in the People's Republic of China 1949–1979* (Berkeley: University of California Press, 1984), pp. 3–35. Jack Belden's *China Shakes the World* (New York: Harper, 1949) conveys the excitement of the time; see especially Chapter 17, "A Beggar Writer," and Chapter 22, "Class Society in the Classroom."

[42] "The Yenan [Yan'an] Revolution in Mass Education," *China Quarterly* 48 (October–December 1971), p. 641.

[43] Jane L. Price, *Cadres, Commanders, and Commissars: The Training of The Chinese Communist Leadership, 1920–1945* (Boulder: Westview Press, 1976).

[44] Zhang Difei, quoted in De Francis, *The Chinese Language*, p. 247.

the beauty of foreign alphabets with which to write down what common people could already hear on any village corner, or worse, to write some city dialect found only in books.

The ultimate CCP strategy, which Seybolt calls a "revolution in education," was to recognize the reality of a dual school system: the central government withdrew from local direct school administration and supported a small number of formal schools, mainly in the larger towns. Scarce resources were to be focused in the cities, on cadres and party members, and in sectors which could finance schools on their own.[45]

The Peoples' School (*minban xuexiao*) was to be the key to village hopes, just as it had been in James Yen's Rural Reconstruction at Ting Hsien. Local government and party cadre would encourage surrounding institutions, such as the Winter Evening School, the literacy circle, the circulating library, the little teacher, again on the Ting Hsien precedent. A leading CCP general and administrator was at pains to say that the new policy was not a matter of cut and run; one suspects that some were making just that charge, and that there was something to it:

> The policy of popular management cannot be divorced from that of government assistance. Popular management schools cannot be allowed to run their own course; it is incorrect to think that we will lighten our responsibilities through popular management; in fact, the reverse is true.[46]

Another authoritative official stated the intended balance clearly:

> Some think that popular management is just a matter of solving the funding problem—that is, getting the masses to pay. Others think that popular management does not need public [government] aid or does not need supervision. [Both of these types of opinion are] one type of misunderstanding. There is also another kind of misunderstanding, which takes an imperious approach to popular management, so called "bureaucratic enforcement of popular management." The first kind is a bias toward surrendering leadership, the second kind is a form of vile bureaucratism; both are wrong.[47]

The policy, in a chastened tone, concludes that "under this program, we must in the future work towards having a popular management school in every village; through cooperation, the village schools will be able to run winter study programs, night schools, and reading groups so as to achieve the goal of completely eliminating illiteracy in the Border Region."[48]

Thus, the Communist Party in the 1940s reached a balance between ideals and budgets of time and money. They set up a program of education and literacy

[45]Peter Jordan Seybolt, *Yenan Education and the Chinese Revolution, 1937–1945* (PhD thesis, Harvard University, 1969), esp. pp. 256–276.
[46]Chairman Lin Boqu *et al.*, "Border Region Government Directive on Promoting the Study of Model Schools and On Experimentation with Popular Management Primary Schools (April 18, 1944)," translated in *Chinese Education* 4.4 (Winter 1971), pp. 272–273.
[47]Lo Mai, "Promote The Mass Education Movement on a Large Scale," (Statement in the General Meeting on Education in the Shen-Gan-Ning Border Region, November 15, 1944), translated by Ellen Widmer in *Chinese Education* 4.4 (Winter 1971), p. 317.
[48]Lin, "Border Region Government Directive," p. 272.

gradually expanding from the most central to the peripheries; they used government money only for key functions, such as training cadres and maintaining city schools. On the peripheries, they settled for local administration under party supervision and by implication defined literacy in a broader sense, that of social and political mobilization. Where earlier reformers had assumed that the people could only participate as citizens in a republic they could read about, Mao largely bypassed print in reaching down to the countryside. Like all modern nation-states, jealous creatures that they are, the Chinese revolutionary government has also tried to wipe out local and particular literacies in favor of a unitary, nationalized, "modern" literacy.

USE OF THE LITERACY HERITAGE IN THE PEOPLE'S REPUBLIC

The government of the People's Republic that came to national power in 1949 drew on several generation's worth of aspiration and experimentation; they coordinated a flexible and diverse structure for increasing literacy that drew on roots as diverse as the Manchu and Nationalist formal school systems, the YMCA's health campaigns, the literacy movements in the Soviet Union, and the Chinese village school.

Without trying to narrate in detail the initiatives and changes launched in the 1950s and 1960s, much less the awe-inspiring conflicts of the Great Proletarian Cultural Revolution (1966–1976), we can make some comments on China's literacy experience since 1949. The most striking and important fact is the continued commitment, within rather stringent economic constraints, to the spread of literacy and popular education; China must rank high on any world scale in this respect.

A rambunctious divergence of opinion exists on the extent and significance of the literacy achievement. There has been much praise. A laudatory report to UNESCO in 1982 concluded that "China's efforts in anti-illiteracy are clearly the greatest experiment in mass education in the history of the world," and that China has "become a nearly literate society."[49] Estimates of overall literacy have ranged as high as eighty percent. Indeed, on the occasion of the 1984 World Literacy Day, the UNESCO General Director conferred the Noma Literacy Prize on rural Bazhong County, Sichuan for reducing its illiteracy rate from over eighty percent in 1949 to a present rate of under ten percent.[50]

On the other hand, the Chinese government itself does not claim nationwide literacy rates to match those of the most advanced areas, but recently announced once again the determination to eliminate illiteracy in the age-group from twelve to forty throughout the country: "We shall mobilize all our efforts and resources to eliminate illiteracy and to promote various forms of adult

[49]H. S. Bhola, *Campaigning for Literacy* p. 80, as quoted in Robert Arnove, "A Comparison of the Chinese and Indian Education Systems," *Comparative Education Review* 28.3 (August 1984), pp. 381–382.
[50]Coincidentally, Bazhong is James Yen's home county. Xinhua News report, Beijing, September 8, 1984, in *Foreign Broadcast Information Service* CHI-84-179.

education for cadres, workers and farmers in urban and rural areas."[51] Some analysts doubt the usefulness of the level of literacy China has attained: "on the assumption that most of the [Chinese] who are classified as literate can comprehend no more than 1,500 characters, it is questionable whether the cause of rural development has been greatly advanced," for "so modest an understanding of the written language does not really enable a peasant to obtain more than a very limited understanding of a farm manual or guide on how to repair a tractor or any of the myriad publications through which scientific knowledge is transmitted."[52] A leading Chinese anthropologist, Fei Xiaotong, returned in 1981 to the rather well-off village he had studied in the 1930s. He sadly reported that "strictly speaking, those with only one or two years of schooling could also be considered illiterate, for they can recognize little more than their own names and those of their family members. Thus approximately one-half the villagers are illiterate."[53]

These conflicting estimates suffer from imprecision in the concept of literacy. Just as we saw in imperial times, there must still be various *types* (not merely various levels) of literacy. We will have a hard time reconciling different estimates before we recognize the differing significances of economic, political, psychological, social, or even geographic dimensions of literacy. We must understand that any particular concept of literacy is a political and even moral abstraction beyond the reach of empirical data.[54] Let us look at the literacy movement after 1949 in the light of the broad twentieth-century movement.

The new government in the 1950s vigorously expanded the formal education system, especially in the cities. The main feature of the period was the steady, virtually unavoidable use (indeed continuation) of the "two-track system for dual tasks." Except for comparatively short periods during the Great Leap Forward (1957–59) and the Cultural Revolution of the 1960s, the organizing argument has been, as summarized by one level-headed scholar: "for China to modernize quickly, a large number of experts are needed; to quickly turn out these experts at a time when resources are limited, it is necessary to concentrate limited resources on a few 'key point' schools. These 'key' schools are for the training of experts, while the 'non-key' schools are for raising the cultural level of the masses."[55] The main problems were, in the countryside, the vastness

---

[51]"Vow Against Illiteracy" (Xinhua report from Paris), *China Daily* March 22, 1985, p. 1. Moreover, in the chastened opinion of another outside education expert, the worldwide experience calls for statistical skepticism, for "national literacy statistics are the least trustworthy, and probably the most inflated, of all published educational statistics." Philip H. Coombs, *The World Crisis in Education: The View From the Eighties* (New York: Oxford University Press, 1985), p. 268.

[52]Dwight Perkins and Shahid Yusuf, *Rural Development in China* (Baltimore: Published for the World Bank by The Johns Hopkins University Press, 1984), p. 172.

[53]Fei, *Chinese Village Close-Up* (Beijing: New World Press, 1983), p. 241. Some estimates based on field observation put the rates as low as twenty to forty percent, with at most half the population capable of reading a novel. Perry Link, "Fiction and the Reading Public in Guangzhou and Other Chinese Cities, 1979–1980," in Jeffrey C. Kinkley, ed., *After Mao: Chinese Literature and Society, 1978–1981* (Cambridge, Mass.: Council on East Asian Studies, 1985), pp. 250, 312 n. 47.

[54]Levine, "Functional Literacy," p. 294.

[55]Billie L. C. Lo, "Primary Education in China: A Two-Track System for Dual Tasks," in Ruth Hayhoe, ed., *Contemporary Chinese Education* (White Plains: M. E. Sharpe, 1984), pp. 47–64.

of the numbers involved, and, in the city, the imbalance in production between teachers and babies. When the wave of births from the early 1950s hit the schools, the system was inundated; many of the ensuing problems were demographic, not ideological.[56] In spite of these problems, however, the system has maintained a steady growth in size and sophistication.

If the main force of literacy development was through the formal school system, the paraliteracy movement, or social education, was still given remarkable attention. Literacy campaigns were mounted every few years through the 1950s, with some obvious effect. In 1957, before the inane inflation of statistics of the Great Leap Forward, the government reported more than seven million students in anti-illiteracy classes; since James Yen claimed five million in Mass Education Movement classes in the mid-1920s, the figure seems plausible. National organizations such as the Anti-illiteracy Commission of 1951 and the Anti-illiteracy Association of 1956 mobilized local committees through work-place and residential organizations, which used their own finances.[57] Literacy campaigns were but one tool, standing side by side with efforts in Worker–Peasant Education, language reform, Spare Time Education, Youth Organizations, and so on.[58]

By the time of the Great Leap Forward, however, the tenacity of illiteracy began to make itself felt. Frustration with the conventional school system and its elitist, urban bias combined with Maoist enthusiasm for rapid development based on the creativity of the masses, especially in the countryside. The Peoples Schools were called upon to take up the slack.[59] But once again, extravagant hopes for a magic solution dissipated, and literacy was recognized as a complicated, painstaking matter. National publicity was given to the experience of Wanrong county in Shanxi as a teaching example; a 1958 survey found that of the 34,000 people who had gone through the literacy programs, one-third had already relapsed into illiteracy, and that most of the rest couldn't read a national newspaper.[60]

In the area of language and orthographic reform, the hopes of reformers and fears of conservatives were even-handedly dampened. Vast energy was unleashed—between 1950 and 1958, more than 1,700 schemes for the alphabetization of Chinese were submitted, an outpouring rivalled in the West only by the search for a perpetual motion machine. By the mid-1950s, utopian plans for finally rationalizing the written language gave way to a chastened program in three parts: simplification of the characters by reducing the number of strokes used to write them; the spread of *pinyin* (romanization) though primarily as a

[56] Jonathan Unger, *Education Under Mao: Class and Competition in Canton Schools, 1960–1980* (New York: Columbia University Press, 1982), pp. 16–17.

[57] Bhola, "Anti-illiteracy Campaigns," p. 89.

[58] Leo Orleans, *Professional Manpower and Education in Communist China* (Washington: National Science Foundation, 1961), p. 49. For a more detailed description see Theodore Chen, *Chinese Education Since 1949*, (New York: Pergamon Press, 1983), Chapter Three, "The New Educational Agenda."

[59] Jean Robinson, "Decentralization, Money, and Power: The Case of People-run Schools in China," *Comparative Education Review* 40.1 (Winter 1986), pp. 53–86.

[60] George Jan, "Mass Education in the Communes," in Stewart Fraser, ed., *Education and Communism in China*, cited in DeFrancis, *The Chinese Language*, p. 209. For Wanrong, see also Lin Feng, "All Out Effort in Cultural Revolution" from New China News Agency, June 1, 1960, in Stewart Fraser, ed., *Chinese Communist Education* (Nashville: Vanderbilt University Press, 1967), p. 377.

means of indicating the standard pronunciation, not as an independent phonetic script; promotion of a homogenized national standard dialect (*putonghua*), based on spoken Northern Chinese. Many expressed disappointment at the limited nature of these changes, though it is hard to understand criticism from English-speaking countries which have yet to adopt as rational a reform as the metric system, much less phonetic spelling. As John DeFrancis points out, "in broad perspective, Chinese writing reform is not merely a minor matter of tinkering with the symbols used in writing," but is a "major change amounting to nothing less than the most far-reaching cultural revolution in all Chinese history."[61] Nation-wide use of an alphabetic system for general writing of the language must await nation-wide use of the national dialect, itself dependent on the universalization of primary education in Mandarin.

On the other hand, if we accept the argument made above about the nature of literacy learning in Chinese in the traditional period, we do not need to be pessimistic; literacy is possible without supplanting the everyday use of characters. Doubters should observe Taiwan, where the strong primary school system, built up starting under Japanese rule from 1895 to 1945, has brought nearly universal literacy—without even simplifying characters, much less abolishing them. (A phonetic system is used to give standard pronuciation, however.) Attacks on "feudal" orthography have as much to do with the psychology of the Chinese New Culture intellectual as with practical pedagogy. In the Peoples Republic there is now debate over the nature and future of traditional characters, questioning whether their reform or abolition is desirable, necessary, or even possible.[62]

In the mid-1980s, with China in the throes of normalcy and concerned with economically rational development, government policy is aimed at conserving capital while fostering investment. Nowhere is the tension between constraining reality and social ambition more evident than in the area of mass education, that is, primary schools and adult literacy. The long announced goal of universal five-year education, while surpassed in a number of cities that have reached seven-year school systems, has been reached in the country as a whole in only about a quarter of the populated areas. The census data of the early 1980s show that there are around 230 million illiterates and semi-illiterates, mostly older people, women, and rural residents.[63]

[61] DeFrancis, *The Chinese Language*, Chapter 15, "Writing Reform." His position is, however, that China's sole reliance on characters has "shown itself unsuccessful in producing mass literacy," and that "it seems certain that many if not most of the people will be doomed to perpetual illiteracy" (pp. 286–287).

[62] See Zeng Xingchu, "An Appeal for Justice for Chinese Characters," *Chinese Education* 16.4 (Winter 1983–84), pp. 50–81, and the extremely useful but not entirely convincing rebuttal in "The Continuing Debate on Chinese Characters," *Chinese Education* 18.2 (Summer 1985), pp. 3–20.

[63] "Decision of the CPC Central Committee on Reform of the Educational System" (May 27, 1985), translated in *Foreign Broadcast Information Service*, May 30, 1985; official explication is given in Wan Li, "Speech by Wan Li at the National Education Conference 17 May 1985," translated in FBIS, June 3, 1985; an unusually detailed description of the consultation and decision process is Yang Ruiming, "Pointing the Way to Reforming the Education System," *Liaowang* (Outlook), June 10, 1985, translated in *Foreign Broadcast Information Service*, June 26, 1985.

The rural areas outside prosperous suburbs, comprising another quarter of the population, are largely left with the traditional Peoples Schools. To be sure, we assume that they follow a more modern curriculum than did their Qing dynasty forebears, and certainly they are far more closely supervised, but local officials recently complained that enrollment follows a "three-six-nine" pattern: ninety percent of the school age population enrolls, sixty percent attend, and thirty percent pass. Since the curriculum is set at the national and provincial levels, and since there is little or no chance that the rural classes prepare their students to exam their way into higher schools (which are almost all in the cities and townships), incentive is low. The dropout rates are highest for females, especially since the latest round of economic reforms means that their labor is well rewarded in the fields.[64] Still, the rural economy in general appears to be doing very well in the reforms, and the papers are full of reports that newly prosperous villages are putting money into schools. One of the fascinating questions is whether this development will mean greater local influence on the curriculum, and whether the old diversity of literacies will reassert itself.[65]

We have now reviewed China's experience with promoting literacy in the twentieth century, and can summarize some conclusions. The main conclusion is that China has been successful during this period in making good progress, but that much remains to be done. Progress has come primarily from the steady expansion of the school system, supplemented by adult or social education; there have been no silver bullets or quick solutions, in spite of the range of creative, and sometimes inspired, innovations. The spread of the formal school system appears, for instance, to be much more effective than any of the proposed or partially implemented reforms in the writing system; and literacy campaigns are useful mainly for low-cost mopping up operations and social mobilization.

---

[64] Lo, "Primary Education," pp. 55–60.
[65] See, for example, "Villagers Raise Cash for Schools," *China Daily*, June 5, 1985, p. 3.

CHAPTER 8

The 1961 National Cuban Literacy Campaign

MARVIN LEINER

In 1986, 27 years after its Revolution, Cuba's highest flag is still the banner of education. Almost one-third of the people—three million—including nearly all children between the ages of six and twelve, are enrolled in school. The number of teachers committed to the educational enterprise continues to be a source of national pride.[1]

Yet, on the eve of its revolution in 1959, only fifty percent of the island's children were enrolled in school, and among peasant families, less than half the adults had ever had any education. The Cuban Census of 1953 identified 23.6% illiterate, a total of 1,032,849 adults, with 11.7% located in urban areas and forty-two percent in the rural areas.[2]

As early as 1957, the guerillas in the mountains had decreed in the Manifesto of the Sierra Maestra that, since education was central to the developmental process, the Revolution would immediately start a campaign against illiteracy. Richard Fagen, in one of the earliest analyses of the Cuban education effort, pointed out that "from the very beginning the attack on illiteracy was viewed by the Cuban leadership as not simply a technical or pedagogical problem. It was seen as a profoundly political effort, one tied intimately to the revolutionary transformation of society and the economy."[3]

This theme is a consistent thread in Fidel Castro's speeches. He frequently referred to education as the key to understanding the interconnections between development and revolutionary changes.

This chapter is adapted from a section of the forthcoming book *The Transparent Blackboard: Looking at Cuba through the Schools* (University of California Press).

[1] José R. Fernández, *Desarrollo de la Educación en Cuba*, Speech delivered at the Pedagogía 86 Congress, Jan. 27–31, 1986 (Havana: Ministry of Education), pp. 38, 58.

[2] For documentation of an educational system that had "steadily deteriorated," see Hugh Thomas, *The Cuban Revolution* (New York: Harper and Row, 1971), pp. 349–353; International Bank for Reconstruction and Development, *Report on Cuba* (Baltimore: Johns Hopkins University Press, 1951), pp. 405, 425, 434; Anna Lorenzetto and Karel Neys, *Methods and Means Utilized in Cuba to Eliminate Illiteracy* (UNESCO Report), (Havana: Instituto del Libro, 2nd edition, 1971), p. 15.

[3] Richard R. Fagen, *The Transformation of Political Culture in Cuba* (Stanford: Stanford University Press, 1969), p. 35.

MARVIN LEINER • Department of Elementary and Early Childhood Education, Queens College, Flushing, New York 11367.

> The lack of education is the best index of the state of political oppression, social backwardness, and exploitation in which a country finds itself. The indexes of economic exploitation and economic backwardness coincide exactly with the indexes of illiteracy and the lack of schools and universities. The countries that are more exploited economically and most oppressed politically are the countries that have the most illiterates. . . . Only a revolution is capable of totally changing the educational scene in a country, because it also totally changes the political scene, the economic scene, and the social scene.[4]

During the years following the 1959 victory, Cuba's city streets and rural roads were dotted with banners proclaiming education as a primary theme of the Revolution: "The path up from underdevelopment is education"; "The school plan is your responsibility."

The success of the government's efforts to popularize this philosophy is confirmed by data from the 1985–1986 school year. With 14,600 schools (nearly doubled since 1959), approximately 265,000 teachers and professors, more than 96,000 in the primary schools, and more than 100,000 in the secondary schools, the teaching population is more than eleven times higher than before the Revolution, with 140,000 added to the teaching force since the early 1970s.[5]

There is a huge investment in education in Cuba. The budget of over 1.5 billion pesos with an allotment of 170 pesos per inhabitant compares to eleven pesos per inhabitant before 1959. In 1979, the Cuban per capita figure of 130 dollars per person far surpassed the average spent in Latin America ($73), Asia ($56), and Africa ($33). Cuba had moved to a front position on educational funding among developing countries which was $31 per capita in 1979.[6]

Most observers of the Cuban revolution have acknowledged these tremendous strides in the field of education. In 1979, Erwin Epstein, former president of the Comparative and International Educational Society, praised the Cubans' "heroic effort to raise their standard of education and make learning a natural part of their everyday lives." He observed that "by any measure, the last 20 years of Cuban education have been remarkable. . . . illiteracy has been virtually eliminated. . . . Few if any other nations can claim the use of schools to achieve such a pervasive transformation of social, political, and economic life."[7]

A member of a U.S. science delegation reported that "Cuba's leap into twentieth century science and engineering in only one generation has hurtled the island in most fields beyond its Latin American neighbors." These advances are not restricted to such areas as health care, cattle breeding, and world leadership in sugarcane by-product research. Cubans have pushed "into more sophisticated terrain—computers, interferon, tissue culture and biotechnology."[8]

How was this profound transformation accomplished in such a short time—and in such a tiny and underdeveloped country?

---

[4] Fidel Castro, *Revolución*, Sept. 7, 1961, p. 6. Cited in Fagen, p. 35.
[5] Fernández, pp. 38, 58.
[6] Ibid., pp. 63–64. For additional data on Cuba's ranking in social expenditures, see Ruth Leger Sivard, *World Military and Social Expenditures, 1983: An Annual Report on World Priorities* (Washington, D.C.: World Priorities, 1983).
[7] Erwin H. Epstein, book review of *Children Are the Revolution* by Jonathan Kozol, *Comparative Education Review* (October, 1979), p. 456.
[8] Robert Ubell, "Cuba's Great Leap," *Nature* (April 28, 1983), p. 745.

The pivotal event in Cuban educational change was the National Literacy Campaign of 1961. That campaign, which lay the groundwork for the Cuban philosophy of education and all literacy efforts to follow, inspired in the people the pride, the spirit, and the national will necessary to achieve seemingly impossible goals. It is viewed as a cornerstone in Cuban history, another victorious "battle." Like the Revolution, it had both national and international repercussions. A study of its evolution offers much to literacy efforts around the world.

The Literacy Campaign is a major achievement of the early stages of the Cuban Revolution, representing a "large-scale government effort to advance the level of education and break down the psychological barriers to participation by adults in efforts to educate them."[9] This dramatic nationwide mobilization of teachers, students, workers, and farmers vividly demonstrated a fundamental and repeatedly stated value of Cuban society—namely, that revolution *equals* education—or, in the words of Fidel Castro and Che Guevara, "Revolution and education are the same thing. . . . society as a whole must become a huge school."[10]

Overall, the Campaign utilized the services of 250,000 literacy workers, including 100,000 young people. In the spring of 1961, these students moved to different parts of the Cuban island, especially to the heavily illiterate countryside areas, to identify and teach the illiterate. When the Campaign ended eight months later, the level of illiteracy was reduced to 3.9%.

The view of Cuba as "one large school" extended to all levels and promoted a national political will of "educación permanente," lifelong education. The Campaign utilized the model of revolution (including its language, e.g. campaign, brigades, battle) to inspire mobilization, organization, and commitment. It produced a ripple effect of major, radical changes in schooling at all levels from day care through university, as well as a corresponding impact on the economy and on Cuba's ability to provide qualified candidates for entrance into advanced science, medicine, and technology. It has been called one of the leading international educational and revolutionary stories of the 20th century.

DEVELOPMENT OF THE LITERACY CAMPAIGN OF 1961

The Dilemma

The concept of mobilizing an entire nation to reduce illiteracy may sound good on paper or at a conference—but how does one put it into practice? What educational route does one travel when there are no previous "models" to follow?

Who is to be mobilized? What methodology should be used? Which pedagogic strategies? For example, does one set up thousands of classrooms? Or,

---

[9]Jorge I. Domínguez, *Cuba: Order and Revolution* (Cambridge: Harvard University Press, 1978), p. 165.

[10]"Universidad Popular," *Educación y Revolución*, 6th series (Havana: Imprenta Nacional de Cuba, 1961), p. 271. John Gerassi, ed., *Venceremos! The Speeches and Writings of Che Guevara* (New York: Simon and Schuster, 1968), p. 391.

since Cuba had one of the highest per capita TV set ratios per household in Latin America, should a TV "blitz" be implemented? What about motivation—the historic fear, anxiety, and hopelessness shown by illiterates in previous efforts throughout the world? What about the universal gap between the city and the countryside—the high illiterate rate and the isolation of the peasant? Do the primitive conditions and the rural terrain realistically force the exclusion of the often neglected and invisible peasant population?

Further, how does one even identify the illiterates—location, literacy level, and so forth? Previous efforts by the revolutionary Cuban army, the agrarian reform mobilization, and religious groups were piecemeal efforts. They had opened the door to literacy, but how does one then usher in an entire illiterate population—in Cuba's case, twenty-five percent of the country, one in four adults, or approximately one million people?

The Process

The study of these questions resulted in a fourfold campaign strategy: (1) identifying the illiterate population; (2) recruiting the literacy workers; (3) training the literacy workers; and (4) organizing and implementing the Campaign.

Identifying the Illiterate Population

An illiteracy census was carried out in 1960 and 1961 by teachers and volunteers from mass organizations such as the women's federation, trade unions, and the farmworkers federation. The purpose of the census was to gather statistical data and to gain practical information for the Campaign. Questionnaires were designed to determine residence, occupation, hours of work, history of schooling, and so on.

The difficulty of securing such data has been an international problem of literacy efforts, since illiterates "tended to hide their situation, some for fear of losing their jobs, and others unwilling to confess their ignorance. They resorted to all sorts of subterfuge, even to that of learning by memory the few paragraphs they had to read to prove their knowledge."[11]

According to the census, undertaken both before and after the Campaign, 979,000 were illiterate; 707,212 were taught by literacy workers during the Campaign, reducing the number of illiterates to 3.9% of the population. Of those taught, 476,155 (sixty-seven percent) were located in rural areas, for example, in Oriente province; 237,487 of 300,226 illiterates were in the countryside, usually remote mountainous areas.[12]

[11]Lorenzetto, p. 27.
[12]Richard Jolly, "Education," in Dudley Seers, ed., *Cuba: The Economic and Social Revolution* (Chapel Hill: The University of North Carolina, 1964), pp. 194–195; Also see Lorenzetto, p. 29.

Table 1. Educational Level and Participation of Conrado Benitez *Brigadistas*[a,b]

School level	All *brigadistas*	*Brigadistas* among all those eligible
Primary	52.2	36.3
Junior high school	31.6	47
Senior high school	4.3	23.9
University	4.5	22.6
Teacher	2.6	—
Others	4.8	—
Total	100.0	

Source: Data on characteristics of *brigadistas* are available from Ministry of Education and the Literacy Museum, Havana. These data are from Richard Fagen, *The Transformation of Political Culture* (Stanford: Stanford University Press, 1969), p. 45
[a]Numbers are percentages.

Recruiting and Training the Literacy Workers

The Cubans developed a program of individual teaching by *alfabetizadores* (adult volunteers) and *brigadistas* (volunteer brigades of school-age youngsters).

In April and May of 1961, a media blitz—TV, radio, newspapers, billboard posters—urged youngsters to join the army of *brigadistas*. The appeal, which was frequently emotional, emphasizing that the peasant families and the Revolution needed them, brought forth 100,000 young people from elementary, secondary, and university classrooms.

Forty percent of the *brigadistas* were in the ten- to fourteen-year age level, 47.5% were fifteen- to nineteen-year-olds; the average age was fourteen to sixteen. Fifty-two percent were girls. Almost three-quarters of them came from urban homes, and were assigned to rural provinces, with the easternmost province, Oriente, receiving the largest number (62.1%).[13]

As Table 1 shows, many of the volunteer literacy teachers were older boys and girls who were enrolled in elementary and junior high schools, a reflection of the increased enrollment in 1961. Some of these youngsters had not been enrolled in school at all before 1959. When the revolutionary government called for parents to send all children to school as both a right and a responsibility, preadolescents and teenagers were admitted, not on the basis of age, but according to academic level.

Young people were excited about joining their peers in a brave, bold, and patriotic project. For many of them, it meant traveling to remote country areas in what would be their first trip away from home. For some, permission from parents, who were concerned about health, safety, and separation, was the first hurdle to be faced. *Brigadista* Leonela Relys Díaz recalled that when the call

[13]Ibid., p. 200. See also Lorenzetto, p. 29; Fagen, pp. 45–46.

came in 1961, she was in her first year of junior high school, living with her
family in the province of Camaguay.

> I was thirteen years old. . . . We were given forms to be signed by our families. All my
> friends and classmates were involved in this and I wasn't going to be left behind. We
> all got together, some of us with more support from our families than others, but we
> all decided to fulfill this duty. . . . Nobody [in my family] wanted to sign. . . . I signed
> it myself . . . when the time came, I got on the bus with nothing but the clothes I had
> on, and off I went.[14]

In some families, where parents and older siblings had actively participated
in the Revolution, the youngsters viewed this as their chance to become active
in the process they had witnessed as young children. Rene Mujica explained, "I
felt that I had to do something for my country, even though I was very young.
I felt that I had the responsibility and that I could do it. . . . I was 12 years old
and had just completed primary school."[15]

Training the Literacy Workers

The young volunteers went to the Training Center for the *Brigadistas* at
Varadero Beach, a former tourist area an hour from Havana, for eight to ten
days. Cuban periodicals reported on Varadero with articles and pictures of
brigadistas in their dormitories and classes. "The most beautiful beach in Cuba
and one of the most beautiful in the world is no longer the setting for the
privileged classes. . . . In recent weeks Varadero has been a center for the
brigadistas."[16]

The training included (a) teacher training (instructions on methodology
and familiarization with the key materials: the Primer, *Venceremos*), and the
teacher's manual, *Alfabeticemos*, and (b) orientation to the countryside.

Teacher's Training: (1) The Primer. One and a half million copies of *Venceremos* were printed so that each illiterate could receive one. The teaching strategy utilized what Cuban educators call "social motivation." Political, social, and
economic aspects of the Revolution provided material for the text, in order to
politicize the learner.

The direct political approach is evident from an examination of the fifteen
lessons in the primer: OEA (Organization of American States); INRA (National
Institute of Agrarian Reform); The Cooperative Farm under the Agrarian
Reform; The Land; Cuban Fishermen; The People's Store; Every Cuban; A
Home Owner; A Healthy People in a Free Cuba; INIT (National Institute of
Tourism); The Militia; The Revolution Wins All the Battles; The People at Work;
Cuba is Not Alone; The Year of Education; and Poetry and the Alphabet.

The lesson, La Organización de Estados Americanos (OEA, or Organization
of American States) was chosen to introduce the primer and to begin the reading

[14] Interview with Leonela Relys Díaz, Havana, 1984.
[15] René J. Mújica, "Some Recollections of My Experiences in the Cuban Literacy Campaign," *Journal of Reading* 25 (Dec. 1981), p. 222.
[16] "Los Brigadistas Toman Varadero," *Verde Olivo* 2 (May 14, 1961), p. 18.

program by teaching the vowels. Thus, the instructional usefulness of the OEA letters was coupled with the political significance of the lesson's content—Cuba had been expelled from the OEA just before the Campaign. Similarly, the second lesson focused on INRA (National Institute of Agrarian Reform), an agency which, in 1961, very much affected the lives of Cubans, particularly the peasants.

Abel Prieto, a leading Cuban educator and official at the Ministry of Education, explained the integration of the political and the pedagogical:

> We decided that in addition to the appropriate didactic method adult illiterates required a book whose contents would reflect the reality, offer information on the revolutionary changes, and awaken in people the desire to know more by reading. The *Venceremos* primer was based on this premise, in which the content and method were in harmony. . . .
>   The didactic character of the method is related to the content of the lessons. It is a compound method that combines the global aspect with analysis and synthesis, after having promoted the desire to act and to learn. Moreover, learning to read and write proceed simultaneously. The method guides the literacy worker and provides the illiterate with a way of learning in a conscious and orderly manner. It is based on the characteristics of the literacy worker and the illiterate as the subject of learning. The simplicity of the primer expresses its functionality.[17]

At the beginning of each lesson was a photograph intended to stimulate conversation between the student and the teacher (the *global* aspect). In this way, the teacher learned about the illiterate's experience and knowledge, and had the opportunity to clarify concepts, while helping to overcome timidity and promote expression in the student. Next, using the orientation provided in the manual, the teacher covered the essential points of the lesson, inviting the student "to read."

Following this (the *analysis*), the teacher presented the short phrases which were separate from the main text, reading key words syllable by syllable and emphasizing the syllable chosen for that lesson. Students then practiced, combining the learned sound with each vowel (the *synthesis*). Uniting the syllables, they first formed words with the teacher, then, through reading and writing, formed phrases by filling in the missing words. Auditory recognition was developed through dictation, and cursive writing was begun (see sample lesson from the primer, Figure 1).

Teacher Training: (2) The Teacher's Manual. The stated goal of the manual *Let's Teach How to Read and Write (Alfabeticemos)* was to provide technical assistance, that is, to guide the literacy teacher and to provide content background for the themes of each lesson. It was also designed to heighten the political awareness of the teachers. The revolutionary themes included: The Revolution; Fidel is Our Leader; The Land is Ours; The Cooperative Farms; The Right to Housing; Cuba Had Riches and Was Poor; Nationalization; Industrialization; The Revolution Converts Army Barracks into Schools; Racial Discrimination; Friends and Enemies; Imperialism; International Trade; War and Peace; International

---

[17] Abel Prieto Morales, "The Literacy Campaign in Cuba," *Harvard Educational Review* 51 (February 1981), pp. 35–36. In addition to Prieto's article, other key references on the literacy campaign are Lorenzetto, Fagen, Jolly; and Jonathan Kozol, *Children Are the Revolution* (New York: Delacorte Press, 1978).

A.   The photograph
      A plowed field with a farmer seated on a tractor and another man standing nearby waving
      to each other.
B.   The introductory text
                          INRA
      La Reforma Agraria nació en la Sierra.   [The Agrarian Reform was born in the
                                                       Mountain.]

      La Reforma Agraria da tierra a los   [The Agrarian Reform gives land to the
        campesinos.   peasants.]
      La Reforma Agraria avanza.   [The Agrarian Reform advances.]

C.   Exercise Set A
      1. Vamos a leer. ["Let's read."]
                  La reforma Agraria
                  La Re - for - ma
                  la   le   li   lo   lu
      2. Vamos a leer primero y a leer y escribir despues. ["Let's read first, and read and write
         later."]
                  Lala ala leo
                  Lola ele lea
                  Lula ola lei
                  Lila Ela lio
      3. Vamos a leer primero y a leer escribir despues.
                  El ala ["The wing"]
                  La ola ["The wave"]
                  El lee ["He reads"]
      4. Ponga la palabra que falta. ["Supply the missing word."]
      El_____

      _____ola.

      El _____
      5. Se dictara lo anterior.
             ["The preceding will be dictated."]
      6. Copie con su mejor letra.
             ["Copy with your best handwriting."]

Figure 1. A sample lesson from the *Venceremos* Primer. [a] from Abel Prieto, "Cuba's National Literacy
Campaign," 25 *Journal of Reading* (December, 1981), p. 2117. Adapted from INRA (The National
Institute of Agrarian Reform), Unit 2 in *Venceremos* primer (Havana: Ministry of Education, 1961).

Unity; Democracy; Workers and Farmers; The People, United and Alert; Freedom of Religion; Health; Popular Recreation; The Abolition of Illiteracy; The
Revolution Wins All the Battles; and The Declaration of Havana.

   Orientation to the Countryside. The second area of the Varadero training
provided an education for the urban *brigadistas* regarding the differences in
rural living. Most of them were unfamiliar with the hardships of peasant life:
one-room houses, the lack of electricity and water access, outhouses, different
food customs, hard daily work routine, difficult sleeping accommodations, and
so on. Yet despite this concerted effort, it was understood that nothing could
actually prepare them for "La Realidad" ("the reality") of the work situation.
Learning to teach and to meet the challenge of peasant life could only occur
"out there," among the people.

Each *brigadista* received an equipment package that included the primer and the teacher's manual, a pair of books, two pairs of socks, an olive green beret, two pairs of pants, a hammock, and a shoulder patch of Conrado Benitez (the student teacher who was killed in late 1960 by a counterrevolutionary band, and for whom the student brigade was named). Also included was a lantern to provide light for lessons in homes without electricity, and for travel on unlit country roads. The lantern, a Coleman-type adjustable lamp, was sometimes called the "Chinese lantern" by the *brigadistas* because it was a gift from the Chinese People's Republic. The paraffin lamp became an important symbol, depicted on posters, stickers, and pins, and remembered on anniversaries of the Campaign.[18]

Organizing and Implementing the Campaign

The Pilot Program. The Literacy Campaign was preceded by pilot programs to test materials, evaluate the utilization of young people as alphabetizers, and see what would happen in areas where there were counterrevolutionary groups trying to intimidate and sabotage change—from agrarian reform and improved health care to the literacy efforts.

Raúl Fernández Alech, who was 14 years old in 1961, volunteered to be a part of the pilot program in January.

> I lived in the house of a peasant, a very poor family. . . . I became like another son. In fact, when it was time for me to go, we had truly established a bond of affection.
>
> There were some people who were really hard to teach. . . . At first there were problems with some who couldn't see because of their age. The Revolution gave them all glasses. Everyone was called to a public hall and their eyes were examined for free so that they could read. . . .
>
> The older ones had great difficulty. For example, their hands were the hands of a worker . . . awkward hands for a delicate tool like a pencil. They had trouble holding that insignificant stick of wood. . . . For their whole lives, for thirty or forty years, they had been swinging machetes, axes. . . . We had to take their hands, guide them, until they gained confidence. Because, as they learned to write each word, or letter, they would feel proud and have more interest to keep working. After a while we began to see that they would go into the fields with their workbooks. During their breaks, you would often see them writing. This was proof of their motivation, and it was because they had accomplished something new. . . .
>
> We had a run-in or two with the counterrevolutionaries. On several occasions we were threatened. Since it was in that area where the Bay of Pigs took place, the counterrevolution was rather strong. . . . We were threatened . . . dolls were hung outside our doors with signs, "The next one will be you!" or . . . they threw rocks at us at night, coming out in white sheets to scare us. . . . [But] we became stronger, firmer in our commitment in the face of these pressures. They were trying to stop us from teaching peasants to read and write. . . .[19]

The Assignments. The training period of the adolescent volunteer was then followed by the actual assignment. The experiences vary—depending on the

[18]Marta Rojas, "El Símbolo Fue el Farol" (*Granma*, December 30, 1968), p. 9.
[19]Interview with Raul Fernàndez Alech, Havana, 1984.

particular setting, the personalities, the family dynamics. In rural surroundings where interdependence was the key, the *brigadista* learned to rely on the peasants for security of self and for guidance in survival, and, in turn, became the teacher, the person in command in the area of reading and writing. Leonela Relys Díaz described her experience after the Varadero training:

> When I got to the house where I'd been placed, I was met by a couple who were quite old. The man was about sixty-five and the woman maybe fifty-eight. . . . I cried a lot that night. It was a very dark place. The only light they had was a lamp in the living room. . . . And I was from the city where everything was so bright. But I had my lantern from the Campaign. When I would light it, it would change everything . . . the couple was very warm. . . . They began to be very fond of me, and I of them—so much so that when I left, the tears flowed, as much me as from them. I'd been with them for nine months by then . . . I loved them as if they were my grandparents—my family.
>
> Some of the illiterates were young (nineteen, twenty-five, thirty-six) and they learned very quickly. This, despite my not having any pedagogical experience whatsoever, I didn't know what I was doing. I was doing a job out of this love, my youth, and the desire to do something, but not out of experience . . . it was the actual practice with the people that taught us *how* to teach.
>
> We were able to completely, *completely* make literate four *compañeros*. Totally, fully literate, so today they either have a career or they're studying. With the two from my house, Juan and Eloisa—with her we were able to teach her to read pretty well, and to write somewhat . . . Juan was a man who was 65 years old—very strong—and he said that at this point he had no reason to learn. However, whereas he used to sign by writing an X, we were able to get him to write his name . . . he became so fond of us that he'd come and sit and listen to the class, and so he learned to write his name. More would not have been appropriate; gaining his confidence was quite enough, for he had been totally opposed to learning.
>
> For the four people I did teach to read and write the effect on me has been great. I felt an *enormous* satisfaction to know that I had before me someone who didn't know the letter "a" and that when I finished he was able to pick up a paper and read it. This made me very happy.[20]

In some cases, the entire family was involved in the Campaign—parents and children. Marcelino de la Peña Toranzo remembered not only his working class family commitment and involvement in the Literacy Campaign, but also his participation with peasants in isolated areas of Oriente province.

> I was thirteen and I lived in Holguin . . . In my house we all became involved; my mother, my father, and I all began to work in the campaign. We were what was called "Popular Literacy Workers." That is, we would work with one or two people right near our own home. But then, in May 1961, I joined the brigades . . . [and went to] a zone that was very isolated, a very poor area. They put me in the house of a peasant and his wife and their son who was a bit older than I.
>
> The peasant is a very respectful person. They themselves had offered their homes. I never felt that they manifested any negative attitudes because of my youth. In fact they always called me "usted" [formal usage of "you"]. When we were studying they were always very attentive and respectful.
>
> We tried to help the peasants in their work whenever possible. When we didn't have classes we'd go with them to the fields. In this we learned a great deal. For instance, peanuts—what you get peanut oil from—I'd never seen a peanut plant before. He grew peanuts. I'd go out with him and help him gather the peanuts . . . I missed my

---

[20] Relys Dìaz interview.

family very much. I'd never been away from them. But I was determined to carry out the Campaign as I had decided to.

I recall it was difficult because in addition to teaching them to read and write, we also had to explain the Revolution: the issues, how life was in the past, the things the Revolution planned to carry out, those which it had already done. And in that aspect I must say I did have difficulty. For, as much as they did explain to us, at that age, there were still things I didn't understand. Sometimes the students, the peasants themselves, though they couldn't read, had lived more, so it was they who would explain things to us. The OEA [OAS] for example. I had some idea of what it was but the peasants, they knew. They had knowledge—I'd call it a historical knowledge—related to the history of Cuba—what they had lived through and what they'd heard spoken of.

The Campaign was a great experience for me—in all respects. Firstly because I experienced collective living for the first time, with people from other places, kids from the city with other customs, other styles, kids who were more aware than we were. I experienced life with the peasants as well. This all laid the groundwork for me later to join the scholarship program. Since then I've lived here in Havana. I completed my secondary schooling here and the University with a scholarship. . . . These days the youth celebrate the anniversaries of the Campaign. My children are always proud to be able to say, "My dad was a *brigadista* . . . my dad was a *brigadista*."[21]

Maria Antonieta Paster Escaiy was seventeen when she graduated from teacher-training school in 1961, and answered the call for teachers. She was responsible for supervising other teenagers while also working with her own illiterate students.

I had never before left home. I had been brought up, as we say, "under my mother's skirts" . . . There were eight *brigadistas* under my charge. I also taught three peasants to read . . . We helped the woman of the house. We would go to a stream to wash the clothes and she would teach me because I had no experience at this at all. We would go there with a big pile of clothes and we would hit them on a rock. And we'd also rinse the clothes there and then bring them back home. They also taught us to cook several dishes.

I was responsible for several *brigadistas* . . . At times there were lessons about farming, for example, and I'd help them see they could take advantage of their surroundings—the countryside, the animals, to relate it to words, the lessons.[22]

STAGES OF THE CAMPAIGN

On a recent trip to Cuba, I visited the municipality of Melena del Sur, in the province of Havana. Melena del Sur holds a special distinction: on November 5, 1961, it was declared by Fidel Castro to be the "first territory free from illiteracy." Melena del Sur symbolized the beginning of victory in the final stage of the battle against illiteracy (see Table 2).

A museum—like the larger one in Havana—displaying *brigadista* uniforms, the lantern, samples of the final exam letters written to Castro, and other artifacts, was established there to commemorate the Campaign. To my knowledge, these are the only museums in the world (besides the one in Managua, Nicaragua) that celebrate a national literacy campaign.

[21] Interview with Marcelino de la Peña Toranzo, Havana, 1984.
[22] Interview with María Antonieta Paster Escaiy, Havana, 1984.

Table 2. Literacy Results: Municipality of Melena
del Sur, "First Territory Free From Illiteracy"

	Number	Percentage
Attending school	0	0
Taught	2,269	79.11
Still illiterate	412	14.37
Transferred	61	2.13
Deaths	23	.80
Incapable of learning	103	3.59
Total	2,868	100

Source: These data are from Ana Lorenzetto and Karel Neys, *Methods and Means Utilized in Cuba to Eliminate Illiteracy* (UNESCO Report), 2nd Ed. (Havana: *Instituto del Libro*, 1971), p. 48.

Table 3. The Teaching Force in the Literacy
Campaign

Literacy workers	Number
"People's Teachers" (*Alfabetizadores Populares*)	121,000
"Patria o Muerte" Worker Brigade	15,000
Professional School Teacher Brigade	35,000
Conrado Benitez Student Brigade	100,000
Total teaching force	271,000

Source: These data are from the final report of the National Literacy Commission ("Literacy in Cuba," Havana MINED mineographed, Dec. 21, 1961), p. 28; Richard Jolly, "Education" in Dudley Seers, ed., *Cuba: The Economic and Social Revolution* (Chapel Hill, N.C.: University of North Carolina Press, 1964), p. 197.

The Initial Stage: January 1–April 30, 1961

In this stage, the structure was established. The first to be mobilized were the people's *alfabetizores*—those men and women who volunteered to teach, contributing their free time. This group totalled 121,000 (see Table 3).

The National Literacy Commission, the agency in charge of the Campaign, then decided to close the schools on April 15th and extend the Campaign to the 100,000 school adolescents organized in the Conrado Benitez Brigade. These students, together with the people's *alfabetizores* and a workers' force added in August 1961, totalled 236,000, in addition to the 35,000 supervising teachers.

The Consolidated Structure: April 1–September 5, 1961

During this period, the structure was revised with strong decentralized support by the mass organizations, such as the Committees for Defense of the Revolution (CDR), Women's Federation, and so forth, which reached out to the most isolated, neglected areas.

The teaching structure was built around a ratio of 2:1, two illiterates to each alphabetizer, and a Literacy Unit composed of about twenty-five literacy workers, a professional teacher, a political advisor, and a chief of unit. Each province and each municipality had Commissions of Coordination, Execution, and Inspection. Thus, the professional teachers and the mass organizations were integrated in a decentralized mode of operation that built on the experiences of the first stage.

Previously, the professional teacher was directly in charge of the illiterates, in a unit called the Literacy Nucleus. In the revised structure, the teaching responsibility was left to the literacy worker, while the professional teacher acted as technical advisor, and the political activist took over such tasks as visiting students, handling absenteeism and other problems, and "striking up enthusiasm." However, where the old system worked well, it was allowed to continue.[23]

The "ideal" relationship of two illiterates to one alphabetizer was embodied in the formula $QTATA^2$, which had been publicized by the leaders of the Revolution and the Literacy Campaign. "To every illiterate an alphabetizer, to every alphabetizer an illiterate" ("Que todo analfabeto tenga alfabetizador, que todo alfabetizador tenga analfabeto"). The slogan was publicized with posters, stickers, and emblems that portrayed a double handshake (one, a white arm and a black arm; the other, a black arm and a white arm) emphasizing the unity and integration of the people in the Campaign.[24]

War Footing: September 5–December 22, 1961

A National Literacy Congress, held in Havana in September 1961, of educators and workers from all over Cuba directly and openly criticized the shortcomings of organizational and technical aspects of the Campaign and led to the concentrated effort in this phase, which is shown in Table 4.[25] As each municipality was declared free or nearly free from illiteracy, the organizers, technical staff, and volunteer *brigadistas* moved out to assist other communities.

Almost half the illiterates were taught in November and December as the mobilization went on a "war footing." Volunteers intensified their work, and new forms of mobilization were initiated: Acceleration Camps, the Revolutionary Vanguard, and Study Coaches.

The Acceleration Camps

The acceleration camps or literacy schools were modeled after a camp for illiterate soldiers established in Melena del Sur in 1959. The new camps offered all-day intensive programs taught by teachers, *brigadistas*, and *alfabetizadores* for those who had not completed the Primer. This was a team effort by the mass

---

[23] Interview with Abel Prieto Morales, Havana, 1969. He was the Director of the Literacy Campaign in the province of Pinar del Rio in 1961. He also served as Director of Primary Education in Cuba, Vice Minister of Education, Director of Adult Education and Advisor to the Minister of Education.
[24] Raúl Ferrer, "Informe de la Comisión Nacional de Alfabetización," *Congreso National de Alfabetización* (Havana: Imprenta Nacional de Cuba, 1961), p. 19.
[25] Ibid., pp. 9–127.

Table 4. Progress of the Literacy Campaign, June–December 1961

	June 30	July 31	August 31	October 31	End of campaign December 21
Illiterates located	684,000	822,000	985,000	988,000	979,000
Persons studying	465,000	594,000	776,000	500,000	n.a.
New literates (cumulative total)	22,000	62,000	119,000	394,000	707,000

Source: Data are from Richard Fagen, *The Transformation of Political Culture*, p. 50, and Richard Jolly in Dudley Seers, ed., *Cuba: The Economic and Social Revolution*, p. 195.

organizations, e.g., members of the CDR, or workers who would enable others by replacing them at their regular jobs to attend literacy classes. (This model of workers doubling up for peers to free them for another community task was later used to ease the Cuban housing crisis in the 1970s.)

The Revolutionary Vanguard

These new mobile teacher teams, organized in the province of Havana, were composed of two groups: one sent by special automobile service to remote areas, and the second sent to work in the slums of the city of Havana.

The Study Coaches

In November, *alfabetizores* were trained to help those municipalities that were having difficulty completing the Campaign. These Study Coaches, after training in the use of the Manual and Primer, also travelled to remote areas that needed more literacy workers.

After Melena del Sur was declared the first territory free of illiteracy, the competitive spirit rose as neighboring communities strove to finish first. With each declaration, the literacy workers moved to the next municipality, creating a surge of excitement locally and nationally in the final stage of the Campaign (see Table 4).

TV, radio, press, public meetings, celebrations of each victory, and diploma-granting events were actively used to encourage illiterates. Poems, hymns, and popular songs were broadcast regularly, increasing as the Campaign progressed. In April, the radio began forty-five-second announcements fifteen times a day. The press published the Primer in installments, in addition to a multitude of announcements, photographs, interviews and articles. In August and September alone, hundreds of articles were published.

The Evaluation Methods

There were three tests in the evaluation process: at the time of the census, to determine literacy levels; midway through the work, to determine the progress of the student; and at the end, to determine whether the person was literate. (This final test was composed of reading two short paragraphs from the Primer, a brief dictation, and writing a letter to Fidel Castro.)

CHARACTERISTICS AND STRATEGIES OF THE LITERACY CAMPAIGN

National Goals and Educational Changes

The literacy campaign must be viewed as part of an overall Cuban national strategy for the development of society. The revolutionary leadership immediately set Cuban education on a new path. By providing large budgets for school construction, program development, teacher training, and the national mobilization to eliminate literacy, the new government halted stagnation and gave education the highest priority, both in planning and in practice. Schooling was made available to all, especially the poor in rural areas. Education was redirected to achieve national goals, that is, "to replace the rigid class structure of capitalist Cuba with a classless and egalitarian society; to eliminate sexism and racism; to end the city's economic and cultural domination over the countryside."[26]

In addition, education became a tool for promoting development through the training of a skilled and technically proficient population. This strategy also drastically altered the traditionally hostile attitudes toward science, technology, and modern agricultural methods.

Why did the Cubans choose the strategy of closing the schools—of dedicating so many months of concentrated, focused attack on the illiteracy problem at the sacrifice of the regular school schedule? The Cubans had concluded that "the only way for education to truly be part of our revolution is to make it possible for everyone to learn [and to] teach."[27]

> There is a very positive correlation between our economic and social development and the literacy campaign. We closed the schools for eight months so that *everyone* would get into the teaching, students and teachers. Also, those who were already in school could wait a year, but we felt that the illiterates *could not wait*!
>
> One question that they have asked us at international conferences is, "why did you rush so much?" To develop a country like ours, which was in a state of absolute underdevelopment, we needed technicians, middle-level technicians, qualified personnel . . . we couldn't wait for years. The plan worked: many of those who were illiterates in 1959 are today doctors, architects, engineers, department heads, directors, leaders.[28]

---

[26]Samuel Bowles, "Cuban Education and the Revolutionary Ideology," *Harvard Educational Review* 41 (November, 1971), p. 474.

[27]Interview with Raul Ferrer, 1969. He was a leader of the National Literacy Campaign of 1961, executive secretary of the National Literacy Congress (1961), and National Director of Adult Education. He is currently advisor to the Minister of Education.

[28]Interview with Fernando García Gutierrez, a veteran educator who was an administrator (Head of the Department of Educational Aids) in the Institute of Pedagogic Sciences, Ministry of Education, Havana, 1983.

Nationwide Participation: Cuba's "Epic Poem"

In 1969, Raul Ferrer, reflecting on the lessons of the Literacy Campaign, explained to me what he called the "Primary Law of the Campaign," that "there is no mass education without the support of mass organizations."

> The Ministry of Education alone cannot satisfy the demand for education in our country. If this support is missing, the adult masses—the illiterate, semi-literate or those who have not yet completed elementary school—do not have the opportunity to make study a regular part of their lives.[29]

This "primary law" makes it difficult to answer the question, "What were the costs of the campaign?" or "What is the cost of adult education?" because the Ministry of Education statistics do not give the full picture of expenditures. According to Ferrer, though the Ministry spent some fifteen million pesos in 1969, other organizations, such as the Women's Federation or unions, spent much more. Through their own initiative, they invested in material and physical resources, teachers, personnel, equipment, publishing, and so forth.

Abel Prieto views Cuban strategy as a "national poem" and emphasizes the need to eliminate the source of illiteracy.

> I think a literacy campaign *must be for the masses*. The enthusiasm must be national, *it must be taken up like an epic poem*; then nationwide, encouragement must be offered to all within that suffocating atmosphere in which illiteracy exists.
>
> If you pick a narrow base, you can conceivably do a better job qualitatively—but for a select, small number of people. But if you choose narrow work horizons, you'll never get rid of illiteracy. This is something that's very important in our literacy campaign. It was based upon two key principles: one, if you can find illiterates among the lower classes, you will also find literacy teachers. And the second principle is that whoever knows a little bit more much teach those who know less. . . . In conjunction with the literacy campaign, an efficient national system of education must be created, which will prohibit the further production of illiterate people.[30]

Strengthening of City–Country Bonds

Again and again, Cuban educators emphasized that a key goal, and accomplishment—perhaps as important as the actual literacy results—was the cultural exchange, communication, and strengthening of ties between the urban and the rural population, that is, the industrial worker and the agricultural worker. Besides increasing awareness concerning agriculture, it also increased the mutual respect and recognition of the city person and the *campesino* through their alliance in a joint cause of national development and self-improvement. Together they experienced the power to change their lives, and learned how national unity could make possible the gargantuan strides needed to move Cuban society into the twentieth and twenty-first centuries. Ferrer notes that this was possible because of a "revolutionary conception of the Literacy Campaign."

[29] Ferrer interview, 1969.
[30] Prieto interview, 1969.

Changes in People's Lives

The experience of the Literacy Campaign had a powerful effect on young people and adults. New literates utilized previously untapped potential by continuing their education and developing new skills and occupational opportunities. This enabled them to pursue more technical and professional responsibilities. When I asked one campesino in the mountains of Oriente, "What is Cuban Communism?", he said, "I don't know what Communism is, but agrarian reform, free doctors and hospitals, and my chance to read and write is what the Revolution means to me."

At the same time, the young teachers had an opportunity to confront the facts about their country, to learn about Cuba's problems and the real meaning of underdevelopment.

The Effects of the New Pedagogy

"The National Literacy Campaign had opened the way to participation of the masses in education. It established a direct dialogue which never existed before between the different social strata in the population . . . *participation* became the crux of the pedagogy."[31]

The lessons of the new pedagogy developed during the Campaign became the basis for changes in school level structures from 1961 to the present. Developmental changes in education are often cited with reference to the Literacy Campaign. For example, the secondary education programs of the School to the Countryside (1960s) and the School in the Countryside (1970s) were unique Cuban models that emphasized the participation of high school students in both academic activities (peer tutoring and group study), and organizational activities (responsibility for productive farm work, recreational programs, and living arrangements).[32]

A Model to Resolve the Manpower Dilemma

In Cuba, the exodus of many middle-class professionals after the Revolution at the same time as the opening of schools resulted in a critical lack of trained personnel. Yet, the Literacy Campaign accomplished educational goals with a minimum of trained personnel through its advocacy call of "They who are literate teach the illiterate." It tapped the resources of young people by deemphasizing credentials and allowing thousands to become teachers. This strategy enabled them to move with the present resources on a broad mass base, and then, at a later stage, to focus on raising the quality of teaching personnel. Changes in the construction of society were not forfeited because the "ideal"

[31] Raul Ferrer, interview, 1980.

[32] Gaspar Jorge García Galló, "La Escuela al Campo," *Educación en Cuba*, 1 (January–February, 1967), p. 8. Also see Marvin Leiner, "Cuba's Combining Formal Schooling with Practical Experience," in *Education for Rural Development: Case Studies for Planners*, edited by Manzoor Ahmed and Philip Coombs (New York: Praeger Publishers, 1975), pp. 61–110.

personnel were not available. Later, when public day-care centers were opened for the first time in Cuban history, the Cubans again turned to the "paraprofessional solution" by mobilizing the teenage population and the underutilized potential of older women.[33]

In the 1970s, with the next step of radical change—the tremendous expansion in secondary education—Cubans drew upon recent graduates of their own secondary schools to solve the teacher shortage. The teacher-training approach of "learn and teach" at the same time, which uses the *en campo* (in the countryside) school as a training center, is an approach that merits careful attention by developing nations facing similar shortages in personnel.

Structural Flexibility

The basic organizational structure was modified according to the actual experience during the Campaign. This flexibility provided a mobilization apparatus and a rhythm of centralized support, while also permitting local autonomy in order to weigh the resources, needs, and characteristics of a particular region. It supported a principle that organization is most effective and best developed when it comes from experience and is not superimposed.

Similarly, the policy of delimiting the Campaign opened it to bold and dramatic approaches, while at the same time setting realistic goals that were not overambitious and self-defeating. The Campaign did not take over other aspects of revolutionary work such as family planning and agricultural improvements, which might defeat the specific literacy objectives by attempting too much.

Uniqueness of the Cuban Campaign

Cuban educators viewed the Campaign as a uniquely Cuban experience with motivational factors that stemmed from the Revolution and the political character of the Campaign. When questioned about its differences with other developing countries or the undeveloped areas (e.g. the inner cities) of the developed countries, they acknowledged that Cuba did have certain conditions that were favorable for a national campaign:

> Cuba's twenty-five percent was a lower illiteracy rate than for many other countries. . . .
> [There was] one sole language for the whole country. . . . We have great homogeneity.
> But our greatest advantage is not language homogeneity or that only one in four adults
> were illiterate, it is that we are in revolution, with a tremendous enthusiasm.[34]

This enthusiasm or motivation exists, according to the Cubans, because a better life will follow from their efforts. This is part of the political character of the Campaign.

Abel Prieto questioned the possibility of transferring the Cuban experience

---

[33] For further discussion of Cuban day care personnel problem and the "paraprofessional solution," see Marvin Leiner, *Children Are the Revolution: Day Care in Cuba* (New York: Penguin Books, 1978), pp. 33–50.

[34] Prieto interview, 1969.

without a radical restructuring of society and without consideration of significant conditions.

> We had the unique presence of a prime minister who was practically the first to head the campaign. That is to say, the State doesn't simply observe with approval and satisfaction, but rather the head of state himself is most concerned with carrying out the campaign, and he supplies both the resources and the enthusiasm; he created the environment, the sensibility; he helps us in all that work. . . . [These] are elements that made the literacy campaign easier for Cuba.
>
> We also had a literacy force of some sixty or seventy percent of the population. There are countries where ninety-eight of every hundred people are illiterate. . . . To make a simple comparison to other countries is completely unscientific. Comparative education is a very difficult science, because if you're lacking the sensibility to be able to comprehend the subtleties, the characteristics of the nations, the idiosyncracies of their peoples, you can easily be deluded. . . .
>
> Now, when a change occurs in the social structure, the resources are multiplied. The same thing could happen in a Latin American country with several languages— in Peru, Bolivia or any other. Immediate solutions present themselves. There's a phrase I've used many times in literacy congresses: One cannot lose sight of the fact that the illiterates are found among the people, but so are those who will teach them. . . . [but where] the literacy force is minimal, then outside help is needed. . . .
>
> Of course every country must carry out its own literacy campaign. When I say its *own* literacy campaign, it's because each country has its own characteristics. What seems inevitable is this: for a country to carry out a far-reaching literacy campaign, it must undergo a complete revolution. That is to say, without agrarian reform of considerable breadth and depth, it's very difficult to undertake the work of literacy. The two things are linked.[35]

Fernando García Gutierrez, an administrator in the Institute of Pedagogic Sciences, Ministry of Education, in response to the same question, states that revolution alone is not enough. Literacy, a pivotal keystone for development depends upon important variables of genuine material commitment and use of mass methods. A radical change in the economic and social system is not an exclusive prerequisite.

> Any nation which liberates itself [and] which wants to develop has to begin by eradicating illiteracy because a country with millions of illiterates cannot develop.
>
> Massive literacy work can only be done on a mass scale with mass methods. In other words, where there are mass numbers of illiterates, only mass methods can resolve the illiteracy; there is no other route. Now, this is a problem of the willingness of the government. I wouldn't want to say that it is necessary to have a revolution, but it is necessary that the government understand that it must alphabetize the entire population and that it put into action the whole power of the society for this task . . . that it must mobilize all of the people.[36]

THE FOLLOW-UP

The striking achievements of the Literacy Campaign provided the impetus for continued expansion of educational programs since 1961. Abel Prieto pointed out, in a conversation about the concept of literacy, that

[35] Prieto interview, 1969.
[36] Gutierrez interview, 1983.

Cuba has not rested on its laurels, nor will it ever rest. We know that a residual illiteracy remains. The massive campaign had to be done first, to stimulate education on all levels. However, there is a difference between follow-up and our campaign. In the literacy campaign, the illiterate person was furnished with a reading teacher right in his house. After the campaign, adult classrooms were created, which made it necessary for the adult to go and get his next steps in education in a school or a factory class.

At the end of our campaign, we'd completely finished with illiteracy in Cuba, but not with illiterates. People get confused; illiteracy is one thing and an individual illiterate is something else; illiteracy is a social phenomena. There continue to be illiterates in Cuba but we've eliminated illiteracy as a social phenomenon.[37]

With the nation at a beginning level of education, the next step in the literacy movement was the Battle of the Sixth Grade. In 1963, Lazaro Peña, leader of the Cuban trade union movement, instituted an academic testing program for all workers. The results showed that of 1,102,153 workers tested, 81.1% had a level below sixth grade. Thirteen years later, the 1974 census revealed that 39.3% were still below the sixth grade level.[38] At the thirty-fourth Council of the Cuban Workers Federation (CTC), held in February 1975, a new literacy program was proposed. Fidel Castro announced strong support for the proposal to achieve a minimum grade level of sixth grade for all workers by the year 1980.

A national commission was established, and the resources of the nation were mobilized to see that workers and farmers achieve this literacy level, reiterating the words of Castro and Guevara that "without this minimum of knowledge [6th grade level], it is difficult to participate with efficiency in the process of revolutionary changes and the construction of socialism."[39]

The strategy and guiding principles were: (1) the minimal sixth-grade level was accepted as crucial to "the production of work and the quality of services"; (2) active support and cooperation by the agencies of the state, the trade union movement, and other mass organizations were necessary for the success of the plan; and (3) the problem of teacher shortage was to be solved by a twofold team effort—selection of teachers by the trade unions and preparation by the Ministry of Education. "The working class guarantees the teachers" was the slogan adopted to solve this problem.

Table 5 shows the results of the strides in adult education for the five-year period 1975–1980. During this time, 848,812 adults completed the sixth grade, whereas 535,100 farmers and workers graduated during the thirteen years before.

How was this accomplished? Once again the nation was mobilized, though this time young people's schooling was not interrupted. The Battle of the Sixth Grade was spearheaded by the full force of the trade union movement and other mass organizations such as the Cuban Federation of Women and the Organization of Small Farmers. Thousands of "advanced workers" attended seminars

[37] Prieto interview, 1969.
[38] Rosario Fernández Perera, Raul Ferrer Pèrez, Teodomira Aguilar Abreu, Jaime Canfux Gutiérrez, Lorenzo Rabre Alvarez, *La Batalla por el Sexto Grado* (Havana: Editorial Pueblo y Educaciòn, 1985), pp. 7, 86–88.
[39] Ibid., p. 11.

Table 5. The Battle of the Sixth Grade: Adult
Education Sixth-Grade Graduates

	Sixth-grade graduates
1961–1974	535,106
1975–1980	848,812
1980–1984	118,177
Total	1,502,095

Source: Rosario Fernández Perera, Raúl Ferrer Pérez, *et al.*,
La Batalla por el Sexto Grado (Havana: Editorial Pueblo y Educación, 1985), p. 53.

and were trained in teaching methodology. The adult education structure that
had been developed since 1961 was utilized and expanded.

Adult education is one of the major subsystems in the Cuban educational
structure, given high priority, alongside general education (elementary and secondary) and higher education. The adult education structure includes Worker
and Farmer Education Programs (EOC) (four semesters equivalent to elementary
level), Worker and Farmer Secondary Education Program (SOC) (four semesters
equivalent to junior high level), and Worker Farmer Faculty Programs (FOC)
(equivalent to senior high level), an independent study program (utilizing TV
and radio programming), classes in factories, and farm centers, night schools,
and classes in alternative settings, such as community centers.

The Cubans have found that workers (peer teachers) with special training
became the most effective instructors. Thus, in 1976–1977, fifty-three precent
of the 24,200 adult education teachers were workers. Thousands of new texts
were developed to achieve the advanced literacy goals. Texts in Spanish, mathematics, natural sciences, geography, and history were issued with new editions
and revised curriculum. Flexible academic calendars were adjusted to specific
working conditions in different industries.

Table 6 shows the curriculum for the Worker Farmer Education Program.
Mathematics and science received forty percent of the class time, following the
fifty percent for language arts. This emphasis is consistent with a very strong
current focus in Cuban schools on science and mathematics. Cuban educational
strategy hopes to overcome a historic Latin American tradition of heavy curriculum time on literature and philosophy with a neglect of the sciences. Castro
has stated that this unbalanced tradition must be challenged and changed if
Cuba and other Latin American countries are to become developed nations.[40]

A fundamental factor in providing solutions to the complex problems presented in the Battle of the Sixth Grade was the use of a plan called *Emulación.*

---

[40] Closing Speech by Fidel Castro at the Pedagogy 86 International Congress held in Havana, 1986;
also see Marvin Leiner, "Cuba's Schools: 25 Years Later," in Sandor Halebsky and John Kirk, eds.,
Cuba: Twenty-Five Years of Revolution 1959–1984 (New York: Praeger Publishers, 1985), pp. 33–
35.

Table 6. Curriculum in Worker-
Farmer Education [EOC]: Number of
Hours in each Subject Area

Subject	Hours
Spanish and literature	320
Reading	200
Handwriting	60
Spelling	80
Mathematics	440
Sciences	80
Geography	60
History	40
Total	1,280

Source: Rosario Fernández Perera, Raúl Ferrer Pérez, *et al.*, *La Battala por el Sexto Grado*, p. 93. See also *Informe Sobre la Educación de Adultos en Cuba* (Consulta Regional Sobre la Educacion de Adultos en America Latina y el Caribe, 5–9 de septiembre de 1983). (MINED: Cuba, 1983), p. 68.

A Cuban system of "socialist competition" to motivate and challenge individuals, work centers, and communities, *Emulación* was implemented through "The Movement of Four Steps for the Sixth Grade." These four steps corresponded to the four semesters or levels in the Worker Farmer Education Program (EOC) needed to reach the equivalency of the Sixth Grade. A card was given to each adult, and four stamps were pasted on the card as he/she passed each semester.

When I visited factories, day care centers, or any work center, I saw murals posted with the number of workers involved in the campaign and with such information as attendance, target dates, academic progress, and, of course, the "successes"—numbers of workers who were involved and had completed levels of study. Also prominently displayed were banners of *emulación*, of "victory over illiteracy," and of centers and municipalities that had won the Battle of the Sixth Grade. "Best units" were defined by highest percentages of students who attended classes and who passed the course levels.

There were mass graduations of students, with ceremonies to celebrate the "Victories of the Sixth Grade" in provinces, municipalities, work centers, and union halls. Outstanding workers and centers received "material and moral rewards." More than a million people participated in these events, which were held in plazas, parks, provincial and municipal main streets. Leading popular musical groups and singers performed. "This constituted a social recognition that included warm enthusiastic support by the top leadership of the country, of the party, the government, the CTC, and other mass organizations. . . . *Emulación* always influenced matriculation, the attendance of students, the promotion, the search for the appropriate teacher for every classroom in every collective."[41] In short, the Cuban reward system stated very explicitly that

[41] Fernández Perera *et al.*, pp. 12, 43.

production figures were not enough; educational progress was a significant criterion in evaluating the achievements of a work center.

The Battle of the Sixth Grade was followed by a campaign for the next level, and on January 30, 1986, the Cuban press proclaimed in banner headlines that Cuba had also won the "Battle of the Ninth Grade." During this period 1980–1985, 672,123 workers had completed those adult education course requirements.[42] On the university level, fifty percent of the current student body works, and higher education is not only tuition-free but students receive support in the form of lodging, board, and stipends as well.

Problems of growth and development continue to surface. In my visits to adult education classrooms over an 18-year period, I have noted the difficulties presented by utilizing an unevenly trained teaching force, including peer teachers. Though I have witnessed creative and exciting lessons in progress, I have often observed a rigidity in classroom style that is characterized by the monotonous copying of chalkboard notes. Cuban educators have indicated an awareness of this dilemma and have stated that, with the goal of *basic* literacy fulfilled, they now seek to emphasize the improved quality of instruction that was sacrificed for quantitative change.

It has been noted that the literacy level achieved through the 1961 Campaign represented a first-grade, rather than a fourth-grade level, which is considered by some experts as the requirement for "functional literacy."[43] However, Cuban educators hold that the success of the Campaign was to bring illiterates to a *beginning grade level of reading*, the crucial breakthrough for all further schooling, and the foundation for their principle of "life-long education." This is the vital factor in evaluating the Cuban venture: that the transformation continues, with unwavering support for a universal free system of education, and a series of impressive achievements that have not daunted the desire for more.

These achievements are the culmination of a twenty-five year follow-up program that was put into operation after the 1961 Literacy Campaign, which remains the Cuban benchmark of national pride in educational "victories." This Cuban experience has been viewed as a model for developing countries, especially in Latin America. The Cubans demonstrated both that massive nationwide literacy mobilization and participation can be achieved and that national modernization can be advanced by integrating literacy education within the historical and contemporary context of the society.

At the Pedagogía 86 International Congress in Havana, a teacher from Argentina, one of 3,500 delegates from 35 countries, said to me, "I think the Cubans have an obsession." She smiled and added, "The obsession is education. At the rate they are going they will have a school and a teacher for every person."

---

[42] Dulce Maria Hernández, "Ganô Cuba La Batalla por el Noveno Grado," *Juventud Rebelde* (January 30, 1986), p. 1.

[43] Prieto commented on the UNESCO drive towards "functional literacy": "The teaching of 'functional literacy' is a concept which states that the illiterate person does not stop being illiterate until he has acquired a level of skill that permits him to do better, to reach a better standard of living. But that better standard of living is conditioned by the social structure. Because of that it's a contradiction, like taffy being pulled."

Indeed it was this national "obsession" that, in 1961, became a magnificent "epic poem" involving the whole country in the commitment to eliminate illiteracy. And in 1986, the "obsession" persists, beyond the Battles for the Sixth and Ninth Grades, moving Cuba further into the educational spotlight, in its quest for "educación permanente" for all.

CHAPTER 9

The Experimental World Literacy Program

A Unique International Effort Revisited

ARTHUR GILLETTE

INTRODUCTION

The preceding chapters of this book have looked at a number of national efforts, past and recent, to come to grips with adult illiteracy. Illiteracy has not, however, been a solely national concern; nor has literacy work been an exclusively national enterprise. Since the end of World War Two, for example, many international nongovernmental organizations have been active in this area, as have a number of bilateral government-to-government programs of aid and cooperation.

At the multilateral level, the United Nations Educational, Scientific and Cultural Organization (UNESCO) was entrusted, from its creation nearly forty years ago, with both a standard-setting responsibility and a technical-cooperation function concerning adult education generally and adult literacy more specifically.

A high point in UNESCO's literacy efforts came in the period from 1967 to 1974 with the organization of the Experimental World Literacy Program (EWLP). EWLP was an unprecedented, and remains in educational history an unequalled, multilateral literacy venture in terms of international resources mobilized, political and technical interest aroused, and controversy unleashed. These unique dimensions, coupled with the unusually large body of relatively reliable and comparable data generated by EWLP and analyzed in its final report, *The Experimental World Literacy Program: A Critical Assessment*,[1] suggest that it may be worthwhile to revisit the Program, with the purpose of attempting to derive some still-valid lessons for national and international planners and practitioners.

---

[1]*The Experimental World Literacy Program: A Critical Assessment* (Paris: The Unesco Press and UNDP, 1976). See also *Documents from the Experimental World Literacy Program* (Paris: Unesco, 1979).

ARTHUR GILLETTE • UNESCO, Paris 75007, France. The views expressed in this chapter are solely the responsibility of the author and do not reflect those of the organization where he is employed.

This return trip cannot be relaxed tourism, however, because there is still disagreement over the value, results, and even intentions of EWLP. Also, to do justice to its object, this chapter's itinerary, while proceeding as dispassionately as possible, must not take evasive detours around any of the landmark (or stumbling block) issues that continue to raise controversy even today.

To situate the climate of discussion about EWLP in proper perspective, the chapter will look first at the dispute that surrounded the publication of the Program's final report. It will then, by turns, outline factually what EWLP actually was, discuss the Program's strategy, attempt to derive some practical lessons from EWLP's major variables, and examine EWLP's results in terms of new literates' profiles; it will end with a word about international cooperation's role in the field of literacy.

MUCH ADO . . . ABOUT WHAT?

Third World illiteracy is not usually deemed important enough news to make the front page of major Western newspapers. With the publication in 1976 of the official EWLP report, cosigned by the Director General of Unesco (the executing agency) and the Administrator of the United Nations Development Program (UNDP—the funding agency), came, however, a spate of front-page dispatches in dailies including the *International Herald Tribune, Le Quotidien de Paris*, and the *New York Times*, whose article, relayed through the New York Times News Service, was picked up by the *Washington Star, Denver Post, Atlanta Constitution, Minneapolis Tribune*, and *Louisville Courier-Journal*, among others.

Some of this reporting stressed the nature, extent, and consequences of illiteracy, and the difficulties of tackling it through international action (and national action, for that matter). Other articles, unfortunately, seemed more designed to attack UNESCO than to inform readers about illiteracy. Under the headline "UNESCO Hides an Embarrasing Report," *Le Quotidien de Paris* affirmed that "The information service of UNESCO has chosen to 'mute' the text"[2] of the report. This was an incorrect affirmation, since when the article appeared, the report was on sale at the UNESCO Bookshop and could have been had free of charge by any journalist who requested it from the UNESCO Press Room.

The *New York Times* article gave an even more curious twist (to use a polite word) to the facts. Picked up in the *International Herald Tribune* under a front-page headline that read "10-Year-Old Program to End World Illiteracy Fails, UNESCO Admits," the article's lead read: "An ambitious UNESCO project to eradicate illiteracy, begun a decade ago, has been a dismal failure, according to the organization's own report."[3] Had the author of these words bothered to read the opening sentence of the report itself, he would have known that "A fully

[2] Christian Delahaye, "L'Unesco cache un rapport embarrassant," *Le Quotidien de Paris* (28 September 1976), p. 4.

[3] Andreas Freund, "10-Year-Old Program to End World Illiteracy Fails, Unesco Admits," *International Herald Tribune* (6 February 1976), p. 1.

literate world: such was not the immediate aim—still less the main result—of the Experimental World Literacy Program."[4]

Attacking UNESCO for not achieving a goal it had, quite explicitly, not set out to achieve became something of a journalistic sport in the months following the EWLP report's publication. Why did this happen? It seems possible to identify a number of reasons. One was the tone of the report itself. Although a piece in the *Harvard Educational Review* said "it abdicates its major responsibilities,"[5] *Le Monde* called it "a very honest stock-taking."[6] Indeed, its frankness on numerous issues, including self-criticism of UNESCO and UNDP, was unusual for an official document of the U.N. system. Some journalists found the temptation too great, perhaps, and indulged themselves and their readers nearly to the point of intoxication.

The self-criticism of a major U.N. development effort was also grist for the mill of observers who doubted the capacity of intergovernmental bureaucracy to come to grips with such a widespread and complex problem as illiteracy. The pro-development optimism of the early 1960s (amounting to euphoria in some quarters) had waned, as such large multilateral ventures as the First U.N. Development Decade and UNCTAD showed themselves insufficient stimulants and forums to bring about real change in the poor countries—and in the rich countries' attitudes toward the poor countries.

A less flattering factor in the minds of some editors and publishers may have been the wish to sieze on EWLP as a weapon with which to strike back at UNESCO for resolutions adopted against Israel by its General Conference two years before the EWLP report's publication.

Whatever the reasons, the *Critical Assessment* generated, unintentionally and for reasons that may have been largely extraneous to literacy or international cooperation in its favor, so much heat and smoke that light was largely obscured. Despite continuing irritation in some quarters, it does now seem possible, a decade after the report's publication, to seek illumination from it. In the first place, what exactly was the Experimental World Literacy Program?

THE NATURE OF EWLP

The Program had many parents: decolonization, with its attendant demand for basic education, growing acceptance by governments of out-of-school education, the persistent perception of education as a universal human right, and U Thant's call at the beginning of the first U.N. Development Decade for a development that was social as well as economic. The *primus inter patres* was a 1961 U.N. General Assembly that asked UNESCO for a report on world illiteracy

[4]*The Experimental World Literacy Program*, p. 9.
[5]David Harman, "The Experimental World Literacy Program: A Critical Assessment," *Harvard Educational Review* 3 (1977), p. 444.
[6]Guy Herzlich, "Plus de huit cent millions d'adultes sont encore analphabètes," *Le Monde* (10 September 1976), p. 3.

and recommendations for action. According to Kenneth Levine, Unesco reacted "with a massively ambitious plan for a worldwide frontal assault on illiteracy."[7] Even revised, the proposal was to teach literacy to 330 million people, at an approximate total cost of two billion dollars spread over a decade.[8]

Although the 1963 General Assembly offered general support to this plan, it was dropped. One reason was cost. It was at one and the same time too expensive (a two hundred million dollar-a-year sustained outlay for ten years was perhaps not an entirely realistic expectation) and too cheap (a unit cost per new literate of 6.06 dollars certainly seems unrealistically low). An additional reason for the abandonment of the mass design was probably the then-ascendant influence of education-qua-investment economists, for whom literacy work should be focused selectively on the actual or potential producers of a given society.

Whatever the reasons, the mass approach was discarded, or at least postponed, and replaced, at the 1964 session of UNESCO's General Conference, by "a five-year experimental world literacy program designed to pave the way for the *eventual* execution of a world campaign in this field."[9] How would a limited program "pave the way" for a broader campaign? By providing, in the words of the U.N. Secretary General when he presented the new UNESCO proposal to the General Assembly, "valuable information on the relationship of literacy with social and economic development,"[10] that is, through experimental and research activity as well as actual literacy work.

To prepare implementation of the 1964 decision of UNESCO's General Conference (to launch an EWLP as yet without upper-case letters), Unesco convened a World Congress of Ministers of Education on the Eradication of Illiteracy at Tehran, in 1965. This gathering gave political support and technical content to the Experimental World Literacy Program, which began to get under way the next year.

Many countries were involved in EWLP in a variety of ways. The foci of the Program were, however, eleven countries, in each of which took place one or more geographically limited pilot projects executed by UNESCO with UNDP funds. These countries and actual expenditure figures are found in Table 1.[11] The main components of external assistance were experts (policy, programming, training and research/evaluation design and implementation), equipment, fellowships, and some cash transfer for special activities.

Although patterns differed from one country to another, each national sequence included (sometimes in different order): formulation of policy and objectives; determination of the number and kind of people to be made literate; formulation of the administration and organization of the project; appointment,

---

[7] Kenneth Levine, "Functional Literacy: Fond Illusions and False Economies," *Harvard Educational Review* 2 (1982), p. 252.

[8] Mark Blaug, "Literacy and Economic Development," *The School Review*, p. 408, as cited in ibid., p. 252.

[9] Thirteenth Session of Unesco's General Conference, quoted in *The Experimental World Literacy Program*, p. 9 (emphasis added).

[10] U Thant, quoted in ibid., pp. 9–10.

[11] Figures from *The Experimental World Literacy Program*, passim.

Table 1. Respective Actual Expenditure of Governments
Participating in
EWLP and UNDP[a]

		Government[b]	UNDP[a]
Algeria		4,793,100	1,009,500
Ecuador		1,071,400	1,193,800
Ethiopia		1,661,700	1,812,000
Guinea		229,500	756,000
India		4,164,200	143,800
Iran		4,268,900	1,683,300
Madagascar		366,100	558,500
Mali		1,099,600	1,400,700
Sudan		636,700	674,700
Syria		44,700	251,400
Tanzania		2,870,000	1,327,300
	Totals	21,205,900	10,811,000
	GRAND TOTAL	32,016,900	

[a]Amounts expressed in U.S. dollars.
[b]Note that the nature of inputs is not always comparable from country to country.

training, and deployment of instructors and other staff; development of teaching materials; preparation and implementation of a research and evaluation schedule.

The overwhelmingly vocational orientation of the projects is shown in the following two series of figures. In terms of economic activity, eighty-six percent of EWLP learners were identified as in the agricultural sector, while 3.6% were in the industrial sector. From the standpoint of vocational orientation, of the 131 specific curricula that were developed, forty-one percent were agricultural, twenty-eight percent industrial, thirteen percent related to craftwork, and eighteen percent had a more general socioeconomic bias, such as hygiene, child care, civics, and so forth.[12]

Leaving aside figures for a moment, it should also be said that EWLP was, for at least certain UNESCO officials and experts and not a few project-country nationals, a time of exceptionally deep commitment, unusually intensive enthusiasm, and freely accepted, long and active hours, not to forget hardships. There was, at very least at some times and in some places, the sense of belonging and contributing to an important and unprecedented international pedagogical adventure. This feeling has marked, for better rather than worse, many of the individuals involved. It would perhaps not be misleading to suggest that this was a major, if unquantifiable, EWLP legacy. We shall, however, come to qualitative outputs a bit later in this chapter.

For the moment, and in conclusion to this factual outline of what EWLP was, quantitative data are reported concerning how many Program participants reached what stages of literacy at what cost. Figures given here refer to definitions

[12]Marcel de Clerck, *L'Educateur et le Villageois: de l'éducation de base à l'alphabétisation fonctionnelle* (Paris: L'Harmattan, 1984), p. 178.

Table 2. Evolution of Learner Participation in Five EWLP Countries.

	Initial enrollment	Examinees	Pass
Tanzania	466,000	293,600	96,900
Iran	97,400	46,900	13,900
Ethiopia	36,800	21,700	9,300
Ecuador	17,500	10,000	4,100
Sudan	7,400	2,400	600

Table 3. Unit Costs of Learners in Various Stages of EWLP Projects in Eight Countries.[a]

	Total estimated cost per enrolled participant	Total estimated cost per final participant	Estimated cost per final participant excluding research and evaluation (operations only)	Estimated total cost per participant passing final examination
Sudan	7.00	272.00	110.00	269.00
Madagascar	112.00	126.00	48.00	—
Ecuador	70.00	123.00	70.00	300.00
Iran	49.00	100.00	76.00	332.00
Algeria	71.00	99.00	83.00	—
Ethiopia	54.00	92.00	63.00	212.00
Mali	14.00	35.00	17.00	—
Tanzania	7.00	10.00	9.00	32.00

[a]Amounts expressed in U.S. dollars.

of literacy that differed from country to country, and are in any event of varying reliability; no hard and fast comparisons should be drawn from them.

Something over one million people were initially enrolled in the literacy courses offered under EWLP in its eleven focal countries. Table 2[13] offers absolute rounded figures on the number progressing from enrollment through sitting for final examinations to passing those examinations in five countries from which it proved possible to obtain relatively reliable and comparable data on this subject. Even a cursory look at this table suggests two things. First, given the high attrition rate reported, one tends to trust the reporting. Secondly, the attrition rate seems, indeed, very high; only twenty-five percent or less of initial enrollees passed the final exam.

Unit costs per participant at different stages are available for eight EWLP countries covering cost per enrollee, per final (presumably exam-sitting) participant, per final participant excluding research and evaluation costs, and per participant passing the final examination (five countries). Scrutiny of these data in Table 3[14] yields a number of hypotheses of interest.

[13]*The Experimental . . .*, p. 174.
[14]Ibid., p. 185.

The first (obvious, perhaps, but sometimes forgotten in literacy planning and shown here with stark clarity) is that high drop-out rates lead to correspondingly high costs per successful participant. Secondly, the experimental nature of EWLP, with large inputs for research and evaluation, appears to have raised costs considerably in most cases, more than doubling them, for example, in Madagascar and Sudan.

Thirdly, however, one may expect that once the pilot stage of a literacy program is over, unit costs will decline since (a) increased numbers of participants should yield economies of scale, and (b) while some research, development and evaluation expenditure will continue, major outlays in these areas should no longer be necessary (since the initially developed and tested materials, methods, curricula, etc. can, on the whole, be replicated).

It is difficult to test this last hypothesis, since the only EWLP country to have expanded pilot work into a major campaign following the Program, Tanzania (there being a revolutionary hiatus between Ethiopia's EWLP project and its current campaign), had and has continued to have limited research, development and evaluation costs.

Finally, how were costs distributed in terms of budgetary allocations? Data are only reported on one (unnamed) country, which, however, is said not to have been especially atypical in this regard. These figures (which do not cover capital expenditure or the costs of international and some national staff) show the following breakdown into percentages of overall expenditure: remuneration of instructors: 30; preparatory and research studies: 23.5; administration: 21; transport: 8; training of instructors: 6.5; teaching materials: 5; classroom equipment: 4.5; audiovisual materials: 1.5.[15]

THE EWLP STRATEGY

Widely touted as something of a breakthrough, at very least a way of paving the way for a possible future world campaign when there was not the will to launch such a campaign immediately, the EWLP's strategy was never clearly, completely, and definitively spelled out before or during the Program. It evolved as EWLP went along. In retrospect, however, it seems possible to identify five chief components of the strategy: functionality, intensity, selectivity, innovativeness, and experimentation.

Generally opposed to "literacy for its own sake," *functionality* was defined as follows by the 1965 Tehran Congress:

> Rather than an end in itself, literacy should be regarded as a way of preparing man for a social, civic and economic role ... reading and writing should lead not only to elementary general knowledge but to training for work, increased productivity, a greater participation in civil life and a better understanding of the surrounding world and should ... open the way to basic human culture.[16]

---

[15] Ibid., pp. 184–185.
[16] Quoted in ibid., p. 10.

Who would quarrel with the above definition? What major literacy program in process or recently terminated at the time of Tehran advocated literacy for its own sake? At a period when education was increasingly viewed as an important contributing factor to multifaceted development, *dys*functional literacy appeared to be something of a straw man concept.

A real issue did emerge, however, in 1966 and 1967, when the Tehran guidelines of 1965 were forged into operational definitions in the various countries' project documents. On the one hand, as will be seen below, the Program did innovate, insofar as it integrated unusually large quantities of functional material into the literacy curricula, which in turn had repercussions on the kinds of teaching staff required and the methods they used.

On the other hand, however, and in contrast with the broad, balanced, and multipurpose social, economic, civic, and cultural functionality advocated at Tehran, the central (albeit far from only) criterion adopted by the Program was rather narrowly work-oriented functionality. In all participating countries, literacy was closely linked with industrial, agricultural, and craft training, although secondary activity did take place in other areas (e.g. homemaking and family planning for women).

This conceptual narrowing or reduction of functional literacy to a primarily production-related role appears to have been largely the result of economic-oriented thinking then current at EWLP's major funding agency. According to a recent memoir of one of the Program's artisans, "the UNDP had made its participation in EWLP conditional on the orientation of literacy to vocational training."[17]

Looking back, it now seems possible to clarify some of the confusion that has surrounded discussion of functional literacy. The real debate is not between literacy for its own sake and functional literacy, but between different kinds of functional literacy. Seen in this light, the 1980 Nicaraguan Literacy Crusade was, for example, just as functional as EWLP, the difference being that the first had largely political functionality while the second was vocationally functional.

A second element in the EWLP strategy was *intensity*. Much used during the Program, the term seems to have had several meanings. In one interpretation, literacy became intensive when something (usually vocational content) was added to the three Rs. In another, intensity implied that the overall time required to achieve literacy would be telescoped, presumably with more hours of learning per week making it possible to reduce the number of weeks needed. Focusing of resources—more inputs per learner to achieve fuller and/or shorter learning— was a possible related interpretation of intensity.

In sum, it appears that intensity took on a life of its own as a term or slogan (rather than a well-defined concept), meaning different things to different people in different contexts. If such ambiguity did not actually harm the EWLP strategy, it cannot be said to have contributed to its clarity—or solidity.

Selectivity was, in constrast, a sturdy cornerstone of the Program's strategy. According to it, teaching was on the whole focused on groups most likely to turn

---

[17]de Clerck, pp. 178–179.

literacy and allied vocational training into increased production. Thus, EWLP displayed "more than occasional preference for the most favored of the impoverished—a kind of 'élite'—seen as needing only a small educational push to move over the threshold of modernity. . . ."[18] Who were these "élites of the impoverished"? Farmers with access to arable and irrigable land in areas where sharecropping or peonage was the rule, and workers with salaries, no matter how small, in cities where unemployment was widespread.

Such selectivity was perhaps the only realistic approach in certain of the countries participating in EWLP. It did, however, raise the problem of equity, particularly in countries that were anxious, and perhaps able, to move more quickly toward mass literacy action (Guinea, Madagascar, Sudan and possibly Tanzania).

An issue at stake here is the degree of rigidity and uniformity that is necessary and possible in an international literacy strategy. Selective, vocationally functional literacy could have been offered as one possible approach, appropriate for some countries, less so in others. Unfortunately, EWLP thinking seemed to harden into something of a dogma, which assumed that selective, vocationally functional literacy was the best (if not the only) approach. Since EWLP, Unesco has fortunately returned to a much more flexible and diversified policy.

As stated at the beginning of this chapter, EWLP was an unprecedented international effort in the literacy field. As such, the Program was, by nature as well as intent, a breeding ground for educational innovation. *Innovativeness* was, in fact, a major, if largely unstated, element of the EWLP strategy. In country after country, teams of international and national staff worked out new curricula, materials, and methods, developed improved training packages, and generally gave fresh impulse to literacy work and adult education. In Mali and Tanzania, the Program is recalled nostalgically by specialists who took part as something of a halcyon period of innovation.

Yet, EWLP was not exempt from an overemphasis on the technical aspects of its work. Innovation is a necessary, but not sufficient, condition for successful literacy. When the Program was being formulated, a developmentalist (or, more crudely, technocratic) approach to economic growth and social change prevailed in international circles. Thus, literacy work then being carried out was assumed to fail primarily because of inadequate know-how. The problem was thought to be mainly technical in nature, and it was only logical that its solution should also be sought primarily through technical innovation (i.e., the work-oriented functional approach).

It was perhaps also logical (but nonetheless curious) that the EWLP strategists virtually ignored the recently completed Cuban literacy Campaign, which was anything but innovative in technical terms (the actual teaching was very close to directive school pedagogy), which indeed violated several basic EWLP precepts (it was massive rather than selective, it was politically rather than vocationally functional, it used a single curriculum and manual rather than a diversified/adapted approach, and it was definitive rather than experimental)—and which

[18]*The Experimental World Literacy Program*, p. 162.

was nevertheless a resounding success. The Cuban effort demonstrated forcefully that pedagogically *un*innovative literacy action could succeed. It perhaps prompted the EWLP's final report to suggest that "a crucial lesson of EWLP seems . . . to be the need to avoid viewing or designing literacy as an overwhelmingly technical solution to problems that are only partly technical."[19]

A final major element of EWLP's strategy was, as its title indicates, its *experimental character*. What, in global terms, the experiment was supposed to be and do was never made entirely clear, however. The nature and purpose of the experiment seemed to evolve over time and vary as a function of the expectations of different entities involved in the Program.

At first, it was apparently intended to test the hypothesis of a positive correlation between literacy and (particularly economic) development, by determining, with experimental groups of learners and control groups of nonlearners, if and how the acquisition of work-oriented literacy skills went hand in hand with increased productivity, improved consumption patterns, and other manifestations of better socioeconomic well-being. Then, the emphasis shifted from testing—with the possibility for inconclusive or negative results—to demonstrating the hypothesis—with no option for failure. Finally, it seemed that the correlation was assumed to be an already-proven thesis.

Within EWLP, moreover, there were at least two schools of thought on experimentation. For the first, "windtunnel" school, the Program was a laboratory in which technical improvements in various aspects of literacy work would be made through controlled scientific experimentation before massive expansion would take place. For the second, "runway" school, EWLP was a process of incremental pragmatic enrichment, leading naturally to expanded action. It viewed EWLP "as a plane full of passengers rather than a prototype flown by a test pilot."[20]

On the face of it, *conclusions* for strategists emerging from EWLP seem contradictory.

Where the Program did have clear and solid components of strategy—its mainly vocational functionality and its selectivity—they were not well-suited to the policies of all participating countries, and were looked on as something of an imposition by certain of them, accepted mainly in hope of obtaining international resources for literacy that would not otherwise have been available.

On the other hand, EWLP strategy components that were ill-defined, changing, or otherwise elusive—intensity, innovativeness, and experimentation—contributed to confusion and gave rise on occasion to irritation and even conflict, none of which helped the Program, its implementers, or the illiterates it was meant to serve. So it appears that one is damned if one has a clear, solid strategy, and damned if one doesn't.

In the event, however, the double-bind concerned not the fact of having a strategy, but the nature of the components of EWLP's strategy. When clear and solid, they were too limiting; and those that were neither clear nor solid did

---

[19] Ibid., p. 122.
[20] Ibid., p. 129.

not have the virtue of being intentionally flexible and adaptable. Major criteria for a successful international literacy strategy would seem, then, to include a mix of clarity, solidity, flexibility, and adaptability.

MAJOR VARIABLES AND SOME PRACTICAL LESSONS

The previous section concerns the EWLP's architecture, and may be chiefly of interest to international planners; we now look at the Program's nuts and bolts—hopefully of equal concern for national and international specialists. Who staffed the Program? What curricula were used? What methods? What institutional arrangements were adopted? On what premises did classes take place? What languages were used for instruction? What postliteracy follow-up was provided? Answers to these questions will, it is hoped, yield some practical pointers.

Regarding *staff*, and turning first to the top-level policy makers, continuity was a problem in several EWLP countries. The first three years of one project were severely disrupted by no less than seven changes of the Minister of Education. Some policy makers were reticent because they viewed the Program "as designed to disseminate a pre-packaged, self-contained innovation with which national innovators were not expected to tamper."[21]

At the middle level, EWLP found the usual complement of bureaucrats for whom the Program was a wearisome imposition, and field work an exile. Because of its unique nature, however, it also does seem to have sparked enthusiasm in an exceptional number of cadres. In addition, it showed that the link with functional subject matter and the intention to innovate in terms of materials require the mobilization of a wide variety of professionals whose skills are not normally allied with literacy work: extension officers, factory foremen, journalists, graphic artists, and so forth.

The Program did not (and did not set out to) solve the old argument of professional versus volunteer/amateur literacy instructors. In India, most instructors were, in fact, village schoolteachers who worked at literacy part time. At the other extreme was Mali, which used no teachers but called on skilled workers and students. Most participating countries fell in an intermediate position. They used teachers (with special training, as in Tanzania) while also calling on skilled workers, students, literate farmers, and the like (in Algeria, one-third of project instructors had not completed primary school). Training was provided to these nonprofessionals, who in some cases taught vocational subjects as well as (or instead of) three-R lessons. The impression emerged that technicians who taught literacy got better results than schoolteachers who also gave vocational instruction.

In most EWLP countries, a task profile of the ideal literacy instructor appeared that overlaps with, but extends well beyond, the skills profile and attitude pattern of many primary-school teachers. The ideal literacy instructor should be capable of "teaching the three Rs, classroom vocational teaching,

[21] Ibid., p. 132.

practical training via demonstrations, animation and understanding of—and sensitivity to—adults of the least favored socio—economic strata."[22]

Many approaches to training were used in the different national projects. There was, at the end, consensus that long preservice training with no systematic follow-up was not as effective as short initial training followed by regular refresher sessions. The latter method had three advantages: it provided repeated reinforcement; it enabled trainees to use their personal classroom experience as raw material in the follow-up sessions; and it provided instructors—often working in isolated villages—a chance to get together, socialize, and build an *esprit de corps*.

"Integration" was the guiding principle according to which vocational subject matter was added to basic three R teaching in EWLP *curricula*. At one extreme was Sudan, where heavy stress was put on vocational subjects, and relatively less importance accorded to literacy. At the other were Mali and Algeria, where the three Rs occupied 80% of class time. In between were eight other countries where the vocational-to-three-R ratio was 1:2.

The vocational subjects were supposed to be designed on the basis of an analysis of problems actually encountered by workers and farmers during their productive activity. Statistically significant research results suggested that when this happened, literacy programs were "more effective."[23] But who identified the problems to be covered in curricula? Problem-detection surveys were run in all countries, but did not always include the illiterate producers among respondents. In some cases, only supervisory personnel were polled; in two countries, the economic development authorities alone set vocational curriculum objectives; in another, expatriate experts were left to make curricula decisions on their own.

When workers were surveyed, it happened that the problems they identified did not lend themselves to solution through education (e.g. low wages), but required social change. This led EWLP evaluators to postulate that literacy "brings about a change for the better *on condition* that it is associated with a process of genuine innovation (of a political, social, or technical nature) in which the participants themselves are involved."[24] Similarly, it was concluded that vocational subject matter should not be linked too narrowly, rigidly, or mechanically to performance of learners' jobs.

There is perhaps here a kernel of more general wisdom about education and social change. Human beings resist being reduced to machines. It is their humanity, not perversity, that makes the planner's equation

Input (education) + *process* (individual and/or group)

= *Output* (economic development)

often unpredictably dysfunctional. On a recent visit to rural Tanzania, I stopped at a number of village libraries. From carefully kept loan registers, librarians, borrowers, and a look at the shelves, it was clear that books on farming, clean water supply, latrine digging and the like are not best-sellers. Rather, newly

[22] Ibid., p. 134.
[23] Ibid., p. 159.
[24] Ibid., p. 160 (emphasis added).

literate villagers seem to favor love stories and stories more generally, politics, religion, and a biography of the Brazilian footballer Pelé. EWLP's empirical evidence suggests, then, that a general climate of socioeconomic change that personally concerns the lives of illiterates can help motivate them to learn, but also that, once they have learned, they may prefer to read about football rather than food production. Is that somehow futile, wrong? Is not the delivery of choice real empowerment?

In terms of *teaching methods*, EWLP experience seems to have confirmed the validity of three tenets of andragogy that, if not particularly new (much less revolutionary), are not yet put into practice where school-based pedagogy is still used with adult learners. The first is an inductive approach to knowledge acquisition. Group discussions were the starting point of each class meeting in several EWLP countries, for example. Naturally, discussion that seems superficially non-directive can be subtly structured by instructors or "natural leaders" present in the group. Nonetheless, several projects explicitly recognized adults' ideas and insights as valid starting points for learning. Albert Meister, critical of many other aspects of EWLP projects he observed, concluded that "overall, the teacher's view of the adult pupil has been enriched by the realization that the illiterate adult knows and understands many things; their approach has therefore become more andragogic."[25]

Experiential learning was a second widespread method used in EWLP. Workshops, fields, demonstration plots, and the like were recognized as legitimate locales for learning. In at least one case, Tanzania, profits from the sale of produce from literacy-demonstration plots helped offset the cost of the classes, although this was not their central purpose, which remained pedagogical.

In Iran, a study attempted to identify different rates of adoption of new crops and techniques between older autonomous farmers, whose classes had demonstration plots, on the one hand, and classes without demonstration plots, on the other. Statistically significant differences judged positive were found. Results suggest that adoption of new-taught techniques is also a function of learners' actual postlearning prospects for applying those new techniques. Thus, positive effects were not found among farmers under 25 years of age with no access to land.[26]

Finally, and although no research was carried out on the subject (which was not an explicit part of the methods tested during EWLP), stimulus variation appeared in a number of projects as a kind of intuitive way of maintaining adult learners' interest. Recourse to a variety of methods and techniques typified classes in Sudan, for instance; there, sequences included oral expositions (by the class instructor, then visiting technicians), group discussion (problem- and solution-oriented), audiovisual aids, individual and joint use of written materials, field visits, and practical demonstrations.

The major lesson to be derived from EWLP as regards the most appropriate *institutional arrangements* for literacy is that there is no magic solution to the problem. At the national level, with the understandable desire to confer a dynamic

---

[25] Albert Meister, *Alphabétisation et Développement* (Paris: Anthropos, 1973), p. 137.
[26] *The Experimental World Literacy Program*, p. 167.

identity on the EWLP project, several countries set up autonomous structures, outside the institutional framework of other educational and developmental activities. This created friction among programs and staffs, and in virtually all cases the responsible structure was merged into preexisting institutions, generally the Ministry of Education.

In turn, a single-ministry setting made it difficult to have access to the services of other vertical parts of the bureaucracy, crucial though such services were for literacy work attempting to integrate vocational and other development-related elements. The predictable result: in one country, agricultural extension workers attached in principle to the project had no contact with literacy instructors who taught the same pupils but were responsible to another ministry.

Even attempts to achieve compromise or intermediate solutions did not have notable success. Cooperation bodies, ranging from national advisory committees to coordinating councils with (in principle) more executive muscle, were created, modified, disbanded, resuscitated, to little avail. In no case does it seem possible to attribute project success or failure to the structural formula ultimately, if uneasily, settled on, or even correlate the with it. "Finally," according to the EWLP evaluation, "there seems to have been no satisfactory and replicable solution to the autonomy/coordination dilemma."[27]

Much the same may be said of the centralization/decentralization question. This is the more regrettable since a measure of local learner self-government was part of the EWLP's approach. In 1973, the UNESCO Secretariat affirmed that

> functional literacy work cannot be designed from outside, in accordance with the mechanistic approaches of traditional pedagogy. It presupposes active participation on the part of those concerned at all stages of preparation and implementation.[28]

Attempts were made in Algeria, Guinea, and particularly Tanzania to provide for a degree of devolution of responsibility to this class itself. In Tanzania, elected class committees were empowered inter alia to enforce participant discipline, spend money made from demonstration plots, and schedule classes. This last function was not without importance, since it could result in classes deciding to extend schedules that, in turn, could require extra government spending for additional teaching hours.

Internationally, the institutional relationships were also complex. UNESCO and UNDP were both involved in all projects, and there was between them, according to the final report signed by both, a "fundamental disagreement at various times . . . about the relative priority to be accorded to literacy programs in the framework of economic development and scarce international resources."[29] Further complicating relationships was the participation in some projects of other technical or funding agencies, both bi- and multilateral.

One disappointment noted by the EWLP evaluators was the unrealized potential for involvement in the Program of international nongovernmental organizations (NGOs) and their national branches in project countries. After

[27] Ibid., p. 145.
[28] Quoted in ibid., p. 146.
[29] Ibid., p. 148.

some initial efforts, "the movement of joint and active international NGO participation in EWLP slowed, and then stopped. . . . Joint action in the framework of EWLP . . . died a premature death, depriving the Program of an important consortium of partners."[30] Why this happened is still not entirely clear. Inter-NGO cooperation has, however, again become a real possibility with the creation by Unesco in 1984 of an annual Collective Consultation of NGOs on Literacy.

As for *premises*, EWLP dealt a body blow to the "edifice complex." Many classes did, of course, take place in rural primary schools, often a village's most modern and (costly) construction, with cement walls and a tin roof. But churches, mosques, factories and other work places, private homes, and even the shade of trees were also used, and shown to be adequate locales in which literacy could be taught successfully.

From the pedagogical point of view, the organization of classes in varied settings offered the advantage of providing a physical link with reality, particularly the reality of learners' actual working situations. Sometimes the link was not fully exploited by instructors who did not themselves view such settings as pedagogically worthy places. Elsewhere, unthinking organizers appear to have followed instructions rather ineptly: one demonstration plot was hardly bigger than the UNESCO expert's office. But on the whole, EWLP did confirm that successful literacy work does not require a "normal" or "modern" classroom.

From the economic point of view, diversification of premises enabled most Program countries to make fuller use of already-existing educational and other plants, thereby reducing costs. Also, economies were achieved when, as in Ethiopia, learners built their own facilities; a similar practice in Tanzania led to a national policy under which villages only receive government assistance to build educational facilities if they themselves provide labor and materials.

With regard to *language*, statistically significant research results led EWLP evaluators to postulate that "the closer the language used to present the content and materials of the course to the workers' everyday language, the more effective the literacy program."[31] This sounds a reasonable, even banal, proposition today; but at the time of the Program there was still considerable reticence about breaking away from the former colonial language as the medium of instruction outside, as well as inside, the school. In Mali, new ground was broken thanks to EWLP: national languages were transcribed, a lexicon and grammar were prepared in Bombasa, teaching materials developed and used, and a popular rural newspaper issued for new literates. Still today, the responsible government unit is called National Directorate of Functional Literacy and Applied Linguistics.

Elsewhere, however, progress was far from remarkable. In some multilingual countries such as India, problems arose in maintaining full fidelity to the meaning of the language in which materials were prepared while making them thoroughly comprehensible to speakers of the language(s) into which they were translated. The international element compounded the complexity on occasion. In one case, original drafting was done in Russian, then translated into English,

---

[30] Ibid., p. 149.
[31] Ibid., p. 170.

then from English into the major national language for distribution to learners who did not speak that language (much less English or Russian). In this connection, the possible use of international funds to promote literacy as a means of spreading the national language to assimilate (subdue?) minority groups appears to have raised sensitive cultural, and thus political, questions in certain instances.

If the Experimental Program's creators gave thought to post-EWLP work, it was primarily with a view to the possible World Campaign toward which EWLP was to pave the way. There was a widespread (if not universal) implicit assumption in the Program that once people had become literate they would stay literate. The major focus had, therefore, to be on making him or her literate.

In reality, EWLP countries encountered serious difficulties in providing *postliteracy follow-up* reading materials. Indeed, "the very term 'follow-up' seems to have lulled several projects into assuming that such materials were of secondary or auxiliary importance only."[32] Nothing, EWLP demonstrated, could have been farther from the truth. Literacy, of the levels to which it was taught in most national projects, was not self-sustaining. Unless nourished by periodicals, books, and other reading matter, and unless developed by further education, newly acquired literacy tends to wilt, wither, and die.

Even in highly literate societies, the care and feeding of the three Rs is more than a marginal activity, as Britain, America, West Germany, and France found out when in the late 1970s or early 1980s they discovered that perhaps as many as 15% of Johnnies, Johanns, and Jeannots could not really read.[33] How much more awesome, then, is the task of postliteracy work in situations where the majority is illiterate, where the printed message is an exception rather than the rule, and where writers, publishers, libraries, and other facilities for its production and wide dissemination (often in more than one previously uncodified language)—not to forget opportunities for continuing education—are few and far between.

In such settings, according to the EWLP final report, creation almost *ex nihilo* of indispensible postliteracy facilities "may be tantamount to setting up the material infrastructure of a literate society."[34] This lesson has been well illustrated by a country like Tanzania, whose experimental EWLP project bloomed into a full-scale national literacy campaign which, in turn, has given birth to a whole new written literature in Kiswahili, an extensive network of rural libraries, eight widely read rural newspapers, and a pervasive and varied menu of postliteracy learning opportunities: residential, in villages, and by correspondence.

Yet, the magnitude of the postliteracy work required for initial literacy to have a good likelihood of success appears to be occasionally ignored and often underestimated, even on the part of serious promoters of literacy. Hurried to engage in mass literacy activities as soon as possible after liberating the national territory, the Nicaraguan Sandinista authorities do not, for example, seem to have given sufficient initial thought to postliteracy; and if postliteracy is a working

[32] Ibid., p. 139.

[33] Véronique Espérandieu, Antoine Lion, and J.-P. Bénichou, *Des Illettrés en France* (Paris: La Documentation Française, 1984), p. 32; Ali Hamadache, "Illiteracy in the 'Fourth World'," *Unesco Courier* (February 1984), p. 25.

[34] Ibid., p. 140.

proposition today in that country, it is largely a result of psychological mobilization of the population (which could perhaps have been helped by better initial planning for the transition from literacy to postliteracy).[35]

In conclusion, major "nuts-and-bolts" outcomes that can be culled from EWLP may be grouped into four categories.

First, the Program could not but restate certain dilemmas that are as familiar as they seem to be inextricable. No breakthrough was evident with regard to certain institutional problems (autonomy vs. coordination, centralization vs. decentralization, UN interagency relations), and the professional vs. amateur/volunteer staff argument persists unresolved.

Second, EWLP plotted a number of hopeful avenues which, disappointingly, it then explored hardly at all. Among these: full learner participation in preparing and implementing literacy work, and the unfulfilled potential of mobilizing an NGO consortium.

Third, the Program did break ground—or at least reconfirmed earlier ground breaking on a comparatively broad international scale—on some questions. These included: successful integration of functional subjects in literacy curricula on the basis of actual problems facing learners in contexts of socioeconomic change; the pedagogical and economic advantages of using diverse and unusual locales for learning; andragogical methods (inductive, experiential, and varied); staff issues (the possibility of sparking enthusiasm, broadened skill profiles of functional literacy instructors, mobilization of a wide range of technical staff for instructional and backup tasks, and the effectiveness of short initial training followed by periodic refresher encounters).

Finally, EWLP pointed the way (not always intentionally) to certain new issues, or at least called attention to the need to view certain issues with a new intensity. The complex problem of languages used for literacy work was one; the decisive importance of postliteracy follow-up was another.

EWLP'S NEW LITERATES: CREATORS OR CREATURES?

The most critical part of the assessment of EWLP issued in the Program's final report, a section strangely ignored by most reviewers, concerns its human results. How did the new literates change, in terms of socioeconomic behaviors, as a result of EWLP?

Causality proved difficult indeed to establish, as was to be expected. Nevertheless, it does seem that EWLP caused behaviors to change. Some 160 measures and observations were run on various projects, doubtless with differing degrees of reliability. In all, the "influence of functional literacy [on changes observed and measured] was judged to be plausible"[36] in about forty-two percent of the cases.

---

[35] Rosa Maria Torres, *De Alfabetizando a Maestro Popular: La Post-Alfabetización en Nicaragua* (Managua: Instituto de Investigaciones Económicas y Sociales and Coordinadora Regional de Investigaciones Económicas y Sociales, 1983).

[36] *The Experimental World Literacy Program*, p. 176.

Not only "plausible," but "favorable."[37] In other words, the Program assigned positive or negative value to changes that took place, and attempted to determine what favorably valued (and statistically significant) changes attributable to functional literacy took place, in three categories of new literates' relationships with their surroundings. These were: insertion into the milieu, mastery of the milieu, and transformation of the milieu.

Indicators used to assess *insertion into the milieu* reflected, among other things, efforts made to obtain vocational/technical advice, interest in further education, participation in formal organizations and management of personal finances. Eighty-six percent of changes found were judged to be satisfactory, fifty-six percent with statistical significance. Analysis of data from several countries enabled the final report's authors to establish a provisional qualitative profile of the new literate judged to be successfully "inserted" in the milieu. Such a person seemed to

> (a) actively seek information likely to help solve mainly personal problems, generally posed in vocational terms; (b) prefer such activity to participation in formal community organizations; (c) take advantage of his or her new literacy and numeracy skills to maintain personal bank and savings accounts; and (d) aspire to reduce the size of his or her family in exchange for the prospect of a higher material living standard.[38]

Clearly, the Program judged itself most successful "when it reproduced the narrowly economic interpretation of functionality."[39] This kind of functionality reflects, in turn, a certain model of socioeconomic development which, while dominant in certain countries, is far from universally accepted.

The second broad class of intended socioeconomic changes examined concerned new literates' *mastery of the milieu*. Here, such effects as adoption of new technical practices were measured, and ninety-three percent of changes recorded were deemed satisfactory, fifty-one percent significantly so. Focusing its analysis on agricultural subprojects in India, the EWLP final report suggested that a major effect had been to enable small peasants to join the Green Revolution. This step had advantages (higher personal income) but servitudes too (greater expenditure for new seeds and other accessories). Also, the approach is not massively replicable, since the Green Revolution tends to be neither green nor revolutionary outside land irrigated with sure water (about ten percent of cultivated land in India).

EWLP did, then, increase new literates' mastery of the milieu, but in a narrowly technical and productivistic way akin to the kind of functionality promoted with regard to insertion into the milieu, as outlined above. This leaves a number of important and not entirely rhetorical questions to be dealt with:

> In acquiring this kind of mastery of the milieu, to what extent does the new literate become dependent on which external socio-economic processes and forces? Has literacy enabled the new literate to know and understand these processes and forces? To come to grips with them? To have a voice in controlling them? What implications has the

---

[37] Ibid.
[38] Ibid., p. 178.
[39] Ibid.

new literate's accession to mastery of the milieu for the fate of his or her less favored neighbors and compatriots?[40]

The final class of behavior changes sought and measured by EWLP involved *transformation of the milieu*. In this category, attempts were made to detect effects on behaviors concerning, for example, the means and volume of production, cash income, and consumption of goods such as bicycles, sewing machines, and pressure lamps. Of changes recorded, ninety percent were judged satisfactory, forty-one percent significantly so.

One must ask, however, whether increased consumption can (or should) be made a proxy for the humanistic aspiration to achieve mastery over the conditions in which one lives. Proceeding from this line of questioning, the Program's final report outlines a global profile of the positively judged new literate, who

> "inserted into the milieu" has been stimulated by the prospect of personal material gain and equipped with knowledge . . . to supply appropriate response to that stimulus. As a "master of the milieu," the new literate does seem effectively to supply the appropriate response. It is only logical then that, completing the circle, the new literate should be rewarded: he or she (and family) appears to gain access to increased personal consumption of material goods.[41]

This may seem something of a caricature, or at least an oversimplification, considering that during EWLP, over one hundred thousand people were made literate in diverse provinces of 11 very different countries in Africa, the Arab States, Asia, and Latin America. Yet, the Program's basic vocational and productivistic logic made it vulnerable to precisely the kind of stimulus/response and instrumental thinking that pervaded its evaluation design and the values by which results were judged under that design.

Literacy, however, like education more generally, cannot be reduced to behavioral conditioning. It endows people with skills that they can (although do not always) use to receive and emit messages of an almost infinite range, a range that in any event largely escapes the control of those who imparted literacy to them. Literacy is potential empowerment.

President J. Nyerere could have been (but probably wasn't) referring to some of EWLP's excesses on this score when he made "a serious distinction between men and women who are skillful users of tools, and a system of education which turns men and women into tools. I want to make quite sure that [ours] is an education for creators, not creatures . . ."[42]

A FINAL WORD ON INTERNATIONAL COOPERATION

The Experimental World Literacy Program had its ardent devotees, who felt the Program achieved major successes on most fronts, and its dogged detractors, who judged it a nearly total failure. Reality, as this chapter has attempted to examine it a decade later, probably lies somewhere in between.

[40] Ibid., p. 181.
[41] Ibid., p. 182.
[42] Julius Nyerere, "Education for Liberation in Africa," *Prospects* 1 (Paris: Unesco, 1975), p. 67.

True, little more than ten percent of original EWLP enrollees actually passed final literacy tests, according to internationally vetted data. Disappointingly, too, the Program did not lead to mass literacy in participating countries other than Tanzania (and perhaps Ethiopia, but the link there is tenuous), much less pave the way for a World Literacy Campaign. Quite to the contrary, since EWLP's conclusion, UNDP funding available for literacy has decreased, and although Unesco's budget for literacy has received priority for growth, it remains tiny compared with the magnitude of the problem. Also, having examined the conclusions of a study on the feasibility of intensified Unesco action in the field, the 1978 General Conference considered that "the conditions for the success of a possible Unesco literacy decade have yet to emerge" and even stated that "at the present stage, the setting up of an international literacy fund would not help to bring about a marked increase in the amount of resources. . . ."[43]

Why did a World Campaign not emerge from EWLP? Partly because EWLP itself forcefully demonstrated how complex an undertaking multicountry and interagency cooperation for literacy can be, even at the relatively modest level of the EWLP. This state of affairs was all the more disheartening for those involved since, far from a successful test of a breakthrough innovation (functional, work-oriented literacy), EWLP showed that technical innovation could not bring about widespread literacy if the national will to do so is absent.

The passing from fashion, in the early 1970s, of the idea that investment in education produces development also had a dampening effect. And the two billion dollars deemed necessary in 1961 to make the world literate (see note 8 above) were even less likely to materialize a decade and a half later, if only because the first oil crisis took place in the intervening period.

On the other hand, whatever faults may have marred (for example) EWLP's strategy and the kinds of behavioral changes it attempted to bring about thanks to literacy, the Program did make over 100,000 people literate at a unit cost of about three-hundred dollars (high, but not excessive, particularly since exceptional research and evaluation costs are included). EWLP also yielded a number of "nuts-and-bolts" pointers which it has only been possible to summarize in this chapter. As Unesco's Director General told the 1978 General Conference, the Program "can be said to have had a considerable impact on the design and methods of literacy training [going] far beyond [its] immediate impact."[44]

Given this fairly balanced result, why did irritation and even acrimony surround so much of discussion about the Program? Like the journalists who criticized EWLP for not achieving goals it had not set out to achieve, some specialists who took part in EWLP seem to have had unrealistic expectations and assumptions about what international cooperation could and/or should accomplish.

Perhaps frustrated at having their wings clipped when the original World Campaign was scaled down to an Experimental Program, EWLP's designers were

[43]*Records of the General Conference: Twentieth Session-Resolutions* (Paris: Unesco, 1978), p. 42.
[44]*The Organization's Literacy Program: Conclusions and Recommendations of the Director General* (Paris: Unesco, Document 20 C/71, 1978), p. 5.

determined to make the most of even that limited effort. In their largely understandable eagerness, they unfortunately saddled themselves with a single internationally designed strategy (verging on doctrine or dogma) which then had to be marketed to a variety of national authorities. Was this not an overambitious interpretation of the role and capacity of international cooperation, which, although hampered by the complexities of a large administration, is still puny and poor in terms of global problems? And if "insiders" could fall prey to such a misconception of the limits of international cooperation, how much easier it is for the broader public to do so. UNESCO continues to receive letters asking why it has not yet eradicated world illiteracy.

> This is what EWLP's final report calls the World Program's most poignant lesson. Neither literacy nor development can be willed into existence by international agencies that are inter- (but not supra-) governmental. Such agencies probably go awry if they try to replace the muscle of national governments. At best they can prick the conscience [and, one can add in retrospect, help feed and tone the muscle] of national governments. It is perhaps in this role that they can best respond to the hopes of those to whom ultimate ethical, if not yet legal, accountability: "We the peoples of the United Nations."[45]

The most paradoxical outcome of EWLP as concerns international cooperation is that, even seen through the time-polished lenses of a decade's hindsight, it appears to have had no effect whatsoever on the current attacks on UNESCO and multilateral cooperation more generally. Despite the severe pounding that it got at the time from part of the Western press, EWLP's real or supposed problems have, to my knowledge, never been cited by the authorities of UNESCO Member States on withdrawing, or announcing or threatening withdrawal, as exemplifying the accusations of overambitiousness or mismanagement justifying withdrawal. Indeed, such countries have not seldom pointed to literacy work as one of the "good things" UNESCO does. A small mercy, perhaps; but a mercy all the same.

---

[45] *The Experimental World Literacy Program*, p. 190.

CHAPTER 10

Tanzania's Literacy Campaign in Historical–Structural Perspective

JEFF UNSICKER

Tanzania's national literacy campaign merits the attention of both scholars and practitioners of adult education. On the one hand, as indicated in the overview section of this chapter, it is a special case among literacy efforts in the Third World nations: Tanzania's leadership and adult educators have succeeded in mobilizing and sustaining a very large-scale campaign for nearly fifteen years; as a result, Tanzania now has one of the highest literacy rates in Africa, and its campaign has often been suggested as a model for other underdeveloped nations. On the other hand, as indicated in the subsequent section on the campaign's impact, the Tanzanian case is perhaps typical of many other Third World nations: little is really known about the outcomes at the level of the individual, and even less is known about the level of general national development. I argue that more complete impact assessments cannot be made without an understanding of the structural relations of production and power in the Third World and in the relations between the Third World and the First World. As these relations are the product of history, the final sections of the chapter trace the origins and development of Tanzania's national literacy campaign within this historical–structural context. The result is a series of working conclusions, subject to further refinement as subsequent research pursues their implications.

OVERVIEW

On 31 December 1970, in his annual New Year's eve address to the nation, President Julius Nyerere directed that within one year illiteracy should be "completely eradicated" in six of Tanzania's approximately eighty political districts. The following September, even before the results of the quickly mobilized Six Districts Literacy Campaign were known, TANU (the ruling political party) directed that all citizens in the nation should be literate by the end of 1975.

JEFF UNSICKER • World College West, Pedaluma, California 94952.

While such ambitious directives are remarkable in any situation, it is all the more so when one realizes that in 1971 the government estimated that there were 5.3 million illiterates, sixty-seven percent of all Tanzanians over the age of ten (some unofficial estimates placed the figure at over eighty percent). Moreover, as one of the poorest, most underdeveloped nations in the world, Tanzania lacked the financial resources and educated manpower that such a task would seem to require.

On the other hand, the President, as a charismatic leader with "father of the country" status due to his role in the independence struggle during the 1950s, had massive popular support. That support appeared to have increased all the more when the party adopted the Arusha Declaration of 1967, which commited the nation to the progressive ideals of *ujamaa*[1] socialism. Part of that commitment was to use the nation's limited resources in first meeting the basic needs of the rural areas (where well over ninety percent of the population, and an even higher percentage of all illiterates, lived). Thus, as if oblivious to the immense difficulties of the task, the party cadre, the government's Ministry of National Education and over 88,000 teachers, secondary school students, and citizen volunteers rallied to the call, and the national literacy campaign was soon underway. Several foreign nations, and especially the Swedish International Development Authority (SIDA), quickly responded to requests for needed paper supplies and funds. The result, according to the Swedish advisor responsible for assisting in the campaign's planning:

> No country in the world has probably been able to mobilize and enroll the people, to raise the general literacy motivation, and to build up the adult education machinery to the same extent within a few years as Tanzania has managed to do.[2]

In the four year time frame of TANU's directive, over 5 million persons were enrolled in the national literacy campaign. A national examination, designed to test literacy at four different levels (see Table 1), was given to assess the campaign's success. Over 3.8 million persons took the examination. About 1.4 million passed at levels III and IV, the levels at which one was judged functionally literate—thereby reducing the official rate of illiteracy to 39%.

While the examination results thus suggested that tremendous progress had been made, they also indicated that the goal was still far off. In response, the party and government reaffirmed their commitment to total literacy and directed that the campaign should continue until that goal was reached. Moreover, they committed the nation to a variety of other adult programs designed to support the literacy training and the new literates (rural libraries, special newspapers, vocational adult education centers, and so forth).

---

[1] *Ujamaa* is a Swahili noun that literally translates into English as "extended familyhood." Nyerere adopted the term early in his political career to link his vision of a type of Fabian-style, communal socialism with Africa's precolonial past. *Ujamaa* socialism became the official state policy with the adoption of the Arusha Declaration in 1967. Though used here as an adjective to describe this type of socialism, the word has now come to be the general Swahili translation of the noun "socialism."
[2] Olle Osterling, "The Planning of the Literacy Campaign Qualitative Evaluation" (Tanzania, Ministry of National Education, Directorate of Adult Education, mimeo, 1974), p. 1.

Table 1. Definition and Levels of Literacy in Tanzania

In 1975, Tanzania's National Coordinating Committee for Adult Education adopted a definition of literacy that has four levels (and two sub–levels) on a continuum from illiterate to functionally literate. For purposes of the National Literacy Examinations and official literacy statistics, those participants who reach level 3.1. in reading, writing, and arithmetic combined are considered to be literate ("literacy graduates") and those who have achieved level 4 are considered to be "functionally literate."

Level 1. Has enrolled in literacy classes and attended two-thirds of the sessions.

Level 2.1. Able to read words and recognize symbols, to write alphabet letters, numbers, and arithmetic signs.

Level 2.2. Able to read a short meaningful sentence, to write a simple short sentence, to add and subtract one figure numbers.

Level 3.1. Able to read and write as above, to add and subtract two-figure numbers.

Level 3.2. Able to fluently read a simple text (based on the common syllables and vocabularies in the literacy primers or the most frequent syllables and vocabularies, in the Swahili language) with understanding, to write a simple, short message, to add and substract three figure numbers, to multiply two figure numbers and to divide by one figure.

Level 4. Able to read a newspaper in order to keep up with current happenings and obtain information, to read "how to do it yourself" books on better living, better food, better ways of farming, etc., to keep records and solve simple arithmetic problems, to keep a simple book of accounts on income and expenditure.

Source: Compiled from Johnsson, Nystrom, and Sunden, *Adult Education in Tanzania*, "Appendix 1."

The national literacy campaign continues today, almost fifteen years after the initial directive, as do the other elements of the adult education system. While the highly visible "campaign" character has, over time, been replaced by a more institutional approach, relying more heavily on government workers, the record of steady progress remains: the official illiteracy rate fell to 27% after the 1977 examinations, to 21% in 1981, and to 15% in 1983 (see Table 2).

Tanzanian political leaders and adult educators are justifiably proud of the campaign's record. When one evaluates the achievements in light of Tanzania's weak infrastructure (which makes seemingly simple tasks into logistical dilemmas) and limited economic resources, the need to extend the timeline from four to over fifteen years is not an indication of failure. On the contrary, the decisions to extend and reextend the campaign offer an impressive indication of what many Tanzanians and others refer to as the "political will" that is at the foundation of the literacy campaign and other struggles to meet basic human needs and to bring about self-reliant national development. Only in the early 1980s, as the nation was struggling with major economic crises, did a SIDA-commissioned study group detect what they felt was a waning in the political will behind the literacy effort.[3]

---

[3] Anders Johnsson, Kjell Nystrom, and Rolf Sunden, *Adult Education in Tanzania* (Stockholm: Swedish International Development Authority [Education Division Documents No. 9], 1983), pp. 81–82.

Table 2. Results of the National Literacy Examinations, 1975–1983 (in Thousands)

	1975	1977	1981	1983
Total adult population 10 years and over	10,206	10,885	12,366	13,154
Illiterates before the test	5,860	4,597	3,889	3,034
Participants registered for test	5,185	3,546	3,524	2,811
Percent of illiterates	88	77	91	93
Participants actually tested	3,804	2,481	3,108	2,162
Percent of illiterates	65	54	80	71
Percent of those registered	73	70	88	77
Test results				
Below Level I	407	346	918	591
Percent of all tested	11	14	30	28
Levels I–II	1,994	1,328	1,276	892
Percent of all tested	52	54	41	41
Levels III–IV	1,403	806	913	680
Percent of all tested	37	33	29	31
Illiterates after the test	4,457	3,791	2,976	2,354
Official illiteracy rate	39	27	21	15

Source: Goran Andersson, Celia Male, and Karl-Erik Westergren, "New Post-Literacy Curriculum for Adults: Appraisal Report" (Stockholm: Swedish International Development Authority, mimeo, 1984).

IMPACT ON INDIVIDUALS AND NATIONAL DEVELOPMENT

But beyond enrollment statistics and examination results, little is known about the actual impact of the literacy campaign on either the new literates or on the process of national development. While there is a significant body of literature on adult education in Tanzania,[4] it is primarily descriptive. One reads about the President's numerous papers and speeches on adult education, the Party policies, the "work-oriented" or "functional literacy" approach, the structure of the campaign, the methods of recruiting and training teachers, and so forth.

Individual Impact

With regard to the campaign's impact on individuals, the literature is limited. Yusuf Kassam, the former director of the Institute of Adult Education in Tanzania, has reported on a qualitative impact study conducted in 1977. Unfortunately, that research was limited to in-depth interviews or dialogues with only

[4]Among the most comprehensive studies of adult education in Tanzania are: Budd L. Hall, *Adult Education and the Development of Socialism in Tanzania* (Kampala: East African Literature Bureau, 1975), Yusuf O. Kassam, *The Adult Education Revolution in East Africa* (Nairobi: Shungwaya Publishers, Ltd., 1978), Zakayo J. Mpogolo, *Functional Literacy in Tanzania* (Dar es Salaam: Swalo Publications, 1980), and Johnsson *et al.*, *Adult Education in Tanzania*.

eight new literates, and thus cannot be assumed to be representative. On the other hand, at a minimum, Kassam's work suggests the potential outcomes for peasants who have learned to read and write:

> [I]n the majority of cases, if not all, literacy has made a powerful and positive impact on the qualitative aspects of people's development. All the sentiments, perceptions and feelings which have so forcefully and eloquently been expressed by the new literates indicate dramatic changes in the quality of their lives. They have got rid of their former state of marginality, alienation and fear, they feel more self-confident and have begun to be assertive, they have acquired a new awareness of self, they have become politically conscious, they have regained their complete human dignity, they cannot be exploited and humiliated in the same way as before, they have become self-reliant in many ways, they now feel like active subjects rather than manipulable objects, and they have begun to demystify social reality.[5]

In the words of several of the new literates:

> These days when people see me they say to themselves, "You cannot deceive or intimidate this old man—he knows".[6]

> Now that I have become literate I feel that before I was carrying a small lantern but now a pressure lamp has been brought to me.[7]

> The world "education" used to terrify me. . . . [E]ducation now had the aura of some kind of magic. But now I know that anyone can learn and anyone can get education. . . . An educated man is simply one who is made to understand and to know. . . . Education, we thought, was something that was out "there," somewhere far away . . . but now you are told it is right here near the river.[8]

More recently, in conjunction with the 1983 literacy examinations, the Ministry of Education conducted a relatively large-scale study of the impact of literacy and postliteracy classes.[9] In stark contrast to Kassam's sample, the Ministry's study involved interviews with over 5,000 new literates, who in turn were grouped in three categories: currently enrolled in literacy classes, graduated from literacy classes but not continuing to postliteracy classes, and graduated and continuing in postliteracy classes. Interviews were also conducted with 1,680 relatives of the above adults, and questionnaires were used to collect additional data from over 1,000 teachers, adult education coordinators, government administrators and experts, and party leaders. Unfortunately, there appear to be numerous problems with the study's research methods.[10] Some of those problems

---

[5] Yusuf Kassam, *Illiterate No More* (Dar es Salaam: Tanzania Publishing House, 1979).

[6] Ibid., p. 52.

[7] Ibid.

[8] Ibid., pp. 54–55.

[9] Tanzania, Ministry of Education, "Translated Report on the Impact of Adult Education in Tanzania" (A. S. Kamwela, translator) (Dar es Salaam: Department of Adult Education, mimeo, 1985).

[10] While multiple regression and other statistical techniques might offer partial solutions to the technical problem of isolating the effects of literacy in relation to other factors, the Tanzanians did not have access to either the computers or statistical packages which would be needed. Such limitations might not be so important in themselves, since attention to statistical technique too often serves to divert attention from the far more fundamental questions of conceptualizing the process of change and the other factors involved, many of which are not directly observable. Yet the Ministry's study does not demonstrate substantial attention to even the observable factors— and thus has no basis for concluding, "We believe that most of the changes revealed in the evaluation

are common to all efforts of this type (for example, isolating the impact of literacy classes in relation to other socioeconomic and environmental factors when assessing a reported change in farming behavior); others are more basic (for example, the researchers asked about current farming behavior, but not about whether or not the behavior had changed during or since the literacy classes).

On the other hand, the Ministry of Education researchers did ask the same questions to each of the three categories of current and former literacy students, and by comparing their answers, one can make some rough inferences about individual impact (see Table 3). For example, from the findings that the literacy graduates are generally more politically active and slightly more "modern" in their farming and health habits than are those adults who have not yet completed literacy classes, one might infer that the literacy classes have had some positive impact on the participation levels and quality of life for the peasant farmers and workers.

There are, of course, alternative explanations of the Ministry of Education's results. The finding that twenty-two percent of the adults in the postliteracy classes reported they had been elected in a party leadership post (such as a "cell leader" responsible for ten households), compared to eight percent of the adults still in the literacy classes, might have several explanations, including: some (probably small) percentage of the persons in literacy classes in 1983 were young adults who had not been old enough to participate previously, and thus were less likely to hold a leadership post simply as a result of their junior status in a highly age-conscious society; or, those older persons who were most motivated to take on leadership posts were likely to have been in the first cohorts of literacy students and had graduated by 1983. In neither case might literacy itself be considered the cause of the difference between the two groups. Likewise, the finding that sixty-two percent of the postliteracy class adults reported that they participate in the planning and implementation of development projects in their village, neighborhood, or workplace, compared with twenty-five percent of those in the literacy classes, might have a similar explanation. But the overall pattern of these two and other findings does seem to suggest something more substantial may be occurring as a result of the literacy campaign.

National Impact

With regard to the campaign's impact on national development, or on Tanzania's transition to socialism, the literature on Tanzanian adult education is all the more sparse. The intended impact is well known. According to the

---

were caused through the adult education programme" (Chapter 6). Moreover, while the report outlines an impressive effort to select an appropriate national sample, and while a very high percentage of the target sample was reached, the actual data may be somewhat suspect, due to the in-the-field process of selecting the local samples and/or the nature of the interview relationship (government official asking questions to a peasant or worker about issues for which there are politically "correct" responses—perhaps all the better known to the more advanced, postliteracy adults). While it is unfair to criticize the study against the standards of well supported research in the North, it would be equally inappropriate to not utilize the reported findings without extreme caution.

Table 3. Reported Impact of Literacy and Postliteracy Classes, 1983 (Selected Indicators)

	Adults in literacy classes	New literates *not* continuing to postliteracy	New literates in postliteracy classes
Size of sample	1,875	1,590	1,804
Farming impact			
Use fertilizers	39%	49%	52%
Use pesticides	43	53	45
Use hybrid seeds	73	75	77
Use plough	10	15	12
Use tractor	1<	1<	1
Political impact			
Vote in general elections	69%	87%	84%
Can follow party training for becoming member	NA	50	49
Party member	33	62	54
Member of party affiliate	34	44	48
Give ideas at party and government meetings	41	60	59
Take minutes at meetings	16	NA	37
Elected party leader	8	NA	22
Participate in planning and implementing development in village, neighborhood or workplace	25	NA	62
Health impact			
Boil and filter water	38%	43%	47%
Boil or filter water	41	44	42
Total	79	77	89

Source: Compiled from tables in Tanzania, Ministry of Education, "Translated Report on the Impact of Adult Education in Tanzania" (A.S. Kamwela, translator) (Dar es Salaam: Department of Adult Education, mimeo, 1985). NA = not available.

plans outlined in several of Nyerere's most important policy papers—"Education for Self-Reliance" and "Socialism and Rural Development"[11]—literacy would be one important method of empowering the peasants. Armed with the pride, self-confidence, and other qualities that Kassam found, as well as the knowledge of modern farming, technical crafts, and homemaking, the literate peasants would provide more effective members in the over eight thousand *ujamaa* villages into which almost all of the rural population relocated during the late 1960s and 1970s. Largely as a result of the new consciousness, knowledge, and skills the peasants had acquired through literacy classes (as well as through the demonstrations of agricultural-extension agents and community-development workers), Nyerere expected the villages to become increasingly productive economic units—

[11] Julius Nyerere, *Freedom and Socialism* (London: Oxford University Press, 1968).

involved in collective agricultural production and, as resources permitted, adding small-scale or cottage industries. Self-help would reduce dependence on the government treasury in the construction of roads and schools, in the eradication of diseases, and so forth. The nation would become more self-sufficient in food and less dependent on imports and foreign aid. Social class differentiation would be halted, and inequalities between urban and rural areas would be reduced.

While it is certainly not the fault of the literacy campaign, many of Nyerere's national development plans have yet to be realized. In fact, since the campaign was initiated in the early 1970s, Tanzania has experienced increasingly difficult economic problems, becoming less productive and more dependent. As is the case with most Third World nations, the oil price increases that began in 1973 and the deteriorating terms of trade between the products of primarily commodity-producing countries and those of the industrial countries caused Tanzania to experience significant balance-of-trade deficits (by 1980, sixty percent of all foreign exchange earnings were spent on oil). In addition, several of the agricultural seasons were ruined by drought, and the 1979 war that defeated Idi Amin in Uganda cost the nation millions of dollars.

The economic problems, however, may not have been all of an external source. The negative balance of trade appears also to be partially due to reduced actual production in some of the export crops upon which the nation depends for earning foreign exchange (coffee, tea, cotton, tobacco, and sisal), and this reportedly paralleled production declines in major domestic food crops (most importantly, maize). The fall in production is in turn at least partially attributable to the practices of state-controlled marketing boards and crop authorities, or parastatals. These bureaucracies control producer prices and hence incentives for peasant production and eat up a growing share of the income generated by export (the farmers' share of export prices fell from seventy percent to thirty-five percent during the 1970s). The negative trade balance, among other factors, has led to a growing dependence on foreign aid. During the 1970s, the absolute level of aid increased by a factor of ten (even adjusted for inflation, the level doubled), which has made national control over development priorities all the more problematic.

The nation's economic problems are somewhat offset by improvements in social services in the rural areas (from education, including literacy, to health and sanitation), by rising life expectancy and decreasing child-mortality rates, and by the reduction of the gap between the highest and lowest incomes in the nation. But Nyerere was among the first to argue that socialism did not mean the expansion of social services for their own sake (for example, one of the main rationales for universal primary education and literacy was that they would enhance the knowledge, skills, and attitudes for increased production), nor did it mean the equal sharing of poverty.

However, while no analysts have suggested that Tanzania's severe economic problems are the result of the literacy campaign, there is little agreement about what in fact are the major causes. One group of analysts, of whom Nyerere is among the most articulate, argues that the increased import prices, the droughts, and the war with Uganda are the primary causes. Another group of analysts, which include the economists advising the International Monetary Fund in its drawn out negotiations with Tanzania, gives more attention to the inefficiencies in the parastatals and the government's unwillingness to cut back on social services. Tanzania's development strategy, they seem to suggest, is based on "too much socialism." A third group, whose work is based in Marxian class analysis, also point to inefficiencies in the parastatals. However, they argue that those problems are the result of "too little socialism." The parastatal managers and other government bureaucrats are not accountable to the peasants or workers and make technocratic decisions that bring them into alliance with the interests of international capitalism. While Nyerere and other leaders of the party may be willing to go against their own material interests (to commit what Amilcar Cabral called "class suicide"), their failure to recognize class divisions between the bureaucrats, peasants, and workers in Tanzania, and thus their reliance on education instead of class struggle as the means of transformation, has kept them from rallying the type of mass action needed to address the fundamental differences in class power.

Amid such a debate, what can be said about the literacy campaign's contribution to national development? Was it totally inconsequential? Or, was the campaign a positive force for higher productivity and/or socialist consciousness amongst the peasants—even if it was not enough to overcome the more powerful forces of nature and/or the international political economy? Would conditions have been worse if the campaign had not been conducted? Or, was the campaign in fact a negative factor? Did it help the bureaucrats to gain a still stronger control over the lives of the peasants? How would we know? It may be obvious that any attempt to answer those questions is highly conditioned by the analytic framework one utilizes.

GENERAL ANALYSIS

The analytic framework of most of the literature on adult education in Tanzania could be described as functionalist. Like Nyerere (not coincidentally so, given the President's strong role in articulating the philosophy of adult education in Tanzania), most of the authors have assumed that there is an overriding common interest between different actors, specifically the illiterate peasants, the teachers, and the government bureaucrats and party leaders at different levels. Thus, while the alternative framework, based on attention to class conflict, has informed a significant number of the general studies of Tanzania's development and the more specific studies on policies, programs, and outcomes in sectors such as rural development, there are only a few, and relatively recent, studies of adult education that employ the framework of conflict analysis.[12]

[12] Marjorie Mbilinyi, "Towards a Methodology in Political Economy of Adult Education in Tanzania" (Paper for Political Economy of Adult Education Planning Meeting, International Council for Adult Education, Toronto, 1980) and A. N. Kweka, "Functional Literacy and Peasant Education— The Case of Orngadida Village" (Dar es Salaam: Political Economy of Adult Education Project, Institute of Development Studies University of Dar es Salaam [Discussion Paper], mimeo, 1983).

This chapter argues that, though there is not as yet enough empirical data to draw definitive conclusions about the impact of the literacy campaign on individual or national development, conflict analysis provides new insights and can produce a plausible set of initial conclusions. To support this contention, the chapter employs the analytic method of conflict analysis—what is often termed "historical–structural analysis."[13] The remainder of this chapter is thus a brief history of the background and origins of the literacy campaign in the context of the structures of the Tanzanian political economy. From that emerge several initial conclusions, which are in essence working hypotheses for further research. They are:

(1) At the international level, where the impact has been perhaps the most pronounced, the literacy campaign has provided important external legitimation for the Tanzanian state, particularly in relation to the international development agencies; thus it has helped create and especially sustain the very high level of foreign aid to Tanzania, with a full range of consequences.

(2) At the national level, the campaign (and the adult education program more generally) has been the focus of considerable struggle within the state, which partially reflects the ideological conflict between Nyerere and his allies, on the one hand, and the whole bureaucracy, on the other, and which partially reflects a more limited intrabureaucracy conflict over personal privileges.

(3) At the local (village production) level, the campaign does not appear to have had any significant role in the development of the village's leadership or access to power. In fact, the short-term impact has probably been to solidify the power of the bureaucracy more than it has to liberate the peasants. However, in the longer run, the campaign may well have provided a key set of skills that can be utilized by the peasants, should the historical moment provide a realistic opportunity to shift the balance of power.

HISTORICAL CONTEXT

The Party's call for the eradication of illiteracy in four years was the culmination of a number of important events in the development of Tanzania's commitment and approach to adult education. This history helps explain many of the features of the ensuing national campaign. A yet deeper understanding of the literacy campaign is achieved when its history is traced in the context of the changing political and economic structures that have molded Tanzania's overall development, and especially when such structural changes are understood in the context of historical periods, each period with its own set of internal contradictions. In the following pages, four periods will be discussed: colonialism (1890s–1960), nationalism and modernization (1961–1966), voluntary socialism (1967–early 1970s) and frontal-attack socialism (early 1970s–1979). This discussion will lead into a description of the literacy campaign itself. In the final

[13]See, for example, Fernando H. Cardoso and Enzo Faletto, *Dependency and Development in Latin America* (Berkeley: University of California Press, 1979).

section of the chapter, the effects of, and the most recent developments in, the literacy campaign will be discussed in light of the structural conditions of the 1980s.

Colonialism (1890s–1960)

The general structure of the present day Tanzanian economy, polity, and social classes was forged during the first half of the twentieth century, when the nation was first a colony of Germany and then (after Germany's defeat in World War I) of the United Kingdom. The colonial powers, as elsewhere in Africa, developed an economic, political, and physical infrastructure that was based on the expropriation of natural resources and export crops grown with African labor.

When they met resistance, as did the Germans in the *Maji Maji* uprising in 1905–1907, the colonial powers reacted with brutal force. But, in general, the struggle was not so conspicuously violent. Indeed, since the U.K. held control over the territory as a trustee of the League of Nations and later the United Nations, its actions were most often characterized by carefully constructed, if sometimes vacilating and not always wholly effective, laws and policies designed to control the economic possibilities of different social classes.

The major class differences were marked by race. Europeans (British civil servants, missionaries from several nations, and relatively few European settlers) had very few limitations and substantial privileges. Asians were allowed to dominate the trading and commercial sectors, acting as the "middle men" in the process of expropriation of wealth. Africans had very few possibilities, and this low status was worsened by the government's "divide and conquer" tactics. Tribal rivalries and regional inequalities were exploited. In the favored regions where certain export crops did well, peasant farmers were forced to grow and sell those crops in order to pay a head tax. In the less favored regions, termed "labour reserves," peasants were forced to migrate to plantations and mines in order to earn the currency needed to pay their taxes. These rural peasants were in turn divided from a small number of Africans who were educated to perform clerical and assistant functions within the colonial government.

Racially segregated schools played a dominant role in the class divisions, and the African schools were an especially crucial screening device for those who sought the limited privileges of salaried work. The several percent of the total African population receiving more than rudimentary education in "bush schools" were screened for cooperativeness with the colonial administration and then socialized to believe that they were at once superior to other Africans and inferior to the Europeans.

Literacy Programs (Prior to 1960)

The colonial powers' interest in adult education, on the other hand, was limited to the extent that it might enhance the peasant productivity and that it did not raise mass expectations of salaried employment and other privileges reserved for the few. Later, British liberals gained control of some colonial offices in the wake of World War II. In Tanganyika, liberals began to organize a variety of new services through the Department of Social (later Community) Development, including a series of pilot literacy campaigns influenced by the work of Laubach. In general, the scale of such probjects was very limited: several districts were targeted, and overall enrollment was measured in hundreds and thousands, not millions. Many Africans, on the basis of several generations of experience with the colonial powers, distrusted the government's motives; others appear to have actively participated in the programs, perhaps in the hope that literacy would provide a first stepping stone to formal education and then a government post. Both of those responses suggest the difficulty of understanding a literacy program without understanding the structurally conditioned interests of both the illiterates and those who plan and control the program.

Nationalism and Modernization (1961–1967)

The contradictions inherent in the British form of colonial exploitation, especially regarding their education of an African elite to serve the state, eventually led to the independence. Beginning in the early 1950s, this elite African class assumed the leadership role in a broad-based, nationalist independence movement. Julius Nyerere, then a young secondary-school teacher, was the movement's catalyst and spokesman. Partly as a result of the fact that the colony's status as a U.N. trust territory allowed the nationalists to directly petition the general international community, and partly as a result of the (not unrelated) fact that there was no significant European settler population committed to protecting their property interests, the victory came quickly (1961) and with almost no violence. The new nation committed itself to building a nonracial, democratic nation guided by what are now known as "modernization" economic policies. The initial emphasis was placed on Africans assuming the key roles in all branches of the new government—itself a structurally close replica of the former colonial government.

The advice of a World Bank study team became the foundation of the nation's first economic development plans. Capital, technology, and expertise, in forms ranging from aid and concessionary loans to direct investment, were sought from many different Western nations. The formal schooling system was expanded at the higher (secondary and university) levels, in order to rapidly train the thousands of Africans needed to fill government posts.

Literacy Programs (1961–1967)

The new government's interest in adult education and literacy was substantial. During the independence campaign, the movement leaders had urged peasants to participate in the colonial government-sponsored literacy classes. Now, having achieved their goal of an independent Tanzania, the leaders argued that the benefits of adult education needed to be distributed more widely in order to bring about both political and economic changes.

The first five-year development plan argued that "the nation cannot wait until the children have become educated for development to begin." Responsibility for literacy classes and adult education more generally was assigned to the Division of Community Development, a direct carry over from the colonial state, and a British community-development officer of the colonial state was appointed the division's first commissioner. In order to "win the people's commitment to development" (to use the phrase in Community Development's 1964 Annual Report), literacy classes were organized by a mushrooming staff of field assistants—which grew from thirty-two to over four hundred in the five years following independence. Enrollment in literacy classes grew from 132,000 in 1961 to 570,000 in 1965.

However, in relation to formal education and especially secondary and higher education, the funding available to carry out literacy classes and adult education programs was very low. (The United States became one of the main sources of support to Community Development's programs, especially in the area of training the government staff in Tanzania and in the U.S.) Even the efforts that were funded were frought with problems. For example, actual attendance was apparently far lower than enrollment: a UNESCO study surveyed selected districts and found rates ranging from seventy-nine percent to as low as eleven percent; the rate in most districts in most months was around twenty-five percent.[14] Moreover, according to other critics, the literacy classes and other community development activities were "paternalistic" in their approach, based on colonial-period beliefs that peasant farmers were ignorant of their own needs and incapable of planning their own development.[15]

During this same period, at the new University College of Dar es Salaam, there emerged what eventually became a second base for the literacy effort: the Institute of Adult Education (IAE). The IAE was based on the elitist adult education model fo extramural studies departments organized in British higher education, including the universities in British colonies, such as Makerere University College in Uganda. Upon the independence of the three nations that were formerly British East Africa, Makerere became the first of three colleges within the new University of East Africa, joined by Nairobi (Kenya) and Dar es Salaam.

The IAE, like its equivalents in the other two university colleges, initially focused most of its attention on night classes for the well educated Africans living in the capital city. However, its first director, Paul Bertelsen, brought a different perspective. Bertelsen was a Danish adult educator, schooled in the Scandinavian traditions of participatory social movements and folk education, and experienced in the adult education programs of Ghana that had developed during the period of Kwame Nkrumah's progressive influence. During the early 1960s, he built upon his, and Nyerere's own, Scandinavian connections to host several visits by folk educators, including an official delegation from Sweden

---

[14] Jane King, *Planning Nonformal Education in Tanzania* (Paris: International Institute for Educational Planning/UNESCO, 1967), pp. 21–24.
[15] Budd L. Hall, *Adult Education*, p. 118.

charged with assessing SIDA's potential role in assisting adult education in East Africa.

The Voluntary Transition to Socialism (1968–Early 1970s)

The contradictions in development based on Western-style and Western-financed modernization soon became apparent to Nyerere and other key policy makers. As in numerous other Third World nations, the end of political colonialism led to a form of economic neocolonialism. Capital-intensive investments tended to displace traditional craft workers and/or did not support the development of an integrated internal economic system; foreign corporations repatriated profits instead of reinvesting them in Tanzania. The levels of foreign development aid anticipated in the development plans was not forthcoming, and foreign-policy conflicts with the U.K. (over their recognition of the Unilateral Declaration of Independence by white settlers in Rhodesia), with West Germany (over Tanzania's recognition of East Germany), and the U.S. (over accusations of CIA involvement in Tanzania) all led to further cutbacks in the level of foreign aid.

On the internal front, many of the Africans who had assumed roles in the new government were adopting elite lifestyles and attitudes. This trend was brought to a head when the majority of the students at the University of Dar es Salaam organized a protest march to the President's office to complain about a new regulation requiring that they participate in the National Service without salaries equivalent to their educated status. Nyerere responded with a strong admonishment of their elitism and dismissed them from university studies. Though almost all of the students were later reinstated, their protest provided one of the justifications for the party's Arusha Declaration of 1967, which committed the nation to building socialism. A series of nationalizations followed, as did the (often) strict enforcement of a leadership code barring any party or government officials from engaging in any capitalist activities.

In subsequent policy papers, Nyerere argued for a reorientation of national priorities to deal with the rural agricultural sector and the peasants as the foundation of self-reliant development. Central to this plan was the voluntary formation of socialist villages where agriculture could be collectivized and where education and other social services could be made more accessible. The voluntary quality of the villagization process, and, more generally, of the entire strategy of socialist transformation, was considered essential. Socialism, argued the President, is "an attitude of mind" and could never be imposed against one's will.

Literacy Programs (1968–Early 1970s)

The government's interest in spreading development through adult education became all the stronger in the post-Arusha period, as a result of its new rural-development and villagization policies. While the party was adopting socialism, the Division of Community (later Rural) Development was finalizing negotiations with the United Nations Development Programme (UNDP) and

UNESCO for Tanzania's participation in the Experimental World Literacy Programme.[16]

In 1968, the Tanzanian component, or the Work-Oriented Adult Literacy Pilot Project (WOALPP), began operating in the important cotton-producing districts surrounding Lake Victoria in the north. The world program, and thus WOALPP, emphasized a "functional literacy" approach that was supposed to integrate the teaching of reading and numeracy with the teaching of practical skills useful to the illiterate students. By 1972, the end of the initial contract, the project had enrolled more than a half million illiterates in 16,800 classes, which were offered by 13,500 newly trained literacy teachers and adult education staff and supported by primers in seven fields (focused on cotton, banana, and rice production, cattle rearing, fishing, home economics, and political education), each field with two primers organized by level of difficulty. In addition, the project established ninety rural libraries and four rural newspapers, and introduced a rural construction program and a radio education program.

Many Tanzanian adult educators, including Zakayo Mpogolo, a former deputy directory of WOALPP and now the Ministry of Education's Director of Adult Education, have stressed WOALPP's strong influence on the design and operation of the national literacy campaign. They point out the decentralized system of recruiting and training literacy teachers, the use of writers' workshops to produce the primers, the continued use of support programs (libraries, newspapers, radio, and so forth) and the interministerial coordination.

From the perspective of ultimate impact on individual, and especially national, development, the major legacy of WOALPP on the national campaign may have been its functional orientation. While there are several different explanations as to why this emphasis was adopted at the international level,[17] there is agreement that in the case of Tanzania the terminology and many of the basic concepts of the functional approach were carried forward into the national literacy campaign—beginning with the fact that the WOALPP primers became the initial texts for the national campaign. As will be argued later, the functional approach appears to have supported a style of teaching and thinking about literacy-program development that depoliticizes the literacy process and thus solidifies rather than challenges the power relations of the bureaucrats over the peasants.

In addition, the WOALPP experience points to another subplot in the history of Tanzania's literacy and adult education effort: the role of international

[16]See Gillette chapter in this book.

[17]Susan Gitelson, in *Multilateral Aid for National Development and Self-Reliance* (Kampala: East African Literature Bureau, 1976), suggests that the decision to emphasize "functional" literacy was part of UNESCO's efforts to redefine literacy as an economic and not just a human-rights objective, which then rationalized the use of UNDP's economic development funds in such projects. Mwesiga Baregu, a former WOALPP staff and political science faculty member at the University of Dar es Salaam, has suggested in personal communication that the functional approach was supported by UN members who were threatened by a more political or consciousness-raising approach, which had attracted international attention due to Cuba's campaign in the early 1960s and the rising popularity of Paulo Freire's work in Brazil.

aid agencies in relation to the Tanzanian state. Gitleson's study[18] of the nego-tiations between the U.N. and Tanzanian actors indicates a series of conflicts between the two groups. One conflict was over the scope of the project: the Tanzanian planners wanted a national project; while the UNESCO planners wanted a local pilot project that could be carefully monitored and evaluated; UNESCO got its way. Another conflict was over the relative proportion of funds allocated to equipment, expatriate advisors, and training fellowships for local staff: the Tanzanians initially requested $684,000 in equipment and $390,000 for six experts; the final agreement was $252,000 for equipment and $716,000 for nine experts; the level of fellowship funding was reduced by an unspecified amount. Moreover, all of these decisions occurred even though the Tanzanians, at least on paper, were funding $5.2 million of the $6.4 total cost of WOALPP. Gitelson traces similar conflicts between the U.N. experts and their Tanzanian counterparts during the first two years of the project's operation. She specifically discusses philosophical and personality conflicts between the Tanzanian desig-nated as the on-site manager and the head of the U.N. expert team, conflicts that resulted in less than desirable cooperation between the teams the two super-vised. Gitelson's assessment, as she finished her field research in 1969, was that the conflict had been so great that the project was likely to be "low yield" in relation to several other UNDP funded projects she studied in Tanzania and Uganda.

The analysis of such conflicts takes on still greater meaning when one realizes that the head of the U.N. team was Paul Bertelsen, the former director of the Institute of Adult Education, Tanzania's other major base of adult edu-cation. By the late 1960s, the IAE had become the focus of aid from the Swedish International Development Authority, primarily in the form of advisors from the Swedish folk schools, cooperatives and so forth. Two years after the SIDA mission of 1965, the IAE received a commitment of nine Swedish advisors. Later the same year, the IAE was allocated six more Swedes to implement a corre-spondence education program. In the process, the IAE was continuing to refocus its work away from urban elites toward the rural masses. While training adult educators became the central work of the IAE, other programs were underway to directly reach the general population. A campaign involving a series of radio broadcasts and local study groups, based on one of the folk education models of Sweden, was first tried in one or two regions in 1967. In 1969 the Institute coordinated its first national radio study group campaign, focused on gaining public support for the nation's second five-year development plan (1969–74). This in turn provided the framework for a series of several other similar cam-paigns, climaxing with the Man is Health Campaign of 1973 and the Food is Life Campaign of 1975. The former, for example, involved over two million persons in 75,000 study groups concerned with concrete improvements in public health at the village or neighborhood level.

The above dynamics set the context within which Nyerere and other key government leaders decided to take the responsibility for literacy and adult

---

[18]Gitelson, *Multilateral Aid*, pp. 111–114.

education from the Division of Rural Development and give it to a new Department of Adult Education in the Ministry of National Education. While the published histories of Tanzanian adult education uniformly note this change as a key step with universal support, interview data suggests that the change was resisted by Rural Development officials, and that the success of National Education officials was intimately linked to their Scandinavian connections.[19] These personal connections, and the financial support they represented, were not likely the major factor in determining the change. In fact, in a personal interview, the former Party Education Secretary, who reportedly authored the policy paper proposing the change, indicated that it was his belief that the primary schools, under National Education's control, would be necessary for any successful national literacy campaign. But those connections undoubtedly conditioned the timing and nature of the change in ministry, and bring to view a subtle dynamic of the Tanzanian state: if a ministry wishes to grow in size and responsibility, it must be able to successfully manage its relations with external aid agencies and support systems.

"Frontal Attack" Socialism (Early 1970s–1979)

Within a few years following the Arusha Declaration, Nyerere and other key Tanzanian leaders were beginning to realize that the voluntary process of socialist transformation was both slow and caught in a new set of contradictions. This was perhaps most clearly evident with regard to the plan to create *ujamaa* villages. One voluntary, bottom-up village-development effort that had been initiated in the early 1960s—the Ruvumu Development Association (RDA), an umbrella for up to seventeen highly collectivized villages in one of Tanzania's most underdeveloped regions—received substantial national attention, including several visits from Nyerere himself. However, the RDA's autonomy and the example it set for other similar efforts threatened district- and regional-level party and government leaders. In 1969, soon after a Party restructuring gave regional leaders the majority power in the Party Central Committee, they voted to totally disband the RDA.

---

[19]The network of contacts included: Bertelsen (who was in conflict with the Rural Development staff assigned to WOALPP, and whose base was in the Institute, which itself would soon seek more autonomy from the University College of Dar es Salaam through a more direct connection with Education); Barbro Johansson (a member of parliament who had come to Tanzania as a Swedish missionary and teacher, and who eventually became one of Nyerere's closest advisors, especially in the area of adult education); various SIDA officials and Swedish folk educators (including a team whose offer of advisors and some aid to Rural Development was turned down in favor of the UNDP project at the same time that the IAE was accepting a similar offer; and several key party and government leaders who were among a handful of Tanzanians to have lived and studied in Sweden: Reverand Mushendwa (then the Party's Secretary of Political Education, the author of the policy paper recommending the change in ministerial responsibility who had done his religious studies in Sweden and was a close contact of Johansson and the Swedes in both Tanzania and SIDA) and Emmanuel Kibira (who had similar close contacts, and who became the first Director of Adult Education in the Ministry of Adult Education).

Other efforts to create new villages were under the top-down supervision of district and regional leaders. While the record was mixed, with at least several examples of leaders and peasants cooperating to establish socialist-oriented villages, many new villages were only formed in response to promises of credit and/or new services (schools, clean water, etc.), and most villages were formed through "operations." The first, Operation Rufiji in 1969, was begun at the time the RDA was being disbanded. A government directive stated that villagers in the flood-prone Rufiji River valley must move into government-selected, new village sites if they wished to receive famine relief following an unusually heavy flood, and 42,000 peasants were moved in one year. The following year, Operation Dodoma directed that 500,000 persons in a poor, dry, and sparsely populated central region of Tanzania be moved into villages and succeeded in moving 150,000 into 190 new villages. Operation Kigoma followed the next year.

The voluntary villagization period came to a final close in 1973 when a resolution at the Party's biennial conference called for all rural Tanzanians to be living in villages by 1976. In November, Nyerere announced that "to live in a village is an order." In the language of the Tanzanian leadership, the new approach was that of a massive "frontal attack." District and regional officials reacted swiftly. It is estimated that between three and six million peasants were moved into villages in one year. As in the previous operations, government planners hurriedly chose the village sites, often with more concern for road accessibility than quality of farm land. While promises of credit, services, and famine relief (Tanzania suffered a major drought in 1973) were still employed, coercion was also employed in cases where peasants resisted the move—including the burning of homes and crops in areas outside the new village sites.

In terms of numbers moved, the national villagization operation succeeded. Over eight thousand villages were created. However, contrary to the original rationale for villagization, the new villages had little to do with collectivized socialist production. According to the Village Act of 1975, the new villages were "development" rather than "*ujamaa*" villages. Over time, it was hoped, the villages would grow as multipurpose agricultural and cottage industry cooperatives.

The success of the "frontal attack" villagization effort (in the terms just discussed) was largely due to another major government initiative of the period: decentralization. Based on a study by an American business consulting firm (McKinsey and Company), in 1972 the government passed an act that ostensibly was to increase mass participation in government decision-making and to increase the accessibility of services to the rural populations. In practice, the decentralization was the most decisive step in a long series of moves increasing Party and government control over day to day life in the rural areas. A hierarchical chain of command, unbroken due to the removal of the last vestiges of any autonomous local government, allowed the Party and government officials to issue directives for massive operations. The only significant political economic structures remaining outside of direct state control were the agricultural cooperatives. Arguing (not without some justification) that many cooperative leaders were using the institutions for their own personal profit, the Party disbanded the cooperatives in 1976.

Given the Party's stated goal of socialist transformation based on equitable rural development, and given the structures of power and inherent resistance in an underdeveloped social formation such as Tanzania, one should not assume that such a centralization of power is necessarily negative. For example, in 1974 the new government structure allowed the Party to issue, with some confidence, a directive that changed the target date for universal primary education from 1989 to 1977. The decentralized system of government was essential for a massive mobilization of villagers to construct new schools on a self-help basis and for training the thousands of new teachers needed. Moreover, in issuing the directive to speed up universal primary education, the party leaders specifically cited the national literacy campaign as justification that it could be done.

The main issue, then, is who controls the centralized system and to what end it is used. One important analyst of Tanzania's political economy, Goran Hyden (then a professor of political science at the University of Dar es Salaam), argued that the frontal attacks, operations, and other campaigns of the 1970s were attempts by Nyerere and other key socialist leaders to prevent the government officials—from ministry offices in the capital to the villages—from consolidating power.[20] The slogan "we must run while others walk," according to Hyden, described a style of policy making in which the officials, or Tanzania's "bureaucratic bourgeoisie," was kept off balance, always pressured to respond to nearly impossible deadlines to meet the needs of the rural masses (including literacy and primary education). On the other hand, the disbanding of the Ruvuma Development Association and the general style of the villagization efforts suggest that, at least in some of the cases, the government officials were in control of the frontal attack strategies of this period. The highly technocratic orientation in the McKinsey and Company's assessment of government organization, leading to the decentralization in 1972 and also informing the same company's study of village development needs in 1975 (which led to or at least helped justify decisions to post government staff as managers at the village level in the late 1970s), was consistent with the orientation of the officials: "progress" was being blocked largely as the result of the inability of peasants to plan and manage their own development efforts.

The National Literacy Campaign (Early 1970s–1979)

Understood in the above context, the national literacy campaign was one of the first frontal attack efforts by the Tanzanian state. The immediate origins of the campaign were discussed in the chapter's introduction: Nyerere's New Year's eve speech directing that illiteracy should be totally eliminated in six districts during the 1971 calendar year, followed by the Party's directive that illiteracy should be eliminated in the entire nation in just four years. Having established a new Department of Adult Education in the Ministry of National Education, and having solidified a strong line of support from the Swedish

[20]Goran Hyden, "Administration and Public Policy," in J. D. Barkan and J. Okumu, eds., *Politics and Public Policy in Kenya and Tanzania* (Nairobi: Heinemann Educational Books, 1979).

International Development Authority (SIDA), the Tanzanian leaders had laid the foundation for such ambitious efforts. And, with the decentralization of 1972 and the massive national villagization operation that followed, the task was made somewhat more manageable.

Perhaps none of the Party leaders who decided to call for a national literacy campaign really believed that Adult Education could actually meet its four-year timeline, and thus the directive might be considered, in Hyden's terms, a conscious effort to make the government officials "run." On the other hand, perhaps the generally apolitical, "functional" orientation of the literacy effort—due, in turn, to the technocratic ideological orientation of the officials responsible for implementing the campaign, and/or to the very fact that the officials needed to respond quickly, with WOALPP being the only readily available model—resulted in increased control of the bureaucrats over the peasants, rather than increased control of the socialist leaders over the bureaucrats.

As pointed out in the introduction, while it is clear that the literacy effort was supposed to increase peasant power and help build socialist rural villages, we lack the evidence needed to confidently assess the campaign's impact. Moreover, we can expect that the latter will have both short and longer-term effects, that these may be contradictory, and that any impact will necessarily always be in relation to changes in the more general social formation in Tanzania. Nevertheless, the available descriptions of the campaign organization and method used during this historical period do provide the basis for some tentative inferences.

The organization of the national campaign was critical to the enrollment successes. Shifting the responsibility for literacy and adult education from Rural Development to National Education had been rationalized as a means of coopting the resources of all schools, teachers, and students into the adult effort, and the new Department of Adult Education especially benefitted from the designation of every head teacher in primary schools as the local adult education coordinator. However, it appears that an equal, if not more significant, factor in National Education's performance was largely outside the ministry's control: the changes in overall government organization that led up to and culminated in the government decentralization of 1972. Between 1970 and 1975, salaried adult education coordinator posts (and then other adult education posts) were included in the general expansion of government and party staff in every region, then every district, then every division and ward—the administrative levels of governance connecting capital and village. Furthermore, as part of a more general process of making joint appointments, all adult education coordinators were also designated Party education coordinators. With the designation, the power needed to enforce central party directives about enrollment in the literacy campaign.

At the apex of the campaign, the first Director of Adult Education, Emmanuel Kibira (who held the post for approximately ten years), benefited from a close personal relationship to the President and significant other contacts in the Party and (as noted previously) in Sweden. He was known as a very forceful and demanding leader, very willing to draw on those contacts for achieving his goals.

With regard to the literacy campaign, his goal was single-minded: high enrollment. In an interview with the national newspaper, Kibira said that any regional or district leaders who failed to insure full enrollment in the campaign would have to answer directly to him.

Kibira was not known to be particularly concerned with the details of planning or administration. It is perhaps evidence of Kibira's very close relations with various Swedes connected to Tanzania and the Swedish International Development Authority that in 1970 SIDA made the acceptance of a Swedish planning advisor a prerequisite of receiving other Swedish aid. Kibira reluctantly agreed. SIDA immediately began supplying paper for printing primers, and in 1972, as the national campaign was just getting underway, a Swedish planner was assigned to the Department of Adult Education. The pattern of conflict between the Tanzanian responsible for WOALPP and his UNESCO counterpart was repeated once again, though here in an apparently far more low key style.

More importantly, the Swedes by now were deeply committed to the literacy effort in Tanzania. Despite any strains in the relationship between Kibira and their main advisor, SIDA signed a second agreement to support Adult Education in 1973, providing funds for training workshops for adult education staff and literacy teachers and for honoraria to compensate the teachers, as well as for various supporting projects (e.g., rural libraries). The next year SIDA signed another agreement, expanding the amount and scope of the support (especially in the area of purchasing transport vehicles for the adult education staff and in supporting the Adult Education Press). In 1975, as part of SIDA's commitment to establishing sectoral funding agreements that a recipient country might use very flexibly to meet its long-term objectives in a given sector, a five-year agreement was made for Swedish support to Tanzanian education, and adult education was guaranteed stable funding through the end of the decade. In the same year, SIDA also agreed to support the capital development costs of Tanzania's newest adult education effort: the creation of residential Folk Development Colleges in all of the then eighty rural districts of the country. In the process of the 1970 agreements, Swedish aid became the sole source of Adult Education's development budget and often, when the recurrent budget of operating funds from local sources was inadequate, the SIDA funds also covered key costs such as teacher honoraria.

The campaign's hierarchical structure and the expanding, flexible Swedish support allowed the campaign to recruit thousands of literacy teachers (see Table 4). Many were "volunteers" paid only a small, though for most not an insignificant, honorarium of thirty shillings (several dollars) per month. The teachers were trained in workshops organized by regional and district adult education staff, who in turn had been trained by the former WOALPP staff. The teachers initially used the functional-literacy primers developed for WOALPP and designed to teach subject matter relevant to the illiterates at the same time they learned how to read, write, and do simple arithmetic.

The books and all instruction were Swahili, the national language spoken as a second language by nearly all Tanzanians (the major exceptions being

Table 4. Literacy Teachers, 1970–1981

Year	Professional teachers	Voluntary teachers	School students	Others	Total
1970	7,643	663	1,639	2,992	12,937
1971	13,135	487	2,394	13,325	29,341
1972	33,903	46,865	4,031	3,307	88,106
1973	20,672	59,590	2,893	11,107	94,262
1974	13,289	79,648	4,469	10,267	107,673
1975	14,917	94,607	9,409	14,952	133,885
1976					175,185
1977					193,987
1978					207,000
1979					55,550
1980					70,504
1981					114,152

Source: Johnsson, Nystrom, and Sunden, *Adult Education in Tanzania*, p. 16.

nomads or farmers in very remote settings, and especially the women in those situations). The language is spelled phonetically, which simplifies instruction. "Writers' workshops" were formed to modify the original primers and prepare new ones. The Adult Education Press, within the ministry's Department of Adult Education, was responsible for publishing the primers.

The teachers were supported by two weekly radio broadcasts, and the literacy students by a full range of other educational programs. Other weekly radio broadcasts focused on the students—including one which for several years contained "songs for literacy" sung by literacy and other adult education classes. In a Department of Adult Education research study in 1982, approximately one third of the new literates in the survey reported that they listened to the broadcasts. The WOALPP-initiated rural newspapers were combined into one regional paper, and then several other regional papers were initiated during the 1970s. In the same 1982 study, eighty percent of the new literates reported that they regularly read one of the papers. The WOALPP rural library program was continued and expanded, resulting in approximately 2,900 libraries in villages, most staffed by a volunteer librarian who receives an honorarium similar to that of a literacy teacher. Four vans were set up in 1972 to show films in villages, expanding to twenty by the end of the decade. Finally, WOALPP's program of "work-oriented projects" (*vituo maalumu*, which literally translates as "special centers") was expanded. The program provided tools, materials and in some cases workshops for groups of literacy students who then learned carpentry, masonry, sewing, other crafts, and (less often) agriculture by doing. According to government statistics, around 2,300 projects had been established by the end of the 1970s.[21]

In 1976, the Department of Adult Education began postliteracy classes for graduates of the literacy classes. Enrollment grew from 140,000 in the first year

[21] Statistics and evaluation data of the support programs taken from Anders Johnsson *et al.*, *Adult Education in Tanzania*, pp. 20–25.

to approximately 1.3 million in 1981. The courses comprised of subjects similar to the regular school system were divided in three stages called V, VI and VII. The numbering system was built on the four stages in the literacy examinations, but stage VII was misunderstood by many to represent the equivalent of the final year of primary school, known as Standard VII. Stage V initially had eleven books (including Swahili, mathematics, political education, agriculture, home economics, handicrafts, health, political economics, and English) and a similar number was planned for each of the other two stages. However, by the end of the 1970s, only three Stage VI books had been published, and the Department of Adult Education was rethinking the curriculum.

As noted at the beginning of the chapter, the impact of the literacy and postliteracy classes is unclear. Kassam's study suggests very positive outcomes in terms of individual empowerment, but is severely limited by sample size. The Ministry of Education's follow-up study in 1983 had a very large sample, but its methods were questionable, and its findings difficult to interpret. A third and starkly contrasting assessment is contained in an article by Michaela von Freyhold, an expatriate member of the University of Dar es Salaam faculty during the 1970s. Through "somewhat unsystematic observations" made in the course of her fairly extensive research on the villagization efforts and her work as a volunteer literacy teacher in Dar es Salaam, von Freyhold identified a number of "obvious problems that arise from the present system" of literacy education.[22] Some are the same problems that plagued the previous literacy programs organized by Community (later Rural) Development, including WOALPP: inadequate teacher training, teachers who are too young to command the respect of illiterate elders, and so forth.

Von Freyhold's assessment, however, focuses on the political dynamics. For example, she reports that the high enrollment levels often resulted from threats of heavy fines or other pressure from the party, and that the attendance rates dropped dramatically whenever party pressure was relaxed. Agricultural primers carried information that was either overly abstract or uncritically repeated advice inconsistent with the peasants' more intimate knowledge of the costs and returns for different crops—which in turn reflected more general social relations of unequal power and hierarchical authority between government "experts" and peasant farmers. Thus, there was "little interest in using adult education as a base for communal action"[23] and that "education had no organic link to village development."[24] Von Freyhold suggests that those relations were fairly conscious:

> After a visit by Paulo Freire to Tanzania [in 1971] there were some discussions on whether it would be advisable to make the primers more 'problem-posing' and open. In the end this suggestion was turned down. The planners argued that: 'If we allow the peasants to criticize the advice of the extension agent, we undermine his authority.' Nor should there be any discussion of the choice of crops: 'If peasants begin to discuss

---

[22] Michaela von Freyhold, "Some Observations on Adult Education in Tanzania," in H. Hinzen and V. H. Hunsdorfer (eds.), *The Tanzanian Experience: Education for Liberation and Development* (London: Evans Brothers, 1979), p. 162.

[23] Ibid., p. 163.

[24] Ibid., p. 165.

whether they want to grow cotton or not they might decide against it, and if they produce no cotton where are we going to get our foreign exchange from?'[25]

At the local level of campaign implementation, von Frehold suggests that

> where educational campaigns were launched under official auspices, the different people who had to co-operate in implementing them at the local level tended to view them as part of the power struggle going on in the village. The opportunity to 'give' something to the learners—at least in the earlier stages of the campaign when learners were still interested—or the chance to pose to the outside world in front of a group of people doing what the nation wanted—were seen as tactical advantages gained by one side or the other, by government staff [or] the village leadership or by certain factions within the village. Education programs thus came to be seen not as a way of giving the ordinary villagers more power but as excercising power over them.[26]

Von Freyhold's conclusion, while empirically no more valid than Kassam's, is consistent with the latter author's assessment of the short-term outcomes of the literacy campaign:

> Adult education may be designed to make workers and peasants more subservient and dependent or it may be designed to help them to raise their own consciousness, articulate their own interests and make their own choices. The political philosophy of the President of Tanzania sees adult education as a tool for the liberation of the masses, but the way in which adult education has actually been planned and implemented in Tanzania appears to be unrelated to this objective.[27]

The Current Crisis (1980s)

The history of the literacy campaign has now entered a period of economic crisis. Given the analytic orientation of this chapter, it is important to note the relation of the campaign to two of the major contradictions of the "frontal attack" period. Those contradictions have both contributed to the current crisis and directly effected the options for future literacy efforts in Tanzania.

First, the literacy campaign was one of several highly visible efforts during the 1970s (along with universal primary education, health and sanitation programs directed at villages, and so forth) that attracted international attention to Tanzania's development strategy. As the international aid establishment developed a new interest in "basic needs" assistance in the face of the failure of many of their previous efforts to help the poorest of the poor, Tanzania was a highly visible target for channeling such aid. And even though the Arusha Declaration called for a close monitoring of aid dependency, bureaucrats understood that access to aid was essential to building up their own programs—especially as economic conditions beame worse and there was no other reliable source of foreign currency to purchase equipment, vehicles, and certain supplies. Thus, the special connections between Tanzanians in the Ministry of Education (and the Institute of Adult Education) and Scandinavian (especially Swedish) educators and aid officials was essential for the success of the campaign. In this

[25] Ibid., p. 166.
[26] Ibid., pp. 165–166.
[27] Ibid., pp. 166–167.

sense, the literacy effort was made possible by, and contributed to, the growth
of aid dependency.

The contradictions in aid dependency have become more clear in the 1980s,
during which time there has been a significant erosion in external support.
General world recession reduced the commitment of many Western nations to
aid that is not tied directly to their own foreign economic or military interests.
The United States, which in the early 1980s was the second largest single source
of aid to Tanzania, began to lead the criticism of Tanzania's domestic policies,
blaming them for the nation's economic problems. The U.S. argued for free
enterprise and for the austerity measures which the International Monetary
Fund wished to impose as conditions for balance of payment assistance. In 1983,
th U.S. invoked a special ammendment to its aid legislation that justified the
total withdrawal of all foreign aid to Tanzania. The strong international criticism
forced even SIDA, which had become by far the largest single source of aid to
Tanzania, to carefully justify each of its programs to an increasingly skeptical
parliament and public. Thus, unlike the case of highly responsive SIDA assistance
in the early phases of the literacy campaign, the 1980s has been a period of slow
and careful negotiations between the Swedes and the Department of Adult
Education over proposals to restructure and expand the postliteracy classes that
had begun in 1976.[28]

A second important contradiction of the previous period that has become
more evident in the 1980s is the high costs of the extensive, multilevel ("decentralized") bureaucracy which was so essential for implementing the various "frontal attack" operations and campaigns of that period—including the national
literacy campaign. While it is unlikely that the literacy enrollments would have
been so high and sustained without such organization, the large (relative to
national income) civil service payroll has proven to be a major burden on the
peasant agricultural sector. The bureaucracy, and especially the parastatal marketing boards, became the focus of much of the external criticism. Nyerere and
other key Tanzanian leaders were equally self-critical of their own decisions to
eliminate local government and the cooperatives, and new legislation was adopted
for reinstating both. The implementation of that legislation is too recent to assess
whether or not the new structures will continue to be dominated by the bureaucratic class and their self-interests.

In any case, the future of adult education is unclear. The more difficult
and less visible efforts to reach the final fifteen percent of the population that
remains illiterate, and to provide support and continued education to the new
literates, are not likely to provide the Tanzanian state with new international
legitimacy. Those efforts appear to have now become a lower priority for national
leaders and bureaucrats, as they take on the more pressing issues of the economic
crisis. Moreover, if the hierarchical structure of the extensive civil service is once

---

[28] In defense of SIDA's position, the Department of Adult Education's proposals for future postliteracy efforts do appear to have been vague, costly, and oriented toward a classroom approach to
adult learning. SIDA's efforts to clarify and improve the potential of the postliteracy proposals,
which included a special study mission, appear to have produced a program plan which may be
more oriented toward a practice approach to adult learning.

again broken through the reestablishment of autonomous local governments, the status of adult education may become all the more problematic. Responding to local pressure, and especially to the demand for further schooling from the first generations of universal primary-school graduates, those new government structures are likely to prioritize secondary education over adult education.

What is clear is that any future efforts in literacy and adult education will continue to be conditioned by the larger historical and structural developments in Tanzania's political economy. While I share von Freyhold's general assessment of the short-term impact of the national literacy campaign, I suspect that the bureaucratic class may at some point find a literate peasantry to be capable of challenging their power in ways otherwise difficult.

CHAPTER 11

Adult Literacy for Development in India

An Analysis of Policy and Performance

H. S. BHOLA

This study presents an analysis of the role of adult literacy in the development of India, comparing policy against performance and intention against action. A political theory of adult literacy in development provides the conceptual framework. Two general development models are identified: the motivational-developmental model (where the responsibility for development is placed on the individual who must aspire, learn, act, and achieve); and the structural-developmental model (where the state must take the initiative to change political and economic structures). What use is made of adult literacy in development in a particular country depends upon the overall development model being followed.

The conceptualization contributes to an understanding of the role of adult literacy in development in India from the pre-Independence period to the present time. The National Adult Education Program (NAEP, now renamed AEP), launched in 1978, has been given special attention in the analysis presented here. This is so because NAEP constituted the first instance ever in the educational history of India when an adult education and adult literacy program of such scope and size was introduced in the country. A discussion of the ideology and the technology of NAEP is followed with a review of the available evaluations of its impact.

The Indian case reinforces the emerging understanding that technical solutions and pedagogical innovation are much easier to develop than creating and sustaining political commitment. The study also points to the fact that provision (even partial provision) of adult literacy may have far-reaching consequences, and that results may not always be apparent from the ongoing processes. Finally, there is a larger history of many histories of small literacy projects and programs, some successful and some not so successful. This larger history seems to point to the inevitability of universalization of literacy all over the world, if not in the twentieth century, then early during the twenty-first century.

H. S. BHOLA • School of Education, Indiana University, Bloomington, Indiana 47405.

Mohandas K. Gandhi, who would later be called "The Mahatma" (the Saint) and "The Father of the Nation," returned to India in 1915 from South Africa, where he had organized his first passive-resistance campaign against racial discrimination. Back in India, Mahatma Gandhi continued with his "experiments with truth" on a much larger political stage and with much greater resoluteness. It had been Gandhi's task to capture the imagination of the Indian people and to create a mass movement for national independence. The task of establishing a national government for post-Independence India fell to Pandit Jawaharlal Nehru, who became Prime Minister in 1947 and held that office until his death in 1964.

Over the years of struggle for independence, the Indian National Congress, the party that Nehru led into government in 1947, had made solemn resolutions promising economic and social reforms in the country, in line with the "modernization ideology." It was now time to make good on those promises. However, as Gunnar Myrdal[1] has pointed out so insightfully, the Indian "liberation movement was an upper-class protest movement," despite Mahatma Gandhi's appeal to the masses. The party in power was a party of the elite with a narrow social base, and with no pressure from the masses to respond to their needs.

Understandably, India under Nehru followed the pattern of "bold radicalism in principle but extreme conservatism in practice." Universal suffrage did not transfer power to the people, but merely compelled the politicians to build coalitions with landlords, merchants, and moneylenders—the dominant elements in the rural setting.

In this regard, not much has changed in India, since 1964, the year of Nehru's death. The governments of Lal Bahadur Shastri, of Mrs. Indira Gandhi, Nehru's daughter,[2] of Morarji Desai and Charan Singh of the Janata Party, and now of Rajiv Gandhi, Nehru's grandson, have stayed the course. All these governments have declared themselves to be the protectors of the poor and the downtrodden and have indeed passed an impressive body of social legislation. Unfortunately, its implementation has been effectively thwarted by the vested interests entrenched within the Indian body politic. The landowners, the moneylenders, and the urban middle class have defended their privileges both with wile and (sometimes) violence.

EDUCATION FOR DEVELOPMENT

Prime Minister Jawaharlal Nehru, in accepting the Western ideology of modernization, also accepted the Western model of development, based on industrialization and scientific agriculture. In so doing, he accepted the education

---

[1]Gunnar Myrdal, *Asian Drama: An Inquiry into the Poverty of Nations* (New York: Pantheon, 1968), pp. 257–303. Other quotations in this section are also from Myrdal unless otherwise stated.

[2]Mrs. Indira Gandhi, the daughter of Prime Minister Jawaharlal Nehru, and for many years the Prime Minister of India herself, was no relative of Mahatma Gandhi. She got the "Gandhi" surname from marrying Feroz Gandhi, an Indian Parsi, who for many years was active in the Indian independence movement.

and development connection. Education would serve the purposes both of modernization and democratization. Attention would be given to both ends of the educational spectrum: to higher education to produce the manpower needed for bringing about modernization, and to the universalization of primary education to make democratization possible.

India's experience with education as a tool for manpower training and as an instrument of development in general has been subjected to considerable discussion. In some ways the distortions and dysfunctions of the educational system in India are in no way different from those seen to appear elsewhere in the Third World and need not concern us here.[3]

However, one does need to take a quick view of India's effort at the universalization of primary education. As various Unesco policy statements over the years have pointed out, the implementation of universal adult literacy policies will require a dual strategy: universal primary education and nation-wide adult literacy campaigns. One or the other by itself will not do. Both objectives have to be pursued at the same time.[4]

The constitution that came into force in 1950 accepted the obligation to provide approximately eight years of free and compulsory education for all children by 1960. Thirty-five years after the constitutional directive, the task is still not fully accomplished. Targets for 1984–1985 were to enroll 95.2 percent of the children in the age group six to eleven.[5] Stagnation and wastage is endemic in schools in rural and poor urban areas, and as few as thirty-five percent of those who begin may actually complete the primary education cycle of five years. This takes away much of the glow from the otherwise impressive achievements in formal education. This does not augur well for literacy or for modernization and democratization.

The immediate tasks of development could not, of course, have waited for India's children to come out of their schools all prepared for waging battle in behalf of the modernization and democratization of society. The millions of severely deprived adult men and women caught in the structures of colonialism, both external and internal, had to be rescued. To help them to help themselves, they had to be provided with adult education.[6]

Unfortunately, adult education did not receive the attention from politicians and policy makers that it deserved. There was, of course, no lack of rhetoric, but needed resources were not allocated to promote the education of adults to

[3]See Joseph Di Bona, ed., *The Context of Education in Indian Development* (Durham, North Carolina: Duke University Press, 1974). For a global view of the role of education in development, see Philip H. Coombs, *The World Crisis in Education: The View from the Eighties* (New York: Oxford University Press, 1985).
[4]Programme II.1: "Promotion of General Access to Education: Development and Renewal of Primary Education and Intensification of the Struggle Against Illiteracy," *Unesco's Second Medium-Term Plan (1984–1989)*, 4XC/4 Approved, Unesco, 1983, pp. 72–74.
[5]*India 1982* (New Delhi: Publications Division, Ministry of Information and Broadcasting, Government of India, 1982), p. 46.
[6]Some of the other terms used to describe adult education are adult basic education, social education, fundamental education, continuing education, lifelong education, and, more recently, nonformal education. See H. S. Bhola, "Nonformal Education in Perspective," *Prospects* 13(1983): 45–53.

enable them to participate effectively in the economic, social, and political institutions and, hopefully, to make these institutions responsive to people's needs.
Significantly, adult education was separated from adult literacy. In other words,
literacy was not always a part of adult education.

Dr. V. K. R. V. Rao, an eminent Indian economist, who served both as
member in charge of education in the Indian Planning Commission and as a
Minister of Education in the central government in New Delhi, was invited to
address the Silver Jubilee Conference of the Indian Adult Education Association
in March 1964. In his address, he wondered aloud why, immediately after independence, India had not launched a massive adult literacy program, and expressed
sadness over the fact that even after almost two decades of independence, the
government did not seem particularly bothered about the shamelessly high rates
of illiteracy in India.[7] But there is, indeed, nothing unexpected in regard to
adult literacy policy and performance in India. We should expect to see a congruence between the political culture of a society and its adult literacy policy
and performance. Such congruence does exist in the case of India.

A THEORY OF LITERACY FOR DEVELOPMENT

Developing societies of the Third World can be seen to follow one of two
general development models: a structural-developmental model or a motivation-
developmental model. The two models are not mutually exclusive, but they do
spawn different development policies and very different priorities among those
policies. The motivational-developmental model, for instance, emphasizes individual motivations. Individuals must learn to aspire and should be motivated to
achieve. Social structures are seen to be essentially benign, though some structural adjustments are not ruled out. The motivational-developmental model is
a reformist model. Its uses of education are conservative. Adult literacy is offered
in the context of control, to perform specified vocational-technical functions
within specific development projects and (sometimes) programs.

The structural-developmental model focuses on economic, social, and political structures. Structures are seen to determine the rules of the game. Structures,
therefore, must be changed to integrate the people into new political, social, and
economic relationships. People will learn motivations once they know that the
new structures are helpful rather than oppressive. This is a revolutionary model.
It makes revolutionary uses of education. Adult literacy is typically offered in
the context of nationwide mass campaigns that would teach people to read the
word as well as to read the world.[8]

A theory of literacy for development must, therefore, embrace the two
dimensions of ideology and technology. The prevailing ideology of the power
elite in a particular society will determine whether policy initiatives for literacy

[7]V.K.R.V. Rao, *Adult Education and Development* (New Delhi: Ministry of Education and Youth Services, 1970), p. 2.
[8]H. S. Bhola, *Campaigning for Literacy* (Paris, UNESCO, 1984), pp. 196–199.

promotion will be taken at all, what uses might be made of literacy in the overall developmental process, and what role the people will be assigned in the process of their own alphabetization. The availability and the utilization of technology, both hard and soft, will determine how effectively a policy of literacy promotion is actually planned and implemented. Political will is a necessary condition for successful literacy campaigns and large-scale programs. It might be said that ideology is perhaps both a necessary and sufficient condition. Ideological commitment can often overwhelm merely technical problems. Thus, while technology of planning and instructional design helps, it is seldom the reason for the success of failure of policies of literacy promotion.[9]

HISTORICAL AND POLITICAL CONTEXT OF LITERACY IN INDIA: LITERACY DURING THE BRITISH PERIOD

There was mass education in India before the British arrived, but the British brought a new ideology of adult education to the country. The first contact was destructive of indigenous institutions and traditional modes of mass education. Sohan Singh[10] writes, "In the last years of the 18th century, we find India lying prostrate in economic, political and cultural degradation and ruin. However, as the next century advanced in years new India began to rise from the ashes of the old one, till by 1885 she had recovered her soul as completely as she had lost it."

From 1917 onwards, the fortunes of adult education (which always included adult literacy in one of the local languages) were quite clearly correlated with the tempo of India's struggle for independence. During the postwar years 1918–1927, there was renewed demand for franchise, and literacy became a part of the process of awakening. Gokhale, whom Gandhi himself recognized as his guru, consistently stressed the necessity of eliminating illiteracy in India, and he won over the entire nationalist movement to his point of view. Thus, in the 1920s, literacy campaigns among adults were inaugurated in India for the first time. Again, during the years 1937–1942, there was considerable interest in literacy in the context of the political movement towards freedom. With the advent of popular ministries in the provinces, there was hope and enthusiasm all around. Illiteracy was seen as the "sin and shame" of a nation in shackles.

The political leaders of the time led the way in demonstrating their commitment to literacy. Syed Mahmud, the Minister of Education in the Province of Bihar, stood on the road with a piece of chalk in his hand and a blackboard beside him to teach the unlettered. C. Rajagopalchari, the Premier of Madras, who would later be the President of the Indian Republic, himself wrote little

---

[9]H. S. Bhola, "The Theory of the Mass Literacy Campaign" (Paper Presented to the Seventh Annual Henry Lester Smith Conference on Research in Education, Indiana University, Bloomington, Indiana, February 1–2, 1982). ERIC Document No. ED 211 687.

[10]This section of the paper is heavily indebted to Sohan Singh, *History of Adult Education During British Period* (Delhi: Indian Adult Education Association, 1957).

books in Tamil for newly literate adults to read. In the princely state of Aundh, the royal father and son wandered from village to village preaching the message of literacy. The Prince closed all the primary schools in the state for two to three months so that students and teachers could go into the rural areas to teach reading and writing to peasants, a strategy that Fidel Castro would use in Socialist Cuba twenty-five years later, but on a much larger scale.

It was also during 1937–1942 that literacy became part of the policy agenda of the government. The Central Advisory Board of Education, at its fourth meeting held in December 1938, appointed a committee to consider literacy policy. The committee submitted its report in 1940 and made recommendations that were a mix of the bold and the conservative. Literacy, it said boldly, should not be considered to be an end in itself, but a movement for further education. The teaching of literacy, it added in a conservative note, should be closely related to the learner's occupation, his personal interests, as well as to his social and economic conditions. Voluntary agencies should be associated with the national effort to eradicate illiteracy, but the movement ought not be used for religious or political propaganda. The committee invited special attention to the disadvantage of women and was bold enough to suggest the levying of a tax on those employers in urban areas who did not make adequate provision for the education of their employees.

The *Report on Postwar Educational Development* had outlined a plan to make all adults literate within twenty-five years, at an estimated cost of 127 million rupees (one U.S. dollar is about twelve rupees today). At the rate of half a rupee per adult made literate, the estimate was by no means generous, but the plan in itself was. The Central Advisory Board of Education, at its tenth meeting in January 1944, endorsed this plan and proposed a "complete scheme of adult education" of its own. The eight-point scheme should be of interest to students of adult literacy and is reproduced fully below:

1. Adult education, which, in the first stages, would be mainly literacy work, should be conducted in classes of two kinds: one for men and the other for women. The men's group would include, firstly, classes for boys from ten to sixteen years of age and, secondly, for grown-ups from seventeen to forty. Women's classes would not be divided into age groups and would cater to women from ten to forty.

2. Teaching in the adult education centers would be practical and relate to the activities and the environments of the adults. The centers would also have vocational classes for those who at least to begin with, might not be attracted by the cultural side of adult instruction and might wish to learn some craft.

3. The literacy course should be of a year's duration. The adults would attend classes for about four days a week, and there would be no classes in busy seasons.

4. The teachers at the adult education centers should be fully trained for their work. The inspectors and organizers who would look after the adult education centers should themselves be experts in adult education. Besides, a nucleus of specially trained teachers should be appointed, who would not only teach but also assist in selecting, training, and supervising other teachers.

5. Fullest possible use should be made of audiovisual aids to education. A place should also be found in those centers for folk dances, music, and drama.

6. Every adult education center should have a library or have access to a neighboring library.

7. While the primary responsibility for adult education should be the government's, the latter should welcome the voluntary services of organizations such as employers of labor, commercial firms and other trade associations, big landlords, and so forth. Of course, the voluntary organizations should conform to the general principles of the scheme of adult education and keep to the standards of instructional work required by the government.

8. Particular attention should be paid to the adult education of women.

These policies were bold and insightful, but they were not always translated into concrete actions. Using the reports from the provinces sent to the government of India over the years, Sohan Singh has painstakingly compiled statistics of adults actually made literate (Table 1). Thus, there was clearly a decline in adult literacy activities in the years immediately preceding independence. Nationwide protests against the British rule, Hindu-Muslim riots, and perhaps the largest migration of people in human history directed the nation's attention and energy to other tasks.

Literacy in Postindependence India

In regard to adult literacy policy, there seems to be a complete break from preindependence India to postindependence India. All the declarations of the leaders of the Indian independence movement, and all the formal resolutions of the Central Advisory Board of Education were conveniently forgotten. Adult education was still part of the rhetoric but not of real educational policy. Most significantly, adult literacy was conceptually and operationally separated from adult education for reasons that were never stated.

The First Five-Year Development Plan (1951–1956) included a program of social (or adult) education that government documents described as "ambitious." During the Second Five-Year Development Plan (1956–1961), social education was integrated into the program of community development that paid little attention to the teaching of literacy and focused on the social and cultural promotion of adults. The only bright spot on the literacy horizon of those years was the launching in 1959 of the Gram Shikshan Mohim (Village Education

Table 1. Adult Literacy Activity

Number of adult centers	Enrollment in centers	Number of adults made literate
During 1937–1942		
188,777	7,618,189	2,904,068
During 1942–1947		
130,742	2,884,870	1,522,025

Campaign) of Maharashtra that sought to make the whole state (earlier province) literate within five years.

During the Fourth Five-Year Plan (1969–1974) and the Fifth Five-Year Plan (1974–1979, terminated one year earlier in 1978), little attention was paid to adult education or to adult literacy. The only policy initiative in behalf of literacy taken during those years was the Farmers Training and Functional Literacy project of the government of India, planned and implemented in cooperation with Unesco and UNDP. Under this plan, one million farmers in one hundred districts were to be taught functional literacy to enable them to work better with their land under high yielding varieties of food grains.[11]

The financial allocations to adult education during the five five-year plans tell the story. All figures are in millions of rupees. The figures in parentheses are percentage of total financial allocations to education.[12]

Plan I	Plan II	Plan III	Plan IV	Plan V
50	40	20	59	326
(3.5)	(1.6)	(0.4)	(0.1)	(0.3)

There had been no paucity of rhetoric or policy declarations, however. Nehru himself, while addressing a conference of education ministers in November 1963, had said, "I am quite convinced in my mind that our first plan should be for universal education. Everything else, whether it is industry, agriculture, or anything else which is important for us, will grow adequately only if there is a background of mass education."

The *Report of the Education Commission (1964–1966)*[13] came out strongly in behalf of the eradication of illiteracy through "a massive unorthodox national effort." They conceptualized such an effort as a "nationwide, coherent and sustained campaign . . . supported vigorously by the social and political leadership" and "inspired by a faith in [literacy's] vital significance to national life." *The National Policy Resolution* of 1968, in accepting the recommendations of the *Education Commission Report*, emphasized universal literacy "not only for promoting participation in the working of democratic institutions and for accelerating programmes of production, especially in agriculture, but for quickening the tempo of national development in general." At the same time, they seemed to be inspired by Unesco's Experimental World Literacy Program and talked of functional literacy using the selective approach to literacy promotion.

THE NATIONAL ADULT EDUCATION PROGRAM (NAEP)

In March 1977, Morarji Desai took over as Prime Minister of India from Mrs. Indira Gandhi after her election debacle that followed her emergency rule of twenty-one months. Barely a month later, on April 5, 1977, the Union Minister

[11] S.N. Saraf, *Literacy in a Nonliteracy Milieu: The Indian Scenario* (Paris: International Institute for Educational Planning, 1980), pp. 55–70.
[12] *Report of the Review Committee on the National Adult Education Programme* (New Delhi: Ministry of Education and Culture, Government of India, 1980), p. 9.
[13] *Report of the Education Commission (1964–66): Education and National Development* (New Delhi: Ministry of Education, Government of India, 1966), pp. 423–443.

of Education, speaking on the floor of Parliament, made it known that along with the universalization of elementary education up to the age of fourteen, the new government would give the highest priority to adult education as part of its overall educational and developmental planning.

In the months that followed, the Desai government did indeed come up with the National Adult Education Program (NAEP)[14] as part of the Fifth Five-Year Plan of 1978–1983. (This plan did not run its full course.) To mark the birthday of Mahatma Gandhi on October 2, 1978, a national program would be launched. In five years, this program would make 100,000,000 people in the "economically productive" age group of fifteen to thirty-five years functionally literate, enabling and empowering them to participate in the social, economic, and political life of the nation. People, both at home and abroad, were impressed, and some called it an auspicious moment in the history of independent India.

THE IDEOLOGY OF THE NAEP

The NAEP document declared that the government's thinking was based on the following assumptions:

1. That illiteracy is a serious impediment to an individual's growth and to a country's socioeconomic progress.
2. That education is not coterminous with schooling but takes place in most work and life situations.
3. That learning, working, and living are inseparable, and each acquires a meaning only when correlated with the others.
4. That the means by which people are involved in the process of development are at least as important as the ends.
5. That the illiterate and the poor can rise to their own liberation through literacy, dialogue, and action.

Thus, using the radical vocabulary of participation and liberation, unusual for government prose, the NAEP document committed the government to work in behalf of the disadvantaged—the women, the scheduled castes, and the scheduled tribes.[15] The debt of the NAEP document to the work of Paulo Freire, the Brazilian philosopher and educator, and to the Declaration of Persepolis,[16] is obvious. For the Janata Party government of Prime Minister Desai, the NAEP would serve many different purposes. At one level, the NAEP could be seen as Desai's resolve to push forward the Gandhian revolution that had been lost in

---

[14] *National Adult Education Programme: An Outline* (New Delhi: Ministry of Education and Social Welfare, Government of India, 1978).

[15] Scheduled castes and scheduled tribes are those selected castes and tribes which have been listed in special schedules appended to the Indian constitution. The constitution directs that these scheduled castes and tribes be accorded special protection of the constitution and affirmative action be taken in their behalf to provide them education and employment.

[16] Paulo Freire, *Pedagogy of the Oppressed* (New York: Herder and Herder, 1970). See also Leon Bataille, ed., *A Turning Point for Literacy: Proceedings of the International Symposium for Literacy, Persepolis, Iran, 1975* (Oxford: Pergamon Press, 1976).

the post-Independence period and had never been given a real chance. It would seek to end Indira Gandhi's personality cult and the politics of charisma. At another level, the NAEP could be seen as a strategy for a positive platform for the Janata Party, a move to legitimize the power of the Party by acting in behalf of the people, and thereby to keep Mrs. Indira Gandhi out in the wilderness.

THE TECHNOLOGY OF THE NATIONAL ADULT EDUCATION PROGRAM

We have talked earlier of the theory of literacy for development. We suggested that such a theory is two-dimensional, involving both ideology and technology. Ideology first determines policy choices: whether adult literacy will be considered central to the process of social transformation of a society, and what priorities will be assigned to different competing educational and development needs at a particular historical time in society. The prevailing ideology and the existent political culture then determine what planning assumptions are made, and what technological choices are made in regard to resource generation, recruitment of participants and pedagogues, institutional arrangements, communication, and instruction. The "literacy for development theory" model[17] will be used to describe and analyze the NAEP.

1. *Birth of the mass literacy campaign.* It should be noted at the very outset that the government scrupulously avoided the use of the word "campaign" in its discussion and documentation related to the NAEP. Also, it was called an "adult education" program, not an adult literacy program.

As a strategy of literacy promotion, the campaign has been dismissed by some development planners as a staged event of relatively short duration with the purpose of achieving quick and dishonest political gains and without any long-term commitment either to literacy or development. Again, it has been seen as something that is possible only within socialist states that are not shy of demanding participation from their people.

None of the above characteristics attributed to a campaign are necessarily inherent in the campaign strategy. As Gandhi's own campaigns of nonviolence in India should teach us, the campaign strategy is not the sole preserve of socialist societies, and socialism need not be the only source of inspiration for campaigns. Campaigns may draw their inspiration from the history and cultures of peoples they seek to mobilize for action. Campaigns need not be undertaken for quick and dishonest gains, but may indeed be central to long-term structural reform in behalf of the people. The mode of mobilization in campaigns need not be coercive, but may be a genuine invitation to people to engage in praxis—the process of reflecting on their reality and acting to transform it. Literacy campaigns, in particular, can be "campaigns within campaigns," including a multiplicity of local initiatives within an overall national vision that is continuously kept alive. These campaigns may begin small and then expand incrementally

[17] H. S. Bhola, *Campaigning*, pp. 176–195.

over time and space. A campaign should thus be seen as a political definition of mode of planning and of action. It must have a sense of urgency and combativeness about it. It must be run like a crusade. The commitment must be intense, involvement must be deep, and perseverance must be inexhaustible.[18]

We have already speculated about the driving forces behind the launching of the NAEP and the political motives of the Janata Party. The planning assumptions of the NAEP need another critical look. Rightly enough, development was defined as fulfilling the "basic needs" of the poorest of the poor; and rightly enough, literacy was seen to be an essential tool that the poor and the powerless had to acquire to improve their lot. Quite rightly again, the universalization of elementary education and adult literacy were seen as mutually interdependent.

A bold operational assumption was made. It was that the government would be made to work on behalf of the disadvantaged through its functionaries and through voluntary agencies that would be invited to participate. In their policies, governments have previously favored the poor and the disadvantaged. However, they have often been revolutionary governments with well-organized party machines and committed cadres. It was somewhat fanciful for the NAEP planners to think that government officials—salaried, career-oriented, and middle-class in orientation—would do so. Most significantly, there was no real or visible attempt to change surrounding social, political, and economic realities. NAEP was the unusual program within the overall political climate of business as usual.

2. *Institutionalization of policy initiatives.* Attempts were made to institutionalize the policy initiative. A National Board for Adult Education was set up at the center, and all state governments were invited to establish state boards for adult education to coordinate thinking and action at the state levels. These were, however, advisory boards, unable to lead or to impose their will on the systems of action.

The institutional location of the NAEP was not the Prime Minister's office or some other new structure superior to all existing developmental ministries. In locating the NAEP in the Ministry of Education, all other ministries were, in a sense, left off the hook. They were supposed to be involved, but they did not develop a sense of ownership of the program. On the positive side, the already existing Directorate of Adult Education in New Delhi was considerably strengthened to enable it to function as a National Resource Center for the NAEP.

Funding for the total program was estimated at 10,560 million rupees. About half of the total estimated expenditures would come from the budgets of state governments and localities and two thousand million rupees were provided within the central budget. More was promised on request. Considering that no more than 460 million rupees had been provided for under all the preceding five-year plans covering some twenty-seven years since 1950–1951, the current funding was generous, to say the least.

The goals of the NAEP were well codified. These were to give the poor and disadvantaged—especially women, scheduled castes, and scheduled tribes—

---

[18]H. S. Bhola in collaboration with Josef Müller and Piet Dijkstra, *The Promise of Literacy* (Baden-Baden: Nomos Verlagsgesellschaft, 1983), pp. 206–207.

literacy, functionality, and awareness. With literacy as a tool, they would learn functional knowledge to become economically more productive. They would also use literacy to "read the world," becoming aware of the social and political roots of their problems, and learning to find solutions to such problems, depending upon their own collective wisdom and strength. But part of the language of policy justification was clearly elitist. Functionality may have been understood by the common man, but not awareness and liberation and conscientization. The language may have mystified rather than mobilized.

3. *Study of preconditions and preplanning.* Too often, failure of literacy campaigns or programs is explained in terms of conditions not being right or lack of proper preparation. The truth is that the politicians and policy makers fail literacy rather than that literacy fails them. It can indeed be asserted that no preconditions are too adverse for a literacy campaign or mass-scale program, if the political will exists. Preconditions therefore need to be studied not for a go/no-go decision on a literacy initiative, but to improve implementation. Again, while preparation helps, action is the best teacher.

NAEP could easily be characterized as the best prepared literacy program in recent times in the world. Earlier national experiences in the area of adult literacy and adult education were systematically analyzed. Visits were made to successful literacy programs all over the world: to Thailand, Vietnam, China, Iraq, Tanzania, Brazil, and other countries. All aspects of mobilization, administration, field organization, program development, pedagogy, training, and evaluation were discussed in national forums, and the best possible solutions were developed.

4. *Mobilization of the masses and mobilization of the state.* Mobilization of the state resources is comparatively easier than the mobilization of the people. In the case of the NAEP, the mobilization of the state resources themselves was not easy. In India, education is a state subject, within the authority of the twenty-two state governments and nine union territories. While the central government can and does exert considerable power over the development policies of states through the instrument of the Planning Commission and through funding centrally sponsored programs, there is a limit to how much the center can demand from the states. Thus, while the resources of the central government may be said to have been somewhat effectively mobilized for launching the NAEP, the same cannot be said about mobilization at the state government level.

In the mobilization of the masses, there were several problems and contradictions. There was no organized party machine. Indeed, the Janata Party itself was a child of a marriage of convenience between several nonsocialist parties in parliament. Decentralization of action necessary for the success of such programs does not succeed without continued centralized visions. The plans for the delivery of the program through the center, the states, and the voluntary agencies did not decentralize the program, it fragmented it. The people were not mobilized. Interestingly enough, government documents kept on equating mobilization with more effective administration and coordination.

5. *The establishment of administrative structures.* There were at least three administrative challenges facing the planners of the NAEP: (a) to develop

interministerial coordination at the center and interdepartmental coordination at the state, district, and field levels; (b) to establish a system of coordination between the center and the states; and (c) to establish interfaces, in each state and union territory, between the state's program and the work of the voluntary associations that were to carry a large burden in the delivery of the program.

The main responsibility for overseeing the NAEP was given to the Ministry of Education. The problem of interministerial coordination was "solved" by establishing a National Board of Adult Education, on which representatives from all development ministries served as members. Interagency coordination at the state and lower levels would also be achieved through similar organizational mechanisms such as state boards of adult education and district committees. In regard to integration between the center and the state, the existing institutional mechanisms were to be used.

An administrative fact of great significance in the case of the NAEP was the governmental decision to work through voluntary associations—NGOs or PVOs in the current international parlance. As many as eight thousand voluntary associations, big and small, have been estimated to exist in India, feeding, healing, caring, teaching, and organizing in villages and slums. The government was to undertake direct responsibility to administrative programs only in areas where no one else would take the initiative. Once again, voluntary associations had to be reached and funded, often through the state governments and not directly by the center. Nothing special was done to coordinate the work of the voluntary associations, and, as we learned, voluntary associations almost succeeded in undoing the program.

A reorganized Directorate of Adult Education (DAE), within the Ministry of Education and Social Welfare, was put at the apex of the administration and technical system. The DAE would function as the center for coordination and catalyzation for the national program as well as act as the source of technology and innovation. At the state level, the DAE promoted the appointment of separate directors of adult education, who would not be subordinate to the directors of general education, but would function autonomously in regard to the NAEP and related adult education programs. Similarly, the appointment of separate and autonomous adult education officers was promoted at the district level.

The most significant administrative unit within the overall administrative network for the NAEP was the project. A project area would be administratively and culturally homogeneous and no larger than two development blocks, including 150–500 adult education centers, run by government and/or voluntary agencies, and serving anywhere from five thousand to sixteen thousand adult participants.[19]

Each project was to be headed by a project officer who would have all the necessary administrative and program staff. Depending upon the number of centers run within the project area, the project officer would have between five

---

[19]The block as a development unit was invented during the heyday of the community development movement in India, when the whole country was divided into some five thousand development blocks. A block typically is made up of one hundred villages.

and twenty supervisors, each supervising some thirty adult education centers. Voluntary associations would have their own supervisors and would feed their reports to the project office.

The NAEP also tried new administrative norms and procedures. They talked of a new administrative culture, based on collegial, instead of hierarchical, relationships. The project officer was made part of the developmental administration rather than of the educational administration, in that he or she was to be supervised by the district collector and not the director of education. The project officer was also authorized to spend the budget without item-by-item clearance from the finance department, as long as expenditures were within the sanctioned budget and allocated to different budget heads.

6. *Technical structures for conducting the NAEP.* A parallel technical structure, referred to as "resource structure" in the NAEP documents, was conceptualized, again going from the DAE at the center, through the states and districts, down to the project level. The DAE was expected to, and did indeed, provide important technical assistance to the whole NAEP program, in regard to conceptualization, training, materials, production, monitoring, and evaluation.

The most important innovation within the technical system was the development of State Resource Centers (SRCs). Each state, as a general rule, was to have its own resource center that would become the nerve center for all technical resources available in the universities, research centers, government departments, and voluntary agencies in the area. Such a resource center would pool these available resources to (1) produce need-based instructional materials in regional and subregional languages for learners and teachers; (2) provide training for functionaries at various levels from the state through the project down to the field; (3) provide technical assistance to individuals and organizations requiring such assistance; and (4) conduct applied research and evaluation and monitoring at the state level. There was the hope that, in due course, there would also be district level resource centers, and that each project office would become a resource center, producing low-cost instructional materials or adapting what was received from outside to the special needs of local communities and specific groups of learners.

The Coverage of the Program

The NAEP sought to cover 100 million adult men and women in the age group fifteen to thirty-five (Table 2). The program was to cover the entire country and was to have projects in all of the twenty-two states and the nine union territories. The teacher–learner ratio was assumed to be 1:30; supervisor-teacher ratio was, again, to be 1:30. Project officer-supervisor ratio was set at 1:10. Thus, beginning with some five hundred project officers, five thousand supervisors, 150,000 literacy instructors, and 4.5 million learners in 1979–1980, the program, in its final year (1983–1984) would be dealing with four thousand project officers, forty thousand supervisors, over a million instructors, and 35,000,000 learners. The program assumed a wastage of up to one-third through dropouts. At the end of 1983–1984, it was to become a diversified program of lifelong education, suitable for a learning society.

Table 2. Coverage of the National Adult Education Program

Year	Annual coverage in millions	Cumulative coverage in millions
1978–1979[a]	1.5	1.5
1979–1980	4.5	6.0
1980–1981	9.0	15.0
1981–1982	18.0	33.0
1982–1983	32.0	65.0
1983–1984	35.0	100.0

[a]The year of preparation.

Curricular Goals of the Program

These goals were conceived to be in three parts: literacy, functionality, and awareness. The curriculum design and delivery would be *relevant* to the environment and learners' needs, *flexible* regarding duration, time, location, instructional arrangements, and so forth, *diversified* in regard to curriculum, teaching and learning materials, and methods, and *systematic* in all aspects of organization. Thus, the overall curriculum planning orientation was to create a mass program with the quality of planning and implementation of a selective program.

At the operational level, the NAEP was a program of adult education, with "literacy as an indispensable component." To ensure functionality, the NAEP program had to relate, on the one hand, with the government's development objectives and, on the other hand, with the needs and realities of the lives of those it would serve. Literacy promotion strategy would fit the development planning strategy, namely, intensive area planning and emphasis on income generation. Wherever possible, literacy work was clearly and directly linked with programs of integrated rural development, integrated tribal development, employment-oriented area planning, and so on.

Awareness was to be an important part of the curriculum, but was not always understood, even by middle-level functionaries. Ideally, the objective was to make learners aware of the things happening around them, to help them understand the roots of their disadvantage and the sources of their problems, to enable them to understand the mechanisms for improving their conditions, and, finally, to give them the conviction that something could be done about all this. In reality, nothing of this was even reflected in the curriculum, and field-level workers, if not unsympathetic ideologically, were ill-prepared to teach these ideas in the context of "dialogic action."

Recruitment and Training of Functionaries

Instructional work was to be done by "paid volunteers," who would receive fifty rupees per month—four to five days' wages of an unskilled laborer. They would come from among the ranks of school teachers, university students serving under the National Service Scheme, unemployed and underemployed village youths, exservicemen, government extension workers doing extra work, and voluntary social workers. Instructors would normally come from the communities where they would teach. At least half of the instructors would be women.

Considerable attention was to be given to training.[20] The NAEP would provide training of no less than twenty-one days, with additional refresher courses and experiences, to *all* functionaries, so that they could be taught both the values and objectives of the program and the basic techniques of their work.

Instruction and Instructional Materials

It was envisaged that learners would be provided three hundred to 350 hours of instruction over a period of nine months, using, as far as possible, the spoken language of learners as the language of literacy. There would be a division of labor in the production of materials, some being produced at the state level, others at the district level, and some even at the project level. A whole variety of instructional media would be used, including folk, print, and electronic media.

It was not going to be possible for districts and projects to float teams that could prepare suitable reading materials in spoken languages, tailored to their clients, in the very first year of prepreparation. As a purely interim measure, therefore, it was decided that the State Resource Centers (SRCs) would prepare materials in standard regional and subregional languages and dialects. By the second or third years, local projects should have produced their own materials to read in the early stages, before switching to the regional languages.

Postliteracy Materials and Programs

Due attention was to be paid to the production of follow-up reading materials to ensure against relapse into illiteracy. Those who wanted to enter the formal education system were to be provided with suitable entry points. Most important, interfaces had to be built between literacy and social, economic, and political institutions of the society to enable people to put literacy to use in their lives.[21]

Monitoring the NAEP and Evaluating its Effects

Considerable time and effort was put into designing systems for the monitoring and evaluation of the NAEP. The designs of the overall evaluation plan and of instruments for data collection were exemplary.[22] Actual

---

[20] *Training of Adult Education Functionaries: A Handbook* (New Delhi: The Directorate of Adult Education, Ministry of Education, 1978).

[21] *Report of the National Seminar on Strategies for Post-Literacy, Follow-up and Continuing Education, Hyderabad, Andhra Pradesh, September 24–30, 1982* (Hyderabad: State Resource Center, Osmania University, 1982). Also, Anil Bordia, "Plans and Management of Post-Literacy Programmes," in G. Carron and A. Bordia, eds., *Issues in Planning and Implementing National Literacy Programmes* (Paris: Unesco International Institute for Educational Planning, 1985), pp. 179–197.

[22] *Monitoring the NAEP* (New Delhi: Directorate of Adult Education, Ministry of Education and Social Welfare, Government of India, 1979).

implementation of the monitoring and evaluation systems was quite another matter, however.

MRS. GANDHI RETURNS TO POWER: FROM NAEP TO AEP

There were several contradictions in the conception, as well as in the planning, of the NAEP as launched by Prime Minister Morarji Desai. These contradictions, however, did not have the time to surface. Differences among the followers of the Janata Party, with nothing but their opposition to Mrs. Gandhi to hold them together, came to the surface sooner. The Janata Party broke up during the latter part of 1979, and Mrs. Gandhi was back in power in January 1980, her excesses of the emergency all but forgiven.

The important political task before Mrs. Gandhi, an astute politician, was to paint the Janata Party as an aberration, and to discount its policies and programs. The NAEP had to be dealt with appropriately as well.

THE RENOVATION OF THE NAEP

The NAEP could not simply be terminated. Apart from the fact that it had found an institutional nitch in the Union Ministry of Education, as well as in some of the State Departments of Education, it was already being seen as a program for the people. Mrs. Gandhi, therefore, renovated the program as part of the process of assuming ownership of it.

She started by accusing the NAEP of having been captured by voluntary associations that were communal in character and that did not serve the secular and democratic interests of the nation. This, incidentally, was a concern often expressed by the Central Advisory Board of Education during the British rule. Hurriedly, a review committee was established that was asked to examine the program and come up with the recommendations on how it should be revised to serve the "real" educational needs of the people.[23]

The Government of India document, entitled *Adult Education Programme*, published in February 1984, provides an interesting record of how the program of adult education changed, or did not change, under Mrs. Gandhi.[24] First, the name of the program was changed from National Adult Education Programme to merely Adult Education Programme (AEP). Second, there were new figures for illiterates to be covered by the program and new time schedules to cover them. The target now was to enroll 110 million illiterate adults in the age group fifteen to thirty-five in ten years, 1980 to 1990 (Table 3).

---

[23] *Report of the Review Committee on the National Adult Education Programme* (New Delhi: Ministry of Education and Culture, Government of India, 1980).

[24] *Adult Education Programme: Policy Perspective and Strategies for Implementation* (New Delhi: Ministry of Education and Culture, Government of India, 1983).

Table 3. Time Schedules of the Adult Education Program

Sixth Five-Year Plan			Seventh Five-Year Plan		
1980–1981	2.6	million	1985–1986	11.5	million
1981–1982	3.1	"	1986–1987	14.0	"
1982–1983	4.3	"	1987–1988	17.0	"
1983–1984	6.5	"	1988–1989	20.5	"
1984–1985	9.0	"	1989–1990	24.5	"
	25.5	"		87.5	"

A third, and perhaps the most important point to note in regard to the new program was that the instructional process was conceptualized to last three years, with the following three phases:

Phase 1 of about 300–350 hours spread over a year, including basic literacy, general education with emphasis on health and family planning, functional programs relating to learners' vocations, and familiarity with laws and policies affecting the learners.

Phase 2 of about 150 hours spread over a year, to reinforce literacy skills and their use in daily life. This phase included appreciation of science in relation to one's environment, elements of geography, history, and the country's cultural heritage. It would also contribute to the improvement of all vocational skills.

Phase 3 of about one hundred hours spread over a year, to achieve a reasonable degree of self-reliance.

Mrs. Gandhi's government also sought to use university students more fully in the implementation of the program. During the first phase of university involvement, to end March 31, 1985, all affiliating-type universities and about 1,500 colleges would be involved in organizing fifteen to twenty thousand centers. In a second phase, ending March 31, 1990, the number of centers was to rise to about fifty thousand by involving *all* the universities and colleges in the country.

To seal the process of ownership of the old government's program by the new government, it was included in the Prime Minister's Twenty-Points, and 1,280 million rupees were allocated for it for the duration of the plan period.

PERFORMANCE OF LITERACY POLICIES UNDER NAEP AND AEP

Any evaluation of performance of literacy policies in India under the NAEP/AEP years 1978–1985 is tricky, to say the least. Whose performance is being evaluated, anyway—that of the Center, the States, or of voluntary organizations? The only statistics that are available come from government sources, and they are always figures for adults enrolled in the program rather than for adults made literate. However inadequate these figures may be, they are still useful in getting some fix on the situation. For example, the following figures have been apparent recently in various government reports:

1971–1981   5.0 million (made literate)
1980–1981   2.6 million (actually enrolled)
1981–1982   3.1 million (actually enrolled)
1982–1983   4.3 million (actually enrolled)

Of the 4,261,480 adults enrolled in 1982–1983, 2,531,550 (59.4%) were males and 1,729,930 (40.6%) were females. Again, of the total covered, 1,085,689 (25.47%) belonged to the scheduled castes and 768,686 (18%) belonged to the scheduled tribes.

Qualitative evaluations are even more difficult. While no nationwide evaluation of effects has been undertaken, various small-scale evaluations are available. These have been conducted in different areas of the country, at various times, and have dealt with groups coming from different socioeconomic environments. Different questions have been asked using different instruments and different levels of research skills. But together, they do provide a montage of what may be happening and what may not.

The First Year of the NAEP

After a year of operation of NAEP, the reorganized Ministry of Education and Culture issued an official review (not a systematic evaluation) of the first year of the program.[25] The report expressed satisfaction with the "interest evinced in the programme by the various sections of society—the political leaders, teachers, development agencies, and the vast masses of illiterate people." Wishing that the available data were more complete and that there had been opportunities to verify some of the reports from voluntary agencies, the review report was sure that the program had indeed "got off to a good start."

Since the states did not have the will to implement NAEP, said the report, the progress had been uneven. Delays in the development of administrative arrangements and delivery systems had necessitated deferment of the new program in Utter Pradesh, Rajasthan, Maharashtra, Karnataka, Andhra Pradesh, Haryana, Manipur, and Sikkim. In most other states, while there was no formal deferment, full steps for the start of the program were not taken.

There had been a mushrooming of voluntary agencies in the country, now that government funding was available for literacy work. This problem was partially solved by giving money only to those organizations which had been in existence for at least one year. By September 1, 1979, 603 voluntary agencies had been approved to run 27,956 adult education centers and promised a funding of 47,318,000 rupees. Overall, the total number of centers run by government and voluntary agencies were 94,181, with a maximum total enrollment of some 2.8 million learners at any one time.

The performance of the NAEP in the implementation of the technical system was quite satisfactory. Boards of adult education and steering committees had been established in all states and union territories. Six states had established

---

[25] *National Adult Education Programme: The First Year* (New Delhi: Ministry of Education and Culture, Government of India, 1979).

full-fledged directorates of adult education, while others had appointed separate officers within the existing directorates of education to deal with the subject of adult education. One hundred and sixty-three administrative units had been sanctioned to be established at the district level in thirteen different states. But effective implementation of the program did not follow. The appointment of women within the administrative and technical structures was, again, at a level lower than that envisaged.

Fifteen SRCs were already in place serving nineteen states. Four of these SRCs were located in the universities, and eleven were located within voluntary agencies, with long experience in literacy work. The report indicated that reasonably satisfactory materials were available in all regional languages, as well as in several important dialects. A beginning had been made in the production of materials in the tribal languages, and sixteen major tribal languages had already been covered.

The first-year report talked of failures in the training of functionaries and of the functionaries' preoccupations with targets rather than with the creation of dynamic and development-oriented learning. But it asserted that the program had also shown that "if a proper environment is created, if the organizers of the programme are serious, and linkage with development programmes is visible, the inert and illiterate masses respond to the call with simplicity and enthusiasm."

FROM THE PERSPECTIVE OF THE NAEP FUNCTIONARIES

In early 1980, two researchers[26] developed an appraisal of the NAEP based on the perceptions of key functionaries of the NAEP itself. One hundred and ten questionnaires were sent to the top and intermediate level functionaries of adult education in the country, including academicians, central and state government officials, heads of voluntary associations, and teachers in universities. Those who responded complained about recruitment practices that emphasized academic qualifications and ignored both commitment and competence. They also pointed to favoritism in appointments. Decentralization in the production of materials had not worked. The respondents had made the conservative suggestion of moving from the field to the laboratory for the design of materials. Three-fourths of respondents favored working through the voluntary agencies, while others cautioned against the abuse of funds by voluntary agencies and their threat to democratic values, because many of those agencies were communal and sectarian. The majority of respondents thought that the objective of conscientization in the curriculum was impossible, and might even prove disastrous in cases when aspirations could be raised with subsequent frustrations. Most complained of the lack of commitment among functionaries of the program, of bureaucratization within the administrative and technical systems, and they pointed out the need for the government to come in and help in the liquidation

---

[26]G. Haragopal and A. Ravinder, "Perceptions of the Key Functionaries about NAEP—A Critical Appraisal," *Indian Journal of Adult Education* 41 (May 1980).

of local vested interests too strong for field-level workers to confront. Only one-third showed any optimism for the success of the program.

Six Studies of Impact Reviewed

In 1981, a DAE document summarized the results of six different regional studies of the NAEP/AEP program conducted during 1980–81 and pointed out that while enrollment of women was low, enrollment of scheduled castes and tribes was quite encouraging. Fifteen to twenty-five year olds were most represented among those participating in the program, the age group twenty-six to thirty-five was underrepresented, the average enrollment per center was 28.2, and an average of twenty attended daily. Classes were in "flux"—sometimes 100 percent of those who began a class were replaced by others—and instructors were of very low educational levels needing systematic training to compensate for their inadequate formal preparation. There were too few women instructors, though, happily, instructors from scheduled castes and tribes were well represented. Instructors found the honorarium of 50 rupees a month too low; there were delays in the distribution of teaching materials; there were few appropriate places to hold classes; there was no interest shown by development departments of the states, and as a result the program did not become functional. And finally, conscientization was a challenge hardly ever met.[27]

An Evaluation of the Program in Bihar

An evaluation of the AEP in the Tamar Block in Ranchi District, Bihar, published in April 1981,[28] came to similar conclusions. The average attendance at the centers studied was fifty-three percent, though 84.39 percent of respondents felt that they were attending regularly. While 62.61 percent read satisfactorily, barely fifty percent were satisfactory in writing and numeracy. In regard to acquisition of functional knowledge and skills, 24.84 percent felt greatly benefitted, while 53.47 percent felt somewhat so. Unfortunately, fifty percent of respondents intended to abandon the rural areas and to move to a city or township after completion of the program, in the hope of more earnings.

For lack of any baseline data, respondents' level of awareness cannot be attributed to attending learner groups. In any case, awareness turns out to be a mixed bag. Social awareness was good enough. Of the learners who responded, 68.49 percent did not care what the caste of their literacy instructor was, fifty percent were aware of the illegality of giving or receiving a dowry, but only 5.46 percent knew of the minimum legal age for marriage for boys and girls, and, on the average, they desired three to four children—a number higher than

[27] Anita Dighe, R. S. Mathur and Prem Chand, "Appraisal Studies of the Adult Education Programme: Their Implications for Policy, Planning, and Management" (New Delhi: Directorate of Adult Education, Ministry of Education and Culture, Government of India, 1981).

[28] *Adult Education for Social Change* (Patna: Directorate of Adult Education, Government of Bihar State (India), 1981).

the one the government promotes. Political awareness was lower: while 92.21 percent were aware of the problems in their villages, 44.40 percent ascribed causes for these problems to nature, and 63.43 percent felt that there are no solutions. One can only surmise whether these responses indicated a lack of awareness or a realistic appraisal of the situation on the part of the respondents.

An Evaluation of the Program in Maharashtra

A study by Muthayya and Prasad published in January 1982,[29] based on six villages in Pune district of Maharashtra, found that adult education officials, as compared with their colleagues in the general education branch, had fewer facilities and fewer powers granted to them. There was lack of structural as well as operational coordination between the adult education department and all other development departments. Development officials, right from the block development officer down to the village level worker, had no orientation to the AEP. Understandably, the involvement of development agencies and their functionaries in the implementation of adult education programs was negligible. On the other hand, adult educators at various levels of the system had very little knowledge about the various development programs.

The study found that the training of instructors and supervisors was based on predetermined content, rather than on the assessment of real needs and knowledge gaps. Instructional materials in use did not reflect local realities. Supervisors had graduate degrees but little knowledge of the village setup. They were reluctant to make field visits, and they could not go far anyway with a limit of sixty rupees a month on travel and daily allowances. Most instructors were high caste and inadequately trained for handling management tasks. They were reluctant to go for training that involved leaving their homes and work. Local leaders were also uninvolved, their function being restricted to providing accommodation for the adult education center, and persuading the learners to attend. In spite of all this, learners are positive towards the program, desiring it to be more functional and to offer useful vocational training. They also want recreational facilities and access to media like radio and TV.

CONCLUDING REMARKS

The Indian case study does provide evidence that a theory of literacy promotion now exists. Policy makers and planners can make use of existing knowledge to manage the calculus of ideology and technology, so as to implement national literacy programs and campaigns with some expectation of success. The Indian case also points out that ideological commitment is not easy to articulate

---

[29] B. C. Muthayya and Hemalatha L. Prasad, "Adult Education in Rural Development: A Study of the Process of Implementation in a Block," *Journal of Rural Development*, 1 (January 1982), pp. 72–113.

or to sustain. Literacy is a political act and, by its very nature, is difficult to protect from changes in the political wind.

The technology of literacy promotion and its pedagogy are much better understood. In the Indian context, as in other literacy projects, programs and campaigns, there were several innovative solutions in organization and instruction. The development of a network of resource centers, going from the center down to the district and block levels, was but one example of such innovations.

One can, but need not, be cynical about the rise and fall of literacy promotion in India, and shed tears over the many distortions and contradictions that have been introduced in the implementation of the NAEP. The launching of NAEP by Prime Minister Desai in 1978 remains an historic event, and its significance cannot be buried under the dust of history. Mrs. Indira Gandhi, when she returned to power in January 1980, tamed and renovated the program, in the process of exorcising it from the ghost of Desai and putting her own soul in it. The program has been limping since, but it is not dead.

The situation of literacy in India is a reflection of the political situation in the country and of the structures of privilege and poverty on which the Indian polity rests. Adult education is inherently progressive, and adult literacy is even radical in its assumptions and consequences. Naturally, governments and the power elite like to handle literacy with care. Nevertheless, there is hope. The historical processes let loose on the world stage may be stronger than the strongholds of power and privilege in individual countries. Universal literacy worldwide may be inevitable.[30]

---

[30] H. S. Bhola, "Literacy: Destiny of the Human Species" (paper presented to the Annual Meeting of the American Library Association [OLOS Session on Literacy], Chicago, Ill., July 6–11, 1985).

CHAPTER 12

The 1980 Nicaraguan National Literacy Crusade

ROBERT F. ARNOVE

The 1980 Nicaraguan National Literacy Crusade was born of the struggle to depose a repressive political regime and establish a new social order. One year prior to coming to power, the broad-based coalition of insurgent forces led by the Sandinista National Liberation Front (*Frente Sandinista de Liberación Nacional*, FSLN) issued a twenty-five point umbrella program of reform that included, as point 14, the following:

> The Frente Sandinista will dedicate itself from the very start to fight against illiteracy so that all Nicaraguans may learn how to read and write; and everyone, including adults, will be able to attend school to prepare for a career and to excel.[1]

As early as 1969, the FSLN, in Chapter 3 of its "Historic Program" had articulated the intention to "push forward a massive campaign to immediately wipe out illiteracy" and develop national culture.[2]

It is therefore not surprising that within fifteen days of coming to power in mid-July 1979, the new FSLN-dominated Government of National Reconstruction announced that, among other sweeping reforms—including confiscation of property belonging to the Somoza family and immediate associates, nationalization of the banks and the mining and lumber industries, land reform, the unionization of workers, and the devolution of decision-making power to mass organizations—there would be a national literacy crusade. The literacy campaign initiated on March 23, 1980, was to symbolize, more than any other

---

Earlier versions of this chapter appeared as "The Nicaraguan National Literacy Crusade of 1980," *Comparative Education Review* 25 (June 1981): pp. 244–59, and "A View from Nicaragua: Literacy Campaigns and the Transformation of Political Culture," in Jack W. Hopkins, ed., *Latin America and Caribbean Contemporary Record, Vol. 2: 1982–83* (New York: Holmes & Meier, 1984), pp. 245–60. This chapter also appears in slightly different form in my 1986 book, *Education and Revolution in Nicaragua*, Chap. 2.

[1]"Documents: Why the FSLN Struggles in Unity with the People," *Latin American Perspectives* 20 (Winter 1970), p. 108.

[2]Sandinista National Liberation Front (FSLN), "The Historic Program of the FSLN," in *Sandinistas Speak* (New York: Pathfinder Press, 1982), p. 142.

ROBERT F. ARNOVE • School of Education, Indiana University, Bloomington, Indiana 47405.

event or process, the transformations occurring in Nicaragua in the initial stages
of its revolution. Indeed, 1980, the first year following the revolution, was declared
the Year of Education.

To the question, "why literacy?" the Nicaraguans answer that the high
illiteracy rate that characterized the country—and particularly the rural areas,
where illiteracy ranged from between sixty and ninety percent of the population—
was an outcome of the feudal system of the Somoza dynasty, one that kept the
majority of the population ignorant. Previous literacy activities of the Somoza
campaign, such as the Plan Waslala, far from constituting efforts to extend
enlightenment to the countryside, were part of counterinsurgency activities aimed
at rooting out and eliminating the FSLN revolutionaries.[3] The few notable efforts
to promote literacy were undertaken by the private sector and, in particular,
religious groups. Still, illiteracy levels had languished at approximately one-half
the adult population for over a decade, while the absolute number of those who
could not read and write was increasing.[4]

As the Ministry of Education's description of the Great National Literacy
Crusade (*Cruzada Nacional de Alfabetización*—CNA) notes: "to carry out a literacy
project and consolidate it with a level of education equivalent to the first grades
of primary school, is to democratize a society. It gives the popular masses the
first instruments needed to develop awareness of their exploitation and to fight
for liberation. Therefore, literacy training was something that the dictatorship
could not accept without contradicting itself."[5]

Extending education to the vast masses of the people represented, sym-
bolically and substantively, a conferral of the rights of citizenship. The literacy
campaign constituted a fundamental mechanism for integrating the country—
rural and urban populations, the middle and lower classes—for mobilizing the
population around a new set of national goals. In the process, the Sandinista
political leadership hoped to win the majority of people to its vision of a society
organized according to a different model. While, as Richard Fagen has observed,
Nicaragua is not a socialist country, socialism is very much on the historical
agenda.[6] Presently, the Sandinista government is nationalist, populist, and
pluralistic.

It is important to note that the masses of people who rose up in arms
against Somoza and the National Guard[7] represented all political persuasions.

[3] Valerie Miller, *Between Struggle and Hope: The Nicaraguan Literacy Crusade* (Boulder, Col.: Westview Press, 1985), p. 21.
[4] Robert F. Arnove, *Education and Revolution*, Chap. 1.
[5] Nicaraguan Ministry of Education, "The Great National Literacy Campaign: Heroes and Martyrs for the Creation of Nicaragua," mimeographed report, translated and edited by the National Network in Solidarity with the Nicaraguan People (Managua: Nicaraguan Ministry of Education, January 1980), p. 1.
[6] Comments made by Richard Fagen to the panel on "The Nicaraguan Revolution: A New Model?" (9th National Meeting of the Latin American Studies Association, Bloomington, Indiana, October 18, 1980).
[7] For a detailed study of the role of the National Guard in maintaining the Somoza family in power for a period of four decades, see Richard Millett, *Guardians of the Dynasty* (New York: Orbis, 1977).

They were not fighting for socialism, but against a corrupt and brutally repressive regime. They fought in the name of heroes such as Augusto César Sandino, who led a popular insurrection against occupation of the country between 1927 and 1933 by the United States marines, and in the name of the martyred Carlos Fonseca Amador, founder of the Sandinista National Liberation Front in the 1960s (both Sandino and Fonseca had initiated literacy activities among their militants, as part of the struggle to change the status quo), and for the countless Nicaraguans, among them children and adolescents, who died in the struggle against the ruling elite. They were fighting for a more just social order—yet to be defined.

To transform the political culture of the country, to inculcate a new set of values (based on more egalitarian social relations, cooperative forms of labor, workers' participation in decision making, a sense of sacrifice for others, and international solidarity with the struggles of peoples in other countries for self-determination and justice), it would be necessary to establish a massive program of education and reeducation. And this education had to take not only the form of education *for* socialism—that is, schooling, media, and mass campaigns to prepare people for new roles and behaviors and outlooks—but education *within* socialism. The latter means, to paraphrase Arthur Gillette,[8] placing people, particularly youth, in nonalienating situations where they can engage in socially productive work that contributes to the general welfare and collective advancement: it is an education that puts theory into practice. The mechanism for this engagement of youth, as well as diverse adult populations, was the literacy campaign.

The new Sandinista political and educational leadership consciously built on past twentieth century campaigns, such as those of Cuba and Tanzania, but imparting its own vision of the crusade's nature and outcomes, in accordance with the realities of Nicaraguan society.[9] It was viewed as an intense national effort that could be accomplished within a limited period, involve massive numbers at a reasonable cost to the country, and make manifest to the population the intention of the government to extend social benefits to the most disadvantaged groups.[10] It also would manifest the expectation of the national political leadership that the populace at large was to play an active part in the processes of national reconstruction and social change.[11]

This chapter will describe the scope, organization, and content of the Nicaraguan National Literacy Crusade of 1980 and its aftermath. Special attention will be given to those aspects of the campaign that relate to the goals of integrating previously excluded groups, stimulating and consolidating national unity, strengthening mass organizations, and encouraging widespread participation in

---

[8] Arthur Gillette, *Cuba's Educational Revolution* (London: Fabian Society, 1972), p. 20. Gillette actually distinguishes between education *for* communism and education *in* communism.

[9] For discussion of international advisors and the CNA, see Miller, *Literacy Crusade*, pp. xxii, xxiv, 185, 215–17.

[10] Ibid., pp. 44–45, 69.

[11] Ibid., p. 38.

decision making by those individuals and collectivities that were previously the objects, but not the subjects, of history.[12]

SCOPE AND SYMBOLISM

The extent of the mass mobilization was nothing less than incredible, considering the socioeconomic situation of Nicaragua. The all-out attack on illiteracy occurred in a country devastated by a protracted civil war, with many of the country's youth killed and maimed, with a national economy in ruins, and a foreign debt per capita among the highest in the world.[13] A campaign of this magnitude and brevity had not been taken anywhere. To reduce the illiteracy rate from fifty percent to approximately fifteen percent within a period of six months meant that initially, almost every person who knew how to read and write would teach those who did not, and moreover, as adult learners gained minimal literacy skills, they would, in turn, help those who lagged behind.

Only with mass mobilization, with everyone studying, would it have been possible to find adults willing to face the painful, public embarrassment of attempting to write their names on a blackboard. Only with the universal participation of people of all ages would it have been possible for adults over sixty years of age to learn from youngsters of 12 and 13.

A number of the colorful posters and billboards that adorned the landscape captured the spirit and significance of the literacy campaign. One poster stated:

> *En cada casa un aula.*
> *En cada mesa un pupitre.*
> *En cada Nica un maestro!*

> Every home a classroom.
> Every table a school desk.
> Every Nicaraguan a teacher!

Another consists of two scenes: the top one depicting armed people in the streets behind barricades fighting against the National Guard; the bottom one a rural thatched-roof hut with a literacy worker, book open, teaching an entire family (mother, father, and children). The captions read, "Yesterday's Struggle" (next

---

[12] For a statement of the CNA as a political priority of the Sandinista government, see Guillermo Rothschuh Tablada and Carlos Tamez, *La Cruzada Nacional de Alfabetización de Nicaragua: Su Organización y Estrategias de Participación y Mobilización* (Paris: UNESCO, 1983), p. 56.

[13] Statistics that highlight the destruction wrought by the civil war include: over forty thousand killed; 100,000 wounded, of whom forty thousand required continuing medial attention; forty thousand orphaned children; 200,000 homeless families; and $1.8 billion in total material costs (i.e., approximately $581 million in physical damage, $630 million in revenues lost due to a reduction of the Gross Domestic Product, and $600 million of losses in foreign exchange reserves due to capital flight and illicit withdrawals. These data are cited from the Fact Sheet of the Center for International Policy, "The Impact of Civil War in Nicaragua," mimeographed (Washington, D.C.: Center for International Policy, n.d.). When Somoza fled in July 1979, he left 3.5 million dollars in foreign reserves in the central bank and a deficit of 1.6 billion dollars.

to the scene of the barricades) and "Today's Struggle" (next to the family learning to read and write together).

The imagery and vocabulary of struggle and a national war loomed large in the symbolism of the CNA. Just as six guerrilla armies victoriously converged on Managua on July 19, in the wake of Somoza's flights from the country, so, on March 24, 1980, six "armies" left Managua to wage war on illiteracy. The six national fronts of the People's Literacy Army consisted of some 55,000 *brigadistas* (literacy workers), mostly high school students, who would live in the rural areas of the country to work with, learn from, and teach the largely illiterate peasantry. The six fronts were divided into "brigades" at the muncipal level, and the brigades, in turn, were divided into "columns" at the hamlet level. The columns had four "squadrons" of thirty *brigadistas* each; the squadrons consisted of youth of the same sex and roughly the same age, who often were from the same school.

In the cities, the People's Literacy Teachers (numbering approximately 26,000) comprised a parallel war effort.[14] These teachers included factory and office workers, professionals, and housewives, plus high school and university students who for health or family reasons could not leave the city. The urban-based teachers taught after work or during their spare time. The usual pattern was two to three hours of instruction a day, Monday through Friday—although during the final stages of the campaign instruction also took place on the weekends.

Out of a total population of 2.4 million, of whom 717,000 were at least ten years old and literate, over 250,000 youths and adults volunteered to teach.[15] Although no one was officially required or compelled to teach or become a *brigadista*, schools were required to participate, and students who did not participate risked the danger of losing credit for the academic year.

STRUCTURE OF CNA

The deployment, logistical support, and protection of the literacy army members required the support of every national ministry and mass organization. Literacy workers had to be transported to the remotest corners of the country, often inaccessible by road and four-wheel vehicles;[16] they had to be housed, fed, and safeguarded. The dangers *brigadistas* were exposed to in the countryside reflected not only the ravages of underdevelopment—the lack of potable water,

---

[14] The People's Literacy Teachers (*Los Alfabetizadores Populares*—AP) consisted of two types: over twenty thousand "Urban Literacy Guerillas," who taught in the urban neighborhoods, and some three thousand worker-teachers who taught in the factories and comprised the "Workers' Literacy Militias."

[15] For further discussion on the recruitment of literacy teachers, see Jan L. Flora, John McFadden, and Ruth Warner, "The Growth of Class Struggle: The Impact of the Nicaraguan Literacy Crusade on the Political Consciousness of Young Literacy Workers," *Latin American Perspectives* 36 (Winter 1983), pp. 53–55.

[16] Detailed description of logistical problems posed by the CNA is found in Chapter V of Rothschuh, Tablada, and Tamez, *Cruzada Nacional*.

the scarcity of food, and endemic diseases such as dysentery and malaria—but the imminent threat of terrorist attacks by several thousand exguardsmen who had fled to neighboring Honduras and slipped across the border to terrorize and murder *brigadistas*—symbols of the revolutionary changes occurring in Nicaragua. Nine literacy workers were assassinated during different stages of the crusade by counterrevolutionaries known as *contras*. In case of illness or injury there was a need for emergency medical services, and in case of counterrevolutionary attacks, there was a need for a permanent communications network to alert defense officials.

Complementing these efforts to place and support the *brigadistas* were activities to publicize the literacy crusade, identify those who did not know how to read and write, and encourage them to attend literacy units and complete the literacy process.

A National Coordinating Commission was established under the auspices of the Ministry of Education to determine broad policy and facilitate implementation of all these efforts. The commission consisted of twenty-five ministerial, political, military, educational, cultural, religious, and mass organizations. Parallel coordinating commissions for the CNA were established at departmental and municipal levels. According to outside observers, the national and departmental committees were but shadow organizations; it was the municipal level where the crusade took form, where organizational involvement was most intense and the mass of people participated.[17] And it was the mass organizations that were to play the principal role in implementing the literacy campaign.

MASS ORGANIZATION PARTICIPATION

The mass organizations that were instrumental in overthrowing the dictatorship were the key to the success of the CNA. Organizations in Nicaragua had been formed at factory and neighborhood levels by workers, women, and youth; they involved tens of thousands of Nicaraguans who provided supplies to the revolutionary army, set up communication networks, administered first aid, obtained and distributed weapons, and erected barricades to do battle during the uprisings of 1978 and 1979.

Following the victory, these mass organizations, in many cases renamed and reconstituted, took their place in the battle against illiteracy. The Sandinista Workers Central (CST) assumed responsibility for literacy-related activities in the factories, forming, with some three thousand of its members, Workers' Literacy Militias; similarly, the Rural Workers Association (ATC) assumed responsibility for rural areas, and recruited a contingent of its affiliates to serve as literacy teachers in Peasant Literacy Militias. In the cities, the Sandinista Defense Committees (CDS) were the major organizing force. Nationwide, the Nicaraguan Womens' Association "Luisa Amanda Espinoza" (AMNLAE) mobilized women

[17]See Charles L. Stansifer, "The Nicaraguan National Literacy Crusade," American University Field Staff Reports, South America, No. 41, 1981, p. 5.

to participate in the campaign and, through various support groups, attended to the welfare of the *brigadistas*. Teachers were another group whose participation was essential to the successful implementation of the CNA. Over nine thousand teachers assisted in the preparation, supervision, and in-service training of the literacy workers. Notable among their efforts was the formation of a "red and black flag" brigade to serve in the most rote and dangerous areas of the country. In addition, they helped maintain educational, cultural, and recreational activities for youth while schools were officially closed between March and September; furthermore, they established special educational programs for child street vendors. Assisting the National Teachers' Association (ANDEN) were university-level School of Education majors.

CONTENT AND PEDAGOGY OF LITERACY MATERIALS

Learning activity centered on the basic reader *Sunrise of the People*.[18] The reader, based in part on the pedagogical ideas of the Brazilian adult educator Paulo Freire, contains twenty-three generative themes. Each theme, accompanied by a photograph, consists of generative polysyllabic words that can be broken down into basic sound and meaning units (phonemes and morphemes) and recombined by the learner to form new words. The initial themes pertain to the revolutionary heroes Augusto César Sandino and Carlos Fonseca Amador and progressively cover the topics of the struggle for national liberation, the termination of exploitation by foreign and national elites, the role of the mass organizations and the Popular Sandinista Army in defending the revolution, the rights and responsibilities of the citizenry of the new society, the achievements of the Government of National Reconstruction in undertaking land reform and in expanding and extending health care, education, and other social welfare services, the liberation of women from subservient roles, the integration of the long-abandoned Atlantic Coast region into the national society, and, finally, the commitment of the new revolutionary regime to solidarity with other progressive governments of the world.[19] At the core of these themes are emotionally charged phrases and words. Appropriately, the first such word is *revolución*. Pedagogically, the words *la revolución* contain all the vowels of the Spanish alphabet. Other generative words include *liberación*, *genocidio*, and *masas populares*. To summarize the sequence of pedagogical activity: with the introduction of each photograph there was to be a group discussion of approximately one hour duration, followed

[18]Instruction in mathematical concepts using the primer *Calculo y Reactivación: Una Sola Operación* was of secondary importance and was usually not undertaken until the student had successfully completed lesson 7 of the literacy primer.

[19]It is interesting to note that the photograph used in Lesson 23 of the literacy primer to indicate solidarity with liberation struggles in other countries is of the prime minister of Vietnam and two members of the Government Junta, Alfonso Robelo and Violeta Chamorro, who left the government in the spring of 1980, and have since become opponents of the Sandinista regime. The revised 1984 literacy primer, which is being used in the ongoing program of adult education, needless to say does not have this photograph.

by one hour of practice related to reading the text and decoding and encoding the generative words. The format of group discussion, however, was frequently not followed—given the inexperience of the teachers and the reluctance of students to discuss issues publicly or question authority.

Sheryl Hirhson, a United States teacher who volunteered her services as a supervisor of a group of twenty-five brigadistas in the northern mountainous province of Matagalpa, vividly describes the difficulties of implementing this innovative pedagogy in her book, *And Also Teach Them to Read*. According to Hirshon, the first step of each lesson—the dialogue between the literacy instructors and the adult students—was the most difficult to conduct: "the *brigadistas* found it a frustrating and confusing assignment. What was it for? Certainly *they'd* never been taught that way. In all too many of the classes it was done badly, or ignored altogether."[20]

The CNA endeavored to put into practice a number of Freire's pedagogical concepts—principally those which (a) conceive of adult education as a political process involving consciousness raising and which (b) stimulate individuals to see themselves as makers of culture and transformers of their environment. But the CNA also departed in significant ways from his educational model, which stresses the necessity of developing materials in dialogue with the learning community and on the basis of a sociocultural analysis of that community.[21] According to Freire's ideal, literacy workers should not arrive in a community with a prepared text.

Such an approach was not really possible in Nicaragua, where an all-out assault on illiteracy using the volunteer labor of minimally trained and mostly young people could not have been accomplished by strict adherence to the ideal model of Freire concerning content development.[22] A primer was developed by a national team of educators in consultation with top political leaders. To the credit of the Nicaraguan campaign, the literacy materials reflect careful pedagogical planning in the selection and sequencing of content. The materials appear to be based on solid scholarship, as well as on respect for the experience and social world of the adult learners.[23]

The most common criticisms of the literacy materials pertain to the pro-FSLN content of the literacy crusade. Those who object to political propagandizing as part of the literacy process are oblivious to the indoctrination that occurs in all education systems.[24] What differs from one system to another is

[20]Sheryl Hirshon with Judy Butler, *And Also Teach Them to Read* (Westport, CT: Lawrence Hill & Co., 1983), p. 104.

[21]See Paulo Freire, "The Adult Literacy Process as Cultural Action for Freedom," *Harvard Educational Review* 40 (May 1970), pp. 205–23, and his *Pedagogy of the Oppressed* (New York: Herder & Herder, 1970).

[22]A parallel situation existed in Cuba. See the discussion of Jonathan Kozol, "A New Look at the Literacy Campaign in Cuba," *Harvard Educational Review* (Summer 1978), pp. 341–77, especially p. 354.

[23]Paulo Freire visited Nicaragua for a nine-day period prior to the commencement of the CNA. After consulting with the team of educators designing the campaign, he announced his enthusiastic support for both its content and pedagogy.

[24]See, for example, the discussion of Kozol, "Literacy Campaign in Cuba," p. 364.

the subtlety of the indoctrination, the content of the messages, and the socio-political purposes of instruction.

To repeat the fundamental question posed by Freire, is the object of a literacy campaign domestication or liberation?[25] Are the educational programs designed to provide limited information so that people can better fit into the existing hierarchical structures and do the bidding of dominant groups,[26] or is the literacy process designed to provide an indispensable base of knowledge that opens up options for formerly dispossed people, providing them with the understandings, skills, and attitudinal dispositions that equip them to play a decisive role in forging a new society?

The Government of National Reconstruction posited that under successive regimes of the Somoza dynasty (1937–79), education worked to legitimate an inequitable social order that prepared elite groups for leadership roles while denying fundamental knowledge and skills to the vast majority.[27] In contrast to the passivity and fatalism fostered in the masses by the previous reigmes, the new Sandinista-led government proposed to instill a different set of values and a radically different ideology. The materials used in the literacy and postliteracy educational campaigns are designed to prepare people to play an active role in creating a more prosperous and just society. Consonant with the characteristics of the present political leadership of the country, the values of nationalism and populism are stressed—but also emphasized are the values of a country attempting to follow a model of development based on collective work efforts, personal sacrifice, and national austerity to create greater abundance. It also should be noted that, unlike the values stressed in literacy instruction during the guerrilla phase to topple the Somoza regime,[28] the content of materials in the CNA tended to downplay notions of social class struggle and instead emphasized the common interests and goals of all segments of Nicaraguan society.

Despite the laudable goal of actively involving the mass of Nicaraguan citizens in social change, it is still open to debate whether or not the actual pedagogy employed fostered critical consciousness or top down indoctrination. Hirshon narrates the difficulties involved in depending on poorly prepared

---

[25] For further discussion along these lines, see Robert F. Arnove and Jairo Arboleda, "Literacy: Power or Mystification?" *Literacy Discussion* 4 (December 1973), pp. 389–414.

[26] See, for example, Martin Carnoy, *Education as Cultural Imperialism* (New York: McKay, 1974), esp. Chap. 1.

[27] Eighty percent of the children in rural areas were not in school and twenty-one percent of the illiterates in the country were accounted for by youths in the age group ten to fourteen. Under twenty-five percent of the appropriate age group thirteen to eighteen were enrolled in secondary school, while according to the *Encyclopedia of the Third World* (ed. George Thomas Kurian, New York: Facts on File, 1978, 2: 1065), 5.38 per one thousand (about eight percent) of the appropriate age group were enrolled in universities. Nicaragua ranked eighty-sixth in the world in adjusted school enrollment for primary and secondary education, but sixty-first in per capita university enrollment in 1976). For further discussion of educational neglect, see Arnove, *Education and Revolution,* Chapter 1.

[28] For a discussion of the type of consciousness-raising and organizing activities that occurred during the clandestine period of resistance to the Somoza regime, see Omar Cabezas, *Fire from the Mountain* (New York: Crown Publishers, 1985), pp. 37, 210, translated from the original novel in Spanish, *La Montaña Es Algo Mas que una Inmensa Estepa Verde,* by Gonzalo Zapata.

and often impatient *brigadistas* to stimulate the adult learners to reach the stage of independent thought. The following account is taken from a Saturday workshop in which her group of *brigadistas* discussed common problems and concerns:

> I try to do it ([the dialogue]) right, but students say "we don't want to talk politics; just get on to syllables."

> May I speak, profe? Listen, *compa*.[29] If your students say that, it's because you've made them feel that it isn't important. If we just come and teach reading, we aren't doing anything. This crusade was planned so that the workers and peasants could really understand the national reality, and if you just teach letters and syllables, you're not even fulfilling your duty as a *brigadista*.

> That's right, Miguel, but you have to be careful about the opposite danger, too, which is that the exercise becomes more important than letting the students know you are really interested in what they have to say. When I saw your class, you started really well, but when people remained shy, you ended up giving a speech. That's when people get the idea it's some kind of political indoctrination.[30]

Low-income and rural populations reached by the literacy campaign had traditionally been excluded from participation in decision making; they had been taught to defer to authority, to be mute and passive. When they spoke out and challenged authority, the response had almost always been punitive. Thus, it was not uncommon to find that rural people felt uncomfortable discussing their opinions publicly or questioning authority—although that authority might be an adolescent teacher some twenty or thirty years their junior. Asking these learners to be active participants in their own education directly opposed ingrained traditions of subordination and self-deprecation. Taking into account these dispositions on the part of the learners, as well as the inexperience of the youthful instructors, it is not surprising that the CNA, in its final stages, resembled a traditional teacher-directed pedagogy and an almost mechanical approach to literacy instruction. What was supposed to be dialogue often consisted of the literacy worker merely reading notes jotted down from the teacher's guide. Moreover, as the national campaign goals of so many learners reaching lesson 23 and successfully passing the five-part literacy test by mid-August approached, the literacy workers increasingly concentrated on rote drill of phonic sequences (such as pri, pre, pra, pro, pru/ gri, gre, gra, gro, gru). Despite the political consciousness raising objectives of the campaign, it should have been obvious to anyone observing classes that many learners were essentially grappling with letters, sounds, parts and blocks of words—not ideas.

It is possible, however, that the most important political lessons of the crusade resided not in the literacy materials or the teacher-learner encounters, but in the very existence of the campaign itself. The literacy crusade was a symbol

---

[29] The word *compa* is a Nicarguan abbreviated form of the word *compañero*, which may be translated to mean companion or colleague. It is frequently used by people sympathetic to the FSLN, and those who participated in the insurrection against Somoza or who are involved in joint efforts related to national reconstruction.

[30] Hirshon, *Also Teach Them*, p. 105.

of justice, of the concern of the new political regime for the most neglected areas and populations of the country. It involved the extension of national authority and services into previously unreached corners of the society. The commitment of the revolutionary Sandinista regime was most palpably present in the *brigadistas* who went to live with and assist impoverished rural families and in the "urban literacy guerrillas" who worked in the poorest barrios of Managua and other cities. Thus, in studying the political impact of the CNA, it may be more enlightening to study the overall process, structure, and context of learning than the explicit content of instruction.

FOLLOW-UP CAMPAIGN IN INDIGENOUS LANGUAGES

Immediately following the termination of the National Literacy Crusade on August 23, the government began preparing for a campaign in the three major indigenous languages of the Atlantic Coast region of Nicaragua—English, Miskito, and Sumo. Geographically, historically, and culturally, the Atlantic Coast has constituted a distinct and distant population, tenuously integrated with the Spanish-speaking Pacific Coast Region.[31] The Atlantic Coast region contains approximately one-half the territory of Nicaragua, but less than ten percent of its population. In large expanses of the East Coast—along the Río Coco and in the areas of Puerto Cabezas and Bluefields—the majority of the inhabitants speak either Miskito or Creole/English as their native tongue. In scattered pockets along the coast between two and five percent speak Sumo, Rama, and Carib. Many of the coastal peoples, however, speak two or three languages (principally, Spanish, English, and Miskito)[32] with varying degrees of fluency, switching back and forth between them according to the language situation.

According to the October 1979 census, approximately 88,400 individuals, about seventy-five percent of the region's population ten years of age and older, were illiterate.[33] Between March and August 1980, approximately fifty thousand coastal people (costeños) participated in the Spanish-language literacy crusade,

---

[31] For further discussion, see Philippe Bourgois, "Class, Ethnicity and the State among the Miskito Amerindians of Northeastern Nicaragua," *Latin American Perspectives* 29 (Spring 1981), pp. 22–39; also his "Nicaragua's Ethnic Minorities in the Revolution," *Monthly Review* 37 (January 1985), pp. 22–44, and Philip A. Dennis, "The Costeños and the Revolution in Nicaragua," *Journal of Interamerican Studies and World Affairs* 23 (August 1981), pp. 271–96.

[32] According to the Center for Information and Documentation of the Atlantic Coast (INNICA), sixty-two percent of the costeños are Spanish-speaking Latinos, twenty-four percent Miskito-speaking, ten percent English-speaking, 2.5 percent Sumo-speaking, .47 percent Carib-speaking, and .24 percent Rama-speaking. For further discussion, see National Network in Solidarity with the Nicaraguan People, "Atlantic Coast: Miskitu Crisis and Counterrevolution," *Nicaragua* (May–June, 1982), pp. 4–5—reprinted in *The Nicaragua Reader,* eds. Peter Rosset and John Vandermeer (New York: Grove Press, 1982), p. 83.

[33] For discussion of the census taken to ascertain the level of illiteracy in the country, see Fernando Cardenal, S. J. and Valerie Miller, "Nicaragua 1980: The Battle of the ABCs," *Harvard Educational Review* 51 (February 1981), pp. 13–14.

reducing illiteracy to about thirty percent of the inhabitants of the coastal departments of Puerto Cabezas, Bluefields, and Rama. Many of the indigenous-speaking people who opted to acquire literacy in Spanish did so in order to participate in national institutions and communicate with the rest of the country. It also appears that the more pro-Sandinista inhabitants were those who sought literacy in Spanish.

By the end of the National Literacy Crusade, there were still a substantial number of *costeños* who were illiterate and who preferred to participate in literacy classes conducted in English, Miskito, and Sumo.[34] Over 12,500 people participated in and completed the indigenous campaign, which took place between October 1980 and March 1981. With the completion of this campaign, illiteracy had been reduced to approximately twenty-two percent of the Atlantic Coast population.

In the aftermath of the crusade (CNA) and the campaign in languages, students, both young and old, entered the new system of Adult Basic Education (EPB), which was placed under a newly established Vice-Ministry of Adult Education (VIMEDA). The core of this system consists of Basic Education Collectives (*Colectivos de Educación Popular,* CEPs), in which the sole language of instruction is Spanish. The Vice-Ministry of Adult Education has taken the position that knowledge of Spanish is essential to unifying the country, and that it would be neither feasible nor desirable to erect a parallel system of instruction in a second of third language. As achievement of national unity was one of the principal goals of the CNA, it is to this objective as well as other outcomes that the discussion now turns.

OUTCOMES

The outcomes of the CNA may be studied at various levels. The most obvious results are found in the number of adult learners who passed the literacy test or completed so many lessons in the primer. Observers may also point to the physical improvements in communities where literacy workers resided.[35] At a more profound level, the outcomes of the CNA must be evaluated in relation to the transformation of political culture, the integration of previously alienated sectors of the country, the unification of countryside and city as well as the Pacific and Atlantic coast regions, the winning of youth to the revolution, the improvement of the status of women in Nicaraguan society, and the strengthening of mass organizations. All of these were important political priorities of the revolutionary Sandinista government.

---

[34] Illiteracy was relatively low among the English-speaking inhabitants, who tend to be fundamentalist Protestants placing great emphasis on reading the Bible.

[35] According to Bulletin no. 13 of *La Cruzada en Marcha* (Managua: CNA/Ministry of Education, July 1980), p. 7, brigadistas helped build 2,862 latrines, seventy-five wells, ninety-six schools, thirty-four roads, fifty bridges, thirty-seven health centers, and had participated in the planting and harvesting of thousands of acres of various fruits and vegetables.

Literacy Achievements

In the history of twentieth century literacy campaigns, three cases stand out as truly remarkable achievements. In 1970, Tanzania mobilized its population around the theme of adult education; literacy classes sprang up all over the country—in schools, churches, factories, and fields; and by 1977, the illiteracy rate had been reduced from sixty-seven percent to twenty-seven percent.[36] Cuba, on April 15, 1961, declared a national war on illiteracy; the end of that year illiteracy had been reduced from 23.6[37] percent to 3.9 percent of the adult population of four million. Thus, within two years of the revolution that toppled Fulgencio Batista and brought Fidel Castro to power, Cuba became the first country in Latin America to claim that it had eliminated illiteracy.

Even more impressive, and perhaps the single most impressive undertaking in the field of literacy campaigns, is that of Nicaragua. Mounted within the first year of a revolutionary regime, the campaign was able to reduce the illiteracy rate from 50.35 percent ($N = 722,616$) of the population over the age of ten to approximately twenty-three percent in five months. Officials of the campaign claim that the illiteracy rate had been reduced to 12.96 percent; but it should be noted that this lower figure is based on the decision of the government to subtract from the target population of illiterate adults approximately 130,000 individuals who were considered to be unteachable. These were people who because of blindness, debilitating illnesses, advanced age, senility, and institutionalization were not able to participate in the literacy campaign. Whether the Nicaraguan official claim of 12.9 percent or the higher figure of 23 percent is accepted as the illiteracy rate, the accomplishments of the CNA were singularly impressive. Between March 23 and August 23, 1980, a total of 406,056 Nicaraguans had learned to read and write. This achievement occurred in a war torn and economically devastated country. In addition, the campaign in languages on the Atlantic Coast extended literacy skills to another 12,664). Despite attempts by critics to discredit the level of literacy achieved during the five-month campaign, and despite claims that there are people who have literacy certificates who cannot read a single word on their diplomas,[38] the general consensus of independent observers is that there was a systematic effort to assure that the adult students had achieved certifiable literacy skills. The five-part final examination consisted of the learners writing their names, reading a paragraph containing vocabulary from the more advanced lessons (roughly equivalent to a third grade primary education text), answering questions about the paragraph, taking dictation on the paragraph, and writing their thoughts on one of three themes (for example, what the Sandinista revolution meant to them).

[36] For further details, see Chapter 10 above and H. S. Bhola, *Campaigning*, Chapter 7.

[37] Jonathan Kozol, however, in his article "Literacy Campaign in Cuba," p. 360, estimates that by early 1961 the illiteracy rate was less than twenty percent due to experimental programs conducted during 1959 and 1960. Still, as he points out, no other Latin American country had reduced its illiteracy rate to as low as eight percent of its population, and the Latin American median illiteracy in 1960 was 32.5 percent. See also Chapter 8 above.

[38] See, for example, Robert Leiken, "Nicaragua's Untold Story," *New Republic*, October 8, 1984, p. 19.

This level of competency, however, was just the beginning of a process of continuing adult education. At the same time, educational opportunity was to be provided to some 46,600 participants in the CNA who, at the end of the official campaign in mid-August 1980, had not completed the literacy primer and therefore were considered to be semiliterate, as well as to those illiterate adults who, for a variety of reasons, were not able to participate in the CNA.

In recognition of these outstanding achievements in the field of literacy, UNESCO selected Nicaragua as the recipient of the Nadezhda K. Krupskaya award in September of 1980. The international jury cited not only the magnitude of the literacy project in Nicaragua, but also the fact that the Nicaraguan government had given priority to general literacy as a fundamental component of the process of national reconstruction. The jury further recognized that the campaign "offered an enduring testimony to the nobility of human spirit thanks to the exemplary dedication of the voluntary teachers of whom more than fifty gave their lives in service to their compatriots."[39]

Engagement of Youth—Raising Consciousness and Commitment

While a majority of the combatants against Somoza were under twenty-five years of age,[40] it is also the case that many youths did not participate in the armed struggle. The literacy crusade was to provide the golden opportunity for youth—as well as other groups such as teachers—to play an active part in the process of national reconstruction. Whereas some 20,000 youths were involved in the final stages of the general insurrection against the deposed regime, 65,000 youths were involved in the CNA.[41] Their participation in the campaign changed their status from one of being marginal to national life (in fact, young people were considered by Anastasio Somoza Debayle and the National Guard to be public enemies) to being key actors in the creation of a new society. As a result of their involvement in the CNA, many youths were to undergo substantial transformations in their values and their perceptions of themselves and their place in national society.

Although they were sent to the countryside as teachers, the *brigadistas* were also cast in the role of learners—placed in an unfamiliar world far distant from the comfortable middle-class existence most knew. As Don José, a recently literate peasant farmer, wrote to the mother of his literacy worker:

> Do you know I'm not ignorant anymore? I know how to read now. Not perfectly, you understand but I know how. And do you know, your son isn't ignorant anymore either. Now he knows how we live, what we eat, how we work, and he knows the life of the mountains. Your son, ma'am has learned to read from our book.[42]

---

[39] See Hugo Assmann, ed., *Nicaragua Triunfa en la Alfabetización* (Managua: Ministry of Education and San Jose, Costa Rica: Departamento Ecuménico de Investigaciones, 1981), p. 194.

[40] Hirshon, *And Teach Them to Read*, p. 75.

[41] Interview with Carlos Carrión at the headquarters of the Sandinista Youth (JS-19), Managua, June 21, 1984. Carrión is national director of the organization.

[42] Valerie Miller, "The Nicaraguan Literacy Crusade," in Thomas W. Walker, ed., *Nicaragua in Revolution*, p. 244.

Beverly Treumann, one of a handful of United States citizens who served as a volunteer in the CNA, provides an account of the metamorphosis in her middle-class friend Julia: Before becoming a *brigadista*, Julia had described herself as a snob who would not greet the *campesinos* (peasant farmers) who came into town, who fussed a lot about dressing-up and putting on make-up, and who filed and painted her toenials. But according to Treumann's account,

> Julia now (at the end of the campaign) knows personally how most Nicaraguans live. She spent five months eating beans and tortillas, sleeping with fleas, getting up at 4 A.M., sharing a bedroom wth a whole family, hiking for miles through mud and rock without the convenience of even an outhouse. She knows lots of once-illiterate people whom she regards as far more talented and intelligent than herself [the members of her peasant family].[43]

As the Minister of Education, Carlos Tünnermann Bernheim, noted: "The CNA was a great school for the brigade members; one often asks oneself: who learned more, the literacy-teachers from the peasants or the peasants from the literacy-teachers? Many literacy-teachers have said they thought it was actually they who learned more during their stay in the countryside."[44]

The most striking evidence of these changes in youths are found in personal histories. Learning about the countryside was stimulated by the requirement that all *brigadistas* keep a diary. The diary, as outlined by the administration of the CNA, was to include a detailed description of all major aspects of the community in which the volunteer resided: the history of the community, physical features, principal economic activities, social agencies and developmental activities undertaken, and so on. In addition, cultural brigades consisting of some 450 students organized by the Ministry of Culture and the National University gathered systematic data on archaeological sites, folk traditions, artisan activities, and, in general, compiled an oral history on the popular insurrection against the Somoza regime.

Beyond the intimate learning about rural conditions that was to take place, the other major change that the *brigadistas* describe is a great gain in self-confidence and a resolve to work wherever they are needed by the revolution. Treumann ends her account of Julia this way: "Julie, who had once viewed the crusade as a five-month act of routine patriotism after which life would return to its normal worries, has become courageous and self-sacrificing."[45] As Carlos Carrión, head of the general staff of the CNA, has noted, "the youth of the country don't have to convince themselves that they can play a role in society. They have already proven it."[46]

Following the literacy campaign, many of the brigadistas continued their active involvement in the Sandinista Youth organization (*Juventud Sandinista 19*

---

[43] Beverly Treumann, "Nicaragua's Second Revolution," *Christianity and Crisis* 41 (November 2, 1981), pp. 297–98.

[44] Carlos Tünnermann Bernheim, "One Year Later," in Jan Kaspar, ed., *Nicaragua for the Eradication of Illiteracy* (Paris: International Union of Students and UNESCO, nd).

[45] Treumann, "Nicaragua's Second Revolution," pp. 297–98.

[46] Interview of June 21, 1984.

de Julio—JS-19), participating in militia service and health campaigns, and contributing voluntary labor for different crop harvests. Besides these indicators of the commitment of youth to participate in the tasks of national reconstruction, data are available on the impact of the CNA on the political consciousness of young literacy workers. In what is perhaps the only study of this kind undertaken in Nicaragua to date, Flora, McFadden, and Warner surveyed 1079 third-year high school students from Managua, Estelí (Nicaragua's fourth largest city), and the rural community of San Rafael in the Department of Jinotega; the sample consisted of *brigadistas*, urban literacy workers who lived at home during the CNA, and a control group of students who did not participate in the campaign.[47] The researchers conclude that "the national literacy crusade, in spite of problems in recruitment, training, and logistics arising from the rapidity with which the campaign was put together and from the fact the bourgeois *brigadistas* were often supervised by conservative teachers, had a positive impact on the young participants which was independent of their involvement in the insurrection. Those who did not participate in the insurrection showed greater growth in support for the revolution than those who did."[48] Although the researchers found that "working-class students are more committed to the revolution in word and deed than are their higher class companions, participation in the crusade was associated more strongly with subsequent revolutionary attitudes and activities for middle- and upper-class students than for working-class students."[49]

Participation in the crusade, however, was not always associated with an increase in support for the revolution. In the above study, for thirteen percent of the *brigadistas,* participation in the CNA was cited as the determining factor in decreasing revolutionary support.[50]

Ambiguous and even contradictory outcomes of involvement in the CNA may be a consequence of individuals' past biography and class position, as well as changing opportunity structures within the country. For example, returning one year after the termination of the literacy campaign, Treumann once again observed Julia:

> Julia was a different story. She continues to volunteer for such things as health brigades and coffee harvesting, but when I asked about the revolution she wrinkled her nose, smiled and said she was "contra"—short for counter revolutionary. "She's joking," said a friend of hers, but I didn't think it was wholly a joke. And yet, when I asked her about her future, she said she wants to become an agronomist—an intriguing career choice much favored by the revolution; no other change could put her closer to the heart of the important social change. Her father frowns on it: "Not a good choice for a woman." But her boyfriend not only approves but would like to study also.[51]

It would be difficult to speak of a new Nicaraguan person characteristized by such values as altruism and a willingness to sacrifice for others. However, the

[47] Flora, Mcfadden, and Warner, "Impact of Literacy Crusade," pp. 49–51.
[48] Ibid., pp. 56–57.
[49] Ibid., p. 59.
[50] Ibid., p. 53
[51] Treumann, "Nicaragua's Second Revolution," p. 299.

literacy crusade provided an opportunity for many youths to put into practice this value and demonstrate a maturity that far exceeded their years. Hirshon has said that for many of the city bred youths, the rural experience with the CNA represented "a move from intellectual to physical and emotional commitment. Fighting for an abstract idea wasn't the same as fighting for a lived conviction."[52] Among the abstractions to take on concrete meaning for *brigadistas* were the *campesinos* with whom they lived.

But also for the *campesinos,* a number of abstractions were to acquire intimate meaning. The changes in the rural populations, the raising of consciousness and participatory levels of peasant farmers, as well as the linking-up of countryside and city, is the next topic of analysis.

Integration of Rural Populations into National Life

According to Hirshon, "The literacy crusade had been basically conceived as a dialectic—a meeting of opposites: city kids with country people, intellectual with manual work, independence with discipline, traditional thought patterns with revolutionary new ideas."[53] The crusade also has been described by a distinguished Nicaraguan poet as a national *entrevivencia,* a coming together and sharing of living experiences of urban and rural populations.[54] The encounters of these two distinct worlds was to engender mutual respect and understanding, as well as more equalitarian social relations. The gain in self-confidence reported by so many literacy workers was to be matched by similar developments in many of the peasant farmers, who learned more than just to read and write during the crusade. Previously self-deprecating before city people, especially those who might have a secondary or higher education, they were now more self-assertive. As Anita Mikkonen, an international volunteer from Finland, observed: "During the Literacy Campaign, the [rural] adults enormously expanded their view of the world and became more self-confident; instead of being the forgotten part of the population they were beginning to realize that they were the protagonists of a gigantic national effort."[55]

The involvement of the newly literate peasants in the tasks of national reconstruction is manifest in a variety of ways, including membership in farming cooperatives and workers associations and participation in rural militias. Perhaps the best indicator of their heightened commitment is the fact that they comprise the bulk of instructors in the over twenty thousand adult education collectives formed in the aftermath of the CNA. Not only commitments were awakened. The CNA also contributed to expectations of expanded national services in previously neglected areas such as health, and to demands for consumer products that were unfamiliar to most rural households prior to the arrival of the *brigadistas.* The *brigadistas* were provided with two rations of basic food commodities

---

[52] Hirshon, *And Teach Them to Read,* p. 211.
[53] Ibid., p. 62
[54] Interview with Pablo Centeno-Gómez, at his home in Managua, June 2, 1984.
[55] Anita Mikkonen, "The Literacy Crusade and the Children," in Kaspar, ed., *Eradication of Illiteracy.*

to feed themselves and to assist their host families. Moreover, as Cardenal and Miller note, "Weekend visits by parents and care packages from home helped improve the community diet."[56] One unforeseen result of the CNA was a tremendous—and inflationary—increase in the rural demand for such products as refined sugar, salt, cooking oil, and poultry products.

While the *brigadistas* were expanding the horizons of rural populations, it is also the case that urban populations were discovering at first hand the countryside. According to the mother of three literacy teachers, "The Literacy Crusade taught us two things. One, what our children are capable of doing and of becoming. Two, what our country is like and how gentle and how poor our people are in the countryside."[57] Not only the *brigadistas*, but thousands of middle-class parents who were to visit their children during the crusade, gained an appreciation of the *campesinos*, who are now considered family members. It is not uncommon for the *brigadistas*, for example, to refer to their hosts as their *campesino* mother or father. It is also quite common at holiday time, particularly Christmas, to see thousands of former literacy workers boarding buses in the cities on their way to visit their *campesino* families.

To conclude this section, the CNA played a critical role in helping to liberate rural populations from their previous isolation and neglect, and initiated the long-term process of integrating the rural sector into national development efforts. The aroused political consciousness of the peasantry went hand in hand with the acquisition of literacy skills and the opening of economic opportunities with large-scale agrarian reform. In turn, the economic and social transformations occurring in the rural areas since 1979 were to place increasingly greater demands on rural farmers and workers for more sophisticated technical skills and knowledge.

Improving the Status of Women

Among the other changes that were to be accelerated and magnified by the CNA was the liberation of women from their marginal positions in the society. During the large-scale fighting of 1978–1979, women not only formed support groups, but played an active role in combat, comprising up to one-third of some guerrilla units—and in the case of León, five women were in command of the capture and running of the city.[58]

The literacy crusade brought even more women into important public roles. It has been described as the first national task in which women had equal participation.[59] By far the most educationally neglected group in the country, women seized the opportunity to teach and study during the crusade—the CNA was to

---

[56] Cardenal and Miller, "Nicaragua 1980," p. 12.

[57] Ibid., p. 25.

[58] Warren Hoge, "Women Win New Role in Nicaragua," *Austin American Statesman*, January 15, 1981, p. E-4.

[59] Interview with Fernando Cardenal, Managua, June 7, 1984, at the national headquarters of the Sandinista Defense Committees.

be their own personal vindication of past abandonment and subordination. During the CNA, women comprised the majority of teachers (sixty percent) and technical personnel. In the follow-up adult education programs, they comprise approximately forty-six percent of the students and instructional personnel.

As with the mobilization of youth, once women were engaged in the process of national transformation through new teaching–learning roles, they became available for a variety of other tasks such as militia duty and voluntary participation in agricultural production. In 1983, for example, women comprised eighty percent of the over seventy thousand health *brigadistas* involved in immunization campaigns, and seventy-five percent of the nearly nine thousand health workers in the country. Women also represent forty-eight percent of militia members and sixty percent of those involved in revolutionary viligance (night time guarding of public property against sabotage by counterrevolutionary forces).[60]

At the same time, the Sandinista government, with the prompting and support of AMNLAE, has instituted a number of positive policies to both expand job opportunities for women and end past practices that involved the commercial exploitation of women.[61] AMNLAE, itself, as a mass organization with representation on the Council of State (1980–1984) played a leading role in introducing legislation to protect the rights of women and to insure male responsibility for household chores.[62]

These laws articulate ideals yet to be achieved, but as statements of public policy they are nonetheless important. It is unrealistic to expect that traditional sex-role perceptions and modes of interaction will completely change within a span of five years. Indeed, the high incidence of reported divorces and separations attests to the tensions that accompany such changes.

The AMNLAE statement, "Women's Participation in the New Nicaragua," summarizes the current situation: "Machismo, as part of the heritage of a society based on exploitation, still persists in many men and women. Unfortunately, it is much easier to destroy oppressive and repressive political and economic structures than the people's mental structures. . . . Nicaraguan women are fully convinced that women will be free to the extent that both men and women become free: that liberty is not granted but won."[63]

Strengthening of Mass Organizations

Another significant outcome of the CNA was the strengthening of mass organizations as valid and effective means of popular participation in the postwar period of reconstruction. The continued democratization of post-Somoza Nicaragua depends on the vitality and expansion of these organizations. Furthermore, given the poverty of the country, these organizations are critical to

---

[60] For further details, see *Asociación de Mujeres Nicaraguenses "Luisa Amanda Espinoza"* (AMNLAE), "Women's Participation in the New Nicaragua," in *Contemporary Marxism* No. 8, special issue entitled, "Nicaragua under Seige" (Spring 1984): 122–128, esp. pp. 126–27.

[61] The ban applies, for example, to mass media advertising; see Hoge, "Women Win New Role."

[62] AMNLAE, "Women's Participation," pp. 126–27. .

[63] Ibid., p. 127.

mobilizing people to contribute voluntary labor and to stimulating workers to higher levels of productivity.

At the beginning of the crusade, many of the mass organizations were in a fledgling state. As Treumann notes:

> We [the *brigadistas*] brought organization and more services. The *campesinos* had organized to receive us and part of our work was to help those first committees expand into community organizations, farmworkers' associations, women's groups and the people's militias. Or, as the members of these groups now like to say, it was during the literacy crusade they "put in the batteries" and got going.[64]

As a case in point, the Rural Workers' Association (ATC), before 1979, only had organizational influence in the four different departments of Managua, Carazo, Rivas, and Chinandega. By 1980, the association had more than doubled its membership to well over one hundred thousand affiliates. The ATC, which helped recruit peasant literacy militias, was able to use the CNA as a vehicle for unionizing rural workers and helping farmers to organize into cooperatives.[65]

The National Teachers' Association (ANDEN) gained new strength and an enhanced self-image through its participation in the crusade. It was the vehicle for mobilizing teachers. As with students and women, the CNA provided the first major opportunity for teachers to become involved on a massive scale in revolutionary activities. Teachers, as an occupational group, had suffered political repression under the outgoing Somoza regime, which prevented them from unionizing and which used all the powers at its command to punish militant teachers and reward loyal servants. Many members of the teaching force, therefore, were either politically apathetic or acquiescent. According to Nubia Pallavaccini of the national executive committee of ANDEN, the crusade made teachers feel, once again, that they had much to give.[66] Their participation as trainers and supervisors in the countryside and cities was to help overcome the gulf—if not the hostility—that existed between them and many of the youths who had participated in the rural guerrilla struggle or the urban insurrections. These youths were often contemptuous of their teachers, who they considered collaborators of the old system or cowardly in their character.

The Sandinista Youth Organization, as another case in point, had only fifteen hundred members at the commencement of the CNA. These militants served as heads of brigades during the crusade; they were responsible for discipline and conduct, as well as the political education of the brigadistas. (Not infrequently they also served as political mentors of the teacher supervisors.)[67] By the end of the crusade, membership in the JS-19 had mushroomed to over twenty thousand, and as of 1984 to approximately forty thousand militants.

[64] Treumann, "Nicaragua's Second Revolution," p. 295.
[65] Interview with Edgardo García at the national headquarters of the Rural Workers Association, Managua, May 22, 1984.
[66] Interview with Nubia Pavallaccini at the national headquarters of the National Teachers Association, Managua, June 15, 1984.
[67] See, for example, the descriptions of the role played by the brigade leader in Hirshon, *And Teach Them to Read.*

The linkage between participation in the CNA, membership in Sandinista political organizations, and involvement in national revolutionary tasks is seen in the overlapping roles played by the delegates to the Sandinista Youth Organizations national youth assembly in Managua, December 19–21, 1981. Of the 560 delegates in attendance, 547 were militants of the Sandinista National Liberation Front (FSLN), 467 had been production *brigadistas*, 322 were veteran guerilla fighters from the struggle to overthrow Somoza, and 496 had been literacy teachers in the CNA.[68]

The crusade also extended these mass organizations into regions that had a paucity of social services and little experience in unionization or political interest articulation. On the Atlantic Coast, for example, the CNA is credited with greatly strengthening the National Teachers Association. And according to Ministry of Education personnel in Puerto Cabezas, the literacy workers also helped organization the Association of Rural Workers.

Integrating the Atlantic Coast

The campaign in indigenous languages in 1980–1981 signaled the intentions of the national government to begin integrating the Atlantic Coast with the rest of the country while respecting its cultures. Philippe Bourgois describes the campaign's intended outcomes in this way: "By emphasizing . . . what appears superficially to contradict national unity—the distinctive identities of the ethnic minorities—a greater trust and sympathy for the government is actually promoted."[69] In keeping with this thrust, the government made special efforts to train indigenous instructional personnel—over three-fourths of the literacy teachers in the campaign came from the region—and to revise the literacy materials from the CNA to reflect (in the photographs, drawings, and content) the people, terrain, economy, and cultures of the Atlantic Coast.

Among the integrative outcomes of the literacy campaigns on the East Coast are a greater familiarity with written Spanish on the part of the indigenous population, an awareness of national symbols and figures like Sandino, and a sharing in the folk culture of the Pacific Coast peoples. Furthermore, the campaigns brought with them access to other important services, particularly in the area of health: thousands were furnished with eyeglasses, inoculated, and referred to health centers.

Serious problems also have beset the literacy campaigns and the follow-up programs in adult education. Steadman Fagoth, a leader of the Miskito people and the indigenous association MISURASTA (Miskitu, Sumu, Rama, Sandinistas "United Together"), used the campaign to help reach and organize Miskitos to demand a degree of autonomy for Atlantic coast inhabitants that was considered by the Sandinista government to be prejudicial to national unity. In February 1981, when Fagoth was detained by the Sandinista government, a great number

---

[68] Onofre L. Guevara, "La JS 19: Una Posición Ganada en la Lucha," *Barricada*, December 22, 1981, p. 3.
[69] Bourgois, "Miskito Amerindians," p. 37.

of Miskito Indians pulled out of the language campaign, and when Fagoth subsequently escaped to Honduras in May of 1981, thousands went with him.

Since late 1981, large tracts of the Atlantic Coast have comprised a war zone. This is particularly true of the area bordering Honduras, where many Miskito villages are located. There have been innumerable incursions by counterrevolutionaries (*contras*), many of them Miskito Indians. Needless to say, educational activities and other national social services have been disrupted by the conflict.

The integration of the Atlantic Coast remains problematic. The region still contains separatist and hostile elements and many more who are taking a cautious wait-and-see approach; and even among the government supporters who worked actively in the literacy campaign, there is a strong sense of regionalism and a desire for more resources to be channeled to the coast. While the CNA and follow-up educational activities stimulated greater national awareness on the part of the people and strengthened several mass organizations that are national in scope, the progressive integration of the region will depend, more fundamentally, on major improvements in transportation and communication systems, on the availability of capital for economic development, and the working out of a modus operandi by which the natural resources of the Atlantic Coast can be jointly exploited by indigenous communities and the national government to the satisfaction of both sides.[70] This modus operandi, in turn, will have to be part of an overall negotiated settlement, in which the autonomy of the indigenous populations will be congruent with the Sandinista goals of a unified nation in which all segments can participate and benefit.

THE LITERACY CRUSADE AS A MODEL OF EDUCATIONAL AND SOCIAL CHANGE

The CNA served as a model of voluntary collective effort to resolve pressing social needs. This model has been applied to subsequent efforts in nonformal education, and to other areas such as health. For example, in October 1981, over seventy thousand trained volunteers were mobilized for a three-day period to distribute antimalarial pills to approximately seventy-five percent of the Nicaraguan population.

The above mobilization was based on the multiplier model of training first demonstrated in the literacy campaign. The model takes the form of a pyramid of trainers. In the case of the CNA, eighty trainers (half teachers and half university students) were first prepared in a fifteen-day course followed by one month of field experience. These eighty then trained 560. The multipler effect then proceeded in this fashion: from 560 to more than twelve thousand (mostly teachers) to over 100,000 literacy workers. The process took approximately three months. Thus, large numbers of people can be prepared in a brief period.

---

[70]William Ramírez, "El Problema Indígena y la Amenaza Imperialista en Nicaragua," in the magazine section *Vergara, Barricada,* January 6, 1982, pp. 13–14.

The national literacy crusade further demonstrated the philosophy of the Sandinista regime that when the people want a basic service they can provide it to themselves through their communal efforts. The role of the government is to assist with mobilizing the population and providing necessary material support, training, and technical advice. This approach breaks with the elitism of a model based on professionals monopolizing knowledge and exclusively controlling delivery of services in essential areas such as education and health.

The Ecuadoran educator Rosa María Torres succinctly summarizes the new model of education:

> The Crusade had been, in effect, the great laboratory where they tested the ingredients of a new model of education congruent with the historical project of the Revolution, in which the people are the principal actors and objects of this project.[71]

For people to view themselves as the principal actors in a process of national reconstruction, they must undergo a change of mentality and political consciousness. As Torres goes on to note, the transformation of consciousness, as exemplified by the CNA, "is not an individual act but a basic social process of formation of collective consciousness . . . and the formation of that new collective conscience cannot be accomplished at the margin of concrete social practice, but in the process of transforming reality."[72]

QUESTIONS AND CONCLUSIONS

What impact did the literacy campaign have on the political culture of Nicaragua, on the stated goal of the "humanistic transformation of Nicaraguan society"?[73] Some seven years after the termination of the crusade, it is possible to point to positive outcomes. The CNA played a critical role in helping to overcome the inequities between countryside and city, males and females, the Atlantic and Pacific Coasts. It contributed to the mobilization and induction of previously marginal populations—peasantry and women, the youth and the aged—into new roles related to national reconstruction. The crusade also played an important role in strengthening mass organizations—notably the Sandinista Youth (JS-19), the National Teachers' Association (ANDEN), and the Nicaraguan Women's Association (AMNLAE).

Another important outcome is the notion that people are not only recipients, but creators, of culture.[74] In the land of Rubén Darío, recently literate peasants are writing poetry, and hundreds of poetry workshops have been established in factories, union headquarters, army bases, and farming cooperative

---

[71] Rosa María Torres, *De Alfabetizando a Maestro Popular: La Post-Alfabetización en Nicaragua* (Managua: *Instituto de Investigaciones Económicas y Sociales,* 1983), p. 10. My translation from Spanish.

[72] Ibid.

[73] Carlos Tünnermann Bernheim in *Primer Congreso Nacional de Educación Popular de Adultos* (Managua: Ministry of Education, June 6–7, 1981), p. 21.

[74] "Pluralism and Popular Power: An Interview with Sergio Ramírez Mercado," in *Contemporary Marxism,* "Nicaragua under Seige," p. 172.

centers.[75] At the same time, the mass consumption of Nicaraguan and Latin American classics in another facet of the remarkable cultural changes occurring in the country. The public demand for inexpensive literature, and printed material in general, has increased dramatically over the past five years. Prior to the CNA, there was no national publishing industry in Nicaragua. The literacy campaign, among other milestone events, marked the beginnings of that industry, in that the CNA produced and distributed over one million different texts and pamphlets; the follow-up adult education program was to place even greater demands on the national publishing capacity.

Finally, the CNA established a new model of social change, based on substantial devolution of decision-making powers to the grass-roots level. It demonstrated that communities, through their own efforts and in conjuction with the government, can provide basic social services. According to Torres, the crusade initiated the process of administrative decentralization of the country,[76] whereby the country is divided into nine regions and substantial authority is delegated to local governmental entities and mass organizations.

The limitations of the campaign must also be noted: male–female relations do not change that easily, the integration of the Atlantic Coast involves a substantial number of obstacles, and the initial good will and regime support engendered by the CNA—widely regarded as perhaps the single most outstanding achievement of the revolution—is also contingent upon government initiatives in other areas. Also problematic is the level of literacy skills attained by people in such a brief period. And how reasonable is it to expect significant changes in individual life circumstances or community living standards because of enhanced literacy skills?

In many respects, the literacy campaign never ended. For even before the mid-August deadline approached for terminating the activities of the brigadistas in the countryside, plans were already under way to select community leaders who would assume the role of instructors in the follow-up adult education program. The process of mass education had merely begun.

[75] See Stansifer, "Nicaraguan Literacy Crusade," p. 49.
[76] Torres, *Post-Alfabetización*, p. 10.

CHAPTER 13

Adult Literacy Policy in Industrialized Countries

LESLIE J. LIMAGE

The title of this chapter may appear rather provocative to any adult educators presently concerned with adult literacy provision in a number of industrialized countries. The provocation lies in the fact that most developed nations are still at various stages of recognizing that there are indeed millions of people in their populations who are completely illiterate or semi-illiterate, and this in spite of a longstanding formal education system through which virtually all adults have passed.

To dignify the types and degrees of national commitment to eradicating adult illiteracy with the term "policy" can, at best, leave adult literacy tutors, organizers, and activists somewhat perplexed. It is the purpose of this chapter, however, to examine just how recognition of widespread adult illiteracy in industrialized countries such as the United Kingdom, France, and the United States has grown; how such recognition has originated for the most part with voluntary bodies and pressure groups; and to what extent some coherent national level response has developed that may truly be considered an adult literacy policy.

Current adult literacy-provision analysis must take two major factors into account, if efforts to truly provide "the right to read" are to operate effectively. This chapter seeks the historic link between the role of formal schooling in Western Europe and the United States and the growth of literacy in the populations of these countries. In order to understand the present situation, it is essential to distinguish the historic aims of formal schooling, as they have been amply documented by social historians in the countries mentioned. Second, attention to adult literacy provision is occurring in an overall context of economic austerity and political conservatism in virtually all the countries concerned. Public

This chapter is a revised version of an article of the same title that appeared in the *Comparative Education Review*, *1*, 1986.

LESLIE J. LIMAGE • UNESCO, Paris 75007, France. The views expressed in this chapter are solely the responsibility of the author and do not reflect those of the organization where she is employed.

schools are under a concerted attack to justify themselves in terms of mythical values of "excellence" that they are accused of no longer conveying. At this level of policy discourse in the Western countries, the arguments are surprisingly similar, although they have been given the greatest publicity and expression in the United States. Even in France, however, with its Socialist government of former teachers and educators, the call from the Minister of Education, J. P. Chevènement, was for a "back to basics" along the same lines as its more politically conservative neighbors among Western nations.

With this contextual background, the chapter will then examine adult literacy efforts in the United Kingdom, France and United States, in order to distinguish their origins, types of provision, and future prospects, and to offer some comparative commentary on similarities and differences found in these countries. The chapter closes with reflections on possible national commitments and policy in this area. Given the rather widespread withdrawal from the democratization of education reforms of the 1960s and early 1970s in industrialized countries, this discussion can only hazard some suggestions in demystifying current official educational policies. It joins Jonathan Kozol's conclusion in the face of such retrenchment:

> Illiteracy, when widely recognized and fully understood, may represent the one important social, class and pedagogic issue of our times on which the liberal, the radical and the informed conservative can stand on common ground and toil, no matter with what caution and what trepidation in a common cause that offers benefits to all. Some of those benefits are hard and tough and painfully pragmatic. Others possess a dignified and searching character which recognize an absolute imperative to lessen the ordeal of those who are in pain and to create a less divided nation in a less tormented world.[1]

THE HISTORIC ROLE OF FORMAL SCHOOLING

The "divided nation" referred to by Kozol in terms of the United States in 1985 is deeply reminiscent of descriptions employed by social and educational historians in a number of industrialized nations to describe and map the growth of formal schooling in their countries. Hence, as this author has more fully documented elsewhere, F. Furet and J. Ozouf[2] in France, B. Simon[3] in the United Kingdom, and S. Bowles and H. Gintis in the United States,[4] to give just a sample, have shown that the history of literacy acquistion does not coincide with the history of formal schooling, and that one cannot be used interchangeably to describe the other. This author believes, as do these historians, that schools in

---

[1] Jonathan Kozol, *Illiterate America* (Garden City, New York: Anchor Press/ Doubleday, 1985), p. 199.

[2] François Furet and Jacques Ozouf, *Lire et Ecrire* (Paris: Editions de Minuit, 1977).

[3] Brian Simon, *The Two Nations and the Educational Structure, 1780–1870; Education and the Labour Movement, 1870–1920; The Politics of Educational Reform, 1920–1940* (London: Lawrence and Wishart, 1974).

[4] Simon Bowles and Herbert Gintis, *Schooling in Capitalist America* (London: Routledge and Kegan Paul, 1976).

industrialized countries have never had as their fundamental mission the transmission of literacy and numeracy skills; that historically schools have had a social-control function that forms the framework in which they transmit any knowledge, including reading and writing. Furthermore, throughout the Western industrialized world, schools contributed to developing literacy and numeracy only when the surrounding population already possessed a certain level of these skills.

A brief review of the findings of Furet and Ozouf may illustrate the eminently political role of the school. Prior to the French Revolution, the school was the focus of political conflict between Church and monarchy. After the Revolution, the school became the battleground between Church and State, as the proponents of the Revolution attempted to unify a highly diverse country into a Republican nation. Reading and writing had no significant place in the existing schools, except for a minority of ecclesiastics and aristocrats. The major conflict, which in many ways persists to this day in France, is one of promoting a centralized republican state without interference from religious or political interests. Since the French Revolution, the lay teacher has been seen as a sort of pioneer going out into a culturally, linguistically, and economically diverse country in order to convey a republican nationalism previously inexistent, in opposition to the religious interests that had control over the minds of the people. This primary tension, between the political conservatism represented by religious interests and republican values, still wracks France in many ways.

But to return to the historic role of schooling, Furet and Ozouf have shown that the chronology and map of literacy in France is much less related to the establishment of a school system than to the history of social development. In fact, schools, as they became open to wider social groups, severely restricted access to reading and writing. The appropriate form of learning in nineteenth-century schools in France, as in other early industrialized countries, was rote memorization of biblical passages. The transition to include reading on the program was slow and selective. A clear division of labor occurred, first in schools and then in peasant homes. After reading in French was introduced for boys as well as girls in schools, access to writing was generally reserved for boys. Religious justification for such selectivity goes back centuries. Nonetheless, the culture and economy of the rural family home reinforced this separation. Women tended to read in the home for family religious purposes, while men ceased to read and maintained their writing skills only in order to keep family accounts and records and, of course, to maintain any contacts with the larger social world.[5]

As in the United Kingdom, a distinction also has to be made between the growth of literacy occurring outside schools in terms of rural and urban areas. Older urban centers responded more readily to the growth of literacy than newer ones because of their established populations of lawyers, merchants, and artisans. Newer urban areas were characterized by many more poor peasants who had

---

[5]Furet and Ozouf, p. 227.

recently emigrated to these areas of rapid growth. B. Simon's history of British education[6] has also shown that older urban centers were more receptive to literacy acquisition than newer ones. And historians in both countries amply document Kozol's "divided nation" of the poor peasants and working classes, on the one hand, and the wealthier classes, on the other. The former were highly mistrustful of the school as an institution designed to indoctrinate them to accept a certain social order. Comparable mistrust for public education in the nineteenth century has been documented by Bowles and Gintis[7] for the United States. They found that the farming states with strong Populist movements (Minnesota, the Dakotas, Nebraska, Kansas, North Carolina and Alabama) spent much less on public education during that period. Also, many immigrant groups in urban centers strongly resisted the forcible assimilation of their children in American schools.

These historians, and other demographers of literacy, emphasize the distinction that must be made between the gradual spread of literacy to communities ready to receive it and the growth of formal public schooling. Across nations, the pattern is more or less than same. First, the written word is the exclusive possession of an elite. It is then extended by rote memorization to a larger audience, frequently in a language other than the vernacular (first Latin, then French in France, while the majority of the population spoke a variety of dialects and regional languages). When a larger number of people eventually have access to reading and writing, power relationships are likely to change dramatically. Initially only reading was taught in schools. That in itself may or may not allow for extensive control, since reading alone does not facilitate communication. Writing, however, was considered a potentially dangerous acquisition. The reticence surrounding access to writing is illustrated by the fact that it took three centuries for French schools to pass from the purely passive transmission of reading for memorization to include writing. A similar reticence is documented by B. Simon for the United Kingdom. Well into the twentieth century, industrialized countries extended schooling only gradually and with great reluctance. This is not to say that there was no demand for knowledge among the most impoverished and working classes of these nations. Historians amply document initiatives undertaken by these populations to gain knowledge independently. The Irish "hedge schools" of the nineteenth century, in which instruction occurred on pain of punishment by the British, remind one of the kinds of literacy campaigns mounted in revolutionary societies or nations fighting for independence in the postcolonial period, to which we shall refer later on.

In other words, to view the history of formal educational provision as a continuum of progress from which schools in 1985 have somehow deviated is to miss the parallels to be drawn between many industrialized countries' histories of the growth of literacy. It also prevents one from analyzing just how the socialization function of the schools has developed with the expansion of public schooling.

[6] Simon, *Two Nations.*
[7] Bowles and Gintis, *Schooling.*

SOCIALIZATION AND SELECTION

It is beyond the scope of this discussion to trace the various socialization functions that have been assigned to public schools in Western countries. Nonetheless, no discussion of adult illiteracy in industrialized nations can avoid seeking the relationship between the formal schooling experience and the existence of millions of adults who have gone through the system and come out completely or semi-illiterate. Without giving at least passing attention to the socializing and selection functions of schools, it is too easy to simply "blame the victim," as many current governments tend to do when acknowledging the existence of large numbers of adult illiterates in their midst.

An illustration of the heavy socializing responsibility of schools in the American context is thoroughly documented by Bowles and Gintis.[8] A particularly eloquent resumé of successive social expectations attached to schools is supplied in a recent article by B. Finkelstein.[9] In a way, one comes away from her analysis wondering if American schools could possibly fit basic literacy and numeracy into their programs if they were to truly attempt to accomplish all the tasks set for them. She begins with early forefathers such as Washington and Jefferson who, although unable to convince states and local governments to set up schools, clearly paved the way, as in France, for the idea of the school as an "agency of cultural uniformity and an instrument of political liberty."[10]

The nineteenth century reformers, who actually succeeded in inspiring the creation of public schools, envisaged a tool to manage social change by instilling certain values in a culturally and economically diverse population of immigrants and natives. They prepared the way, as in the United Kingdom, for a docile and controlled labor force to suit the needs of a rapidly industrializing society. In fact, schools were seen as straightforward "sorting machines" for the needs of industry according to Finkelstein as well as Bowles and Gintis. Such sorting involved a whole host of social responsibilities that schools were expected to engage in efficiently. On the other hand, since the mid-1950s, schools have been charged with the tasks of eliminating many of the inequalities of society—racism, ethnocentrism, sexism, sectarianism—and to "prevent car accidents, pregnancies, alcohol and drug dependence."[11] Diane Ravitch more fully documents the increasing and complex pressures placed on American public schools in terms of greater accountability to more and different authorities as well as more numerous responsibilities.[12]

And by 1985, reformers were calling for reversal of social commitments from those of the mid-1950s and 1960s:

[8] Ibid.

[9] Barbara Finkelstein, "Education and the retreat from democracy in the United States, 1979–198?", *Teachers College Record* 86, 2 (Winter 1984), pp. 275–283.

[10] Ibid., p. 276.

[11] Ibid., p. 276.

[12] Diane Ravitch, *The Troubled Crusade: American Education, 1945–1980* (New York: Basic Books, 1983); *The Schools We Deserve: Reflections on the Educational Crises of Our Time* (New York: Basic Books, 1985).

> the educational visions of contemporary reforms evoke historic specters of public schools
> as crucibles in which to forge uniform Americans and disciplined industrial laborers.
> They echo traditional commitments to public schools as agents of cultural imposition
> and economic regulation.[13]

In other words, while indicting American schools for lowering standards of
academic excellence, current official policy rhetoric calls for yet another set of
socializing commitments, in many ways negating the commitments called up over
the last twenty years to provide equality of access and opportunity for all young
people regardless of economic or ethnic origin. This new role not only contradicts
other egalitarian roles, but sets up a whole new battery of selection and elimination procedures to insure that fewer and fewer young people actually learn
to their potential. The emphasis is on measurement, testing, evaluation, and
exclusion, and this in ever more overt collaboration with the private sector and
industry as a whole. Such a reversal is also called for at a time of continuing
cutbacks in educational and social expenditure, affecting not only the United
States but other industrialized countries as well. The justification, then, for
decreasing national investment in education in the United States, France, the
United Kingdom, Canada, and other industrialized nations is said to be that
schools are no longer doing their job and are unworthy of such investment.
Indeed, all the categories for selection and exclusion that have been set up over
the years to separate out children who do not perform to a fixed norm are to
be strengthened and expanded. Failure and underachievement in school are
once more the fault of the victim and no longer a social responsibility. The
denunciation of testing for overt social selection that has been made over the
years, and documented by Jencks and Gould in the United States,[14] Brian Simons[15]
in the United Kingdom, and Pierre Bourdieu and Jean-Claude Passeron[16] in
France, to give just a few examples, will no longer be heard in the current political
and economic climate. What then is the situation and outlook for adult literacy
provision against this background of retrenchment?

THE RIGHT TO READ: ADULT LITERACY PROVISION

An extensive body of literature exists to define and redefine what is meant
by literacy, illiteracy, and the host of related terms such as functional literacy,
computer literacy, and so forth. It is this author's view that the time for such
academic niceties as debates on definition is long past. Briefly, the possession of
literacy, the capacity to read and write, distinguishes the possessor from the
illiterate, or, as Kozol has once again so eloquently put it:

[13] Finkelstein, "Retreat from Democracy," pp. 276–277.
[14] Christopher Jencks *et al.*, *Inequality: A Reassessment of the Effect of Family and Schooling in America*
(New York: Basic Books, 1972). Stephen Jay Gould, *The Mismeasure of Man* (New York: Norton
and Company, 1984).
[15] Brian Simons, *Intelligence, Psychology and Education: A Marxist Critique* (London: Lawrence and
Wishart, 1971).
[16] Pierre Bourdieu and Jean-Claude Passerson, *La reproduction* (Paris: Editions de Minuit, 1970).

> The illiterate . . . has been crippled in at least three ways: first, by economic and societal exclusion; second, by the inability to see historic precedent for that exclusion and thereby to make use of what has already been said by others; finally, by the inability to render eloquence accessible, and suffering believable, by use of written words.[17]

The recognition that sizeable numbers of adults in industrialized countries are unable to read or write to a level enabling them to fully participate in their societies is of fairly recent date. A few industrialized countries are still reluctant to make such an admission, yet alone undertake some commitment to remediate the situation. The most recent country to officially recognize a problem is France, with a report to the Prime Minister of January 1984 entitled *Des illettrés en France*.[18] Until this past year, France, like a number of other European countries, responded to official inquiries, such as the one conducted by the Commission of the European Economic Community in 1981, that adult illiteracy was not a problem.

It is beyond the scope of this text to give a complete description of the growth of awareness and ranges of measures taken over the past fifteen or so years in all industrialized countries. It is, nonetheless, possible to draw upon the experience of three countries, the United Kingdom, the United States, and France, to illustrate similarities and differences in approach to the recognition that up to a third of the adult population in each country is semi- or completely illiterate.

It is fair to say that the vast bulk of research, experience, and literature on adult literacy has developed in direct relation to UNESCO's commitment to assist in the eradication of illiteracy in developing countries. Although this chapter is concerned primarily with the situation in industrialized nations, it is useful to provide a brief review of the stages of UNESCO's response to the problem. UNESCO has altered its programs and priorities over the past twenty-five years in response to the political realities of member states. Thus, its sensitivity to history is relevant to our discussion and certainly allows some perspective on conditions in industrialized nations.

The Universal Declaration of Human Rights adopted on December 10, 1948 states in Article 26:

> Everyone has the right to education. Education shall be free, at least in the elementary and fundamental stages. Elementary education shall be compulsory. Technical and professional education shall be made generally available and higher education shall be made equally accessible to all on the basis of merit.

Subsequent declarations, and the work of UNESCO, have been based on this Article. Clearly, however, the right to education is closely linked to the other human rights outlined in the Universal Declaration, and it is in a changing world political environment that the two major thrusts of UNESCO's programs have been carried out: the encouragement of efforts to provide universal primary education, and adult literacy campaigns and programs. In its initial phase,

---

[17] Kozol, *Illiterate America*, p. 170.

[18] Véronique Espérandieu, Antoine Léon, and Jean-Pierre Bénichou, *Des Illettrés en France* (Paris: La Documentation Française, 1984).

UNESCO encouraged the introduction of mass adult literacy campaigns for developing countries. In the postwar environment of newly-independent nations, the political climate appeared conducive to major social mobilization to effect both political and economic change. Research of the period tended to show the return in both economic and political terms to mass campaigns. The lesson was learned through those mass compaigns as well as in the earlier mass literacy campaigns of the Soviet Union that people learn better, and a literacy effort has more hope of success, in such a climate of general social mobilization.[19]

As the political and economic climate changed in the world, UNESCO developed the Experimental World Literacy Programme in response. As of 1967, the emphasis was no longer on an attempt to provide for the entire population of developing countries. "Functional literacy" programs and projects were set up on a highly selective basis in key sectors of industry and agriculture and on the basis of government priority areas. Countries were no longer assumed to be willing or able to provide for universal education. Indeed, if the proceedings of the Fourth International Conference on Adult Education of UNESCO that took place in Paris, March 19–29, 1985, provides some gauge of current commitment to adult literacy and adult education, it would appear that resources and commitment in these areas are becoming scarcer and scarcer around the world.[20] At the same time, political discourse tends to suggest that a choice has to be made, in such a state of penury, between providing primary schooling for children and adult literacy/education for adults. Educators and activists around the world plead for their interrelation, and for the necessity of seeing that today's children are tomorrow's adults, that illiterate parents are particularly handicapped in assisting their children with school work, and that, although illiteracy does not reproduce illiteracy, it can in no way assist the growth of literacy. For the first time also, industrialized countries have made use of the forum of the International Conference on Adult Education to seek exchange and cooperation concerning adult illiteracy with developing countries. It is prudent, however, to interpret this latter development in the light of recognition and provision actually existing in industrialized countries.

We thus turn to an examination of three types of response, as illustrated by experience in the United Kingdom, the United States, and France, to provide an overview of the state of adult literacy provision in industrialized countries. In each of these countries, recognition and provision are at different stages and have evolved according to specific conditions. Nonetheless, similarities can be

---

[19] See Leslie Limage, *Alphabétisation et culture: Etude comparative. Cas d'études: l'Angleterre, la France, la Répulique Démocratique du Viet Nam et le Brésil* (Doctoral Thesis, Université René Descartes, Paris V, 1975); "Illiteracy in industrialized countries: a sociological commentary," *Prospects* 10 (2, 1980), pp. 141–155.

[20] UNESCO, Fourth International Conference on Adult Education, *Draft Final Report* (Paris: March 19–29, 1985). For a critical analysis of UNESCO's transition from support for mass literacy campaigns to selective functional programs, see Albert Meister, *Alphabétisation et développement: le rôle de l'alphabétisation fonctionnelle dans le développement économique et la modernisation* (Paris: Editions Anthropos, 1973) and UNESCO and the United Nations Development Programme, *The Experimental World Literacy Programme: A Critical Assessment.*

found among these three countries in certain areas, and each illustrates the situation in several other industrialized countries.

ADULT LITERACY IN THE UNITED KINGDOM

Origins of the Campaign and Adult Literacy Provision

In 1985, the United Kingdom celebrated the tenth anniversary of an adult literacy campaign that has drawn considerable interest in many industrialized countries. Although these pages cannot provide a detailed description of this effort, an outline of its origins and prospects will be presented to provide some basis for the comparative discussion to follow (the campaign has been amply documented elsewhere).[21]

The United Kingdom, like many other industrialized countries, has a long history of voluntary and charitable bodies mediating between the wealthy and the poor. This tradition has its roots in nineteenth-century humanitarian efforts to alleviate some of the suffering caused by rapid industrialization and lack of social and labor legislation. Indeed, B. Simon, in his histories of British education referred to earlier, speaks of two nations on the verge of confrontation, the laboring poor and the wealthy middle classes, which voluntary bodies sought to reconcile. In particular, the voluntary body with which we are most concerned here, the British Association of Settlements, was created with this goal in mind. Canon Barnett of St. Jude's had the notion that civil conflict might be avoided if young men from the universities of Cambridge and Oxford established "settlements" in the heart of working class districts and there provided some instruction to the laboring poor. It was thought that young university students would not be distrusted as would actual emissaries of the capitalist middle classes.

The settlements carried out various educational endeavours. As social and political conditions evolved, such associations identified other areas in which they might mediate and serve. Thus, in the early 1970's, the British Association of Settlements was providing basic literacy and numeracy tuition and leading the way among other voluntary bodies to demand national commitment to their charter, "A Right to Read: Action for a Literate Britain" (1974). At that time, it was estimated that some five thousand adults were receiving literacy tuition. On the other hand, the figure of two million semi- or completely illiterate adults was advanced to draw attention to the size of the problem. (We shall return to the role of advancing numbers in the initial stages of an awareness-raising campaign in our comparative discussion.)

It is useful to refer to the "Right to Read" charter's recommendations to provide some indicator of the level of response and success of the campaign. The charter demanded that the Government of the United Kingdom undertake

---

[21] See for example, Limage, *Alphabétisation et Culture*, and "Illiteracy in industrialized countries," H. A. Jones and A. H. Charnley, *Adult Literacy: A Study of Its Impact* (Leicester: National Institute of Adult Education, 1977) and Audrey M. Thomas, *Adult Illiteracy in Canada*, Occasional Paper 42 (Ottawa: Canadian Commission for UNESCO, 1983).

a commitment to eradicate adult illiteracy by a reasonable date, in particular, 1985. Secondly, it insisted that any attempt to deal with adult literacy should take into consideration the findings of the Bullock Committee and its report on reading, "A Language for Life." An analysis of the teaching of reading in schools should be linked to the adult illiteracy problem. Thirdly, it was suggested that a special fund be created, as well as a national body to assist local authorities and voluntary bodies in extending literacy provision. An awareness-raising campaign should also be undertaken to acquaint adult illiterates and the general public with learning possibilities. All provision that would be created should be free of the usual budgetary conditions attached to adult education provision: classes opening and closing on the basis of maintaining numbers, fees waived for participants, usual formalities for enrollment eliminated, and so forth. Tutors and organizers should be recruited, trained, and paid according to the usual pay scale for teachers in public schools, in order to insure their quality and continuity of service. Although volunteers and voluntary bodies had heretofore provided virtually all of the provision, excessive dependence upon them should no longer be the rule. Finally, the charter requested that other sectors and public services assist educators in identifying needs and providing tuition: industry, social welfare and health and community workers, trade unions, book publishers, and the mass media.

The first response to this charter came from the British Broadcasting Corporation (BBC), which committed itself to a three-year series of programs and publications to be produced jointly with the British Association of Settlements and other bodies. The programs produced by the BBC were aimed at both potential learners and potential volunteer tutors in an awareness raising campaign. The programs were intended to suggest that illiteracy is not a shameful state and that assistance is available. A telephone referral service was included, and the programs themselves were broadcast at peak viewing times. Simultaneously, the BBC jointly produced training materials for tutors and organizers with the British Association of Settlements. Subsequently, the Minister of Education, Gerry Fowler, announced a grant of one million pounds sterling, and the creation of an Adult Literacy Resource Agency to allocate funds to local authorities and voluntary bodies. It is interesting to note that although these funds were to be disbursed only after local authorities had already committed themselves to providing tuition, and specifically excluded their use to pay teachers' salries, all available funding was rapidly committed by the beginning of the campaign itself (April 1975 to March 1976).

State of Provision: Campaign Results

As an awareness raising effort, the adult literacy campaign surpassed its initial goals in terms of the response from potential learners and tutors. Approximately twenty thousand adults responded to the first phase of the campaign. Local authorities were scarcely prepared within the traditional frameworks of adult education institutes to cater to this new, unknown client, the adult illiterate. As in most other industrialized countries, adult education provides leisure and nonvocational courses to an already relatively affluent and educated public. It normally involves fees. Also, classes are opened and closed on the basis of numbers enrolled and actually attending. These classes are usually held in public schools during the evening. Although most local authorities provide some in-service training for adult education tutors, at the time, they had no prior experience in training large numbers of volunteer literacy workers. Thus, local education authorities were called upon to undertake a major training effort simultaneously with the opening of the campaign.

In addition, adult education was the focus of another government report prepared by the Russell Commission entitled "Adult Education: A Plan for Development" (Department of Education and Science, HMSO, London, 1973). This report, coming out at the beginning of cutbacks in educational spending in the United Kingdom, barely mentioned adult illiteracy and certainly suggested no commitment to integrate provisions into a sector already considered marginal in local authorities' education budgets. It focused on the many other ways in which traditional adult education for leisure-time activities might reach a larger clientele.

In spite of the relatively unfavorable economic climate, the campaign, in its initial three-year period, drew forth 155,000 adults to participate in some form of literacy provision: one-to-one tutoring, small group classes in adult education institutes, and even home tutoring. Hence, approximately one-thirteenth of the estimated target population were reached by the various types of provision. A mixed reaction was given to the BBC's awareness-raising program "On the Move." Its use of working-class male characters in comic situations, and its overt use of publicity/commercial techniques to draw learners, were not always well received by potential clients.[22] The stereotype of the adult illiterate as a male of working-class origin did not always correspond to adult illiterates' image of themselves. Adult learners who first came forward for tuition were by and large functioning successfully in their professional and family lives. They were not necessarily of working class background. In any case, their illiteracy was not a humorous or humiliating condition, to the extent that it was compensated for by skillful means of subterfuge or assistance by friends or family. As is discussed later, adults who came forward spontaneously in the initial stages were already quite motivated and nearly functional in their own terms and for their own personal purposes. It is to the credit of the BBC that the second and third series of programs attempted to overcome earlier criticism of stereotyping and the employment of childish commercial techniques (for example, a letter of the alphabet was introduced in each program and animated in cartoon form, as it might be in a children's educational television series).

The central government agency itself has had its mandate and budget renewed on a shoestring and year-to-year basis. It never received extra funding to attempt to reach further than those adults with learning needs who came forward spontaneously. It is remarkable that the agency, now called the Adult Literacy and Basic Skills Unit, has continued to function to this day, and has

---

[22] Documented in Limage, *Etude Comparative*, 1975.

provided continued guidance as the needs for numeracy provision and actual basic education were revealed.

Future Prospects

In terms of the "Right to Read" charter's demands, then, the following conclusions may be drawn:

(1) The central government has not undertaken a longterm commitment either to eradicate illiteracy or to examine the linkages between failure and underachievement in schools and adult illiteracy.

(2) Cutbacks in educational expenditure, which began in 1973, have involved, as in other industrial countries, school closures, larger class sizes in primary schools, extensive teacher unemployment, and virtual stoppage of the efforts to transform the selective secondary schools of the United Kingdom into the comprehensive-school model encouraged by the earlier Labor Governments and educational reforms of the 1960s.

(3) Adult education institutes already under severe financial restrictions remain the primary sources of adult literacy provision.

(4) Heavy reliance on volunteer tutors remains the rule rather than the exception despite the call for adequately paid teachers.

(5) Although the numbers of school-leavers without any qualification continue to appear for schemes designed to respond to youth unemployment, there is no linkage between the various agencies and referral services called upon in the Right to Read charter to effect a joint effort at eliminating illiteracy.

(6) Nonetheless, the British experience has provided a wealth of knowledge upon which other industrialized countries can and do draw. It shows how the commitment of organizers and tutors has successfully maintained provision in a generally unfavorable climate. Approximately 200,000 adults have received tuition since the beginning of the campaign.

ADULT LITERACY IN FRANCE

Origin of Adult Literacy Efforts

France, like a number of other industrialized countries, has been extremely slow in recognizing that it may also have a large number of adult illiterates in its own population. Part of the explanation for this reticence has been analyzed by the author elsewhere.[23] Since the early twentieth century, France has had a declining population and has continually encouraged immigration from former colonies to provide the unskilled labor required in many economic sectors. Hence, up until the early 1970s and economic recession, large numbers of migrant workers from North and West Africa, the Mediterranean Basin, and Turkey have been welcome along with their families. The situation changed dramatically

[23]*Ibid.*

with the closure of official immigration in the mid-1970s, but the presence of large numbers of migrants (over five million, according to certain official sources), frequently illiterate in their native languages, and even more frequently with little or no knowledge of French, has drawn considerable attention.

Over the past fifteen years, numerous voluntary associations have been created to provided "alphabétisation" or literacy classes to migrant workers. In fact, these bodies dispense French as a second language, which is some cases is indeed literacy instruction, but in a foreign language. Literacy in the mother tongue is provided exclusively by governments of the countries of origin and migrant associations themselves.

Hence, when the first agreements between government and industry were reached concerning the right to lifelong education in 1971, the provisions that became available for the disadvantaged in France tended to be in terms of French as a foreign language for migrant workers. The logic behind this limited approach was clear: a totally illiterate workforce in the automobile industry or the construction sector, where migrants were heavily represented, could constitute a material danger both to the worker and the employer. Schemes accepted by employers and financed according to the terms of the "Loi sur la formation permanente" were definitely functional and work-oriented. For the most part, the already existing voluntary bodies continued to provide French as a foreign language, along the same lines as the voluntary and charitable associations of other countries. Yet, little or no attention was paid to the possibility that French citizens might have similar needs. Many of the voluntary bodies also developed with political motivations stemming from the ferment of May, 1968 in France. Students and political activists turned to the most visible disinherited, the migrant workers, at a period in which they might have equally well made the discovery of deprivation among the French population at large. This particularity of voluntary bodies in France distinguishes the French context from that of some other industrialized countries, and may help explain why France has been particularly slow in recognizing adult illiteracy in its own nationals.

Indeed, the several hundred voluntary associations concerned with assistance to migrant workers are quite distinct from the various charitable bodies that in many cases go back to the nineteenth century in the United Kingdom. They are relatively recent, frequently partisan in origin, and after an initial phase of unsuccessfully seeking to undertake further political mobilization among migrants, have become pragmatic in their field of action and ability to negotiate government subsidies for their educational undertakings. Over the past ten years, it has been the custom, when looking at underachievement in schools or adult illiteracy, to note that it must be a "migrant problem." Consequently, an abundant body of research on the education of migrants' children and adult migrants exists with a wealth of comparative European experience. The same is not true for the needs of adult nationals.

The first official recognition that France, too, might have an adult literacy problem came in 1981, with the publication of the *Oheix Report* on poverty in France. Among its numerous recommendations, it called for an adult literacy campaign. Its wide-ranging analysis of social and economic inequalities includes

the conclusion frequently found by social research of recent years: schools have
not been able to combat broader aspects of inequality in industrialized countries.
In fact, approximately 100,000 school leavers in France each year are virtually
illiterate and invariably destined for the most precarious jobs or, more likely
still, unemployment.

One of the many propositions made by this major report was that a working
group be constituted on an interministerial level to study the problem of adult
illiteracy, and then to suggest how a campaign might be mounted. It is important
to bear in mind that the origins of the French effort are to be found in the
context of the search for measures to deal with poverty and deprivation. It is
not, as in the United Kingdom or the United States, an effort from the nearly
grass-roots level of voluntary agencies or pressure groups.

At the same time, the discovery of adult illiteracy in France was also being
made in some of the various youth-employment schemes and vocational training
programs created in the early 1980s to deal with increasingly grave youth unemployment. Time and again, such schemes became basic education courses, to the
surprise of their organizers. It had not struck the French consciousness that
nationals, as well as migrants, might have serious learning problems.

The one major voluntary body to recognize adult illiteracy in France and
throughout Europe, however, *Aide à Toute Détresse-Quart Monde* (Aid to All Suf-
fering-Fourth World), had also been focusing its efforts on the link between
severe deprivation and illiteracy. This association has a longstanding experience
of activism among the most disadvantaged and consistently links its efforts in
the field of literacy to overall deprivation. Its portrayal of the "Fourth World"
has, in fact, colored French perception of the adult illiterate as singularly deprived
in all aspects of his or her life. Thus, the governmental response of 1984 is in
some ways no surprise.

Recognition of the Problem

As a response of the *Oheix Report*, the newly-elected Socialist Government
in France set up an interministerial commission on January 23, 1983, which in
turn saw to the preparation of the report to the Prime Minister, *Des illettrés en
France*, in January, 1984.[24] This report outlines the state of knowledge concerning adult illiteracy in France, examine existing provision, and makes specific
proposals for national commitment. Among these proposals are the creation of
a permanent body to coordinate the eradication of illiteracy at interministerial
level the conduct of a research program to ascertain the extent of provision
already available (the report only mentions a few fragmentary efforts), the pro-
curement of finance for the training of adult literacy tutors, the inclusion of
adult literacy in a reexamination of national policy on reading, the integration
of literacy work with youth employment and training schemes, as well as efforts
for other target populations in penal institutions and so forth.

---

[24] Espérandieu, Léon and Bénichou, *Des Illetrés.*

It is significant that the French initiative originates neither in the Ministry of Education nor with voluntary bodies applying pressure, as in the United Kingdom. The Secretariat of the interministerial group is within the Ministry of Social Affairs and National Solidarity (which includes aspects of health, employment, the family, and social welfare). Indeed, the Ministry of Education has appeared relatively reluctant to be actively linked to this effort. Over the past year, as consciousness-raising regional meetings have occurred in France, the participants have tended to be social workers more frequently than teachers.

So far, an inventory of adult literacy provision has only brought up a handful of efforts exclusively devoted to basic education. For the most part, the agencies aware of adult illiteracy tend to be social welfare bodies or those concerned with target populations.

In addition, the publicity surrounding the publication of the official report includes the by now familiar figure of two million adult illiterates in France. It would appear that, in the light of an insufficient knowledge base, any figure is better than no figure.

Future Prospects

France has thus taken the first steps in recognizing adult illiteracy among its nationals. Given the lack of funding other than for small-scale research initiatives, it is difficult to be optimistic for the future.

As this author has argued elsewhere,[25] France has, in its legislation for the right to lifelong education, the ideal potential instrument for providing adults with literacy and basic education on an other than *ad hoc* basis through adult education institutes or charitable bodies. The experience of the past twelve years of trade unions and working people in negotiating with employers for the educational leave to which they are entitled indicates that the most unqualified workers, hence those most in need, are rarely able to take advantage of their rights. Should basic education classes be offered, it would undoubtedly be these workers who would be the major clientele. yet, they rarely obtain recognition of their rights for any professional training.

On the contrary, the instrument of educational leaves for training purposes has proved most readily available to the highly skilled and professional sectors. It would require relatively forceful government intervention to alter this state of affairs. Also, given the retrenchment in educational spending and the recent capitulation by the government to conservative forces seeking to maintain the autonomy of the private, primarily religious schools subsidized completely by the nation, along with the recent "Back to Basics" discourse of the present Minister of Education, it appears unlikely that France will undertake a major effort to eradicate adult illiteracy.

[25] Leslie Limage, "Adult literacy in France: Some historic and socio-economic considerations," *Adult Literacy in Industrialized Countries: An International Seminar*, Report of the Proceedings of the Seminar, September 28 through October 2, 1981, Eastbourne, United Kingdom (Leicester: National Institute of Education).

ADULT LITERACY IN THE UNITED STATES

Origins of Efforts

The existence of adult illiteracy in the United States has been recognized to some extent for many years. Among industrialized nations, the United States belongs to the group that has at least given passing attention to the problem without fanfare or a full-scale national campaign.

It took the publication of Carman St John Hunter's and David Harman's study for the Ford Foundation in 1979[26] to call attention to the size of the problem. Although sources and statistics provide differing figures, these authors come up with a figure representing nearly one-third of the adult population in the United States as being semi- or completely illiterate acording to various definitions of literacy levels. Once again, the figures have primarily a shock value. What is behind them, however, should come as little surprise given our earlier discussion of the various roles attached to American schools over the past century.

At the turn of the century, on the whole, schooling, where it existed, was seen as a means of Americanizing immigrants and preparing an adequate labor force. Literacy skills were only marginal in this effort. Until after the Second World War, awareness that adult illiteracy might be dangerous to national well being went unrecognized. Not until the early 1960s did the federal government begin to become directly involved in measures with an adult-literacy component. Specifically, in 1962, the Manpower Development and Training Act established a program with a functional literacy component, adult basic education, for workers unable to take advantage of retraining schemes. In 1694, the Economic Opportunity Act provided direct funding for adult literacy to target groups such as the unemployed, the undereducated, socially, culturally, and economically deprived adults, migrant and seasonal workers. Federal intervention subsequently took the form of the Higher Education Act of 1965, allowing for the training of teachers for economically disadvantaged areas. In 1966, adult literacy was included in what later became the Adult Education Act. All the endeavors, including the 1971 "National Right to Read Program," aimed at enabling adults to become more employable and responsible citizens.

Current Adult Literacy Provisions

Adult literacy provisions and efforts currently exist in four different forms. The government officially sponsors provisions through Adult Basic Education and the military. It also gives direction to the Adult Literacy Initiative of 1983. Finally, two prominent voluntary bodies, Laubach Literacy and Literacy Volunteers of America, provide the bulk of the remaining provisions. Many very small-scale community initiatives exist but, as we shall discuss, all these measures taken together are in no position to address the size of the problem.

Adult Basic Education is the largest provider of adult literacy tuition. It has had federal funding for the past sixteen years, but at a level that prevents

[26]Carman St. John Hunter and David Harman, *Adult Illiteracy in the United States* (New York: McGraw-Hill Book Company, 1979).

its further expansion. It claims to serve some two million adults, but has a dropout rate from its programs of four in ten and waiting lists of hundreds of thousands.[27] Kozol is also critical of outcomes for participants. He notes that of those participants who have completed Adult Basic Education courses, only 8.5 percent actually obtain employment as a result of their course, and fewer than 2 percent report that they have voted for the first time as a result of their instruction. As with the British instruction provided through adult education institutes, it is significant to note that adults who tend to seek this type of instruction are already highly motivated and nearly "funtional." The most deprived are never reached by this type of provision. They are very likely discouraged by the reminder of a school setting, the very institutional arrangements that affected adult education, hence literacy provision, in the United Kingdom.

The U.S. military also provides literacy instruction, but on a limited basis. In any case, it does not accept recruits with lower than a fifth-grade reading level.

The two major voluntary bodies, Laubach Literacy and Literacy Volunteers of America, reach approximately fifty thousand and twenty thousand adults, respectively.

Municipal and state-run programs also reach limited numbers of adults. For example, the California Literacy Campaign allocates some 2.5 million dollars. On the other hand there are an estimated five million adult illiterates in the state. All of these measures, in addition to the numerous local and community efforts, have only a limited range and success rate. The newest undertaking, the federally sponsored Adult Literacy Initiative, is also far from impressive. It was first presented in the autumn of 1983 by Secretary of Education Terence Bell. Of the eight proposals announced, only three actions were not already in existence. Only one initiative involved any new funding, and that of a very limited amount. Indeed, the various actions involved advising, providing liaison, and facilitating exchange of information concerning existing provision, and in no way prepared the way for a concerted national effort worthy of the term.[28] Indeed, Kozol's evaluation of this most recent federal effort is eloquent for the purposes of our analysis of the prospects for an adult literacy policy in the United States:

> The government's "initiative," therefore, was even more deficient than that timid word implied. It wasn't a struggle. It wasn't a campaign. Above all, it was not a demonstration that the federal government had finally perceived its own responsibility to sponsor and directly fund an all-out answer to a crisis which it had defined as being national in scope and danger.[29]

A final (though nongovernmental) initiative of 1983 was the bringing together to share efforts and experiences of the major volunteer bodies previously mentioned—Adult Basic Education and two major scholarly associations involved in reading in a coalition with the American Library Association and the major bookseller, B. Dalton, at the instigation of the ALA and Dalton's. The

[27] Kozol, *Illiterate America*, p. 43
[28] Ibid, p. 50.
[29] Ibid, p. 51.

advantages of drawing these groups together in a coalition appear numerous. It is too soon to evaluate the outcome of such an endeavor from the point of view of influencing national policy making.

Future Prospects

Hunter and Harman in 1979, and Kozol in 1985, all make a plea for a national commitment to eradicate adult illiteracy in the United States. Indeed, Kozol lays out a courageous "Plan For Mobilizing Illiterate America" in the face of severe retrenchment in educational spending and high level criticism of the "excellence" potential of American schools (no more reference is made to their potential for providing equality of educational opportunity and access).

As Hunter and Harman mapped illiteracy and poverty in the United States and came up with figures approaching one-third of the adult population, and other authors who share Kozol's commitments note and annotate the ever-renewed cycle of underachievement in schools, the dropout rate, and adult illiteracy, the urgency of the problem appears abundantly clear. But, as was noted for the other countries briefly analyzed, the political will is lacking and can be expected to remain inadequate in the near future. Universal adult literacy is no more on the agenda in the most advanced industrialized nations than in so many developing countries that suffer from many other, even graver, material needs.

COMPARATIVE COMMENTARY

This too-brief review of aspects of the historic role of literacy, schooling, and adult-literacy provisions in three industrialized countries allows for some analysis of similarities and differences in attending to the problem. These countries were originally selected for their representativity of a large group of industrialized countries that have similar patterns of provision and recognition. In other words, a more in-depth analysis might show that the degree of recognition in the United Kingdom is comparable to that of some Scandinavian nations, while that of France is close to that of Belgium, Switzerland, the Federal Republic of Germany, Italy, Spain, and New Zealand. The United States seems to have some similarities with Canada and Australia. These categories are not exclusive, however. In the following discussion, we shall take up several points that an examination of all three groups of countries shows to be useful areas of comparison.

Concern for Definitions and Figures

In each of the countries examined, there appears to be a clear-cut cleavage between the initial interests of adult literacy activists and those of policy planners or government and the mass media. In the United Kingdom, the figure of two million adult illiterates was in no way a serious evaluation based on empirical evidence of the extent of adult illiteracy in the country at the time of the campaign. Indeed, the various voluntary bodies led by the British Association of

Settlements were keen to show the urgency of the need for a national commitment, after which they were prepared to encourage research and census taking. The government, and particularly the mass media, however, required a number. In the United Kingdom, in France, and in the United States, the mass media (newspapers, television, and radio) deal in "events," not processes. Interestingly, a shock figure was required and supplied in France as well, just as in the United Kingdom. It appears that the media treatment of adult illiteracy could only obscure the whole process by which adults in industrialized countries are unable to read and write. First of all, the French radio, television and newspaper accounts of "cases" of adult illiteracy emphasized the isolated character of the phenomenon and the sense of shame and embarrassment associated with being unable to read and write. Interviews were publicized of individuals who spoke of their experience. More analytical accounts of the actual extent of the problem or of its origins are extremely rare. As in other industrialized countries, no media recognition is given to the links between underachievement in schools, unemployment or underemployment of young adults, and illiteracy. Above all, the media made serious inroads into separating the whole issue from its socioeconomic context. In a similar manner, government response in each country was fragmentary.

Educational Infrastructures for Adult Literacy

In both the United Kingdom and the United States, it has been seen that the bulk of adult literacy provision has been attached to the most marginal sector of formal education, traditional adult eduction. In both cases, classes take place in schools, frequently with similar methods and materials and with the usual problems associated with schools. Adults cope with distance, as well as memories of dropout, failure, and discouragement. Adult literacy tutors in both countries have been drawn from school teachers of the young and, in some cases, adult-education instructors used to catering to a middle-class clientele seeking leisure activities. The use of volunteer tutors in both countries is seen as both an advantage in terms of flexibility and a serious hindrance in terms of insuring a national commitment and continuity of instruction, and is a direct disincentive to governments at all levels to provide trained and adequately paid teachers in an area where present training is minimal, if not nonexistent. Even the British Association of Settlements called for paid and trained adult literacy tutors, although the campaign went forward almost totally without them, and indeed the British government refused to finance teachers' salaries in a first instance.

The Link between Schools and Adult Illiteracy

Once again, in all industrialized countries, there is a distinct demand among adult-literacy educators that the role of formal schooling be examined in a total attempt at eradicating adult illiteracy, and there is a parallel governmental reluctance for just such a national commitment. In the United Kingdom, the *Bullock Report* on reading in schools and the *Russell Report* on adult education (which were both prepared to assist in government policy formulation) neglected the adult literacy component. Simiarly, in the United States and in France, there is no serious attempt, either in various "excellence" or "risk" reports in the former, or even in the *Oheix* and *Espérandieu, et al.* reports in the latter, to draw the necessary linkages enabling a coherent national policy on universal adult literacy through effective schooling.

Recognition of the Problem

Recognition of the existence of adult illiteracy has taken similar paths in many industrialized countries. Although the statistics concerning recruits to the military have been available for years in all countries, real incentives have frequently originated with voluntary bodies serving as advocates on behalf of adult illiterates. Alternatively, as in the case of France, target group illiteracy appeared as a result of youth employment and training schemes. But in all industrialized countries, the scale of youth employment and training schemes, as well as those for adults in general, is so minimal as to barely provide cause for recognition if taken on its own. In all cases, the danger in token recognition, as illustrated by the American Adult Literacy Initiative, is that the public will consider that something is truly being done. The French report on illiteracy, *Des Illettrés en France*, and accompanying publicity, is another case in point.

Those Who Are Never Reached

Despite all the provision for adult literacy in the countries discussed, it is clear that the vast majority of adult illiterates have not, and will not, be reached by the methods now employed. In addition to inadequate means, there is no sign of the total national mobilization that would be necessary to reach such a scale of provision. Hence, a national commitment is the only solution, and none of the various measures or means taken on its own can replace such an undertaking. There is, indeed, a certain inconclusiveness surrounding almost any mode of teaching taken in isolation. We have seen the advantages and drawbacks of reliance on volunteers in a context of isolated charitable undertaking. Various media, and television in particular, also are characterized by contradictions. By its nature, television invites passivity and is only effective when encompassed in a global learning approach that includes face-to-face dialogue. Kozol and others repeatedly report the over-reliance of adult illiterates on television for all communication with the outside world. No mode or media is sufficient on its own, and all have both a constructive and counterproductive potential. Hence, the conclusion that all modes of learning, including the very vital community-based projects, require a larger policy commitment to universal adult literacy.

Is Literacy a Basic Human Right?

It has been argued that policy discourse in industrialized countries is in some ways similar to that of many developing nations in this period of economic austerity. Governments tend to state that they must choose between schooling the young and providing for adults. Even though public schooling is under attack in most Western countries for not living up to mythical earlier standards, such putative shortcomings fuel justifications for not providing adequate financing and commitment for programs serving adults with learning deficiencies, adult illiterates in particular.

This brief review of the history of literacy and the roles attributed to formal schooling argues that literacy has never been formally enshrined as a basic human right, other than in international declarations of intent. In fact, the trend is clearly towards blaming the victim: either by showing that adult illiterates are not motivated enough to help themselves, or that their state of illiteracy is in no way harmful to their own and their communities' needs. In such a climate, it appears unlikely that educational policy will be formulated in the near future in terms of human rights. As Kozol noted, such commitments may not be forthcoming during the next ten years. Nonetheless, it is up to all who are concerned with education, including adult-literacy activists, to continue to indicate the way forward.

Index

315